# Strategic Approaches to Intrusion Detection in Cloud-IoT Ecosystem

**Scrivener Publishing**
100 Cummings Center, Suite 541J
Beverly, MA 01915-6106

## Advances in Learning Analytics for Intelligent Cloud-IoT Systems

**Series Editor(s): Dr. Souvik Pal and Dr. Dac-Nhuong Le**

The role of adaptation, learning analytics, computational Intelligence, and data analytics in the field of Cloud-IoT Systems is becoming increasingly essential and intertwined. The capability of an intelligent system depends on various self-decision making algorithms in IoT Devices. IoT based smart systems generate a large amount of data (big data) that cannot be processed by traditional data processing algorithms and applications. Hence, this book series involves different computational methods incorporated within the system with the help of Analytics Reasoning and Sense-making in Big Data, which is centered in the Cloud and IoT-enabled environments.

The series seeks volumes that are empirical studies, theoretical and numerical analysis, and novel research findings. The series encourages cross-fertilization of highlighting research and knowledge of Data Analytics, Machine Learning, Data Science, and IoT sustainable developments.

*Publishers at Scrivener*
Martin Scrivener (martin@scrivenerpublishing.com)
Phillip Carmical (pcarmical@scrivenerpublishing.com)

# Strategic Approaches to Intrusion Detection in Cloud-IoT Ecosystem

Edited by

**Partha Ghosh**

*Dept. of Information Technology, Netaji Subhash Engineering College, Kolkata, India*

**Rajdeep Chakraborty**

*Dept. of Computer Science and Engineering, SAGE University, Indore, Madhya Pradesh, India*

**Anupam Ghosh**

*Dept. of Computer Science and Engineering, Netaji Subhash Engineering College, Kolkata, India*

and

**Ahmed A. Elngar**

*Faculty of Computers and Artificial Intelligence, Beni-Suef University, Beni-Suef City, Egypt*

Scrivener Publishing

WILEY

This edition first published 2026 by John Wiley & Sons, Inc., 111 River Street, Hoboken, NJ 07030, USA and Scrivener Publishing LLC, 100 Cummings Center, Suite 541J, Beverly, MA 01915, USA

For more information about Scrivener publications please visit www.scrivenerpublishing.com.



**Wiley Global Headquarters**
111 River Street, Hoboken, NJ 07030, USA

For details of our global editorial offices, customer services, and more information about Wiley products visit us at www.wiley.com.

The manufacturer's authorized representative according to the EU General Product Safety Regulation is Wiley-VCH GmbH, Boschstr. 12, 69469 Weinheim, Germany, e-mail: Product_Safety@wiley.com.



***Library of Congress Cataloging-in-Publication Data***

ISBN 978-1-394-34194-8

Front cover antenna image courtesy of Wikimedia Commons
Cover image: Generated with AI using Adobe Firefly
Cover design by Russell Richardson

Set in size of 11pt and Minion Pro by Manila Typesetting Company, Makati, Philippines

Printed in the USA

10 9 8 7 6 5 4 3 2 1

# Contents

# Preface

The rapid growth of Cloud Computing and the Internet of Things (IoT) has transformed various industries by enabling real-time data collection, processing, and automation. However, this increasing interconnectivity also introduces significant security challenges, including data breaches, unauthorized access, and cyber threats. Ensuring the security and privacy of Cloud-IoT environments requires advanced intrusion detection mechanisms, privacy-preserving strategies, and efficient resource management.

Intrusion Detection Systems (IDS) play a crucial role in securing Cloud-IoT ecosystems by identifying suspicious activities and mitigating potential threats. Various approaches, including Machine Learning (ML), Federated Learning (FL), Blockchain, and Hybrid Detection Models, have been explored to enhance intrusion detection capabilities. In addition to IDS, memory management techniques, anomaly detection frameworks, and encryption methods contribute to strengthening security. These aspects are discussed throughout the book, with a focus on AI-driven security mechanisms, behavioral profiling, and energy-efficient solutions for Cloud-IoT systems. By exploring different threat detection strategies, risk mitigation techniques, and cybersecurity frameworks, this book aims to provide a comprehensive understanding of modern security solutions in Cloud-IoT environments.

This book is organized into two parts. The first provides a detailed exploration of security mechanisms essential for Cloud-IoT environments. The second part focuses on various mechanisms to enhance the existing intrusion detection mechanisms.

**Part I: Intelligent Cloud-IoT Security**

Chapter 1 summarizes the need for intrusion detection in Cloud–IoT systems, outlining key architectures, challenges, techniques, and future research directions. Chapter 2 examines how Artificial Intelligence enhances early cyber-threat detection in cloud-based IoT networks, comparing existing IoCST approaches and emphasizing AI's growing importance.

Chapter 3 introduces memory-allocation and data-storage frameworks—particularly the CA-based MCMS—and demonstrates their efficiency through comparative analysis. Chapter 4 presents Federated Learning as a privacy-preserving strategy for Cloud–IoT environments, showing its advantages over traditional methods in accuracy, bandwidth, latency, and security.

Chapter 5 explores Machine Learning algorithms for anomaly detection in Cloud–IoT systems, comparing multiple models and highlighting their respective strengths and weaknesses. Chapter 6 details the Smart Shields framework, which uses ML algorithms to provide adaptive, real-time security for Cloud–IoT environments and outperforms traditional defences.

Chapter 7 evaluates AI and ML techniques for detecting and preventing cyber threats in Cloud–IoT environments, including a comparison of traditional and generative AI approaches. Chapter 8 investigates Deep Learning–based Encryption for cloud security, outlining a heteromorphic DLE framework with dynamic, adaptive cryptographic mechanisms and demonstrating its efficiency.

**Part II: Intelligent Intrusion Detection for Cloud-IoT System**

Chapter 9 analyzes adversarial attacks on IoT systems and presents deep-learning-based detection and defence strategies, highlighting key vulnerabilities and future research directions. Chapter 10 examines how Federated Learning and Edge Computing can be integrated to create effective intrusion detection systems for Cloud–IoT environments, demonstrating their advantages against evolving cyber threats.

Chapter 11 outlines behavioral profiling as a dynamic anomaly-detection method for Cloud–IoT networks, summarizing key components, techniques, and comparative insights from existing profiling approaches. Chapter 12 introduces an agent-based blockchain framework for intrusion protection in Cloud–IoT environments, combining decentralization with intelligent key management and evaluating its benefits over traditional methods.

Chapter 13 presents a hybrid intrusion detection system for Wireless Acoustic Sensor Networks that integrates signature-based and machine-learning anomaly detection to address WASN vulnerabilities and improve accuracy and efficiency.

We extend our gratitude to all the contributors whose dedication, expertise, and scholarly commitment made this book possible. We also express our appreciation to Martin Scrivener and the team at Scrivener Publishing for their guidance and support throughout the development of this project.

**Dr. Partha Ghosh**
**Dr. Rajdeep Chakraborty**
**Dr. Anupam Ghosh**
**Dr. Ahmed A. Elngar**

# Part I

# INTELLIGENT CLOUD-IoT SECURITY

# 1

# Intrusion Detection in Cloud-IoT Systems: Challenges and Opportunities

**Anindita Raychaudhuri[1]* and Inadyuti Dutt[2]**

[1]*Department of Computer Science, Sarojini Naidu College for Women, Kolkata, West Bengal, India*
[2]*Department of Computer Applications, B. P. Poddar Institute of Management & Technology, Poddar Vihar, Kolkata, India*

***Abstract***

Intrusion detection in Cloud-IoT systems is essential for safeguarding data, ensuring regulatory compliance, maintaining operational continuity, and protecting against the evolving landscape of cyber threats. Cloud-IoT systems collect huge amounts of data from diverse sources, including human-to-human, human-to-thing, and thing-to-thing interactions. These systems leverage cloud computing to process and study the data, delivering real-time insights seamlessly. The data in such systems become very vulnerable to intrusions as they can be compromised at the client's end, where the exchange of data primarily takes place. The data can also be prone to security issues in the cloud environment where the cloud servers can be exposed to attacks. Apart from firewalls that are positioned intelligently, there are needs for Intrusion Detection Systems (IDS). Intrusion detection in Cloud-IoT systems is a multifaceted but essential job to ensure the security and integrity of these environments. By exploiting leading-edge technologies like machine learning, deep learning, edge computing, and collaborative approaches, it is possible to develop robust IDS solutions that can successfully detect and alleviate threats in these dynamic and heterogeneous systems. Intrusion detection in Cloud-IoT systems is a fast-growing domain, with various research avenues developing to tackle the distinct challenges arising from the integration with the internet of things (IoT). This chapter offers a detail review of different strategies, tools and technologies for intrusion detection as well as explores future research directions.

**Corresponding author*: aninrc@gmail.com

Partha Ghosh, Rajdeep Chakraborty, Anupam Ghosh and Ahmed A. Elngar (eds.) Strategic Approaches to Intrusion Detection in Cloud-IoT Ecosystem, (3–30) © 2026 Scrivener Publishing LLC

***Keywords*:** Anomaly detection, cloud-IoT systems, denial of service, intrusion detection system, IoT security, machine learning

## 1.1 Introduction

The importance of cloud-IoT security is rising daily due to the fast expansion of connected devices and the growing dependence on cloud infrastructure for managing, processing, and storing large volumes of data [1–9]. IoT devices frequently gather and send sensitive information. Implementing strong security measures, like encryption and secure communication protocols, is essential to safeguard this data from unauthorized access. A single compromised IoT device can act as an entry point for attackers to breach the entire network [10, 11]. Many IoT applications especially healthcare applications require real-time data availability. Due to the limited computing power and storage, IoT devices rely on cloud infrastructure for these resources [12, 13]. The cloud also enables real-time analytics, data storage, and application hosting for IoT networks. Intrusion detection in cloud-IoT systems is essential because these systems are susceptible to a variety of unique and diverse threats [14–19]. This is because the integrated cloud-IoT systems combines the complexities of cloud computing with the vast and widespread landscape of heterogeneous IoT devices [20–22]. Attacks like Distributed Denial of Service (DDoS) can disrupt cloud services, making it impossible for IoT devices to function properly, with potentially life-threatening consequences in critical sectors [10, 11, 23]. Cloud platforms themselves have vulnerabilities, such as insecure APIs, data breaches [24]. Security breaches can compromise the performance of IoT systems, resulting in inconsistent and unreliable operations. Securing cloud-IoT systems helps in managing risks related to service disruptions, data loss, and hardware failures. By implementing robust security frameworks, organizations can better handle threats and recover quickly, reducing downtime and operational risks [25–27]. Securing cloud-IoT systems is a multi-layered challenge, requiring collaboration between IoT device manufacturers, cloud service providers, and end-users to build trust and ensures protection of critical infrastructures from cyber threats.

***Layout of the chapter***

Section 1.2 presents the overview of the cloud-IoT system. Section 1.3 discusses the challenges in cloud-IoT Systems. Section 1.4 summarizes the key security issues in cloud-IoT systems. The evolution of Intrusion Detection Technologies (IDTs) is briefly explained in Section 1.5. Section 1.6 summarizes the techniques and algorithms for Intrusion Detection and compares different studies based on datasets, methodologies, attack types, and performance indicators. Section 1.7 highlights prominent application areas of Intrusion Detection in Cloud-IoT Systems. Section 1.8 explores future directions and research opportunities. Finally, Section 1.9 concludes the chapter.

## 1.2 Overview of Cloud IoT Systems

The Internet of Things consists of a network of connected physical appliances that gather and exchange data. These devices, including everything from sensors to smart appliances, produce substantial amounts of data. The integration of cloud computing and IoT facilitates scalability, flexibility, and power of cloud services with the widespread, real-time data generation capabilities of IoT devices [12, 13].

*Key Benefits of Cloud-IoT Systems:* The combination of cloud computing and IoT technologies provides numerous essential features that enhance data processing, storage, and analytics [20, 21]. These facilities include:

- **Data Storage**: IoT devices produce massive volumes of data, often exceeding the capacity of local storage and can be manageable by cloud platform.
- **Real-Time Analytics**: Cloud platforms can analyze IoT data instantly, enabling organizations to make prompt decisions.
- **Scalability**: Cloud systems can dynamically scale to accommodate fluctuations in the volume of data and device activity.
- **Machine Learning and AI Integration**: By leveraging AI/ML models on IoT data, the cloud facilitates advanced analytics, including predictive maintenance and anomaly detection.
- **Remote Monitoring**: Cloud integration enables users to oversee and manage IoT devices remotely, providing greater flexibility and improved resource management.
- **Enhanced Collaboration**: Multiple users can access and interact with IoT-generated data through cloud platforms, improving operational efficiency.

## 1.3 Challenges in Cloud IoT Systems

Cloud-IoT systems offer significant benefits, but they also come with several challenges that can hinder their full potential [21, 22]. Below are the key challenges

- **Heterogeneity:** IoT ecosystems consist of a wide variety of devices, each built by different manufacturers with different communication protocols, data formats, and capabilities.
- **Limited Processing Power, Memory, and Energy on IoT Devices:** Several IoT devices like sensors and microcontrollers works in resource-limited environments. They have limited CPU power, memory, and energy (battery), which restricts their ability to handle complex computations, encryption algorithms, and large data transmissions.
- **Data Privacy and Compliance Concerns:** IoT devices generate sensitive data e.g., health information, location tracking, and behavior patterns. Companies must implement policies that comply with local data protection laws
- **Dynamic Environments:** In IoT systems, devices are often mobile, and network topology can change dynamically as devices connect, disconnect, or move across different network environments. Network reliability and device availability can fluctuate frequently.
- **Real-Time Processing:** Applications like autonomous vehicles, smart healthcare requires real-time processing of data. However, sending data to the cloud for processing introduces latency, which may not be acceptable for time-critical applications.
- **Interoperability and Standardization:** There is a lack of unified standards, making it difficult for different IoT devices and cloud systems to collaborate seamlessly.

## 1.4 Security Issues in Cloud Systems

Security is a critical concern in cloud-IoT systems due to the integration of vast, interconnected devices and cloud-based infrastructures. The complex interaction between IoT devices and cloud computing introduces several security risks [1–9].

Table 1.1 summarizes the key security issues in cloud-IoT systems, common threats and vulnerabilities and its possible solutions. By addressing these security issues, organizations can better protect their cloud-IoT systems from cyberattacks, ensuring the safety, privacy, and reliability of their IoT ecosystems [10, 11, 23, 28–41]. The abbreviations used in this chapter are summarized in Table 1.2.

**Table 1.1** Security issues in cloud-IoT systems.

| Category | Common threats and vulnerabilities | Solution | Publication |
|---|---|---|---|
| Unauthorized Access | Weak passwords, Insecure APIs | Multi-factor authentication (MFA), robust identity management systems, and token-based authentication | Suleski, T., *et al.* [28] |
| Data Breaches | Lack of encryption, Man-in-the-middle attacks | Implement strong encryption, protocols such as MQTT with SSL/TLS (Secure Sockets Layer/Transport Layer Security) | Paris, I. L. B. M., *et al.* [30] |
| Denial of Service (DoS) Attacks | Overwhelming traffic, IoT botnets | Limiting rate, cloud-based DDoS mitigation services and Intrusion detection and prevention systems (IDPS). | Bhushan, K., *et al.* [32] |
| Physical Security Risks | Tampering, Theft of IoT devices, Introduce Malware | Implement tamper-resistant hardware designs, physical locks, and access control measures to protect devices from physical threats. | Nunoo-Mensah, *et al.* [36] |
| Vulnerabilities in IoT Firmware | Outdated/Unpatched firmware, Exploitable bugs | Regular security updates, secure firmware designs, and conducting vulnerability assessments can mitigate these risks. | Nadir, I., *et al.* [23] |
| Insecure Communication Channels | Use of Unsecured communication Protocols (e.g. MQTT/CoAP) leads to insecure communication | Implement SSL/TLS protocols to encrypt the communication connecting IoT devices with cloud servers. Implement Virtual Private Networks (VPNs). Use protected IoT gateways. | Zakaria, Mohd Idzaney, *et al.* [37] |

**Table 1.2** Summary of abbreviations.

| Abbreviation | Definition | Abbreviation | Definition |
|---|---|---|---|
| ABC | Artificial bee colony | IDTs | Intrusion Detection Technologies |
| ACO | Ant colony optimization | IoT | Internet of Things |
| AFS | Artificial Fish Swarm | LSTM | Long Short-Term Memory |
| AI | Artificial Intelligence | MFA | Multi-factor authentication |
| ALO | Ant Lion Optimization | ML | Machine learning |
| BPNN | Back Propagation Neural Network | NIDS | Network Intrusion Detection Systems |
| CNN | Convolutional Neural Network | R2L | Remote to Local |
| CS | Cuckoo Search | RNN | Recurrent Neural Network |
| DL | Deep learning | SSA | Salp swarm algorithm |
| DR | Detection rate | SSL | Secure Sockets Layer |
| FCM | Fuzzy C-means clustering | SVM | Support Vector Machine |
| GTO | Gorilla troops optimization | TLS | Transport Layer Security |
| GWO | Grey Wolf Optimization | U2R | User to Root |
| IDS | Intrusion detection systems | VPNs | Virtual Private Networks |

## 1.5 Evolution of Intrusion Detection Systems

Intrusion detection systems have evolved from simple anomaly detectors to complex AI-driven systems. Attackers continually develop new methods to exploit vulnerabilities in IoT devices and cloud services. Intrusion detection helps detect these evolving threats before they cause significant damage. Effective intrusion detection ensures that IoT devices and cloud services operate efficiently and securely, minimizing the risk of disruptions and operational inefficiencies. Intrusion detection in cloud-IoT systems is critical due to the unique challenges these environments present, such as large-scale deployments, heterogeneous devices, and complex data flows. The concept of IDS was initially introduced by Jim Anderson in 1980 [42]. The timeline spans from the 1980s with basic statistical methods, through the introduction of signature-based methods, to modern machine learning and AI-based IDS. Figure 1.1 presents the timeline of the evolution of IDTs.

### 1.5.1 Evolution of IDTs in IoT-Cloud Systems

The evolution of IDTs in IoT-cloud systems is crucial for maintaining the security and integrity of these increasingly complex and interconnected environments. Table 1.3 presents an overview of this evolution:

**I. Early Approaches: Basic Network Intrusion Detection Systems (NIDS)**

Initially, intrusion detection was primarily focused on traditional network-based systems. These systems were designed to monitor network traffic for known attack signatures or anomalies within a local or enterprise network [43, 44].

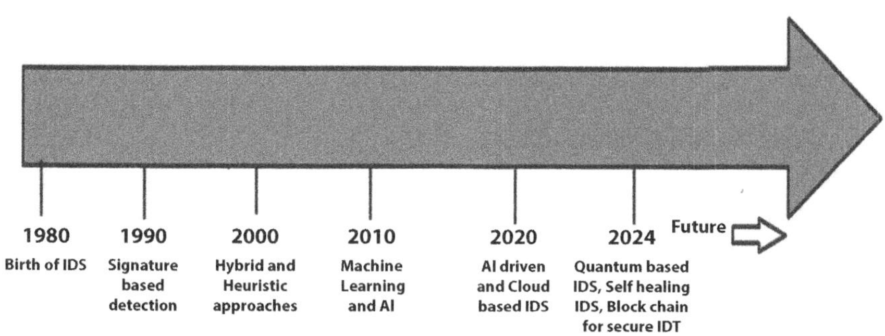


**Figure 1.1** Evolution of intrusion detection systems.

**Table 1.3** Evolution of intrusion detection technologies in IoT-cloud systems.

| Stage | Key features | Technologies/ approaches | Challenges |
|---|---|---|---|
| Early Approaches [43, 44] | Traditional NIDS, Signature-based detection | Basic Network Intrusion Detection Systems (NIDS) | - Ineffective for IoT devices<br>- Limited protocol support |
| First Generation: IoT-Centric [45, 46] | Protocol-specific solutions, Focus on known vulnerabilities | IoT-specific NIDS, Protocol analyzers (MQTT, CoAP) | - Limited cloud integration<br>-Resource constraints |
| Second Generation: Hybrid/Cloud [47, 48] | Hybrid detection, Cloud-based monitoring | Hybrid IDTs, Cloud-based Intrusion Detection | -Scalability<br>-Handling dynamic cloud environments |
| AI-Driven IDTs [44, 49–53] | Behavioral analysis, Anomaly detection | AI/ML-based anomaly detection, CNN based behavioral modeling | - High false positives<br>- Need for large datasets |
| Advanced IoT-Cloud Solutions [54, 55] | Edge computing, Decentralized learning | Edge-based IDTs, Federated learning | -Latency concerns<br>- Data privacy |
| Current & Future Trends [56, 57] | Autonomous IDTs, Blockchain security, Quantum resilience | Autonomous systems, Blockchain-based integrity, Quantum-safe algorithms | - Real-time response<br>- Quantum threat mitigation |

**II. First Generation IoT-Centric IDTs**

As IoT devices became more widespread, specialized IDTs were developed to monitor specific IoT communication protocols like MQTT, CoAP, and Zigbee. These early systems focused on identifying known vulnerabilities and misconfigurations in IoT devices [45, 46].

**III. Second Generation: Hybrid and Cloud-Based IDTs**

To address the limitations of early IoT-centric solutions, hybrid intrusion detection systems were developed. These systems combined network-based, host-based, and application-based IDTS to provide more comprehensive security coverage [47, 48].

**IV. Machine Learning and AI-Driven IDTs**

The integration of ML, DL and AI into IDTs marked a significant leap forward. These systems could learn from normal behavior patterns in IoT-cloud environments and detect deviations that may indicate an intrusion [44, 49, 53]. In this respect convolutional neural network (CNN) based behavioral modeling is noteworthy.

**V. Advanced IoT-Cloud Specific Solutions**

IDTs now operate closer to IoT devices at the network's edge, which decreases latency and enhances the real-time response to threats. In addition, federated learning allows for the training of intrusion detection models across multiple devices or locations without needing centralized data storage. This feature enhances privacy and reduces the risk of data breaches [54, 55].

**VI. Current and Future Trends**

The latest advancements involve the development of autonomous intrusion detection systems that can sense as well as counter the threats in real-time, without human intervention [56]. Researchers are investigating blockchain technology to guarantee the integrity and authenticity of data utilized by IDTs, making it harder for attackers to tamper with detection systems [57]. As quantum computing approaches reality, there is an increasing focus on developing IDTs that are resilient to potential threats posed by quantum computers, which could undermine traditional encryption methods.

This evolution highlights the increasing complexity and sophistication required to secure IoT-cloud systems, reflecting the growing importance of these technologies in modern digital infrastructure.

### 1.5.2 Comparative Analysis of Intrusion Detection Systems

The selection of IDS is influenced by the specific security needs, available resources, and threat landscape. The comparative study of various intrusion detection systems is presented in Table 1.4. It can be interpreted that the overall performance of signature-based IDS is lower than that of the rest of the IDSs being compared [14, 15]. Since the signature-based attacks

**Table 1.4** Comparative analysis of different intrusion detection systems.

| Feature | Signature-based IDS | Anomaly-based IDS | Hybrid IDS | Behavior-based IDS |
|---|---|---|---|---|
| Detects Unknown Attacks | ✗ | ✓ | ✓ | ✓ |
| Computational Overhead | Moderate | High | High | High |
| Adaptable to New Attacks | ✗ | ✓ | ✓ | ✓ |
| Signature/Pattern Updates | Frequent | None | Moderate | None |
| Robust | ✗ | ✓ | ✓ | ✓ |
| Support for Encrypted Traffic | ✗ | ✓ | ✓ | ✓ |
| Cost effective | ✓ | ✗ | ✗ | ✗ |

can only detect known attacks, therefore, it becomes necessary to update the signature patterns regularly in comparison to other IDSs [25, 43, 44].

In contrast, the act of combating with unknown attacks are high for anomaly-based IDS as they mostly depend upon the detection of anomalies in a normal traffic [14, 15, 25]. However, the hybrid-based IDS uses both the frequent signature updates as well as the act of combating with unknown attacks by tracing anomalies [47, 48]. Behavior-based IDS depends mainly of the user-access, sometimes employees' working pattern, data access, file access and network traffic volume for a certain period of time [51].

## 1.6 Techniques and Algorithms for Intrusion Detection

The effectiveness of an Intrusion Detection System often depends on the nature of the environment, the volume of data, and the diversity of threats it faces. Researchers have developed a variety of techniques and algorithms to tackle this challenge [58–97]. Apart from the traditional approaches, bio-inspired approaches have shown significant potential in intrusion detection systems.

The author in the paper [58], used Cuckoo Search Optimization (CSO) along with the concept of neural network. Natesan *et al.* in [59], utilized the MapReduce programming paradigm with Hadoop to furnish the parallel programming in accumulating the big data from cloud network. And that reduced the latency and the computation time for feature selection satisfactorily. In [60], authors used ABC and AFS algorithms to detect anomaly and misuse attacks. Shen *et al.* [61], have improved their accuracy of detection by using Ensemble method with Bat algorithm. Akinyelu *et al.* in [62], used CS-based and Bat algorithm to enhance the efficiency and accuracy of SVM. Idhammad *et al.*, in their work [63], have utilized the data from IoT devices and used Naïve Bayes for feature selection from Cloud data. Mazini *et al.* [64], have developed a model with Artificial Bee Colony (ABC) and Ada-Boost in the cloud environment. Nguyen *et al.*, in their work [65], have addressed the vulnerabilities in all the 3 layers of Edge, Fog and Cloud by developing a system with SVM, Self-Organizing Map (SOM) and Deep Learning Techniques. Roopa Devi *et al.* in their work [66], and Keserwani, in [67], have enhanced their accuracy by incorporating PSO (Particle Swarm Optimization)-based Grey Wolf Optimizer (GWO) algorithm. And they have obtained as high as 99.9% accuracy in an IoT network.

Nguyen *et al.*, in their work [68], utilized Genetic algorithm and CNN to enhance the feature extraction on Bagging learning technique. Ghanem *et al.*, in their model [69], have used Bat and ANN algorithms to determine the abnormal packets from the network. Chen *et al.*, in their work [70], have used ALO, mimicking the hunting techniques of antlions along with clustering technique; whereas, Samadi Bonab *et al.*, in their model [71], have used Fruit fly algorithm and Ant Lions and Ant Algorithm after feature selection. While Alsharafat *et al.* [72], in their work in [72], and also Thirumalairaj and Jeyakarthic in their work [73], have developed Cuckoo Search based models to increase the detection rates. The uniqueness of this algorithm relies on the brood parasitic behavior of cuckoos. While Liu *et al.* in [74], used PSO-based Light Gradient Boosting Machines (GBM) algorithm and Kan *et al.*, in their paper [75], used PSO-based CNN algorithm to enhance the accuracy in IoT-based networks. Ghanem *et al.* [76], used around ten meta-heuristic algorithms to ANN and succeeded in finding global optimal solution. Mehanović *et al.*, in their work [77], have utilized parallel programming paradigm along with Genetic algorithm.

In the work [78], of Halim *et al.*, Genetic algorithm with correlation-based feature selection has been developed which produced high accuracy of more than 99% in IoT network They have also exercised the on real-time intrusions. However, they have faced challenges in addressing repeated iterations and replications during chromosomal selections. Qi *et al.*, also employed a model in their work [79], on real-time intrusions based on BPNN and ABC algorithm in cloud network. In the rest of the works from [80–83], the authors have developed models based on nature-inspired meta-heuristics such as Gorilla Troop Optimizer (GTO), Bat algorithms or based on swarm intelligence along with neural network to enhance the accuracy in IoT network. In works of [84, 85], also the authors have used ALO and ACO based methods. Alzahrani *et al.* in [86], have used transformer design-based method in identifying the intrusions in IoT-Cloud environment.

Abd Elaziz *et al.*, in their works [87], and Aldaej *et al.* in [88], have utilized deep neural network or recurrent neural network to address the attacks in IoT-cloud platform. Kaffash *et al.*, in their work [89], and Alrayes *et al.*, in works of [90], have used K-Nearest Neighborhood with MLP and GTO with Deep Learning (DL) respectively. Guilherme *et al.*, in their work [91], have exercised real-time data in cloud-IoT environment by using Intel S/W Guard Extensions (SGX). Attou *et al.*, in their work [92], have classified attack based on random forest model. Similarly, Biswas *et al.*, in their work [95], have used Random Forest and Decision Tree algorithms to improve the accuracy of detection. Mohamed *et al.*, in their model [93], have used Genetic algorithm and BPNN to address the attacks in cloud-IoT environment; whereas, Okey *et al.*, in the work [94], have employed Deep Transfer Learning Technique which has the capability to utilize the knowledge from previously trained model. Aldaej *et al.* in their model [96], have employed an ID framework in edge network with multiple decision trees called E-trees. Sepide Najafli *et al.*, in their work [97], have proposed a model to detect the attacks in the Fog-Cloud environment with the help of DL based technique.

Table 1.5 compares different studies of Intrusion detections based on datasets, methodologies, attack types, and performance indicators.

## 1.7 Applications Areas of Intrusion Detection in Cloud-IoT Systems

Intrusion detection systems enable organizations to detect, respond to, and mitigate security incidents promptly, thereby enhancing overall system security and resilience. Devices in cloud-IoT systems often communicate

**Table 1.5** Comparative analysis of intrusion detection methods and their performance metrics.

| Author name (publication year) | Dataset used | Method used | Attack types | QoS and VPN support | Stability | Accuracy percentage (%) |
|---|---|---|---|---|---|---|
| Shitharth *et al.* [58] | SIRD, SORD, MIRD, MORD | CSO and Neural Network | Dos, Spoofing | Public network | ✓ | 93.1% |
| Natesan, P., *et al.* [59] | KDDCup 99 | Hadoop MapReduce programming with parallel binary bat algorithm and parallel Naïve Bayes | DoS, Probe, U2R and R2L | Hadoop | ✓ | DR (given): Probe: 93.54<br>R2L: 74.13 |
| Hajisalem, V., and Babaie, S. [60] | NSL-KDD, UNSW-NB 15 | Correlation-based Feature Selection and Fuzzy-based Clustering | DoS, R2L, U2R and PROBE | IoT network | ✓ | 97.50% |
| Shen, Y., *et al.* [61] | KDD99, NSL and Kyoto | Ensemble method with Bat algorithm | Network-based attacks | Public network | ✓ | 98.94% |
| Akinyelu, A. A., & Adewumi, A. O., [62] | CSISA, BISA, and SVM | SVM using CS and Bat algorithm was used | Network-based attacks | Public network | ✓ | 77.83% |
| Idhammad I., *et al.* [63] | CIDDS-001 | Time-based sliding window method | DoS, PortScan, PingScan, Brute Force | Google Cloud Platform | ✓ | 97% with Avg. 0.21% (FPR) |
| Mazini, M., *et al.* [64] | NSL-KDD, ISCXIDS2012 | ABC and Ada Boost algorithm | DoS, R2L, U2R, PROBE, Infiltering, Brute Force, SSH, Botnet | Cloud network | ✓ | 98.90% |

*(Continued)*

**Table 1.5** Comparative analysis of intrusion detection methods and their performance metrics. (*Continued*)

| Author name (publication year) | Dataset used | Method used | Attack types | QoS and VPN support | Stability | Accuracy percentage (%) |
|---|---|---|---|---|---|---|
| Nguyen T. G., *et al.* [65] | CAIDA, KDD Cup 1999 and UNSW-NB 15 | Machine Learning with SVM in Edge IDS, Fog IDS using Self-Organizing Map and Cloud IDS using DL techniques | DoS/DDoS and Probe/ Reconnaissance attacks | × | ✓ | 95.5% |
| Roopa Devi, E., *et al.* [66] | NSL-KDD | Swarm based GWO with enhanced transudative-SVM technique | DoS, R2L, U2R and PROBE | IoT network | ✓ | 99.9% |
| Keserwani, P. K., *et al.* [67] | KDDCup 99, NSL-KDD, CICIDS-2017 | Swarm based GWO and PSO | Network attacks like DoS, Hulk, Port, Scan, DDoS etc. | IoT network | ✓ | 99.66% |
| Nguyen *et al.* [68] | NSL-KDD | Genetic Algorithm, FCM and CNN based feature extractor | Network-based attacks | Public network | ✓ | 98.2% |
| Ghanem, W. A., Janatan, A. [69] | UNSW-NB15, KDDCup 99, ISCX2012, NSL-KDD, | Bat and Artificial Neural Network | Network-based attacks based on standard dataset | Public network | ✓ | 97.48% |
| Chen, J., *et al.* [70] | KDDCup 99 | Quantum-based ALO with hybrid Clustering technique | KDDCup 99 based attacks | IoT network | ✓ | 98.69% |

(*Continued*)

**Table 1.5** Comparative analysis of intrusion detection methods and their performance metrics. (*Continued*)

| Author name (publication year) | Dataset used | Method used | Attack types | QoS and VPN support | Stability | Accuracy percentage (%) |
|---|---|---|---|---|---|---|
| Samadi Bonab, M., *et al.* [71] | UNSW-NB 15, NSL-KDD, KDDCup 99 | Fruit fly algorithm and Ant Lions & Ant Algorithm based method | Network-based attacks based on standard dataset | Public network | ✓ | 99.73% |
| Alsharafat *et al.* [72] | KDDCup 99 | Cuckoo based method | KDDCup based attacks | Public network | ✓ | 98.90% (DR), 0.09% (FAR) |
| Thirumalairaj, A., & Jeyakarthic, M. [73] | NSL-KDD2015, CICIDS-2017 | CS based IDS | Network-based attacks | Cloud-based network | ✓ | 99.95% |
| Liu, J., *et al.* [74] | UNSW-NB 15 | PSO and Machine Learning techniques | Shellcode, Backdoor and Worms | IoT network | ✓ | 86.68%, |
| Kan, X., *et al.* [75] | CIFA-10 | PSO and CNN were used | Zombie host carrying zombie virus | IoT network | ✓ | 95.60% |
| Ghanem, W. A. H., *et al.* [76] | UNSW-NB 15, NSL-KDD, KDDCup 99, ISCX2012 | Multi-Layer Perceptron with ABC method | DoS, R2L, U2R and PROBE, Infiltering, Brute Force, SSH, Botnet | Public network | ✓ | 94.40% |
| Mehanović, D., *et al.* [77] | NSL-KDD | Feature Selection by Genetic Algorithm | Network-based attacks | Cloud network | ✓ | 90.45% |

(*Continued*)

**Table 1.5** Comparative analysis of intrusion detection methods and their performance metrics. (*Continued*)

| **Author name (publication year)** | **Dataset used** | **Method used** | **Attack types** | **QoS and VPN support** | **Stability** | **Accuracy percentage (%)** |
|---|---|---|---|---|---|---|
| Halim, Z., *et al.* [78] | Bot-IoT , UNSW-NB15, CIRA-CIC -DOHBrw-2020, | Genetic Algorithm based method | Network-based attacks based on standard dataset | IoT network | ✓ | 99.80% |
| Qi, G., *et al.* [79] | KDDCup 99 | An Artificial Neural Network based on Back Propagation and ABC algorithm was used | Network-based attacks | Cloud network | ✓ | 98.08% |
| Chaganti, R., *et al.* [80] | IOMT | Machine Learning using CNN technique | Patient data | IoMT network | ✓ | 96% |
| Ethala, S., & Kumarappan, A. [81] | NSL-KDD, UNSW-NB 15 | Swarm Intelligence technique (SMO-HPSO) was used | Network attacks like DoS, R2L, U2R and PROBE | IoT network | ✓ | 99.175% |
| Ahmed, I., *et al.* [82] | NSL-KDD, CICIDS201, BoT-IoT | GTO and CNN methods are used | DoS, R2L, U2R and PROBE | IoT network | ✓ | 99.93% |

(*Continued*)

**Table 1.5** Comparative analysis of intrusion detection methods and their performance metrics. (*Continued*)

| **Author name (publication year)** | **Dataset used** | **Method used** | **Attack types** | **QoS and VPN support** | **Stability** | **Accuracy percentage (%)** |
|---|---|---|---|---|---|---|
| Ghanem, W. A. H., *et al.* [83] | ISCX2012, NSL-KDD, KDDCup 99, UNSW-NB 15 & CICIDS2017 | Bat Algorithm based method for feature selection and optimization | Network-based attacks based on standard dataset | Public network | ✓ | 97.82%<br>0.025% (FAR) |
| Abu Khurma, R., *et al.* [84] | N-BaIoT | SSA with ALO | IoT based attacks | IoT network | ✓ | 99.9 % (TPR)<br>0.029% (FAR) |
| Bangui, H., & Buhnova, B. [85] | DFFNN,<br>DBN,<br>DNN &<br>Deep | ALO and ACO based method | IoT-based attacks | Edge network | ✓ | 95.60% |
| Alzahrani, A.I.A., *et al.* [86] | UNSW-NB 15 | Transformer design-based method | Normal, Generic, DoS, Fuzzers, Reconnaissance,<br>Analysis<br>Worms | IoT cloud | ✓ | 97.22% (multi-class)<br>98.35%<br>(binary) |
| Abd Elaziz *et al.* [87] | KDDCup 99, NSL-KDD, BoT-IoT & CICIDS-2017 | Capuchin Search Algorithm and CNN based method | DoS, Probe, R2L and U2R | IoT-cloud | ✓ | 99.935% -99.994% in KDD & BIoT, CIC2017 |

(*Continued*)

**Table 1.5** Comparative analysis of intrusion detection methods and their performance metrics. (*Continued*)

| Author name (publication year) | Dataset used | Method used | Attack types | QoS and VPN support | Stability | Accuracy percentage (%) |
|---|---|---|---|---|---|---|
| Aldaej, A. *et al.* [88] | BoT-IoT, UNSW-NB15, ISCX2012, NSL-KDD | RNN and LSTM based method | DDoS and DoS | Edge-cloud | ✓ | 99.56% |
| Ali Kaffash *et al.* [89] | IoT23 | KNN for data classification and MLP for suspicious data classification | Benign, C & C-Mirai, DDoS-Mirai, Port Scan-Mirai etc. | Fog network | ✓ | 99.99% |
| Alrayes, F.S., *et al.* [90] | LSTM | Gorilla Troop Optimized and DL based Threat detection | Benign and Malignant attacks | IoT cloud | ✓ | 99.48% |
| Guilherme A., *et al.* [91] | Real-time data | Used Intel S/W Guard Extensions to perform integrity & confidentiality | Physical attacks | Cloud-IoT | ✓ | Latency –few milliseconds Scalability-4 to 6 /sec Time Complexity-O(n) |

(*Continued*)

**Table 1.5** Comparative analysis of intrusion detection methods and their performance metrics. (*Continued*)

| Author name (publication year) | Dataset used | Method used | Attack types | QoS and VPN support | Stability | Accuracy percentage (%) |
|---|---|---|---|---|---|---|
| Attou H., *et al.* [92] | BoT-IoT & NSL-KDD | Random Forest | Network attacks based on datasets | Cloud-IoT | ✓ | 98.3%, 99.99% |
| Mohamed, D., & Ismael, O. [93] | UNSW-NB15, ToN-IoT | Genetic Algorithm based classifier and Back Propagation Neural Network based detection method | Network attacks based on datasets | Cloud-IoT | ✓ | 96.47% 95.36% |
| Okey O. D. *et al.* [94] | CIC-IDS2017 & CSE-CICIDS-2018 | Ensemble transfer learning on CNN method | Bot, Infiltration, DDoS and DoS | Cloud-IoT | ✓ | 99.98% |
| Biswas, S., *et al.* [95] | UNSW-2021, Bot-IoT, UNSW-NB15, NAL-KDD, CIC-IDS2017 | Random Forest | Network attacks based on datasets | Cloud | ✓ | 99% (approx..) |
| Aldaej A., *et al.* [96] | BoT-IoT, UNSW-NB15, NSL-KDD, CICIDS2018 | Ensemble method | DDoS, DoS, Probing, Normal attacks | Edge-cloud | ✓ | 99.56% |
| Sepide Najafli *et al.* [97] | CIC-IDS 2018 | DL and Recurrent Learning based feature selection and detection technique used | Benign, DDoS, DoS, Brute Force, Botnet, Infiltration Web attack | Fog-Cloud | ✓ | 95.97% |

over different networks and protocols, making them susceptible to attacks that exploit these interconnections. Cloud services themselves are attractive targets for attackers due to the potential for large-scale data breaches and service disruptions. IoT devices often collect and transmit sensitive data. Breaches can lead to privacy violations, identity theft, or unauthorized access to personal information. Many industries e.g., healthcare, finance have stringent regulations regarding data protection, making intrusion detection essential for compliance and avoiding legal consequences. Following are a few prominent application areas of IDS:

i. **Industrial IoT (IIoT)**: Prevents unauthorized access to machinery and control systems in manufacturing plants [2, 21, 47].
ii. **Healthcare IoT**: Ensures the integrity of wearable health monitors and cloud-connected medical devices. Prevents manipulation of critical patient data or device malfunctions [28, 38].
iii. **Autonomous Vehicles**: Secures communication between vehicles, cloud systems, and IoT sensors [56].
iv. **Smart Homes**: Identifies unauthorized access to smart devices like cameras, thermostats, or alarms and protects user privacy and home security [44, 98].
v. **Smart Cities**: Protects public infrastructure, like traffic management systems and utility grids, from cyber threats. It also secures IoT sensors and cloud systems used in urban management [99].

## 1.8 Future Directions and Research Opportunities

While considering a practical solution to intrusions at different levels, it is inadvertent to identify an IDS/IDPS that addresses the online or real-time attacks. Few authors have addressed the solution pertaining to such attacks; still there are numerous avenues for future work. In the context of intrusion detection for cloud-IoT systems future directions and research opportunities are diverse and span multiple technological and operational dimensions. Below are key areas to explore:

i. Hybrid Models: Hybrid AI/ML models combining deep learning and traditional approach can improve accuracy.

ii. Few-Shot and Zero-Shot Learning: Enabling IDS to recognize new threats with minimal or no labeled data.
iii. Blockchain-Integrated Intrusion Detection: Exploring blockchain for decentralized and tamper-proof IDS logging and communication
iv. Context Aware IDS: Incorporating context data e.g., location, time for adaptive intrusion detection.
v. Quantum-Resilient IDS: Developing quantum-resistant IDS algorithms and integrating them into Cloud-IoT ecosystems.

## 1.9 Conclusion

The security in cloud-IoT systems becomes challenging due to the fact that there is substantial increase in IoT devices, users, their services and applications day by day. Since, IoT networks are based on smart environments that are largely deficient in security, they are prone to attacks namely DoS, DDoS, Probe and R2L. To overcome such challenges, a single solution based on IDPS can cater the need by addressing not only the intrusion detection and but also its prevention. The identification of a zero-day attacks also becomes a bottleneck to such smart environments. In such situations, where the detection trails are minimum, it is important to furnish a solution that is able to keep traces of small footprints of such attacks. This hindrance is more pronounced due to the fact that these zero-day attacks are novel attacks and cannot be detected without having any earlier footprints. Therefore, for such attacks, it is important to devise a solution that takes into consideration both the misuse-based and anomaly-based detection methods.

Moreover, in IoT networks, both power and other resource consumptions are reasonably high and thus, employing an IDPS would additionally consume more such resources. A lightweight IDPS needs to be devised while considering the design of the solution. Due to the versatility of cloud, it has become invincible and ubiquitous. Yet, cloud faces lot of challenges. Data in transit between the IoT device and cloud faces a lot of challenges while the communication is over the internet. To protect such data, strong encryption must be applied before it is transmitted. Moreover, a substantial attempt needs to be taken to address the zero-day attacks or unknown attacks that are more prevalent in financial institutions like banks, stock markets etc.

**AI disclosure statement:** The author acknowledges the use of AI-based tools for minor language editing or grammatical correction. However, all intellectual contributions, analyses, and conclusions presented in this chapter are entirely the author's own.

## References

1. Bastos, D., Cloud for IoT—A survey of technologies and security features of public cloud IoT solutions, in: *Living in the Internet of Things (IoT 2019)*, IET, pp. 1–6, 2019.
2. Pandey, N.K., Kumar, K., Saini, G., Mishra, A.K., Security issues and challenges in cloud of things-based applications for industrial automation. *Ann. Oper. Res.*, 1–20, 2023.
3. Almolhis, N., Haney, M., Alqhtani, F., Discovering and understanding the security issues in IoT cloud. *Int. J. Comput. Sci. Secur.*, *13*, 6, 255–265, 2019.
4. Sadeeq, M.M., Abdulkareem, N.M., Zeebaree, S.R., Ahmed, D.M., Sami, A.S., Zebari, R.R., IoT and Cloud computing issues, challenges and opportunities: A review. *Qubahan Acad. J.*, *1*, 2, 1–7, 2021.
5. Almolhis, N., Alashjaee, A.M., Duraibi, S., Alqahtani, F., Moussa, A.N., The security issues in IoT-cloud: A review, in: *2020 16th IEEE International Colloquium on Signal Processing & Its Applications (CSPA)*, 2020, February, IEEE, pp. 191–196.
6. Bazgir, E., Haque, E., Sharif, N.B., Ahmed, M.F., Security aspects in IoT based cloud computing. *World J. Adv. Res. Rev.*, *20*, 3, 540–551, 2023.
7. Corno, F., De Russis, L., Mannella, L., Helping novice developers harness security issues in cloud-IoT systems. *J. Reliab. Intell. Environ.*, *8*, 3, 261–283, 2022.
8. Mendez, D.M., Papapanagiotou, I., Yang, B., Internet of things: Survey on security and privacy, *arXiv preprint arXiv:1707.01879*, 2017.
9. Al Nafea, R. and Almaiah, M.A., Cyber security threats in cloud: Literature review, in: *2021 International Conference on Information Technology (ICIT)*, 2021, July, IEEE, pp. 779–786.
10. Bakhshi, T., Ghita, B., Kuzminykh, I., A Review of IoT Firmware Vulnerabilities and Auditing Techniques. *Sensors*, *24*, 2, 708, 2024.
11. Feng, X., Zhu, X., Han, Q.L., Zhou, W., Wen, S., Xiang, Y., Detecting vulnerability on IoT device firmware: A survey. *IEEE/CAA J. Autom. Sin.*, *10*, 1, 25–41, 2022.
12. Sami, N., Mufti, T., Sohail, S.S., Siddiqui, J., Kumar, D., Neha, Future Internet of Things (IoT) from Cloud perspective: Aspects, applications and challenges, in: *Internet of Things (IoT) Concepts and Applications*, pp. 515–532, 2020.

13. Taherkordi, A., Zahid, F., Verginadis, Y., Horn, G., Future cloud systems design: Challenges and research directions. *IEEE Access*, *6*, 74120–74150, 2018.
14. Sicato, J.C.S., Singh, S.K., Rathore, S., Park, J.H., A comprehensive analyses of intrusion detection system for IoT environment. *J. Inf. Process. Syst.*, *16*, 4, 975–990, 2020.
15. Luo, G., Chen, Z., Mohammed, B.O., A systematic literature review of intrusion detection systems in the cloud-based IoT environments. *Concurrency Comput. Pract. Exper.*, *34*, 10, e6822, 2022.
16. Martins, I., Resende, J.S., Sousa, P.R., Silva, S., Antunes, L., Gama, J., Host-based IDS: A review and open issues of an anomaly detection system in IoT. *Future Gener. Comput. Syst.*, *133*, 95–113, 2022.
17. Rebbah, M., Rebbah, D.E.H., Smail, O., Intrusion Detection in Cloud Internet of Things Environment, in: *2017 International Conference on Mathematics and Information Technology (ICMIT)*, 2017, December, IEEE, pp. 65–70.
18. Muhammad, M., Alyas, T., Ahmad, F., Butt, F., Qazi, W., Saqib, S., An analysis of security challenges and their perspective solutions for cloud computing and IoT. *EAI Endorsed Trans. Scalable Inf. Syst.*, *8*, 30, 2020.
19. Aslan, O., Ozkan-Okay, M., Gupta, D., Intelligent behavior-based malware detection system on cloud computing environment. *IEEE Access*, *9*, 83252–83271, 2021.
20. Botta, A., De Donato, W., Persico, V., Pescapé, A., Integration of cloud computing and internet of things: a survey. *Future Gener. Comput. Syst.*, *56*, 684–700, 2016.
21. Bagherzadeh, L., Shahinzadeh, H., Shayeghi, H., Dejamkhooy, A., Bayindir, R., Iranpour, M., Integration of cloud computing and IoT (CloudIoT) in smart grids: Benefits, challenges, and solutions, in: *2020 International Conference on Computational Intelligence for Smart Power System and Sustainable Energy (CISPSSE)*, 2020, July, IEEE, pp. 1–8.
22. Atlam, H.F., Alenezi, A., Alharthi, A., Walters, R.J., Wills, G.B., Integration of cloud computing with internet of things: Challenges and open issues, in: *2017 IEEE International Conference on Internet of Things (iThings) and IEEE Green Computing and Communications (GreenCom) and IEEE Cyber, Physical and social Computing (CPSCom) and IEEE Smart Data (SmartData)*, 2017, June, IEEE, pp. 670–675.
23. Nadir, I., Mahmood, H., Asadullah, G., A taxonomy of IoT firmware security and principal firmware analysis techniques. *Int. J. Crit. Infrastruct. Prot.*, *38*, 100552, 2022.
24. Suryateja, P.S., Threats and vulnerabilities of cloud computing: A review. *Int. J. Comput. Sci. Eng.*, *6*, 3, 297–302, 2018.
25. Otoum, Y. and Nayak, A., As-ids: Anomaly and signature based ids for the internet of things. *J. Netw. Syst. Manage.*, *29*, 3, 23, 2021.

26. Kazim, M., Liu, L., Zhu, S.Y., A framework for orchestrating secure and dynamic access of IoT services in multi-cloud environments. *IEEE Access*, *6*, 58619–58633, 2018.
27. Han, Z., Li, X., Huang, K., Feng, Z., A software defined network-based security assessment framework for cloudIoT. *IEEE Internet Things J.*, *5*, 3, 1424–1434, 2018.
28. Suleski, T., Ahmed, M., Yang, W., Wang, E., A review of multi-factor authentication in the Internet of Healthcare Things. *Digit. Health*, *9*, 20552076231177144, 2023.
29. Ometov, A., Bezzateev, S., Mäkitalo, N., Andreev, S., Mikkonen, T., Koucheryavy, Y., Multi-factor authentication: A survey. *Cryptography*, *2*, 1, 1, 2018.
30. Paris, I.L.B.M., Habaebi, M.H., Zyoud, A.M., Implementation of SSL/TLS security with MQTT protocol in IoT environment. *Wirel. Pers. Commun.*, *132*, 1, 163–182, 2023.
31. Devi, B.K. and Subbulakshmi, T., DDoS attack detection and mitigation techniques in cloud computing environment, in: *2017 International Conference on Intelligent Sustainable Systems (ICISS)*, 2017, December, IEEE, pp. 512–517.
32. Bhushan, K. and Gupta, B.B., Distributed denial of service (DDoS) attack mitigation in software defined network (SDN)-based cloud computing environment. *J. Ambient Intell. Hum. Comput.*, *10*, 1985–1997, 2019.
33. Kambourakis, G., Kolias, C., Stavrou, A., The mirai botnet and the IoT zombie armies, in: *MILCOM 2017-2017 IEEE Military Communications Conference (MILCOM)*, 2017, October, IEEE, pp. 267–272.
34. De Donno, M., Dragoni, N., Giaretta, A., Spognardi, A., DDoS-capable IoT malwares: Comparative analysis and Mirai investigation. *Secur. Commun. Netw.*, *2018*, 1, 7178164, 2018.
35. Srivastava, A. and Giffin, J., Tamper-resistant, application-aware blocking of malicious network connections, in: *Recent Advances in Intrusion Detection: 11th International Symposium, RAID 2008, Cambridge, MA, USA, September 15-17, 2008, Proceedings 11*, pp. 39–58, Springer Berlin Heidelberg, 2008.
36. Nunoo-Mensah, H., Boateng, K.O., Gadze, J.D., Tamper-aware authentication framework for wireless sensor networks. *IET Wirel. Sens. Syst.*, *7*, 3, 73–81, 2017.
37. Zakaria, M.I., Norizan, M.N., Isa, M.M., Jamlos, M.F., Mustapa, M., Comparative analysis on virtual private network in the internet of things gateways. *Indones. J. Electr. Eng. Comput. Sci.*, *28*, 1, 488–497, 2022.
38. Butpheng, C., Yeh, K.H., Xiong, H., Security and privacy in IoT-cloud-based e-health systems—A comprehensive review. *Symmetry*, *12*, 7, 1191, 2020.
39. Abssi, Y., Mishra, S., Shukla, M.K., Cloud Computing and Security in the IoT Era. *Helix-Sci. Explorer Peer Rev. Bimonthly Int. J.*, *10*, 04, 51–58, 2020.
40. Kumar, D.D., Mukharzee, J.D., Reddy, C.V.D., Rajagopal, S.M., Safe and Secure Communication Using SSL/TLS, in: *2024 International Conference on*

*Emerging Smart Computing and Informatics (ESCI)*, 2024, March, IEEE, pp. 1–6.

41. Xie, H., Zhang, Z., Zhang, Q., Wei, S., Hu, C., HBRSS: Providing high-secure data communication and manipulation in insecure cloud environments. *Comput. Commun.*, *174*, 1–12, 2021.
42. Anderson, J.P., Computer security threat monitoring and surveillance. Technical Report, James P. Anderson Company, 1980.
43. Kumar, M., Verma, H.K., Sikka, G., A secure lightweight signature based authentication for Cloud-IoT crowdsensing environments. *Trans. Emerging Telecommun. Technol.*, *30*, 4, e3292, 2019.
44. Visoottiviseth, V., Sakarin, P., Thongwilai, J., Choobanjong, T., Signature-based and behavior-based attack detection with machine learning for home IoT devices, in: *2020 IEEE Region 10 Conference (TENCON)*, 2020, November, IEEE, pp. 829–834.
45. Vijayaraghavan, V., IoT and cloud hinged smart irrigation system for urban and rural farmers employing MQTT protocol, in: *2020 5th International Conference on Devices, Circuits and Systems (ICDCS)*, 2020, March, IEEE, pp. 71–75.
46. Husnain, M., Hayat, K., Cambiaso, E., Fayyaz, U.U., Mongelli, M., Akram, H., Shah, G.A., Preventing mqtt vulnerabilities using IoT-enabled intrusion detection system. *Sensors*, *22*, 2, 567, 2022.
47. Garg, D., Rani, S., Herencsar, N., Verma, S., Wozniak, M., Ijaz, M.F., Hybrid technique for cyber-physical security in cloud-based smart industries. *Sensors*, *22*, 12, 4630, 2022.
48. Salehpour, A., Norouzi, M., Balafar, M.A., SamadZamini, K., A cloud-based hybrid intrusion detection framework using XGBoost and ADASYN-Augmented random forest for IoMT. *IET Commun.*, 2024.
49. Ahmad, Z., Shahid Khan, A., Wai Shiang, C., Abdullah, J., Ahmad, F., Network intrusion detection system: A systematic study of machine learning and deep learning approaches. *Trans. Emerging Telecommun. Technol.*, *32*, 1, e4150, 2021.
50. Hdidou, R. and El Alami, M.O.H.A.M.E.D., Advancements In Intrusion Detection Systems For Internet of Things: A State-of-The-Art and Comprehensive Analysis of Machine Learning Algorithms. *J. Theor. Appl. Inf. Technol.*, *102*, 2, 2024.
51. Abusafat, F., Pereira, T., Santos, H., Proposing a behavior-based IDS model for IoT environment, in: *EuroSymposium on Systems Analysis and Design*, pp. 114–134, Springer International Publishing, Cham, 2018.
52. Tsimenidis, S., Lagkas, T., Rantos, K., Deep learning in IoT intrusion detection. *J. Netw. Syst. Manage.*, *30*, 1, 8, 2022.
53. Dhinakaran, D., Sankar, S.M., Selvaraj, D., Raja, S.E., Privacy-Preserving Data in IoT-based Cloud Systems: A Comprehensive Survey with AI Integration, *arXiv preprint arXiv:2401.00794*, 2024.

54. Fenanir, S. and Semchedine, F., Smart Intrusion Detection in IoT Edge Computing Using Federated Learning. *Rev. Intell. Artif., 37*, 5, 2023.
55. Habiba, M., Islam, M.R., Muyeen, S.M., Ali, A.S., Edge intelligence for network intrusion prevention in IoT ecosystem. *Comput. Electr. Eng., 108*, 108727, 2023.
56. Ali Alheeti, K.M. and McDonald-Maier, K., Intelligent intrusion detection in external communication systems for autonomous vehicles. *Syst. Sci. Control Eng.*, 6, 1, 48–56, 2018.
57. Attkan, A. and Ranga, V., Cyber-physical security for IoT networks: a comprehensive review on traditional, blockchain and artificial intelligence based key-security. *Complex Intell. Syst.*, 8, 4, 3559–3591, 2022.
58. Shitharth, S., An enhanced optimization-based algorithm for intrusion detection in SCADA network. *Comput. Secur.*, 70, 16–26, 2017.
59. Natesan, P., Rajalaxmi, R.R., Gowrison, G., Balasubramanie, P., Hadoop based parallel binary bat algorithm for network intrusion detection. *Int. J. Parallel Program., 45*, 1194–1213, 2017.
60. Hajisalem, V. and Babaie, S., A hybrid intrusion detection system based on ABC–AFS algorithm for misuse and anomaly detection. *Comput. Netw.*, 136, 37–50, 2018.
61. Shen, Y., Zheng, K., Wu, C., Zhang, M., Niu, X., Yang, Y., An ensemble method based on selection using bat algorithm for intrusion detection. *Comput. J., 61*, 4, 526–538, 2018.
62. Akinyelu, A.A. and Adewumi, A.O., On the performance of cuckoo search and bat algorithms-based instance selection techniques for SVM speed optimization with application to e-fraud detection. *KSII Trans. Internet Inf. Syst.*, 12, 3, 1348–1375, 2018.
63. Idhammad, M., Afdel, K., Belouch, M., Distributed intrusion detection system for cloud environments based on data mining techniques. *Procedia Comput. Sci.*, 127, 35–41, 2018.
64. Mazini, M., Shirazi, B., Mahdavi, I., Anomaly network-based intrusion detection system using a reliable hybrid artificial bee colony and AdaBoost algorithms. *J. King Saud Univ. Comput. Inf. Sci.*, 31, 4, 541–553, 2019.
65. Nguyen, T.G., Phan, T.V., Nguyen, B.T., So-In, C., Baig, Z.A., Sanguanpong, S., Search: A collaborative and intelligent nids architecture for sdn-based cloud IoT networks. *IEEE Access, 7*, 107678–107694, 2019.
66. Roopa Devi, E. and Suganthe, R., Enhanced transductive support vector machine classification with grey wolf optimizer cuckoo search optimization for intrusion detection system. *Concurrency Comput. Pract. Exper.*, 32, 4, e4999, 2020.
67. Keserwani, P.K., Govil, M.C., Pilli, E.S., Govil, P., A smart anomaly-based intrusion detection system for the Internet of Things (IoT) network using GWO–PSO–RF model. *J. Reliab. Intell. Environ., 7*, 1, 3–21, 2021.
68. Nguyen, M.T. and Kim, K., Genetic convolutional neural network for intrusion detection systems. *Future Gener. Comput. Syst.*, 113, 418–427, 2020.

69. Ghanem, W.A. and Jantan, A., A new approach for intrusion detection system based on training multilayer perceptron by using enhanced Bat algorithm. *Neural Comput. Appl.*, 32, 11665–11698, 2020.
70. Chen, J., Qi, X., Chen, L., Chen, F., Cheng, G., Quantum-inspired ant lion optimized hybrid k-means for cluster analysis and intrusion detection. *Knowl.-Based Syst.*, *203*, 106167, 2020.
71. Samadi Bonab, M., Ghaffari, A., Soleimanian Gharehchopogh, F., Alemi, P., A wrapper-based feature selection for improving performance of intrusion detection systems. *Int. J. Commun. Syst.*, 33, 12, e4434, 2020.
72. Alsharafat *et al.*, The cuckoo feature filtration method for intrusion detection (cuckoo-ID). *Int. J. Adv. Comput. Sci. Appl.*, 11, 5, 2020.
73. Thirumalairaj, A. and Jeyakarthic, M., Hybrid cuckoo search optimization based tuning scheme for deep neural network for intrusion detection systems in cloud environment. *J. Res. Lepid.*, 51, 2, 209–224, 2020.
74. Liu, J., Yang, D., Lian, M., Li, M., Research on intrusion detection based on particle swarm optimization in IoT. *IEEE Access*, *9*, 38254–38268, 2021.
75. Kan, X., Fan, Y., Fang, Z., Cao, L., Xiong, N.N., Yang, D., Li, X., A novel IoT network intrusion detection approach based on adaptive particle swarm optimization convolutional neural network. *Inf. Sci.*, *568*, 147–162, 2021.
76. Ghanem, W.A.H., *et al.*, An efficient intrusion detection model based on hybridization of artificial bee colony and dragonfly algorithms for training multilayer perceptrons. *IEEE Access*, 8, 130452–130475, 2020.
77. Mehanović, D., Kečo, D., Kevrić, J., Jukić, S., Miljković, A., Mašetić, Z., Feature selection using cloud-based parallel genetic algorithm for intrusion detection data classification. *Neural Comput. Appl.*, *33*, 11861–11873, 2021.
78. Halim, Z., Yousaf, M.N., Waqas, M., Sulaiman, M., Abbas, G., Hussain, M., Hanif, M., An effective genetic algorithm-based feature selection method for intrusion detection systems. *Comput. Secur.*, *110*, 102448, 2021.
79. Qi, G., Zhou, J., Jia, W., Liu, M., Zhang, S., Xu, M., Intrusion detection for network based on elite clone artificial bee colony and back propagation neural network. *Wirel. Commun. Mobile Comput.*, *2021*, 1, 9956371, 2021.
80. Chaganti, R., Mourade, A., Ravi, V., Vemprala, N., Dua, A., Bhushan, B., A particle swarm optimization and deep learning approach for intrusion detection system in internet of medical things. *Sustainability*, *14*, 19, 12828, 2022.
81. Ethala, S. and Kumarappan, A., A hybrid spider monkey and hierarchical particle swarm optimization approach for intrusion detection on Internet of Things. *Sensors*, 22, 21, 8566, 2022.
82. Ahmed, I., *et al.*, Feature selection model based on gorilla troops optimizer for intrusion detection systems. *J. Sens.*, 2022, 1–12, 2022.
83. Ghanem, W.A.H., *et al.*, Cyber intrusion detection system based on a multiobjective binary bat algorithm for feature selection and enhanced bat algorithm for parameter optimization in neural networks. *IEEE Access*, 10, 76318–76339, 2022.

84. Abu Khurma, R., Almomani, I., Aljarah, I., IoT botnet detection using Salp swarm and ant lion hybrid optimization model. *Symmetry*, 13, 8, 1377, 2021.
85. Bangui, H. and Buhnova, B., Lightweight intrusion detection for edge computing networks using deep forest and bio-inspired algorithms. *Comput. Electr. Eng.*, 100, 107901, 2022.
86. Alzahrani, A.I., Al-Rasheed, A., Ksibi, A., Ayadi, M., Asiri, M.M., Zakariah, M., Anomaly detection in fog computing architectures using custom tab transformer for internet of things. *Electronics, 11*, 23, 4017, 2022.
87. Abd Elaziz, M., Al-qaness, M.A., Dahou, A., Ibrahim, R.A., Abd El-Latif, A.A., Intrusion detection approach for cloud and IoT environments using deep learning and Capuchin Search Algorithm. *Adv. Eng. Softw., 176*, 103402, 2023.
88. Aldaej, A., Ahanger, T.A., Ullah, I., Deep Learning-Inspired IoT-IDS Mechanism for Edge Computing Environments. *Sensors, 23*, 9869, 2023.
89. Kaffash, A., Kamel, S.R., Kheirabadi, M., A Two-Layer Intrusion Detection System Based on Fog and Cloud Using Improved KNN and MPNN, 2023.
90. Alrayes, F.S., *et al.*, Enhanced gorilla troops optimizer with deep learning enable cybersecurity threat detection. *Comput. Syst. Sci. Eng.*, 45, 3, 3037–3052, 2023.
91. Thomaz, G.A., Guerra, M.B., Sammarco, M., Detyniecki, M., Campista, M.E.M., Tamper-proof access control for IoT clouds using enclaves. *Ad Hoc Netw.*, 147, 103191, 2023.
92. Attou, H., Guezzaz, A., Benkirane, S., Azrour, M., Farhaoui, Y., Cloud-based intrusion detection approach using machine learning techniques. *Big Data Min. Anal.*, 6, 3, 311–320, 2023.
93. Mohamed, D. and Ismael, O., Enhancement of an IoT hybrid intrusion detection system based on fog-to-cloud computing. *J. Cloud Comp.*, 12, 41, 2023.
94. Okey, O.D., Melgarejo, D.C., Saadi, M., Rosa, R.L., Kleinschmidt, J.H., Rodríguez, D.Z., Transfer learning approach to IDS on cloud IoT devices using optimized CNN. *IEEE Access*, 11, 1023–1038, 2023.
95. Biswas, S. and Ansari, M.S.A., Securing IoT networks in cloud computing environments: a real-time IDS. *J. Supercomput.*, 80, 14489–14519, 2024.
96. Aldaej, A., Ullah, I., Ahanger, T.A., Atiquzzaman, M., Ensemble technique of intrusion detection for IoT-edge platform. *Sci. Rep.*, 14, 1, 11703, 2024.
97. Najafli, S., Toroghi Haghighat, A., Karasfi, B., A novel reinforcement learning-based hybrid intrusion detection system on fog-to-cloud computing. *J. Supercomput.*, 80, 18, 26088–26110, 2024.
98. Ali, B. and Awad, A.I., Cyber and physical security vulnerability assessment for IoT-based smart homes. *Sensors*, 18, 3, 817, 2018.
99. Ramana, N. and Krishna, E.H., Intrusion Detection System Fog Security Model for the Smart Cities and Urban Sensing. *J. Sens. IoT Health Sci.*, 1, 01, 51–63, 2023.

# 2

# Applications of Artificial Intelligence for Early Detection of Cyber Threats in Cloud Networks for IoT Devices: A Sentinel Analysis

**Kaushiki Chatterjee[1] and Soumen Santra[2]***

[1]*Department of Computer Science, RCC Institute of Information Technology, Kolkata, India*
[2]*Department of Computer Application, Techno International New Town, Kolkata, India*

***Abstract***
Traditional security solutions frequently fall short in this changing context. Thus, integrating Artificial Intelligence (AI) for proactive threat detection in IoT networks is critical. The Internet of Cyber Security Things (IoCST) is a rapidly expanding study, which presents new challenges beyond traditional security methods. Artificial intelligence (AI) has emerged as an effective tool for improving IoT security by enabling advanced threat detection and response capabilities. Artificial intelligence systems can continuously monitor network traffic and device behavior, providing real-time insights and alerts. AI can also detect anomalies *via* pattern recognition, allowing machine learning models to learn typical IoT device behavior patterns. Behavioral analysis aids in the detection of abnormalities such as odd access times, unexpected data transfers, or atypical command sequences. Through pattern recognition, AI can also identify anomalies, enabling machine learning models to pick up on the typical behavior patterns of Internet of Things (IoT) devices. Irregularities like odd access times, unexpected data transfers, or strange command sequences can be found with the use of behavioral analysis. Using predictive analytics, AI may also anticipate certain security incidents before they happen. To evaluate the IoT network's vulnerabilities, pinpoint weak points, and put preventative measures in place to lessen risks, it may also simulate different attack scenarios. AI-powered security solutions

**Corresponding author*: santrasoumen230@gmail.com

Partha Ghosh, Rajdeep Chakraborty, Anupam Ghosh and Ahmed A. Elngar (eds.) Strategic Approaches to Intrusion Detection in Cloud-IoT Ecosystem, (31–48) © 2026 Scrivener Publishing LLC

can automatically respond to recognized threats by isolating compromised devices, blocking malicious traffic, and notifying administrators. This guarantees that threats are quickly neutralized, reducing possible damage. AI-driven security solutions will be more and more necessary as the IoT grows to safeguard linked devices against new threats and to guarantee their dependability. The study has introduced different case prospects of cyber security aspects in cloud networks for IoT devices using a sentinel analysis approach.

***Keywords***: Malware attacks, *ad hoc* network, optimization techniques, cloud federated network, data center

## 2.1 Introduction

The Internet of Cyber Security Things (IoCST) ranges from smart home gadgets to industrial sensors that form an intricate web of data and communication. While this connectedness has many advantages, it also poses new security risks and difficulties. AI can also enable self-healing networks, which automatically resolve difficulties caused by attacks, ensuring the continued operation of vital IoT equipment. AI technologies can improve existing security frameworks by adding layers of defense and dynamically adapting to changing threats. They can efficiently handle enormous amounts of data, providing the scalability required to manage increasing IoT networks. Finally, by offering advanced monitoring, anomaly detection, predictive analytics, and automated response, and complementing integration with current security measures, AI can also use predictive analytics to anticipate future security incidents. It may also simulate several attack scenarios to assess vulnerabilities in the IoT network, finding weak points and executing risk mitigation strategies. AI significantly contributes to improving IoT security.

In Figure 2.1, the chapter has shown the different layers of IoT framework in modern application fields [1, 2].

One advanced threat vector is the development and spread of malware and botnets based on IoCST [3]. The disclosure of personal information may lead to enduring impacts on people's lives. Consistent cybersecurity issues have the potential to erode the confidence of the public in IoT technologies [4]. Lack of trust could pose a barrier to the broad acceptance of IoT solutions, thus preventing them from unlocking their complete capabilities.

In the IoCST framework, every layer is interconnected and distinguished by its functions and the equipments. Different viewpoints exist regarding the quantity of layers. According to Ref. [5], a five-layer model

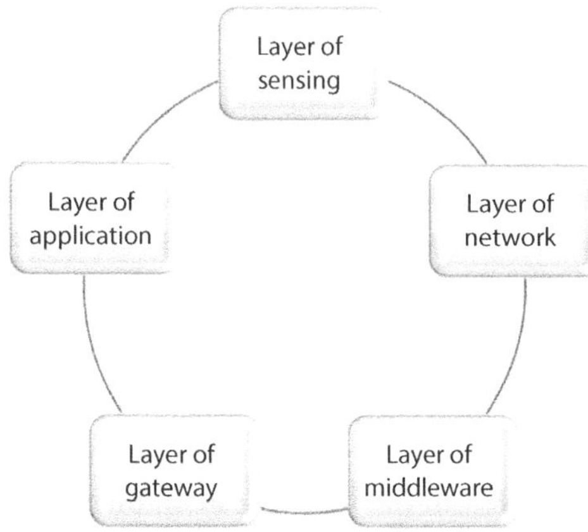


**Figure 2.1** Architecture of IoCST.

is commonly accepted by researchers in the field of IoT. The five layers in question encompass the Sensing Layer and the Network Layer. Utilizing a variety of technologies across different layers presents an array of challenges. Security threats also need to be considered. It is crucial to acknowledge the importance of interaction and relationship.

The environment influences the actions of the actuators as they perform tasks according to provided information. Information collected by these sensors was documented by Jing *et al.* in 2014 [6]. Multiple IoT applications such as GPS, RFID, RSNs, WSNs, and more are being utilized in different scenarios. Yet, the Sensing Layer faces various security vulnerabilities, e.g., potential tampering with sensors, where adversaries could potentially compromise and manipulate sensor devices, controlling actuators in IoCST scenarios to gain command over them. The IoCST application was mentioned in a study by Pathak and colleagues in 2021 [31].

Adversaries can introduce inaccurate data which are stored in the sensors' memory. Updating firmware or software for wireless communication is common among IoT nodes, compromising the facility [7].

Examinations of power usage, laser assaults, and attacks: Timing attacks have the potential to expose sensitive information. In putting the plan into action, the utilization of cryptographic modules could assist in averting such attacks. Eavesdropping and interference are common issues when deploying sensors in open areas. Environments can be compromised, and information can be vulnerable to manipulation. Capturing can occur [8] by endless cycles' result in a sudden increase in energy utilization. The fast drainage of batteries may occur, leading to their quick depletion.

Unfortunately, we are unable to provide the service at this time due to the batteries being depleted [9].

Due to a range of security concerns, phishing attacks can be carried out by adversaries through phishing sites by luring users to deceptive websites with the intention of extracting their account information.

*Qualifications*: These malicious actors acquire this valuable information [10]. DDoS/DoS attacks involve the disruption of services by attackers, impacting legitimate users. Users flood target servers with a massive amount of traffic. Regarding requests, for instance, the Mirai botnet took advantage of this opportunity, exposing vulnerability through the continuous bombardment of inadequately configured IoT devices.

*Manipulation of routes*: In the IoCST system, intruders manipulate tracing routes. Incidents occur while information is being transported. Sinkhole incidents entail redirecting the sensing requests away from an improperly advantageous situation which establishing a routing path. This path draws a multitude nodes which efficiently guide the traffic network. The difficulty of identifying this attack is where the challenge lies, with its ability to monitor network activities discreetly. The changes in the real systems of IoT were made in the study by Agiollo and colleagues in 2021 [32]. The Middleware Layer serves as a crucial connection between two components. On the Internet of Things, the network and application layers work together seamlessly. It can enable efficient computing and communicate functions. It is enhancing storage capabilities and providing APIs to meet the needs of the requirements. According to Zhang *et al.* [11] , this pertains to the Application Layer, which ensures the protection of cloud servers. The compilation of middleware attacks encompasses the man-in-the-middle attack where adversaries gain unauthorized access, gaining entry to the broker's system and positioning it. There is a possibility that they could potentially assume full control.

*Application of the Internet of Things (IoT)*: SQL injection attacks pose a threat to the Middleware Layer. It involves informed sending manipulated commands. Providing instructions to a software application may lead to the recovery of confidential details from the client, and possible modifications may be discussed [12, 13].

Signature wrapping attack transmits inaccurate information. Sending cloud malware can be an attempt made by adversaries to infiltrate computer systems. It is essential in ensuring the seamless connection between users. It is functioning as crucial to act as an intermediary between users and service management. It is securing the transmission of data for safety which is susceptible to risk.

Securing end-to-end encryption to facilitate secure communication by updating the firmware. This firmware is very crucial for maintaining the security of network. The procedure for completing this task is keeping track of records for the latest firmware updates, ensuring the authenticity and verifying signatures while downloading different versions. Updating firmware is crucial for enhancing security within your devices. This assists in avoiding the installation of harmful or unauthorized firmware, securing and maintaining the integrity of the IoT devices that are connected. Passing through the gateway: Security concerns are related to the application layer which is passing through the gateway. The Application Layer interacts directly with end-users, and it is responsible for providing services to clients in various fields including smart technology for residence, intelligent meters, innovative urban areas, advanced grids etc. Nevertheless, this layer is vulnerable to various attacks. Information theft is a common concern as users tend to store private information on IoT devices. Applications may become susceptible to information threats due to certain vulnerabilities. Various methods and protocols are employed to reduce the risk of information theft. Like encryption, the concept of information isolation, along with considerations for client and network security, plays a vital role in ensuring data protection.

Incorrect code transmission attempts, known as false code sending attacks, can be carried out by adversaries using Cross-Site Scripting. Monitoring network activity in IoT applications is varies due to lack of adequate preparation where client secrets can be compromised by adversaries due to it's security protocols. If the programming process is not successful, there is a need to revisit and reprogram the attacks accordingly to collect the data from the application. Because here the skillfully protected opponents might try to alter confidential information from the program which has executed.

## 2.2 Implementing Protective Measures and Following Best Practices to Mitigate Threats from IoCST

Blockchain serves a pivotal function in enhancing security within the given context. The unique characteristic of the previous existing articles has shown in the Table 2.1. The true beauty of permissionless blockchain stems from the ability to easily become part of this network. It does not necessitate any authorization. Bitcoin serves as a prime example of digital currency innovation. Blockchain operates in a permissionless manner, allowing participants the freedom to join or exit at their discretion. This blockchain can maintain a maximum level. The number of nodes has a comparatively lower fan-out. On the other hand, permissioned blockchains function within a clearly established set of regulations.

**Table 2.1** Comparison for existing works on IoCST threats.

| SL no. | Author | Features | Research gap | Remarks |
|---|---|---|---|---|
| 1 | Radovici *et al.* [12] | Secure framework for malwares and threats. | Works only upon software. Hardware based threats not considered. | Broader approach for both hardware and software framework are missing. |
| 2 | Olukunle *et al.* [13] | Threats of cyber security in the time of IoT. | diagrammatic representation is not considered | Security if IoT devices should be analyzed. |
| 3 | Mohammed *et al.* [14] | Application of IoT and threats of security | Cloud based IoT security in federated network is not considered | All kinds of security measures could have been elaborated. |
| 4 | Sahu, S.K., *et al.* [15] | Implemented blockchain for IoT security | Resilience privacy about IoT devices should be stronger | Brief elaboration and connections with existing methodologies should be considered |
| 5 | Rashid *et al.* [16] | Enhancing Cybersecurity in Cyber-Physical Systems with AI | AI enabled methodologies or algorithm should be considered in brief way | AI enabled algorithms to have elaborated in this study. |

Participants are required to comply with joining the network. For those without the need for permission, servers strategically positioned throughout the network are responsible for securely storing encrypted data. Content is available for clients to download. The removal of centralized cloud servers is facilitated by blockchain, improving the security of IoT systems by removing centralization. Decentralization and encryption are employed in this process. Cryptographic hash functions help enhance security by minimizing vulnerability. Centralized cloud servers have focused on the information which are targeting by criminals those who are committed to theft the information. Data is shared among all network nodes, enhancing security measures even more, discovered in a variety of Internet of Things (IoT) applications that utilize fog technology. Irrespective of the circumstances, blockchain offers connectivity between devices despite their geographical distance. It is adjusting the information which requires for making changes. It is modifying the hash function for enhanced security and isolation of the information. The task at hand is to rephrase the provided text in a smooth and refined manner. Clients with integrity can gain access. Information stored in the cloud is secured using hash functions for each data set, which is verified by another network client, thereby reducing the need for authentication. Potential for storing unethical information is present. Utilizing blockchain technology aids in the prevention of information loss and spoofing attacks. This acts as a preventive measure against spoofing attacks on the Internet of Things (IoT) realm. In applications, there are instances where nodes from adversaries try to breach and infiltrate and duplicate within the network.

*The registration of genuine information*: Blockchain makes it easy to interact with clients or devices. Identification and authentication can be conducted independently without the need for dependence. *Certification authorities*: Because of the low-power characteristics of IoT, through the utilization of blockchain technology, information loss is prevented in devices. Additions made to the chain are permanent and cannot be undone. The information can only be accessed by the intended recipient. It is securing the data through encoding technique which improves safety measurements. These issues are commonly found in IoT applications. The proxy-based architecture of blockchain showcases resilience despite its complexities. Built-in security aspects are designed for decentralized settings, such as the Internet of Things (IoT), which also faces limitations in available resources. Proxy-based architecture has come to the forefront. As a promising option, enabling IoT devices to take advantage of blockchain can be utilized without the need to store a cumbersome ledger. The Merkle tree uses as a valuable component in blockchain system. It is enhancing the security of IoT devices through an improved information structure. This method efficiently decreases the quantity and includes blocks within the blockchain and the utilization of hashing at various levels. The Merkle tree gives the security of data at all levels. It is enhancing the integrity of data at a deeper level. IoCST can enhance blockchain's architecture to optimize its efficiency for this particular purpose. The communication patterns are typical of IoCST devices which are different from one another. Various technologies are available, each providing a wide range of applications.

The IoCST is increasingly prevalent in today's technological landscape. It has vastly broadened the world of intelligent devices and applications, it is enhancing the user interactions to provide a more fulfilling experience. In the meantime, cloud computing offers a variety of benefits, e.g., a streamlined solution for storing and managing information to ensure maximum efficiency. The platform is easily accessible from anywhere and has been embraced by many users. *Enterprises*: The widespread adoption of IoT has given rise to an unparalleled situation. The increase in data production is placing a significant strain on the Internet. The development of infrastructure is crucial for the growth of a country. It is used to tackle the obstacles and embrace fresh prospects through the integration of IoT technology within the cloud setting. Nevertheless, the advantages obtained by just integrating cloud services and IoT is not adequate to address the issue effectively in every challenge. Its objective is to target issues. Challenges encountered in the world of IoT can be addressed by providing the solution. The proximity facilitates quicker data processing. By minimizing latency and improving efficiency, it effectively complements the overall performance. The potential of conventional cloud computing within the realm IoCST is being explored. The primary role of fog computing is the oversight of data. The data produced by neighboring IoT devices to facilitate efficient monitoring, requiring a complex architectural design with multiple layers.

*IoCST attack*: It provides an added layer of security. *The cloud or Internet of Things (IoT) system*: All efforts should be directed towards preventing any potential attacks on IoT systems. Salem *et al.* and Hu *et al.* have explained the navigating through the fog layer to facilitate the recognition and reduction of unusual behaviors which were observed prior to the system's operation [17, 18]. Storage provision of details on fog nodes boosts security measures, guaranteeing client safety. The data stays safer and easily accessible [19].

It is listening the private conversations which entails the communication solely between the end customers. Additionally, the presence of fog nodes helps reduce the necessity for routing information across the entire network. This greatly diminishes the chances. Considering the reduced amount of traffic, it is important to be mindful of potential eavesdropping by hostile entities. According to Anajemba *et al.* [8], it was found on the network where the resource limitations need to be addressed. Many IoT devices struggle with resource limitations, making them susceptible to potential manipulation by enemies. Fog nodes are essential in addressing this challenge, aiding edge devices and safeguarding them against potential threats. *Incidents of aggression*: Furthermore, the closeness of these fog nodes enables them to be highly efficient in their operations. Security capabilities should be further enhanced to strengthen security measures.

The overall resilience of the system to potential threats is being evaluated by Imteaj *et al.* [20]. It was found that IoCST systems perform computations near their devices, in locations where data is produced. In the absence of a sufficient intrusion detection mechanism, policy enforcement may be compromised [21]. IoCST could potentially remain undetected and overlooked [22]. Opponents may have the potential to control regional amenities. Fog nodes have the potential to work together with nearby nodes. Nodes are utilized to identify attacks that are aimed at local services. *Observing the situation*: The interaction between programs and host file systems enables the identification of potential issues.

*Verifying one's identity*: Building trust among all parties is essential and presents a significant challenge, amplifying security concerns for IoT services. Shukla and colleagues [23] have analyzed customer data. Consequently, efficient methods for verifying identity are essential. It is necessary to guarantee the provision of secure services. A few suggestions on effective methods for identity authentication have been implemented. Decentralized computations can present various potential risks opponents have. The possibility exists to influence the analyzed outcomes and reveal refined data. Server-assisted computation can be considered. IoT devices can handle tasks within their capabilities, while more advanced tasks can be performed by other means, e.g., the support provided by fog nodes. Nevertheless, it brings along a potential risk of the potential disclosure of information to adversaries, which is a matter of concern, particularly when it involves fog nodes. The method is designed to enhance the security of computing processes, with the goal to minimize the risks connected to handling sensitive information. Dense fog has reduced visibility in the area. Secondly, the importance of having a reliable method to authenticate operations is emphasized. The nodes are precise and have not been tampered with. This guarantees the integrity and accuracy of the dependability of the computation outcomes.

The information stored in IoT devices encompasses a range of data including social gatherings, traffic conditions, and private activities. *The heat level*: Some of this information might be confidential or sensitive. Some things may require a delicate approach, whereas others could be more widely shared with the public. Moreover, the same material could possess different security settings tailored to meet the needs of various users. It is crucial to identify and safeguard vital information, amidst the vast quantities of data.

*Safely sharing information*: One of the essential security practices is encrypting data uploaded to fog servers. Nodes are structured to allow readability solely by their rightful owner. Nevertheless, this encryption presents difficulties when it comes to sharing information. These methods are designed to achieve a specific goal which facilitates the secure and managed sharing of encrypted data.

Encryption is required when sending data to the fog node. Due to security reasons, nevertheless, the implementation of such encryption entails introducing facing obstacles, and trade-offs involve sacrificing certain appealing aspects such as the ability to share exploring and gathering. *Exploring information in a secure manner*: Aligned with the concept of temporary storage, information is the data which is secured with encryption prior to being uploaded. *Seeking or retrieving information*: It becomes challenging for both owners and recipients to decipher encrypted ciphertext. To tackle this issue, methods of searchable encryption can be utilized. The privacy levels of each entity are clearly outlined, establishing a structured framework, to safely access data from encrypted text. Next on the agenda is the aggregation of information to reduce the loss of information while enhancing communication efficiency and to enhance security and prevent information theft. It is necessary to enhance the development of aggregation techniques to attain a high level of security. There are several methods of homomorphic encryption which have been suggested by Doan *et al.* [24] to collate data from various sources. These strategies allow for the utilization of fog. Nodes gather information while ensuring its confidentiality. Data points at an individual level. Decentralized computation is the focus of this section. Decentralized computations present several potential risks. The ability to influence the analyzed findings and reveal them is present.

*Server-assisted computation*: IoT devices can handle tasks that are deemed beyond their capability. They are reducing the potential risks which are linked to handling confidential data. *Nodes for fog computing where computation can be confirmed*: Clients depend on fog nodes to process their data, emphasizing the importance of having a reliable method to verify the fog node's security. *The outcomes of the calculation*: Verifiable computation techniques are crucial. Users have to assured that the calculations carried out by fog in confidence. The nodes are precise and have not been altered. This guarantees the integrity and reliability. *The dependability of the computed outcomes*: Combining Industry 4.0 with the Internet of Things for seamless integration, the idea of interconnectedness is deeply rooted in the concept, facilitating seamless communication between machines and devices. Systems communicate and collaborate independently. In this situation, in the current paradigm, the Internet of Things (IoT) plays a crucial role in establishing the necessary infrastructure to ensure smooth connection and data transmission. *Sophisticated and responsive manufacturing settings*: Incorporating IoT into Industry 4. 0 requires harnessing the capabilities of IoT and utilizing technologies to enhance different facets of industrial processes. This involves overseeing, regulating, enhancing, and making decisions. This integration is geared towards establishing a smart, interconnected, and self-governing system.

## 2.3 Utilizing Diffie-Hellman for Enhancing IoT Security

Figure 2.2 shows the solutions of the IoT framework in different layers. It can participate in blockchain technology for cryptocurrency purposes. It also implements Bitcoin or ethereum virtual machine (EVM) algorithms. Different types of machine learning algorithms can be incorporated with the IoT tools which have worked on dynamic environments like weather forecasting, trade indicating, etc. There are two more wings like fog computing and edge computing. Fog computing elaborates the methodologies for various applications of mobile version outputs where big data has been implemented. In edge computing, the IoT has played a significant role for uploading and downloading big images as output from mobile-based applications where sensors and transducers have been implemented for real datasets.

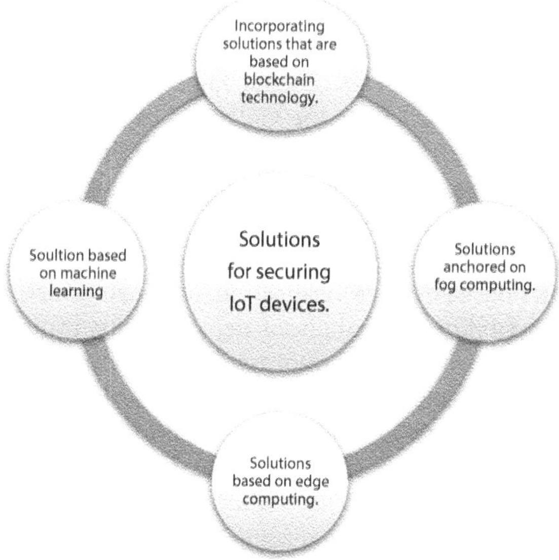


**Figure 2.2** Framework for IoCST security solutions.

Authentication, authorization, and other aspects of IoT security are important to consider. *Defense against a range of potential attacks*: A thorough approach to IoT security would probably require the implementation of various measures. A blend of cryptographic techniques along with secure protocols have utilized and implemented the most effective methods to cater the needs and obstacles in the realm of IoT settings [25].

## 2.4 Utilizing Machine Learning to Enhance Security in the Realm of IoT

A protocol based on MLP has been developed to enhance network security against DoS attacks. Leveraging machine learning algorithms facilitates enhancement. Enhancing the security of IoCST devices is bolstered by the precision of deductions [26]. Machine learning techniques are available to safeguard devices against potential threats. *Listening in on private conversations*: Khan *et al.* has explained the assessment of these plans which were carried out and conducted by means of a range of experiments and reinforcement techniques [27]. The gathering of personal information, including health-related particulars, and the sharing of location data or images could potentially compromise client privacy. To lessen or reduce this risk, the discussion revolves around the protection of privacy through the incorporation of privacy-preserving scientific methods. It is performing the computations using the Parallel Prefix Sum (PPSC) method. It is necessary to establishing the trust in IoCST by implementations and protecting the data against threats. Digital fingerprinting is another useful technique which is consider for the violations of privacy of data. Digital fingerprinting emerges as a fantastic solution to enhance. Ensuring the protection of IoCST systems is crucial for building trust with end-users, e.g., the prevalent nature of the utilization of fingerprints for actions like unlocking smartphones, granting permission for payments, and unlocking vehicle and house entrance verification, due to its widespread acclaim. Due to its affordability and enhanced dependability, traits of the digital fingerprinting have arisen as a significant form of biometric identification. Nevertheless, notwithstanding its benefits, the proficient integration of digital fingerprinting into IoT encounters various challenges, facing various difficulties and obstacles. These encompass matters concerning fingerprint categorization. *Improvement of images and matching of features*: To deal with these issues, numerous machine learning algorithms have been developed to address these challenges [28].

Support Vector Machine optimizes the separation distance in decision-making. This method studies the unique patterns of the fingerprint and it allows for pairing according to the recognized patterns. It can develop the feature vectors through border analysis and training patterns. This is technological advancement. The analysis delves into the unique patterns of the fingerprint and enables accurate mapping with artificial neural networks, commonly referred to as ANN, An algorithm utilized in machine learning that provides numerous benefits [29]. Verification is conducted using network connectivity and fingerprint authentication. Experiential values have been stored in the database, the function performed by machines. In the IoT landscape, acquiring knowledge is crucial to safeguard everything interlinked in systems and devices. The process of machine learning algorithms has been programmed to identify irregularities or undesired actions. In IoT systems, the risk of losing information is minimized by addressing possible concerns to prevent any future problems. As the Internet of Things ecosystem keeps evolving, Machine technology continues to advance and grow through ongoing contributions and developments. Education is crucial for ensuring the security and progress of a society [30–32].

## 2.5 Future

*The potential for the future*: The development and continuous progress of the IoCST environment is required for its success and it can achieve a seamless and effective integration through out different sectors. Utilizing intelligence can be harnessed to create increasingly refined solutions. *Detection and mitigation strategies customized for threats*: IoT settings employ methods to effectively combat continuously changing cyber threats. The incorporation of new technologies is seamlessly integrated with the emergence of cutting-edge technologies like quantum computing. In the realm of homomorphic encryption, potential future studies may delve into their intricacies further. *The relevance of strengthening IoT security*: The use of quantum-resistant cryptographic algorithms has the potential to provide robust security for the Internet of Things, investigating the possibilities in communication and data integrity and utilizing homomorphic encryption for enhanced security and privacy preservation. Areas within IoT networks where data processing takes place are abundant. In a fluid and graceful manner, one can embark on a journey of exploration.

*Privacy-preserving solutions*: When it comes to gathering and analyzing data, efforts are made to protect privacy. There is an increasing demand for solutions that preserve privacy. The secure collaboration should be facilitated for sharing the data. It is conducting the analyses on each person to control the privacy of the rights. Standardization and interoperability are key aspects to ensure seamless compatibility and integration. It is essential to have stringent standards and protocols in place for ensuring the security of IoT, ensuring seamless communication and connection between various IoT devices. Ecosystems can be quite fascinating to study. Future research endeavors can direct their attention towards the development of security frameworks, protocols, and certifications that are standardized means to enhance consistent security procedures and practices to enable smooth integration of IoT devices and platforms. Tools and resources are available to enable active engagement in safeguarding IoT. It is crucial to have devices and networks in place. Future studies can direct their attention to creating security interfaces. These are easy to use for educating the users. It is utilizing various resources by centralization of methods to enhance the security and promoting mindfulness. It is fostering a proactive approach to managing the risks among the stakeholders which involved in the Internet of Things. Factors such as regulatory and policy considerations come into play when considering the adoption of IoT. As the pace of progress quickens, an urgent requirement arises for establishing thorough regulatory structures and policies for governance in the conscientious implementation and functioning of IoT systems. Future studies could delve into the socio-economic consequences to evaluate compliance with IoT security regulations. It is addressing the obstacles and suggesting the methods to promote global unity to guarantee cohesion and effectiveness for the regulatory environment.

## 2.6 Conclusion

The report has outlined a range of roles of the IoCST. It plays the significant role to incorporating the strong security measures like secure authentication, authorization, encryption etc. It also updates software on a regular basis. Additionally, since many IoT devices are positioned in public or remote areas, which raises the possibility of theft or tampering, enterprises should consider the physical security of these devices. Unauthorized access to IoT equipment can be successfully prevented by using physical security measures like locks or tamper-evident tape. Education and training initiatives aimed at aiding individuals and organizations in comprehending the potential risks and outcomes associated with IoT-related attacks can also be implemented. With through collaboration, we have the potential to establish a safer and more secure interconnected world, ensuring that the advantages of IoT technology can be fully enjoyed without jeopardizing security.

**AI disclosure statement:** The author confirms that no artificial intelligence (AI)-generated content or AI-assisted writing tools were used in the preparation of this chapter (including summaries and the abstract). All text, analysis, and conclusions are the result of the author's original work.

## References

1. Ray, P.P., De, D., Chattopadhyay, S., Security in Internet of Things: Issues, challenges, and solutions. *J. King Saud Univ. Comput. Inf. Sci.*, 30, 3, 291–317, 2018.
2. Al-Fuqaha, A., Guizani, M., Mohammadi, M., Aledhari, M., Ayyash, M., Internet of Things: A Survey on Enabling Technologies, Protocols, and Applications, in: *IEEE Communications Surveys & Tutorials*, vol. 17, no. 4, pp. 2347–2376, Fourthquarter 2015, doi: 10.1109/COMST.2015.2444095.
3. Antonakakis, M., *et al.*, Understanding the Mirai Botnet, in: *26th USENIX Security Symposium (USENIX Security 17)*, pp. 1093–1110, USENIX Association, Vancouver, BC, 2017.
4. Jazri, H. and Boudriga, N., Security in the Internet of Things: A review, in: *2017 13th International Wireless Communications and Mobile Computing Conference (IWCMC)*, pp. 1665–1670, 2017.
5. Hassija, V., Chamola, V., Saxena, V., Jain, Goyal, P., Sikdar, B., A Survey on IoT Security: Application Areas, Security Threats, and Solution Architectures. *IEEE Access*, 1–1, 2019. 10.1109/ACCESS.2019.2924045.
6. Jing, Q., Vasilakos, A., Wan, J., Lu, J., Qiu, D., Security of the Internet of Things: Perspectives and challenges. *Wirel. Netw.*, 20, 2481–2501, 2014. 10.1007/s11276-014-0761-7.
7. Jazzar, M. and Hamad, M., An analysis study of IoT and dos attack perspective, in: *Proceedings of International Conference on Intelligent Cyber-Physical Systems: ICPS 2021*, pp. 127–142, Springer Nature Singapore, Singapore, 2022.
8. Anajemba, J., Tang, Y., Iwendi, C., Ohwoekevwo, A., Srivastava, G., Jo, O., Realizing Efficient Security and Privacy in IoT Networks. *Sens. Rev.*, 20, 2609, 2020. 10.3390/s20092609.
9. Sharma, A., Sharma, S., Gupta, D., A Review of Sensors and Their Application in Internet of Things (IoT). *Int. J. Comput. Appl.*, 174, 27–34, 2021. 10.5120/ijca2021921148.

10. Alkhaldi, T.M., Darem, A.A., Alhashmi, A.A., Al-Hadhrami, T., Osman, A.E., Enhancing smart city IoT communication: A two-layer NOMA-based network with caching mechanisms and optimized resource allocation. *Comput. Netw.*, 255, 110857, 2024. ISSN 1389-1286.
11. Zhang, J., Li, T., Ying, Z., Ma, J., Trust-based secure multi-cloud collaboration Framework in Cloud-Fog-assisted IoT. *IEEE Trans. Cloud Comput.*, 11, 2, 1546–1561, 2023.
12. Radovici, C.R. and Şerban, R., A Survey of IoT Security Threats and Solutions, in: *2018 17th RoEduNet Conference: Networking in Education and Research (RoEduNet)*, Cluj-Napoca, Romania, pp. 1–5, 2018, doi: 10.1109/ROEDUNET.2018.8514146. keywords: {Security; Hardware; Binary codes; Browsers; Internet of Things; Kernel; Internet of Things; security; WebAssembly}.
13. Amoo, O., Osasona, F., Atadoga, A., Ayinla, B., Farayola, O., Abrahams, T., Cybersecurity threats in the age of IoT: A review of protective measures. *Int. J. Sci. Res. Arch.*, 11, 1304–1310, 2024. 10.30574/ijsra.2024.11.1.0217.
14. Mohammed, H. and Qayyum, M., Internet of Things: A Study on Security and Privacy Threats, 2017. 10.1109/Anti-Cybercrime.2017.7905270.
15. Sahu, S.K. and Mazumdar, K., Exploring security threats and solutions Techniques for Internet of Things (IoT): From vulnerabilities to vigilance. *Front. Artif. Intell.*, 7, 1397480, 2024. doi: 10.3389/frai.2024.1397480.
16. Rashid, M., Kamruzzaman, J., Hassan, M., Imam, T., Gordon, S., Cyberattacks Detection in IoT-Based Smart City Applications Using Machine Learning Techniques. *Int. J. Environ. Res. Public Health*, 17, 9347, 2020. 10.3390/ijerph17249347.
17. Hu, J.-X., Chen, C.-L., Fan, C.-L., Wang, K., An Intelligent and Secure Health Monitoring Scheme Using IoT Sensor Based on Cloud Computing. *J. Sens.*, 2017, 1–11, 2017. 10.1155/2017/3734764.
18. Salem, R., Saraya, M., Ali-Eldin, A., An Industrial Cloud-Based IoT System for Real-Time Monitoring and Controlling of Wastewater. *IEEE Access*, 1–1, 2022. 10.1109/ACCESS.2022.3141977.
19. Liang, X. and Kim, Y., A Survey on Security Attacks and Solutions in the IoT Network, pp. 0853–0859, 2021. 10.1109/CCWC51732.2021.9376174.
20. Imteaj, A., Rahman, T., Hossain, M., Alam, M.S., Rahat, S., An IoT based fire alarming and authentication system for workhouse using Raspberry Pi 3, pp. 899–904, 2017. 10.1109/ECACE.2017.7913031.
21. Mukherjee, B.K., *et al.*, An SDN Based Distributed IoT Network with NFV Implementation for Smart Cities, in: *Cyber Security and Computer Science*, pp. 539–552, Springer International Publishing, Cham, 2020, DOI: 10.1007/978-3-030-52856-0_43.
22. Verma, A. and Ranga, V., Machine Learning Based Intrusion Detection Systems for IoT Applications. *Wirel. Pers. Commun.*, 2020. 10.1007/s11277-019-06986-8.

23. Shukla, A., Somagattu, P., Singh, V., Kalra, M., IoT-Based Data Storage for Cloud Computing Applications, 2021. 10.1007/978-981-15-3514-7_109.
24. Doan, T., Kayes, A.S.M., Rahayu, W., Nguyen, K., Integration of IoT Streaming Data With Efficient Indexing and Storage Optimization. *IEEE Access*, 1–1, 2020. 10.1109/ACCESS.2020.2980006.
25. Santra, S., Dey, H., Majumdar, S., A Survey with Proposed Approach on Dynamic Load Balancing: *via* VM Migration Strategy in Cloud Computing, in: *IEEE Sponsored Conference Confluence 2013 IN*, Amity University, Noida, 27-28, September 2013, pp. 27–29.
26. Santra, S. and Mali, K., A New Approach to Survey on Load Balancing in VM in Cloud Computing: using CloudSim, in: *IEEE International Conference on Computer, Communication and Control*, 2015, [IEEE Xplore, DOI: 10.1109/IC4.2015.7375671].
27. Salah, K. and Khan, M., IoT Security: Review, Blockchain Solutions, and Open Challenges. *Future Gener. Comput. Syst.*, 82, 2017. 10.1016/j.future.2017.11.022.
28. Santra, S., Dey, H., Majumdar, S., Jha, G.S., New Simulation Toolkit for Comparison of Scheduling algorithm on Cloud Computing, 2014. 978-1-4799-4190-2/14 IEEE at ICCICCT-2014.
29. Santra, S., Mukherjee, P., Deyasi, A., Cost-Effective Voice-Controlled Real-Time Smart Informative Interface Design with Google Assistance Technology, in: *chapter 4*, pp. 63–78, "Machine Learning Techniques and Analytics for Cloud Security", series of "Advances in Learning Analytics for Intelligent Cloud-IoT Systems", Copyright: 2021, ISBN: 9781119762256.
30. Santra, S., Roy, S., Sardar, P., Deyasi, A., Real-Time Vehicle Detection from Captured Images, in: *2019 International Conference on Opto-Electronics and Applied Optics (Optronix)*, IEEE, ISBN: 978-1-7281-0070-8.
31. Pathak, S. and Solanki, V.K., Impact of Internet of Things and Artificial Intelligence on Human Resource Development, in: *Further Advances in Internet of Things in Biomedical and Cyber Physical Systems,* Balas, V.E., Solanki, V.K., Kumar, R. (eds.), Intelligent Systems Reference Library, vol. 193. Springer, Cham, 2021, https://doi.org/10.1007/978-3-030-57835-0_19.
32. Agiollo, A., Conti, M., Kaliyar, P., Lin, T.-N., Pajola, L., DETONAR: Detection of Routing Attacks in RPL-Based IoT, in: *IEEE Transactions on Network and Service Management*, vol. 18, no. 2, pp. 1178–1190, June 2021, doi: 10.1109/TNSM.2021.3075496.

# 3

# Securing the Interconnected: AI-Driven Strategies for Dynamic Cloud-IoT Ecosystem

**Ayan Banerjee[1]* and Anirban Kundu[1,2]**

*[1]Computer Innovative Research Society West Bengal, Kolkata, West Bengal, India*
*[2]Netaji Subhash Engineering College Kolkata, Kolkata, West Bengal, India*

***Abstract***

Authors propose a cloud-based memory capacity management system having distinct layers to access frameworks through multiple entry points such as, user module, administrative module and controller module which have been operated from different geographical locations using distributed approach. Several benefits of industry 4.0 are being achieved using proposed framework. End user has achieved flexible and less time-consuming environment to perform their necessary activities due to usage of cloud services. An efficient memory allocation and data storage are being presented in proposed framework for reducing reallocation and replication transparency. User requirements are being submitted for receiving a suitable resource. Administrative authorities collect memory information from actively interconnected systems and store into server side using AI based automated mechanism. In controller, cellular automata-based mapping is applied on systems' collected memory information for measuring system capacity over the cloud. User requirements should be authorized and analyzed into controller module for mapping an efficient resource within minimum time. Reliability factor, linear time complexity and minimum server load are being measured for realizing system accuracy using cellular automata based proposed algorithms respectively. Maximum system capacity has been measured for each particular user based on number of user inputs. Memory capacity factor is calculated using required dataset for realizing the system efficiency. Comparative analysis is presented for establishing system competency using experimental results. Overall linearity is observed in each particular layer of proposed framework.

**Corresponding author*: ayan871992@gmail.com

Partha Ghosh, Rajdeep Chakraborty, Anupam Ghosh and Ahmed A. Elngar (eds.) Strategic Approaches to Intrusion Detection in Cloud-IoT Ecosystem, (49–98) © 2026 Scrivener Publishing LLC

***Keywords***: Memory capacity nanagement system (MCMS), system capacity analysis, distributed system, cloud services, artificial intelligence (AI), internet of things (IoT), cellular automata (CA), state transition mapping

## 3.1 Introduction

### 3.1.1 Overview

Nowadays, memory optimization is necessary for enhancing system capacities. Several AI strategies and its applications are being designed for analyzing the scope of memory using practical implementations and significant transformations of the fourth industrial revolution. Multiple scenarios such as, server sizing, load testing and server consolidation have been evaluated for increasing system capacities within cloud environment [1]. Cloud computing is an essential technology in modern society for changing the socio-technical structure of resource capacity management. At present organizations, cloud services are applied on software framework for achieving the extraordinary popularity due to greater agility, flexibility of application deployment and efficiency. Various objectives are being concentrated for profitability and longibity of enterprise using AI based cloud computing model [2]. AI is a set of technologies that allow computers to perform tasks, according to human intelligence. Several AI algorithms are being used in hardware for designing memory management framework. AI based heuristics are used in DNN for memory allocation and fragmentation using cloud virtualization. AI is being combined with IoT systems for data mining, managing huge data storage on IoT, and controlling the congestion in network [3]. IoT indicates a set of devices and systems, which are connected and able to communicate between each other through internet. The primary objective of IoT based memory management is to design and configure such system for optimizing resource utility using network based communication. In IoT devices, various memory management algorithms have been used to conserve energy and extend battery life. ICN is being developed for reducing content transfer time and packet loss ratio. CA based encryption is applied on IoT application for generating a random lightweight CA cipher (LCC), maintaining minimum execution time [4]. CA is a discrete model of computation, which is used for simulating a set of cells based on the interaction with their neighbors. CA based VSA is being applied on memory buffer and network for operating infinite data strems with out memory overflow. CA based fault tolerant test structure is designed for identifying the region of defective cache module in microprocessor and memorizing the fault while continuing the test. CA based test structure is comparatively smaller and cheaper in case of VLSI implementation [5]. In the proposed framework, CA based state transition mapping is being applied on all active systems of IoT ecosystem for preparing category wise predefined dataset based on memory capacity analysis. Cloud based communication has been established between user module, controller module and administrative module for executing proposed activities though network. Proposed CA based AI mechanism is being designed in controller module for analyzing user query using predefined memory category wise information. The focus of proposed design is to achieve better reliability and minimum server load with respect to linear time complexity.

### 3.1.2 Aim

The authors' aim is to develop a CA based MCMS using system reliability analysis with maintaining linear time complexity during memory allocation and memory capacity analysis. Following are the major factors to be considered in this research:

- Connection Demand Factor ($DF_{Connection}$)
- Server Load Factor ($LF_{Server}$)
- Harddisk Capacity Factor ($CF_{HDD}$)
- RAM Capacity Factor ($CF_{RAM}$)
- Memory Capacity Factor ($Memory_{CF}$)
- Reliability Factor (RF)

### 3.1.3 Scope

Our system identifies various user queries and performs memory capacity analysis using several factors. CA based linear rules are implemented in proposed system for maintaining IoT ecosystems' condition and to allocate suitable system to user. The proposed model applies two way communication between web server and database server with maintaining minimum server load.

### 3.1.4 Motivation

The authors need to design a CA based MCMS to monitor IoT ecosystem and to analyze memory capacity of each particular system connected through network and further allocate capable system to user based on user requirements.

### 3.1.5 Organization

The rest of the paper is organized as follows: Literature review is described in Section 3.2. CA preliminaries is furnished in Section 3.3. In Section 3.4, CA based MCMS design is presented along with the required figures and algorithms. In Section 3.5, cloud based communication between administrative module and controller module is described for maintaining IoT ecosystems' health. In Section 3.6, CA based functional communication between user module and controller module is presented for user query analysis using conditional activities and state transitional activities. In Section 3.7, CA based controller design is presented for IoT ecosystems' performance analysis and user requirement analysis using single attractor cellular automata (SACA) and multiple attractor based cellular automata (MACA) based state transition activities. Various analytical discussions and theoretical proof are presented in Section 3.8 and Section 3.9 respectively. In section 3.10, experimental results and comparisons are established based on experimental analysis and diagrams. In section 3.11, system efficiency are achieved based on CA based linear rules.

## 3.2 Literature Review

### 3.2.1 Past Researches

In operating system, basic architecture of memory segmentation and its allocation have been described based on virtual memory management and dynamic memory management [6]. Researchers have reviewed the rule of memory management for enhancing performance in OS [7]. Memory and CPU management mechanism have been presented based on cloud computing environment, maintaining distributed approach [8]. AI based architecture has been designed to overcome memory limitation of transformer models [9]. An optimal technique has been designed for realising efficient storage utilization of IoT devices using sequential machine learning approach [10]. An advanced memory management mechanism has been designed to build embedded systems using limited resources [11]. Researchers have proposed quantam dot cellular automata for implementing memory realization processor [12]. CA based neighborhood methodology has been applied to examine the effect of coflicting strategies between economic growth and environment protection in case of urban planning and land policies [13].

### 3.2.2 Challenges

The main challenges of proposed system are to provide better memory capacity management and memory allocation activities than existing approaches as follows:

- Apply linear time complexity in case of IoT ecosystem's performance evaluation and memory allocation to user.
- Apply minimum server load in case of interaction between web server and database server.
- Apply memory capacity analysis using several memory category wise capacity factors.
- Apply system reliability analysis using memory capacity analysis.
- Establish cloud based communication between interconnected modules and client-server modules using several cloud services.
- Design CA based linear MCMS framework using memory capacity analysis.

## 3.3 CA Based MCMS Framework for System Allocation Using Memory Capacity Analysis

In this section, design and activity of proposed CA based MCMS framework is presented.

In Table 3.1, several symbols and corresponding technologies have been furnished for designing proposed CA based MCMS framework. Proposed terminologies have been explained as follows:

**Hard disk (HDD) related User Query (UQ):** A specific set of HDD related user requirement was collected from different geographical locations. HDD related UQs are abbreviated as '$UQ_{HDD}$'. In the proposed system, '$UQ_{HDD}$' has been stored into MCMS controller for memory capacity analysis. $UQ_{HDD} = \{UQ_{hdd1}, UQ_{hdd2}, \dots, UQ_{hdda}\}$;
**Random Access Memory (RAM) related UQ:** A specific set of RAM related user requirement was collected from different geographical

**Table 3.1** Table for explaining the terminologies of proposed MCMS framework.

| **Symbols** | **Terminologies** |
|---|---|
| $UQ_{HDD}$ | Hard disk (HDD) related User Query (UQ) |
| $UQ_{RAM}$ | Random Access Memory (RAM) related UQ |
| NI | Network Information |
| HI | Host Information |
| NH | Network wise Host Information |
| MC | Memory Category |
| HDDI | HDD Information |
| RAMI | RAM Information |
| PC | Predefined Capacity |
| $PC_{HDD}$ | HDD related Predefined Capacities |
| $PC_{RAM}$ | RAM related Predefined Capacities |
| $Resource_{HDD}$ | HDD wise Resources |
| $Resource_{RAM}$ | RAM wise Resources |
| $Resource_{SS}$ | SS wise Resources |
| $CR_{HDD}$ | HDD based Capable Resources |
| $CR_{RAM}$ | RAM based Capable Resources |

locations. RAM related UQs are abbreviated as '$UQ_{RAM}$'. In the proposed system, '$UQ_{RAM}$' has been stored into MCMS controller for memory capacity analysis. $UQ_{RAM} = \{UQ_{ram1}, UQ_{ram2}, \dots, UQ_{ramb}\}$;

**Network Information:** A specific set of network internet protocol (IP) addresses was used in the proposed IoT environment for measuring environmental health. Network information is shortened as 'NI'. In the proposed system, 'NI' has been captured for preparing predefined set of memory information using CA based methodology. $NI = \{NI_1, NI_2, \dots, NI_d\}$;

**Host Information:** A specific set of host IP addresses of each particular network was used in the proposed IoT environment for maintaining network-wise environmental health. Host information is abbreviated as 'HI'.

In MCMS framework, the proposed algorithm has been designed for identifying a live host and to fetch required information for analyzing UQs. HI = {$HI_1$, $HI_2$, ..., $HI_e$};
$\therefore NI_1 \rightarrow HI$;
**Network Wise Host Information:** A specific set of combined information between 'NI' and 'HI' was used for maintaining an index based mapping in IoT environment. Network wise host information is abbreviated as 'NH'. In the proposed framework, CA based mapping has been applied for UQ analysis using predifined memory related information of NH. NH = {$NH_1$, $NH_2$, ... , $NH_f$};
$\therefore NH_1 = \{NI_1 \times HI\}$;
**Memory Category:** A specific set of memory categories was used for preparing a set of memory information based on a particular category. Memory category is shortened as 'MC'. In the proposed framework, CA based mapping has been applied on 'NH' for formulating the set of category-wise memory information based on a particular 'MC'. MC = {$MC_{HDD}$, $MC_{RAM}$, $MC_{SS}$};
**HDD Information:** A particular set of HDD information was prepared based on 'MC' analysis. HDD Information is shortened as, 'HDDI'. In the proposed framework, CA based algorithm has been used for preparing the set of 'HDDI' using 'NH' and 'MC'. $HDDI = \{NH \times MC_{HDD}\}$;
**RAM Information:** A particular set of RAM information was prepared based on 'MC' analysis. RAM Information is shortened as, 'RAMI'. In the proposed framework, CA based algorithm has been used for preparing the set of 'RAMI' using 'NH' and 'MC'. $RAMI = \{NH \times MC_{RAM}\}$;
**Predefined Capacity:** A specific set of capacity indexes was used for analyzing system capacity. In the proposed system, CA based mapping has been applied on each group of 'MC' information for identifying category wise capacity. Predefined capacity is abbreviated as 'PC'. PC = {$PC_1$, $PC_2$, ... , $PC_g$};
**HDD Related Predefined Capacities:** A specific set of capacity was formulated based on mapping between 'HDDI' and 'PC'. HDD related predefined capacities are shortened as, '$PC_{HDD}$'. In the proposed framework, CA based indexing mechanism has been applied on 'HDDI' for preparing a mapping dataset '$PC_{HDD}$'. $PC_{HDD} = \{HDDI \times PC\}$;
**RAM Related Predefined Capacities:** A specific set of capacity was formulated based on mapping between 'RAMI' and 'PC'. RAM related predefined capacities are shortened as, '$PC_{RAM}$'. In the proposed framework, CA based indexing mechanism has been applied on 'RAMI' for preparing a mapping dataset '$PC_{RAM}$'. $PC_{RAM} = \{RAMI \times PC\}$;

**HDD Wise Resources:** A specific set of resources was computed based on '$UQ_{HDD}$' analysis. HDD wise resources are abbreviated as, '$Resource_{HDD}$'. In proposed framework, CA based mapping has been applied on '$UQ_{HDD}$' for preparing '$Resource_{HDD}$' using 'HDDI'. $Resource_{HDD} = \{HDDI \times UQ_{HDD}\}$;
**RAM Wise Resources:** A specific set of resources was computed based on '$UQ_{RAM}$' analysis. RAM wise resources are abbreviated as, '$Resource_{RAM}$'. In the proposed framework, CA based mapping has been applied on '$UQ_{RAM}$' for preparing '$Resource_{RAM}$' using 'RAMI'. $Resource_{RAM} = \{RAMI \times UQ_{RAM}\}$;
**HDD Based Capable Resources:** A specific set of capable resources was generated based on '$PC_{HDD}$'. HDD based capable resources are shortened as, '$CR_{HDD}$'. In the proposed framework, CA based mapping has been applied on '$Resource_{HDD}$' for analyzing '$CR_{HDD}$' using '$PC_{HDD}$'. $CR_{HDD} = \{Resource_{HDD} \times PC_{HDD}\}$;
**RAM Based Capable Resources:** A specific set of capable resources was generated based on '$PC_{RAM}$'. RAM based capable resources are shortened as, '$CR_{RAM}$'. In the proposed framework, CA based mapping has been applied on '$Resource_{RAM}$' for analyzing '$CR_{RAM}$' using '$PC_{RAM}$'. $CR_{RAM} = \{Resource_{RAM} \times PC_{RAM}\}$;

In Figure 3.1, structural design of proposed MCMS framework has been presented. Three distinct gateways have been communicated with proposed MCMS through internet. Multiple set of memory related user requirements are collected from different geographical locations and stored into

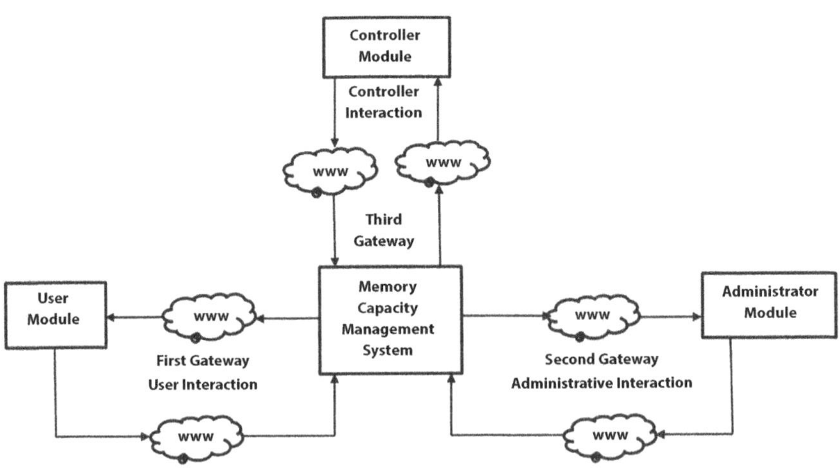


**Figure 3.1** Structural design of proposed MCMS framework.

user module. CA based mechanism is being applied on user requirements for providing capable resource to user, by using state transion mapping. The administrator has interacted with MCMS for maintaining the capacity of IoT ecosystem using CA based approach. Controller module is required for analyzing user requirements and administrative requirements using CA based mapping.

---

**Algorithm 3.1** Memory_Capacity_Management

---

Input: member_credential[], member_type[],user_query[];

Output: Memory Capacity Analysis;
Step 1: valid_member =
Check_Member_Authentication(member_credential[]);
Step 2: if(valid_member)
   Step 2.1: member_category = fetch_member_type(member_type[]);
   Step 2.2: switch(member_category)
      Step 2.2.1: case "Administrator": System_Capacity_Maintainence_
within_IoT_Ecosystem (); [refer Algorithm 3.2]
      Step 2.2.2: case "User": System_Capacity_Analysis_using_User_
Query ( user_query[]); [refer Algorithm 3.3]
Step 3: Stop

---

In Algorithm 3.1, the proposed memory capacity management mechanism has been described. Member credentials, member types, and user queries are incorporated as input. Member id and password are considered as member credentials, and two member types such as, user and administrator are used in Algorithm 3.1 respectively. Memory related user requirements are considered as user query. In Step 1, members' authenticity has been measured based on the validity of member credentials. In Step 2, if member is valid then, member categorization has been executed based on member types in Step 2.1. In Step 2.2, if member categories are 'Administrator' and 'User' then, CA based machine capacity maintainence activity has been executed within IoT ecosystem for generating a list of capable systems in Step 2.2.1 (refer Algorithm 3.2) and CA based machine capacity analysis has been performed for allocating capable resource to user using user requirements in Step 2.2.2 (refer Algorithm 3.3) respectively. The end of algorithm 3.1 has been mentioned in Step 3. The benefit of Algorithm 3.1, is to separate the proposed activities based on member categories, and to analyze machine capacity within minimum time.

## 3.4 Cloud-Based Communication between Administrator Module and Controller Module for Maintaining IoT Ecosystem Capacity

In this section, the administrator is responsible for identifying alive systems in IoT ecosystem and to perform system capacity analysis using CA based mechanism.

In Figure 3.2, structural design of proposed administrative activities has been presented. Cloud based communication has been established between IoT ecosystem, administrator module and controller module. In IoT ecosystem, multiple networks along with their hosts are present. Administrator module is required for collecting memory information from alive hosts and for transmitting information to controller module. In controller module, the proposed CA based memory capacity analysis mechanism has been applied on administrative information for establishing a predefined mapping between size of memory and capacity indexes. Finally, in IoT ecosystem, systems priority have been maintained based on capacity analysis.

In Algorithm 3.2, the proposed mechanism has been designed for maintaining system capacities within IoT ecosystem. Distinct administrative activities and multiple set of network information are considered as input. A set of capable systems along with their memory capacities is considered as output, which has been used as a predefined dataset in the proposed MCMS framework. In Step 1, all active networks have been identified from IoT ecosystem. In Step 2 and Step 3, the list of alive hosts and dead hosts are computed using active networks respectively. In Step 4, a particular

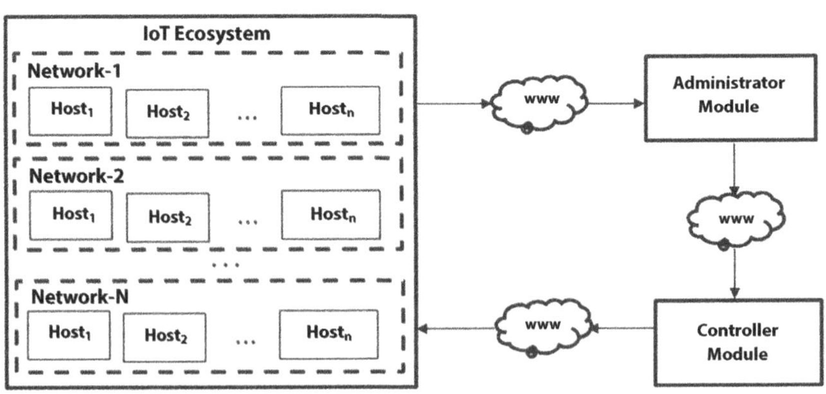


**Figure 3.2** Structural design of administrative activity.

**Algorithm 3.2** System_Capacity_Maintainence_within_IoT_Ecosystem

Input: administrative_activities[], network_information[], network_wise_alive_host[][],
network_wise_dead_host[][], administrator_activity;

Output: IoT Ecosystem Maintainence
Step 1: network_information[] = Network_Identification();
Step 2: network_wise_alive_host[][] = Compute_Alive_Resource_Details (network_information[]);
Step 3: network_wise_dead_host[][] = Compute_Dead_Resource_Details (network_information[]);
Step 4: administrator_activity =
Fetch_Administrative_Activity(administrative_activities[]);
Step 5: switch(administrator_activity)
  Step 5.1: case "Resource Addition": Resource_Addition_in_IoT_Ecosystem (network_wise_alive_host[][]);
  Step 5.2: case "Resource Deletion": Resource_Deletion_from_IoT_Ecosystem (network_wise_dead_host[][]);
Step 6: CA_based_IoT_Ecosystem_Maintainence_Schedular(network_wise_alive_host[][]); [refer Algorithm 3.4]
Step 7: Stop;

administrative activity has been fetched from predefined list for executing further actions. In Step 5, If administrative activities are 'Resource Addition' and 'Resource Deletion' then, new resource has been incorporated within a particular network of IoT ecosystem in Step 5.1 and 5.2 inactive resources have been removed from existing ecosystem respectively. In Step 6, CA-based scheduling activity has been applied on the list of alive hosts for ecosystem's health (refer Algorithm 3.4). The end of algorithm 3.2 is indicated in Step 7. The benefit of Algorithm 3.2 is to identify active networks for measuring system capacities of IoT ecosystem and to establish a predefined mapping between system details and memory capacities using the proposed CA based approach, maintaining linear time complexity.

In Figure 3.3, cloud-based one way communication between administrator module and controller module has been established. The workflows of two modules are throughly described using cloud-based activity. In the administrator module, multiple networks have been identified for analyzing system capacity. Two distinct types of hosts such as, alive host and dead host are separated from each particular network. Several memory

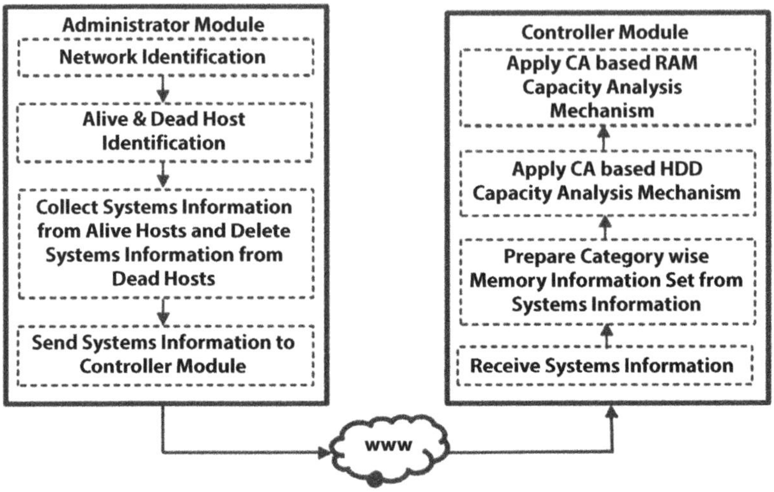


**Figure 3.3** Communicational activities between administrator module and controller module.

information have been collected from each alive host and remove history of all dead hosts respectively through administrative activities. Finally, a set of existing system information are sent to controller module using cloud-based communication. In controller module, system information has been distributed for preparing multiple set of memory capacities based on various memory categories. CA based memory capacity analysis mechanism is applied on user query for generating capable resource based on three distinct memory categories such as, HDD, RAM and Swap-Space respectively. In Figure 3.3, predefined memory information have been collected into controller module for performing CA based memory capacity analysis.

## 3.5 Functional Communication between User Module and Controller Module for Query Analysis

In MCMS, a two way communication are being established between user module and controller module for query analysis based on several CA based functionalities. In this section, user queries are incorporated into proposed controller module for receiving suitable resource with minimum time using CA based user query analysis.

**Algorithm 3.3** System_Capacity_Analysis_using_User_Query

Input: user_query[], query_category[], category_wise_user_query[][], hdd_related_user_query[], ram_related_user_query[];
Output: capable_resource;
Step 1: category_wise_user_query[][] = Apply_Categorical_Mapping_on_User_Query (user_query[], query_category[]);
Step 2: hdd_related_user_query[] = Prepare_HDD_Related_Query (category_wise_user_query[][]);
Step 3: ram_related_user_query[] = Prepare_RAM_Related_Query (category_wise_user_query[][]);
Step 4: capable_resource = CA_based_System_Capacity_Analysis (hdd_related_user_query[], ram_related_user_query[]); [refer Algorithm 3.5]
Step 5: Stop;

In Algorithm 3.3, the proposed CA based mechanism has been described for measuring system capacities using user requirement analysis. A set of user query and distinct query categories are considered as input. A particular capable resource is considered as output. In Step 1, various predefined mapping are established between user queries and query categories for user query classification using query based categorical mapping. In Step 2 and Step 3, multiple set of user queries have been categorized for preparing HDD related queries and RAM related queries based on categorical mapping between user queries and query categories respectively. In Step 4, CA based system capacity analysis mechanism is being used for generating a capable resource using three distinct categories of user queries (refer Algorithm 3.5). The end of algorithm 3.3 is indicated in Step 5. The benefit of Algorithm 3.3 is to measure all active systems capacities and to provide a capable resource to user based on CA based user query analysis, maintaining linear time complexity.

In Figure 3.4, cloud based two way communication has been presented between user module and controller module for preparing a capable resource based on user query analysis. In user module, several user queries are received from different geographical locations. Distinct predefined memory related categories such as, HDD category, RAM category have been used to apply categorical mapping on user queries for generating multiple set of queries. Finally, user queries are sent to controller for preparing a suitable resource using CA based user query analysis.

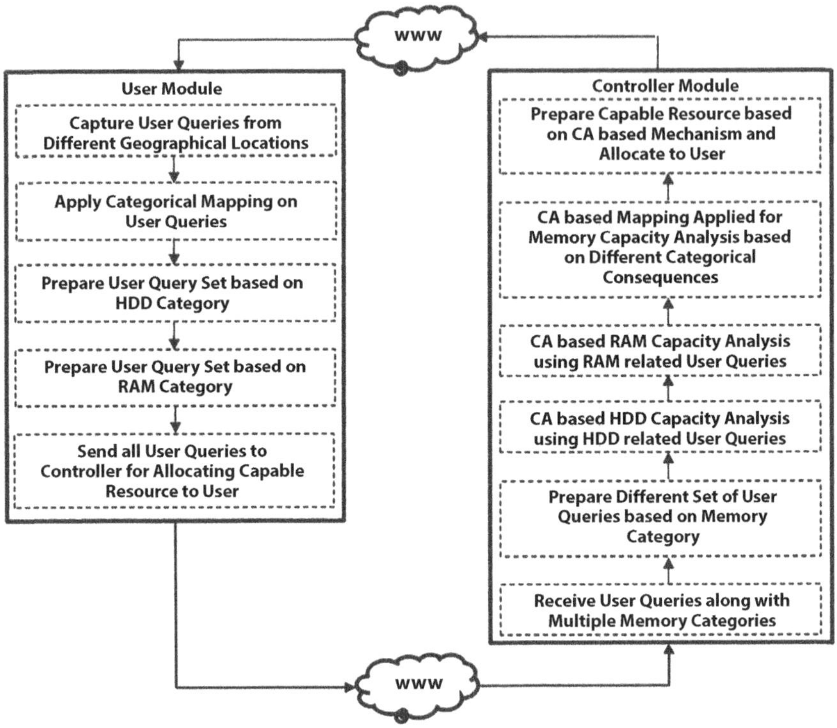


**Figure 3.4** Communicational activities between user module and controller module.

In controller module, CA based HDD capacity analysis and RAM capacity analysis have been applied on each particular user query for computing various set of capable resources. CA based mapping is applied on a list of capable resources for executing memory capacity analysis, maintaining categorical consequences. Finally, in controller module, a capable resource has been generated based on user requirement and sent to user through cloud-based communication.

In Figure 3.5, SACA based state transition activity has been presented for computing capable resource using memory capacity analysis. Three distinct categories of user queries such as, '$UQ_{HDD}$', '$UQ_{RAM}$' and '$UQ_{SS}$' have been incorporated into proposed framework for computing capable resource using CA based analysis. Several user queries are maintained their communication through the network.

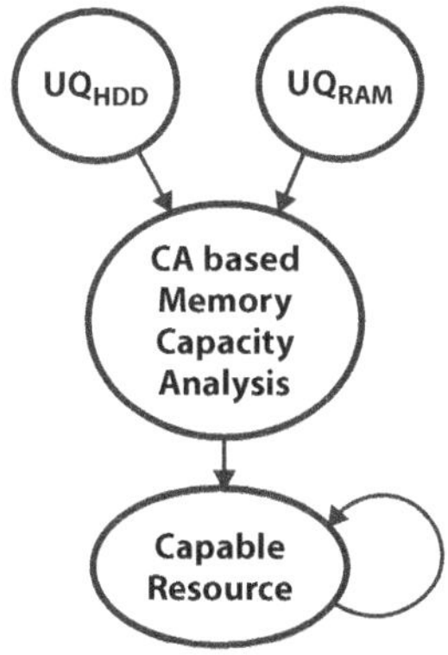


**Figure 3.5** SACA based state transition activity of proposed framework.

Consider, $\{\{UQ_{HDD}\}, \{UQ_{RAM}\}\}$ : two distinct set of user queries (refer Figure 3.5), where, $UQ_{HDD} = \{UQ_{hdd1}, UQ_{hdd2}, UQ_{hdd3}, \ldots, UQ_{hddn}\}$;
$\therefore UQ_{RAM} = \{UQ_{ram1}, UQ_{ram2}, UQ_{ram3}, \ldots, UQ_{ramn}\}$;

$$\therefore \{UQ_{HDD} \cup UQ_{RAM}\} = \left\{\begin{matrix} \{UQ_{hdd1}, UQ_{hdd2}, UQ_{hdd3}, \ldots, UQ_{hddn}\} \cup \\ \{UQ_{ram1}, UQ_{ram2}, UQ_{ram3}, \ldots, UQ_{ramn}\} \end{matrix}\right\};$$

$$\therefore \{UQ_{HDD} \cup UQ_{RAM}\} =$$

$$\{\{UQ_{hdd1}, UQ_{ram1}\}, \{UQ_{hdd2}, UQ_{ram2}\}, \{UQ_{hdd3}, UQ_{ram3}\}, \ldots, \{UQ_{hddn}, UQ_{ramn}\}\};$$

Consider, {CR} : a set of capable resources (refer Figure 3.5) where, $CR = \{CR_1, CR_2, CR_3, \ldots, CR_n\}$;
After applying CA based Mapping on $\{\{UQ_{HDD}\}, \{UQ_{RAM}\}\}$,

$$\{UQ_{hdd1}, UQ_{ram1}\} \rightarrow CR_1 ;$$

$$\ldots$$

$$\{UQ_{hddn}, UQ_{ramn}\} \rightarrow CR_n ;$$

$$\therefore \{UQ_{HDD} \cup UQ_{RAM}\} \rightarrow \{CR\};$$

Therefore, in Figure 3.5, $\{UQ_{HDD} \cup UQ_{RAM}\}$ is used for preparing {CR}.

## 3.6 Controller Design for Measuring System Capacity Using CA

In this section, CA based controller is being designed for measuring system capacities using various scenarios of IoT ecosystem and several user queries. CA based controller is designed for measuring the performance of IoT ecosystem using several memory conditions.

### 3.6.1 CA Based Controller Design for IoT Ecosystem's Performance Sustainability

In this sub-section, a proposed controller has been designed for identifying all active systems within IoT ecosystem and to accumulate each scenario of memory capacities as predefined dataset. In Algorithm 3.4, the proposed CA based scheduling activity is designed for maintaining the memory health of IoT ecosystem, which has been initiated based on a certain time interval. In Figure 3.7, several linear CA rules are established for preparing predefined sets of system capacities based on discrete memory categories.

**Algorithm 3.4** CA_based_IoT_Ecosystem_Maintainence_Schedular

Input: network_wise_alive_host[][], predefine_capacities[][], memory_category[];
Output: IoT Ecosystem Maintainence
Step 1: active_resource = Check_Active_Resources (network_wise_alive_host[][]);
Step 2: If (active_resource)
Step 2.1: predefined_hdd_Information[] = Compute_HDD_Details (network_wise_alive_host[][], memory_category[HDD]) ;
Step 2.2: predefined_hdd_capacity[] = CA_based_Mapping_for_HDD_Capacity (predefined_hdd_Information[], predefine_capacities[HDD][]);
Step 2.3: predefined_ram_Information[] = Compute_RAM_Details (network_wise_alive_host[][], memory_category[RAM]);
Step 2.4: predefined_ram_capacity[] = CA_based_Mapping_for_RAM_Capacity (predefined_ram_Information[], predefine_capacities[RAM][]);
Step 3: time_interval = Wait_for_Time_Interval();
Step 4: If (time interval is terminated)
Step 4.1: Continue Step 1;
Step 5: Stop;

In Algorithm 3.4, CA based schedular's activity has been presented to maintain IoT ecosystems health. A set of network wise alive hosts, predefined memory categories and memory capacities are considered as input. The healthy state of IoT ecosystem is considered as output. In Step 1, the activities of alive resources are being measured for performing further analysis using the set of network wise alive hosts. In Step 2, if resources are active then, in Step 2.1 and Step 2.3, HDD and RAM related memory information have been computed for preparing predefined set of memory information using a set of network wise alive hosts and distinct set of memory categories respectively. In Step 2.2 and step 2.4, CA based mapping is applied on predefined set of HDD information for measuring HDD capacities using the set of predefined capacities in Step 2.2. In step 3, each particular healthy state of IoT ecosystem is being maintained based on the calculation of time interval. In Step 4, if the maximum value is shown as interval of time then, algorithm 3.4 is continued from Step 1 for computing another new healthy state of IoT ecosystem. The end of algorithm 3.4 is indicated in Step 5. The benefit of algorithm 3.4 is to count capacities of all active systems based on predefined memory related information and to preserve the healthy state of IoT ecosystem for a certain time.

In Figure 3.6, MACA based state transition diagram has been presented to calculate system capacities using different memory related information such as, HDD and RAM. In IoT ecosystem, memory category wise system

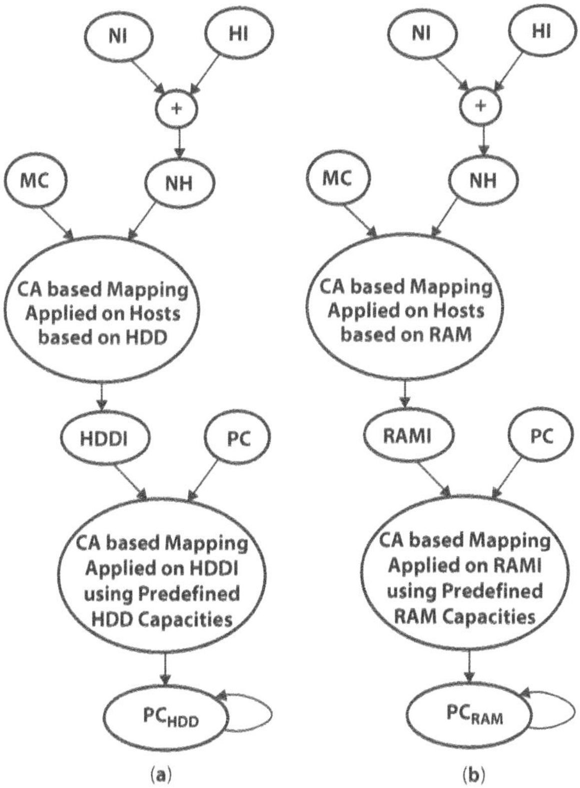


**Figure 3.6** MACA based state transition activity diagram for computing system capacity based on discrete memory categories within IoT ecosystem.

capacities such as, HDD related predefined capacities '$PC_{HDD}$' (refer (a) of Figure 3.6), RAM related predefined capacities '$PC_{RAM}$' (refer (b) of Figure 3.6), are stored as predefined dataset, which have been used for user query analysis.

Consider, {NI} : a set of networks within IoT ecosystem (refer Figure 3.6) where, NI = {$NI_1$, $NI_2$, $NI_3$, …, $NI_x$};
Consider, {HI} : a set of hosts of each network within IoT ecosystem (refer Figure 3.6) where, HI = {$HI_1$, $HI_2$, $HI_3$, …, $HI_y$};
Consider, {NH} : a set of network-host mapping where, NH = {$NH_1$, $NH_2$, $NH_3$, …, $NH_n$}

A relation has been shown between {NI} and {HI} depending on network-host connectivity as follows:

$$NH_1 \rightarrow NI_1 \times \{HI_1, HI_2, HI_3, \ldots, HI_y\};$$

$$NH_1 \rightarrow \left\{\{NI_1, HI_1\}, \{NI_1, HI_2\}, \{NI_1, HI_3\}, \ldots, \{NI_1, HI_y\}\right\};$$

$$\ldots$$

$$NH_n \rightarrow NI_x \times \{HI_1, HI_2, HI_3, \ldots, HI_y\};$$

$$NH_n \rightarrow \left\{\{NI_x, HI_1\}, \{NI_x, HI_2\}, \{NI_x, HI_3\}, \ldots, \{NI_x, HI_y\}\right\};$$

$$\therefore \{NH\} = NI \times \{HI\};$$

$$\therefore \{NH\} = \left\{NI, \{HI\}\right\};$$

Consider, {MC} : a set of memory information categories (refer Figure 3.6) where, MC = {$MC_1$, $MC_2$, $MC_3$, …, $MC_a$};
Consider, {PC} : a set of predefined capacities (refer Figure 3.6) where, PC = {$PC_1$, $PC_2$, $PC_3$, …, $PC_b$};

***Phase 1: Compute HDD Related Predefined Capacities for User Query Analysis***

In Phase 1, HDD related predefined capacities have been calculated using CA based state transition mapping.
Consider, {HDDI} a set of HDD related memory information (refer (a) of Figure 3.6) where, HDDI = {$HDDI_1$, $HDDI_2$, …, $HDDI_n$};
Consider, $MC_1$ contains HDD category;

CA based mapping has been applied on {NH} for preparing {HDDI} depending on $MC_1$ as follows:

$$\therefore \{HDDI\} \rightarrow MC_1 \cap \{NH\};$$

Consider, $\{PC_{HDD}\}$ a set of HDD related predefined capacities, where, $PC_{HDD} = \{PC_{HDD1}, PC_{HDD2}, PC_{HDD3}, \ldots, PC_{HDDm}\}$;
CA based mapping has been applied between {HDDI} and {PC} for preparing $\{PC_{HDD}\}$ as follows:

$$PC_{HDD1} \rightarrow HDDI_1 \times \{PC_1, PC_2, PC_3, \ldots, PC_b\};$$
$$PC_{HDD1} \rightarrow \begin{Bmatrix} \{HDDI_1, PC_1\}, \{HDDI_1, PC_2\}, \{HDDI_1, PC_3\}, \ldots, \\ \{HDDI_1, PC_b\} \end{Bmatrix};$$
$$\ldots$$
$$PC_{HDDm} \rightarrow HDDI_m \times \{PC_1, PC_2, PC_3, \ldots, PC_b\};$$
$$PC_{HDDm} \rightarrow \begin{Bmatrix} \{HDDI_m, PC_1\}, \{HDDI_m, PC_2\}, \{HDDI_m, PC_3\}, \ldots, \\ \{HDDI_m, PC_b\} \end{Bmatrix};$$
$$\therefore \{PC_{HDD}\} = HDDI \times \{PC\}; \tag{3.1}$$

***Phase 2: Compute RAM Related Predefined Capacities for User Query Analysis***
In Phase 2, RAM related predefined capacities have been calculated using CA based state transition mapping.
Consider, {RAMI} a set of RAM related memory information (refer (b) of Figure 3.6) where, $RAMI = \{RAMI_1, RAMI_2, \ldots, RAMI_n\}$;
Consider, $MC_2$ contains RAM category;
CA based mapping has been applied on {NH} for preparing {RAMI} depending on $MC_2$ as follows:

$$\therefore \{RAMI\} \rightarrow MC_2 \cap \{NH\};$$

Consider, $\{PC_{RAM}\}$ a set of RAM related predefined capacities, where, $PC_{RAM} = \{PC_{RAM1}, PC_{RAM2}, PC_{RAM3}, \ldots, PC_{RAMm}\}$;

CA based mapping has been applied between {RAMI} and {PC} for preparing $\{PC_{RAM}\}$ as follows:

$$
\begin{aligned}
&PC_{RAM1} \rightarrow RAMI_1 \times \{PC_1, PC_2, PC_3, \ldots, PC_b\};\\
&PC_{RAM1} \rightarrow \left\{\begin{matrix}\{RAMI_1, PC_1\}, \{RAMI_1, PC_2\}, \{RAMI_1, PC_3\}, \ldots,\\ \{RAMI_1, PC_b\}\end{matrix}\right\};\\
&\qquad\qquad \ldots\\
&PC_{RAMn} \rightarrow RAMI_n \times \{PC_1, PC_2, PC_3, \ldots, PC_b\};\\
&PC_{RAMn} \rightarrow \left\{\begin{matrix}\{RAMI_n, PC_1\}, \{RAMI_n, PC_2\}, \{RAMI_n, PC_3\}, \ldots,\\ \{RAMI_n, PC_b\}\end{matrix}\right\};\\
&\therefore \{PC_{RAM}\} = RAMI \times \{PC\};
\end{aligned}
\tag{3.2}
$$

From (3.1) and (3.2), $\{PC_{HDD}\}$ and $\{PC_{RAM}\}$ are designed as predefined dataset in proposed framework for analyzing HDD related user query and RAM related user query respectively.

### 3.6.2 CA Based Controller Design for User Query Analysis

In this sub-section, CA based controller is designed for incorporating user requirements from different geographical locations and to generate a capable resource based on user query analysis.

In Figure 3.7, SACA based state transition diagram has been presented for analyzing memory capacities based on category wise user queries.

***Phase 1: Generate Capable Resources using HDD based User Query Analysis***

Consider, $\{UQ_{HDD}\}$a set of HDD related user query, where, $UQ_{HDD} = \{UQ_{HDD1}, UQ_{HDD2}, UQ_{HDD3}, \ldots, UQ_{HDDn}\}$;

Consider, $\{Resource_{HDD}\}$ a set of HDD based resources, where, $Resource_{HDD} = \{R_{HDD1}, R_{HDD2}, R_{HDD3}, \ldots, R_{HDDx}\}$;

CA based mapping has been applied on $\{UQ_{HDD}\}$ for preparing a HDD based resource pool depending on {HDDI} (refer Figure 3.7) as follows:

Therefore, $\{HDDI\} = \{Resource_{HDD}\}$;

$$HDDI_1 \times \{UQ_{HDD1}, UQ_{HDD2}, UQ_{HDD3}, \ldots, UQ_{HDDn}\}$$

$$\left\{\begin{matrix}\{HDDI_1, UQ_{HDD1}\}, \{HDDI_1, UQ_{HDD2}\}, \{HDDI_1, UQ_{HDD3}\}, \ldots,\\ \{HDDI_1, UQ_{HDDn}\}\end{matrix}\right\} \rightarrow R_{HDD1};$$

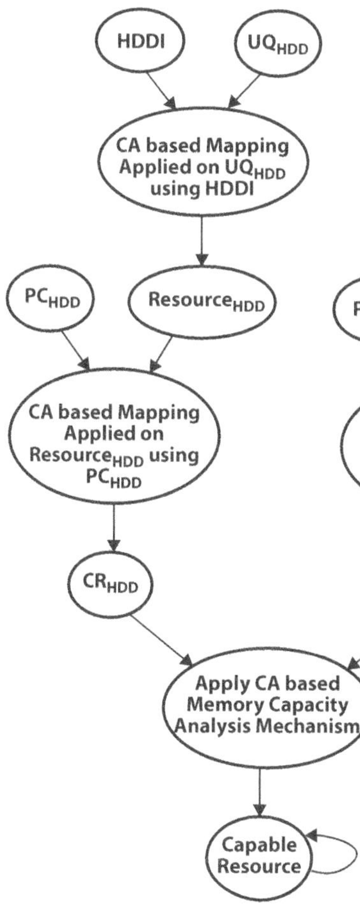


**Figure 3.7** SACA based state transition activity diagram for analyzing memory capacity based on user queries.

Similarly,

$$HDDI_n \times \{UQ_{HDD1}, UQ_{HDD2}, UQ_{HDD3}, \ldots, UQ_{HDDn}\}$$

$$\left\{\begin{matrix}\{HDDI_n, UQ_{HDD1}\}, \{HDDI_n, UQ_{HDD2}\}, \{HDDI_n, UQ_{HDD3}\}, \ldots, \\ \{HDDI_n, UQ_{HDDn}\}\end{matrix}\right\} \rightarrow R_{HDDn};$$

$$\therefore \quad \left\{\begin{matrix}\left\{\begin{matrix}\{HDDI_1, UQ_{HDD1}\}, \{HDDI_1, UQ_{HDD2}\}, \\ \{HDDI_1, UQ_{HDD3}\}, \ldots, \{HDDI_1, UQ_{HDDn}\}\end{matrix}\right\}, \ldots, \\ \left\{\begin{matrix}\{HDDI_n, UQ_{HDD1}\}, \{HDDI_n, UQ_{HDD2}\}, \\ \{HDDI_n, UQ_{HDD3}\}, \ldots, \{HDDI_n, UQ_{HDDn}\}\end{matrix}\right\}\end{matrix}\right\} \rightarrow Resource_{HDD};$$

$$\therefore \{Resource_{HDD}\} = \{HDDI\} \times \{UQ_{HDD}\};$$

CA based mapping has been applied on $\{Resource_{HDD}\}$ for preparing a set of capable resources depending on $\{PC_{HDD}\}$ (refer Figure 3.6) as follows:

Consider, $\{CR_{HDD}\}$ a set of HDD based capable resources, where, $CR_{HDD} = \{CR_{HDD1}, CR_{HDD2}, CR_{HDD3}, \ldots, CR_{HDDx}\}$;
Therefore, $\{Resource_{HDD}\} = \{CR_{HDD}\}$;

$$R_{HDD1} \times \{PC_{HDD1}, PC_{HDD2}, PC_{HDD3}, \ldots, PC_{HDDn}\}$$

$$\left\{\begin{matrix}\{R_{HDD1}, PC_{HDD1}\}, \{R_{HDD1}, PC_{HDD2}\}, \{R_{HDD1}, PC_{HDD3}\}, \ldots, \\ \{R_{HDD1}, PC_{HDDn}\}\end{matrix}\right\} \rightarrow CR_{HDD1};$$

Similarly,

$$R_{HDDx} \times \{PC_{HDD1}, PC_{HDD2}, PC_{HDD3}, \ldots, PC_{HDDn}\}$$

$$\left\{\begin{matrix}\{R_{HDDx}, PC_{HDD1}\}, \{R_{HDDx}, PC_{HDD2}\}, \{R_{HDDx}, PC_{HDD3}\}, \ldots, \\ \{R_{HDDx}, PC_{HDDn}\}\end{matrix}\right\} \rightarrow CR_{HDDx};$$

$$\therefore \left\{\begin{matrix}\left\{\begin{matrix}\{R_{HDD1}, PC_{HDD1}\}, \{R_{HDD1}, PC_{HDD2}\}, \\ \{R_{HDD1}, PC_{HDD3}\}, \ldots, \{R_{HDD1}, PC_{HDDn}\}\end{matrix}\right\}, \ldots, \\ \left\{\begin{matrix}\{R_{HDDx}, PC_{HDD1}\}, \{R_{HDDx}, PC_{HDD2}\}, \\ \{R_{HDDx}, PC_{HDD3}\}, \ldots, \{R_{HDDx}, PC_{HDDn}\}\end{matrix}\right\}\end{matrix}\right\} \rightarrow CR_{HDD};$$

$$\therefore \{CR_{HDD}\} = \{Resource_{HDD}\} \times \{PC_{HDD}\}; \tag{3.3}$$

***Phase 2: Generate Capable Resources using RAM Based User Query Analysis***

Consider, $\{UQ_{RAM}\}$a set of RAM related user query, where, $UQ_{RAM} = \{UQ_{RAM1}, UQ_{RAM2}, UQ_{RAM3}, \ldots, UQ_{RAMn}\}$;
Consider, $\{Resource_{RAM}\}$ a set of RAM based resources, where, $Resource_{RAM} = \{R_{RAM1}, R_{RAM2}, R_{RAM3}, \ldots, R_{RAMy}\}$;
CA based mapping has been applied on $\{UQ_{RAM}\}$ for preparing a RAM based resource pool depending on $\{RAMI\}$ (refer Figure 3.7) as follows:

Therefore, $\{RAMI\} = \{Resource_{RAM}\}$;

$$RAMI_1 \times \{UQ_{RAM1}, UQ_{RAM2}, UQ_{RAM3}, \ldots, UQ_{RAMn}\}$$

$$\left\{\begin{matrix}\{RAMI_1, UQ_{RAM1}\}, \{RAMI_1, UQ_{RAM2}\}, \{RAMI_1, UQ_{RAM3}\}, \ldots, \\ \{RAMI_1, UQ_{RAMn}\}\end{matrix}\right\} \rightarrow R_{RAM1};$$

Similarly, $RAMI_n \times \{UQ_{RAM1}, UQ_{RAM2}, UQ_{RAM3}, \ldots, UQ_{RAMn}\}$

$$\left\{\begin{matrix}\{RAMI_n, UQ_{RAM1}\}, \{RAMI_n, UQ_{RAM2}\}, \{RAMI_n, UQ_{RAM3}\}, \ldots, \\ \{RAMI_n, UQ_{RAMn}\}\end{matrix}\right\} \rightarrow R_{RAMy};$$

$$\therefore \left\{\begin{matrix}\left\{\begin{matrix}\{RAMI_1, UQ_{RAM1}\}, \{RAMI_1, UQ_{RAM2}\}, \\ \{RAMI_1, UQ_{RAM3}\}, \ldots, \{RAMI_1, UQ_{RAMn}\}\end{matrix}\right\}, \ldots, \\ \left\{\begin{matrix}\{RAMI_n, UQ_{RAM1}\}, \{RAMI_n, UQ_{RAM2}\}, \\ \{RAMI_n, UQ_{RAM3}\}, \ldots, \{RAMI_n, UQ_{RAMn}\}\end{matrix}\right\}\end{matrix}\right\} \rightarrow Resource_{RAM};$$

$$\therefore \{Resource_{RAM}\} = \{RAMI\} \times \{UQ_{RAM}\};$$

CA based mapping has been applied on $\{Resource_{RAM}\}$for preparing a set of capable resources depending on $\{PC_{RAM}\}$ (refer Figure 3.6) as follows:

Consider, $\{CR_{RAM}\}$ a set of RAM based capable resources, where, $CR_{RAM} = \{CR_{RAM1}, CR_{RAM2}, CR_{RAM3}, \ldots, CR_{RAMy}\}$;

Therefore, $\{Resource_{RAM}\} = \{CR_{RAM}\}$;

$R_{RAM1} \times \{PC_{RAM1}, PC_{RAM2}, PC_{RAM3}, \ldots, PC_{RAMn}\}$

$$\left\{\begin{matrix}\{R_{RAM1}, PC_{RAM1}\}, \{R_{RAM1}, PC_{RAM2}\}, \{R_{RAM1}, PC_{RAM3}\}, \ldots, \\ \{R_{RAM1}, PC_{RAMn}\}\end{matrix}\right\} \rightarrow CR_{RAM1};$$

Similarly,

$R_{RAMy} \times \{PC_{RAM1}, PC_{RAM2}, PC_{RAM3}, \ldots, PC_{RAMn}\}$

$$\left\{\begin{matrix}\{R_{RAMy}, PC_{RAM1}\}, \{R_{RAMy}, PC_{RAM2}\}, \{R_{RAMy}, PC_{RAM3}\}, \ldots, \\ \{R_{RAMy}, PC_{RAMn}\}\end{matrix}\right\} \rightarrow CR_{RAMy};$$

$$\therefore \left\{\begin{matrix}\left\{\begin{matrix}\{R_{RAM1}, PC_{RAM1}\}, \{R_{RAM1}, PC_{RAM2}\}, \\ \{R_{RAM1}, PC_{RAM3}\}, \ldots, \{R_{RAM1}, PC_{RAMn}\}\end{matrix}\right\}, \ldots, \\ \left\{\begin{matrix}\{R_{RAMy}, PC_{RAM1}\}, \{R_{RAMy}, PC_{RAM2}\}, \\ \{R_{RAMy}, PC_{RAM3}\}, \ldots, \{R_{RAMy}, PC_{RAMn}\}\end{matrix}\right\}\end{matrix}\right\} \rightarrow CR_{RAM};$$

$$\therefore \{CR_{RAM}\} = \{Resource_{RAM}\} \times \{PC_{RAM}\}; \quad (3.4)$$

CA based memory capacity analysis mechanism is applied on $\{CR_{HDD}\}$ and $\{CR_{RAM}\}$ for computing a particular capable resource based on user query analysis.

Therefore, from (3.3) and (3.4),

$$\therefore Resource_{Capable} = \{CR_{HDD}\} \cap \{CR_{RAM}\};$$

where, $\text{Resource}_{\text{Capable}}$ = A specific capable resource based on user requirement; Therefore, $\text{Resource}_{\text{Capable}}$ is calculated to satisfy user requirement using proposed CA based user query analysis, maintaining linear time complexities.

---

**Algorithm 3.5** CA_based_System_Capacity_Analysis

---

Input: hdd_related_user_query[], ram_related_user_query[],
predefined_hdd_Information[],
predefined_hdd_Capacity[],
hdd_resources[], ram_resources[], predefined_ram_Information[],
predefined_ram_capacity[], capable_ram_resource[]
Output: capable_resource;
Step 1: hdd_resources[] =
Apply_CA_based_Mapping_on_predefined_HDD_Dataset
(predefined_hdd_Information[], hdd_related_user_query[]);
Step 2: ram_resources[] =
Apply_CA_based_Mapping_on_predefined_RAM_Dataset
(predefined_ram_Information[], ram_related_user_query[]);
Step 3: capable_hdd_resource[] = CA_based_HDD_Capacity_Analysis
(hdd_resources[], predefined_hdd_capacity[]);
Step 4: capable_ram_resource[] = CA_based_RAM_Capacity_Analysis
(ram_resources[], predefined_ram_capacity[]);
Step 5: capable_resource = CA_based_Memory_Capacity_Analysis
(capable_hdd_resource[], capable_ram_resource[]);
Step 6: Stop;

---

In Algorithm 3.5, CA based system capacity analysis has been presented for generating each particular capable resource based on user query analysis. Two distinct set of user queries such as, HDD related user query and RAM related user query are considered as input. A single capable resource is considered as output. Several categories of predefined information such as, HDD related predefined information, and RAM related predefined information are being used for measuring the capacities of HDD related resources and RAM related resources using proposed SACA based approach. In Step 1 and Step 2, CA based mapping is applied on predefined dataset for identifying a specific set of resources using HDD & RAM related user query analysis. In Step 3 and Step 4, CA based capacity analysis mechanism is being executed for computing capable resources using several categories of predefined information and multiple set of categorical resources respectively. In Step 5, CA based memory capacity analysis mechanism is being applied on capable resources to generate a particular resource for realising user requirement in real time basis. The end of Algorithm 3.5 is indicated in Step 6. The benefit of Algorithm 3.5 is to apply CA based mapping for computing categorical resources and finally a specific capable resource is generated based on CA based memory capacity analysis, maintaining linear time complexity.

## 3.7 Analytical Discussion

In this section, analytical consequences have been formulated using connection based server load analysis, memory capacity analysis based on multiple capacity factors, measurement of system reliability respectively.

### 3.7.1 Connection Demand Analysis Based on Connections between Web Server and Database Server

Connection demand factor is a weightage factor, which has been designed to measure connection based system efficiency using the connectivity between web server and database server. In the proposed framework, it is being calculated using $\text{Actual}_{\text{Connection}}$ and $\text{Maximum}_{\text{Connection}}$. Connection demand factor is known as '$\text{DF}_{\text{Connection}}$'.

$$\therefore DF_{Connection} = \frac{Actual_{Connection}}{Maximum_{Connection}}; \tag{3.5}$$

where,

$\text{Actual}_{\text{Connection}}$ = The total number of actual connections are required between the web server database server for a particular user based on the execution of each modules activity.

$\text{Maximum}_{\text{Connection}}$ = The total number of maximum connections are observed between theweb server database server for a particular user based on the execution of each modules activity.

### 3.7.2 Server Load Analysis Based on Connections between Web Server and Database Server

The server load factor is a weightage factor, which has been generated to measure server load efficiency using the connectivity between web server and database server. In the proposed framework, it is being calculated using $Avg(Actual_{Connection})$ and $Sum(Maximum_{Connection})$. The server load factor is known as '$LF_{Server}$'.

$$\therefore LF_{Server} = \frac{Avg(Actual_{Connection})}{Sum(Maximum_{Connection})}; \tag{3.6}$$

where,

$$Avg(Actual_{Connection}) = \frac{Total\ Number\ of\ Actual_{Connection}\ for\ Proposed\ Framework}{Total\ Number\ of\ Modules\ of\ Proposed\ Framework};$$

$Sum_{(MaximumConnection)}$ = Summation of maximum possible connections of each proposed module.

### 3.7.3 HDD Capacity Analysis

$Input_{HDD\_Capacity}$ and $Output_{HDD\_Capacity}$ are required for HDD capacity.

$$\therefore CF_{HDD} = \frac{Output_{HDD\_Capacity}}{Input_{HDD\_Capacity}}; \tag{3.7}$$

where,
$Input_{HDD\_Capacity}$ = A single unit of HDD capacity, which has been submitted as input into system.
$Output_{HDD\_Capacity}$ = A single unit of HDD capacity, which has been computed after analyzing $Input_{HDD\_Capacity}$

### 3.7.4 RAM Capacity Analysis

$Input_{RAM\_Capacity}$ and $Output_{RAM\_Capacity}$ are required for RAM capacity.

$$\therefore CF_{RAM} = \frac{Output_{RAM\_Capacity}}{Input_{RAM\_Capacity}}; \tag{3.8}$$

where,

$Input_{RAM\_Capacity}$ = A single unit of RAM capacity, which has been submitted as input into system.

$Output_{RAM\_Capacity}$ = A single unit of RAM capacity, which has been computed after analyzing $Input_{RAM\_Capacity}$

### 3.7.5 Memory Capacity Analysis

$CF_{HDD}$, $CF_{RAM}$, $CF_{SS}$ are required for measuring memory capacity ($Memory_{CF}$).

$$\therefore Memory_{CF} = \left[\left(CF_{HDD} * W_{HDD\_Capacity}\right) + \left(CF_{RAM} * W_{RAM\_Capacity}\right)\right]; \tag{3.9}$$

where,

$W_{HDD\_Capacity}$ = A weightage factor of HDD capacity, which has been used to calculate $Memory_{CF}$.

$W_{RAM\_Capacity}$ = A weightage factor of RAM capacity, which has been used to calculate $Memory_{CF}$.

### 3.7.6 System Reliability Analysis

$Memory_{CF}$ and $W_{Quality\ of\ Capacity}$ are required for maintaining system reliability

$$\therefore RF = Memory_{CF} * W_{Quality\ of\ Capacity}; \tag{3.10}$$

where,

$W_{Quality\ of\ Capacity}$ = A weightage factor of HDD capacity, which has been used to measure the quality of memory capacity. Weightage factor ranges between 0 and 1.

## 3.8 Theoretical Discussion

### 3.8.1 Theoretical Perspective on Server Load Evaluation

**Motivation of Theorem 1:** Connection demand factor of proposed design based on total number of users should be realized.

**Theorem 1:** $DF_{Connection}$ is directly proportional to $User_{Count}$.

**Proof:**

Consider, Initial available connection between web server and database server $Initial_{Conn} = 20$;

According to Equation (3.5),

Case 1: $User_{Count} = 1$,

In Algorithm 3.1, $Actual_{Connection} = 2$ and $Maximum_{Connection} = 22$

$$\therefore DF_{Connection} = \frac{2}{22};$$

$\therefore DF_{Connection} = 0.090909$ [Consider, $0.090909 \cong 0.09$];

$\therefore DF_{Connection} = 0.09$;

In Algorithm 3.2, $Actual_{Connection} = 7$ and $Maximum_{Connection} = 24$

$$\therefore DF_{Connection} = \frac{7}{24};$$

$\therefore DF_{Connection} = 0.291667$ [Consider, $0.291667 \cong 0.29$];

$\therefore DF_{Connection} = 0.29$;

In Algorithm 3.3, $Actual_{Connection} = 4$ and $Maximum_{Connection} = 24$

$$\therefore DF_{Connection} = \frac{4}{24};$$

$\therefore DF_{Connection} = 0.166667$ [Consider, $0.166667 \cong 0.17$];

$\therefore DF_{Connection} = 0.17$;

In Algorithm 3.4, $Actual_{Connection} = 7$ and $Maximum_{Connection} = 27$

$$\therefore DF_{Connection} = \frac{7}{27};$$

$\therefore DF_{Connection} = 0.259259$ [Consider, $0.259259 \cong 0.26$];

$\therefore DF_{Connection} = 0.26$;

In Algorithm 3.5, $Actual_{Connection} = 7$ and $Maximum_{Connection} = 27$

$$\therefore DF_{Connection} = \frac{7}{27};$$

$\therefore DF_{Connection} = 0.259259$ [Consider, $0.259259 \cong 0.26$];

$\therefore DF_{Connection} = 0.26$;

Case 2: $User_{Count} = 10000$,

In Algorithm 3.1, $Actual_{Connection} = 20000$ and $Maximum_{Connection} = 20020$

$$\therefore DF_{Connection} = \frac{20000}{20020};$$

$\therefore DF_{Connection} = 0.999001$ [Consider, $0.999001 \cong 1.0$];

$\therefore DF_{Connection} = 1.0$;

In Algorithm 3.2, $Actual_{Connection} = 70000$ and $Maximum_{Connection} = 70017$

$$\therefore DF_{Connection} = \frac{70000}{70017};$$

$\therefore DF_{Connection} = 0.999757$ [Consider, $0.999757 \cong 1.0$];
$\therefore DF_{Connection} = 1.0$;
In Algorithm 3.3, $Actual_{Connection} = 40000$ and $Maximum_{Connection} = 40020$

$$\therefore DF_{Connection} = \frac{40000}{40020};$$

$\therefore DF_{Connection} = 0.999500$ [Consider, $0.999500 \cong 1.0$];
$\therefore DF_{Connection} = 1.0$;
In Algorithm 3.4, $Actual_{Connection} = 70000$ and $Maximum_{Connection} = 70020$

$$\therefore DF_{Connection} = \frac{70000}{70020};$$

$\therefore DF_{Connection} = 0.999714$ [Consider, $0.999714 \cong 1.0$];
$\therefore DF_{Connection} = 1.0$;
In Algorithm 3.5, $Actual_{Connection} = 70000$ and $Maximum_{Connection} = 70020$

$$\therefore DF_{Connection} = \frac{70000}{70020};$$

$\therefore DF_{Connection} = 0.999714$ [Consider, $0.999714 \cong 1.0$];
$\therefore DF_{Connection} = 1.0$;
$\forall User_{Count}$, $DF_{Connection} \propto User_{Count}$ (refer Case 1 and Case 2 of Theorem 1);
Hence, $DF_{Connection}$ is directly proportional to $User_{Count}$.
**[End of Proof]**

**Corollary 1:** $DF_{Connection}$ of the proposed design ranges between 0 to 1.
**Proof:**
According to case 1 of Theorem 1, different values of $DF_{Connection}$ (0.09, 0.29, 0.17, 0.26, 0.26) are nearest to 0.
According to case 2 of Theorem 1, different values of $DF_{Connection}$ (1.0, 1.0, 1.0, 1.0, 1.0) are exactly 1.
Hence, $DF_{Connection}$ of the proposed design ranges between 0 to 1.
**[End of Proof]**

**Motivation of Theorem 2:** Server load factor of the proposed design based on total number of users should be realized.

**Theorem 2:** $LF_{Server}$ is inversely proportional to $User_{Count}$.
**Proof:**
Consider, total numbers of modules present in proposed framework $Proposed_{Module} = 5$;
According to Equation (3.6),
Case 'worst Case Scenario':
For $User_{Count} = 1$

In Algorithm 3.1, Algorithm 3.2, Algorithm 3.3, Algorithm 3.4 and Algorithm 3.5, Required actual connections are 2, 7, 4, 7, 7 and maximum connections are 22, 24, 24, 27, 27 respectively.

$$\therefore Avg(Actual_{Connection}) = \frac{(2+7+4+7+7)}{5};$$

$$\therefore Avg(Actual_{Connection}) = 5.4;$$

$$\therefore Sum(Maximum_{Connection}) = (22+24+24+27+27);$$

$$\therefore Sum(Maximum_{Connection}) = 124;$$

$$\therefore LF_{Server} = \frac{5.4}{124};$$

$$\therefore LF_{Server} = 0.04;$$

For $User_{Count} = 10000$

In Algorithm 3.1, Algorithm 3.2, Algorithm 3.3, Algorithm 3.4 and Algorithm 3.5, Required actual connections are 20000, 70000, 40000, 70000, 70000 and maximum connections are 20020, 70017, 40020, 70020, 70020 respectively.

$$\therefore Avg(Actual_{Connection}) = \frac{(20000+70000+40000+70000+70000)}{5};$$

$$\therefore Avg(Actual_{Connection}) = 54000;$$

$$\therefore Sum(Maximum_{Connection}) = (20020+70017+40020+70020+70020);$$

$$\therefore Sum(Maximum_{Connection}) = 270097;$$

$$\therefore LF_{Server} = \frac{54000}{270097};$$

$$\therefore LF_{Server} = 0.2;$$

$\forall$ $User_{Count}$, difference between $LF_{Server}$ is negligible.

In worst case scenario, $LF_{Server} = User_{Count}$.

Case 'Best Case Scenario':

For $User_{Count} = 1$

In Algorithm 3.1, Algorithm 3.2, Algorithm 3.3, Algorithm 3.4 and Algorithm 3.5, Required actual connections are 2, 7, 4, 7, 7 and maximum connections are 22, 24, 24, 27, 27 respectively.

$$\therefore Avg(Actual_{Connection}) = \frac{(2+7+4+7+7)}{5};$$

$$\therefore Avg(Actual_{Connection}) = 5.4;$$

$$\therefore Sum(Maximum_{Connection}) = (22+24+24+27+27);$$

$$\therefore Sum(Maximum_{Connection}) = 124;$$

$$\therefore LF_{Server} = \frac{5.4}{124};$$

$$\therefore LF_{Server} = 0.04;$$

For $User_{Count} = 10000$
In Algorithm 3.1, Algorithm 3.2, Algorithm 3.3, Algorithm 3.4 and Algorithm 3.5, Required actual connections are 2, 7, 4, 7, 7 and maximum connections are 20020, 70017, 40020, 70020, 70020 respectively.

$$\therefore Avg(Actual_{Connection}) = \frac{(2+7+4+7+7)}{5};$$
$$\therefore Avg(Actual_{Connection}) = 5.4;$$
$$\therefore Sum(Maximum_{Connection}) = (20020+70017+40020+70020+70020);$$
$$\therefore Sum(Maximum_{Connection}) = 270097;$$
$$\therefore LF_{Server} = \frac{5.4}{270097};$$
$$\therefore LF_{Server} = 0.00001999281\,[\text{Consider},\ 0.00001999281 \cong 0.0]$$
$$\therefore LF_{Server} = 0.0;$$

$\forall\, User_{Count}$, $LF_{Server} \propto \frac{1}{User_{Count}}$ (refer best case scenario of Theorem 2);

Hence, $LF_{Server}$ is inversely proportional to $User_{Count}$.
**[End of Proof]**

**Corollary 2:** $LF_{Server}$ is inversely proportional to $DF_{Connection}$.
**Proof:**
Case 1: $User_{Count} = 1$,
According to the proposed algorithms of Theorem 1, required $DF_{Connection}$ are 0.09, 0.29, 0.17, 0.26, 0.26 respectively.
According to the worst case scenario and best case scenario of Theorem 2, required $LF_{Server}$ is 0.04;
Case 2: $User_{Count} = 10000$,
According to the proposed algorithms of Theorem 1, required $DF_{Connection}$ is 1.0;
According to the worst case scenario and best case scenario of Theorem 2, $LF_{Server}$ are 0.2 and 0.0 respectively;

$\forall\, DF_{Connection}$, $LF_{Server} \propto \frac{1}{DF_{Connection}}$ (refer Case 1 and Case 2 of Corollary 3);

Hence, $LF_{Server}$ is inversely proportional to $DF_{Connection}$.
**[End of Proof]**

**Corollary 3:** $LF_{Server}$ is inversely proportional to $DF_{Connection}$.
**Proof:**
Case 1: $User_{Count} = 1$,
According to the proposed algorithms of Theorem 1, $DF_{Connection}$ are 0.09, 0.29, 0.17, 0.26, 0.26 respectively.

According to the worst case scenario and best case scenario of Theorem 2, $LF_{Server}$ is 0.04.
Case 2: $User_{Count} = 10000$,
According to the proposed algorithms of Theorem 1, $DF_{Connection}$ is 1.0.
According to the worst case scenario and best case scenario of Theorem 2, $LF_{Server}$ are 0.2 and 0.0 respectively.
$\forall DF_{Connection}$, $LF_{Server} \propto \frac{1}{DF_{Connection}}$ (refer Case 1 and Case 2 of Corollary 3);
Hence, $LF_{Server}$ is inversely proportional to $DF_{Connection}$.
**[End of Proof]**

### 3.8.2 Theoretical Examination of HDD Capacity Analysis

**Motivation of Theorem 3:** HDD capacity of the proposed design based on input capacity and output capacity should be realized.

**Theorem 3:** $CF_{HDD}$ is directly proportional to $Input_{HDD\_Capacity}$ and $Output_{HDD\_Capacity}$
**Proof:**
According to Equation (3.7),
Case 1: For $Input_{HDD\_Capacity}$ = 1Megabyte and $Output_{HDD\_Capacity}$ = 1Megabyte
After applying CA based mapping, $Input_{HDD\_Capacity\_Index} = 1$ and $Output_{HDD\_Capacity\_Index} = 1$

$$\therefore CF_{HDD} = \left(\frac{1}{1}\right);$$

$$\therefore CF_{HDD} = 1;$$

Case 2: For $Input_{HDD\_Capacity}$ = 1 Megabyte and $Output_{HDD\_Capacity}$ = 8 Terabyte
After applying CA based mapping, $Input_{HDD\_Capacity\_Index} = 1$ and $Output_{HDD\_Capacity\_Index} = 100$

$$\therefore CF_{HDD} = \left(\frac{100}{1}\right);$$

$$\therefore CF_{HDD} = 100;$$

$\forall Output_{HDD\_Capacity}$, $CF_{HDD} \propto Output_{HDD\_Capacity}$ (refer Case 1 and Case 2 of Theorem 3);
Case 3: For $Input_{HDD\_Capacity}$ = 8 Terabyte and $Output_{HDD\_Capacity}$ = 8 Terabyte
After applying CA based mapping, $Input_{HDD\_Capacity\_Index} = 100$ and $Output_{HDD\_Capacity\_Index} = 100$

$$\therefore CF_{HDD} = \left(\frac{100}{100}\right);$$

$\therefore CF_{HDD} = 1;$

$\forall$ $Input_{HDD\_Capacity}$, $CF_{HDD} \propto Input_{HDD\_Capacity}$ (refer Case 3 and Case 4 of Theorem 3);

Hence, $CF_{HDD}$ is directly proportional to $Input_{HDD\_Capacity}$ and $Output_{HDD\_Capacity}$.

**[End of Proof]**

**Corollary 4:** $CF_{HDD}$ of the proposed design ranges between 1 to 100.

**Proof:**

According to the proposed design we know that, the range of $CF_{HDD}$ has been calculated based on $Output_{HDD\_Capacity}$.

In Case 1 and Case 2 of Theorem 3, $CF_{HDD}$ has been measured based on different $Output_{HDD\_Capacity}$ and aparticular $Input_{HDD\_Capacity}$.

According to Case 1 and Case 2 of Theorem 3, $CF_{HDD}$ are 1 and 100 respectively.

Hence, $CF_{HDD}$ of the proposed design ranges between 1 to 100.

**[End of Proof]**

### 3.8.3 Theoretical Examination of RAM Capacity Analysis

**Motivation of Theorem 4:** RAM capacity of proposed design based on input capacity and output capacity should be realized.

**Theorem 4:** $CF_{RAM}$ is directly proportional to $Input_{RAM\_Capacity}$ and $Output_{RAM\_Capacity}$

**Proof:**

According to Equation (3.8),

Case 1: For $Input_{RAM\_Capacity}$ = 1Gigabyte and $Output_{HDD\_Capacity}$ = 1Gigabyte

After applying CA based mapping, $Input_{RAM\_Capacity\_Index} = 1$ and $Output_{RAM\_Capacity\_Index} = 1$

$$\therefore CF_{RAM} = \left(\frac{1}{1}\right);$$

$$\therefore CF_{RAM} = 1;$$

Case 2: For $Input_{RAM\_Capacity}$ = 1 Gigabyte and $Output_{HDD\_Capacity}$ = 128 Gigabyte

After applying CA based mapping, $Input_{RAM\_Capacity\_Index} = 1$ and $Output_{RAM\_Capacity\_Index} = 100$

$$\therefore CF_{RAM} = \left(\frac{100}{1}\right);$$

$$\therefore CF_{RAM} = 100;$$

$\forall$ $Output_{RAM\_Capacity}$, $CF_{RAM} \propto Output_{RAM\_Capacity}$ (refer Case 1 and Case 2 of Theorem 4);
Case 3: For $Input_{RAM\_Capacity}$ = 128 Gigabyte and $Output_{HDD\_Capacity}$ = 128 Gigabyte
After applying CA based mapping, $Input_{RAM\_Capacity\_Index}$ = 100 and $Output_{RAM\_Capacity\_Index}$ = 100

$$\therefore CF_{RAM} = \left(\frac{100}{100}\right);$$

$$\therefore CF_{RAM} = 1;$$

$\forall$ $Input_{RAM\_Capacity}$, $CF_{RAM} \propto Input_{RAM\_Capacity}$ (refer Case 3 and Case 4 of Theorem 4);
Hence, $CF_{RAM}$ is directly proportional to $Input_{RAM\_Capacity}$ and $Output_{RAM\_Capacity}$.
**[End of Proof]**

**Corollary 5:** $CF_{RAM}$ of the proposed design ranges between 1 to 100.
**Proof:**
According to the proposed design we know that, the range of $CF_{RAM}$ has been calculated based on $Output_{RAM\_Capacity}$.
In Case 1 and Case 2 of Theorem 4, $CF_{RAM}$ has been measured based on different $Output_{RAM\_Capacity}$ and a particular $Input_{RAM\_Capacity}$.
According to Case 1 and Case 2 of Theorem 4, $CF_{HDD}$ are 1 and 100 respectively.
Hence, $CF_{RAM}$ of proposed design ranges between 1 to 100.
**[End of Proof]**

### 3.8.4 Theoretical Foundation on Memory Capacity Analysis

**Motivation of Theorem 5:** Memory capacity of the proposed design based on different capacity factors should be realized.

**Theorem 5:** $Memory_{CF}$ is directly proportional to $CF_{HDD}$, and $CF_{RAM}$
**Proof:**
Consider, $W_{HDD\_Capacity}$ = 0.50 and $W_{RAM\_Capacity}$ = 0.50
Case 1: $CF_{HDD}$ = 1 (refer Case 1 of Theorem 3) and $CF_{RAM}$ = 1 (refer Case 1 of Theorem 4);
According to Equation (3.9), $Memory_{CF} = [(1*0.50)+(1*0.50)]$;

$$\therefore Memory_{CF} = 1;$$

Case 2: $CF_{HDD}$ = 100 (refer Case 2 of Theorem 3) and $CF_{RAM}$ = 1 (refer Case 1 of Theorem 4);
According to Equation (3.9), $Memory_{CF} = [(100*0.50)+(1*0.50)]$;

$$\therefore Memory_{CF} = 50.50;$$

Case 3: $CF_{HDD}$ = 100 (refer Case 2 of Theorem 3) and $CF_{RAM}$ = 100 (refer Case 2 of Theorem 4);

According to Equation (3.9), $Memory_{CF} = [(100*0.50)+(100*0.50)]$;

$\therefore Memory_{CF} = 100$;

$\therefore$ $\text{Memory}_{CF} \propto CF_{HDD}$ (refer Case 1 and Case 2 of Theorem 6);

$\therefore$ $\text{Memory}_{CF} \propto CF_{RAM}$ (refer Case 1, Case 2 and Case 3 of Theorem 6);

Hence, $\text{Memory}_{CF}$ is directly proportional to $CF_{HDD}$, $CF_{RAM}$.

**[End of Proof]**

**Corollary 6:** $\text{Memory}_{CF}$ of proposed design ranges between 1 to 100.

**Proof:**

According to the mentioned cases of Theorem 6, $\text{Memory}_{CF}$ are 1, 33.67, 66.34, and 100 respectively.

Hence, $\text{Memory}_{CF}$ of the proposed design ranges between 1 to 100.

**[End of Proof]**

### 3.8.5 Theoretical Discussion on System Reliability

**Motivation of Theorem 6:** Reliability Factor of proposed design based on $\text{Memory}_{CF}$ and $W_{\text{Quality of Capacity}}$ should be realized

**Theorem 6:** RF is directly proportional to $\text{Memory}_{CF}$ and $W_{\text{Quality of Capacity}}$.

**Proof:**

Case 1: $W_{\text{Quality of Capacity}} = 0$;

For $\text{Memory}_{CF}$ = 1 (refer Case 1 of Theorem 6)

According to Equation (3.10), $RF = (1*0)$;

$\therefore RF = 0$;

For $\text{Memory}_{CF}$ = 50.50 (refer Case 2 of Theorem 6)

According to Equation (3.10), $RF = (50.50*0)$;

$\therefore RF = 0$;

For $\text{Memory}_{CF}$ = 100 (refer Case 3 of Theorem 6)

According to Equation (3.10), $RF = (100*0)$;

$\therefore RF = 0$;

Case 2: $W_{\text{Quality of Capacity}} = 0.5$;

For $\text{Memory}_{CF}$ = 1 (refer Case 1 of Theorem 6)

According to Equation (3.10), $RF = (1*0.5)$;

$\therefore RF = 0.5$;

For $\text{Memory}_{CF}$ = 50.50 (refer Case 2 of Theorem 6)

According to Equation (3.10), $RF = (50.50*0.5)$;

$\therefore RF = 25.25$;

For $\text{Memory}_{CF}$ = 100 (refer Case 4 of Theorem 6)

According to Equation (3.10), $RF = (100 * 0.5)$;
$\therefore RF = 50$;
Case 3: $W_{\text{Quality of Capacity}} = 1$;
For $\text{Memory}_{\text{CF}} = 1$ (refer Case 1 of Theorem 6)
According to Equation (3.10), $RF = (1 * 1)$;
$\therefore RF = 1$;
For $\text{Memory}_{\text{CF}} = 50.50$ (refer Case 2 of Theorem 6)
According to Equation (3.10), $RF = (50.50 * 1)$;
$\therefore RF = 50.50$;.
For $\text{Memory}_{\text{CF}} = 100$ (refer Case 4 of Theorem 6)
According to Equation (3.10), $RF = (100 * 1)$;
$\therefore RF = 100$;
$\therefore \text{RF} \propto Memory_{CF}$ (refer Case 1 or Case 2 or Case 3 of Theorem 7);
$\therefore \text{RF} \propto W_{Quality\ of\ Capacity}$ (refer Case 1, Case 2 and Case 3 of Theorem 7);
Hence, RF is directly proportional to $\text{Memory}_{\text{CF}}$ and $W_{\text{Quality of Capacity}}$.
**[End of Proof]**

**Corollary 7:** RF of the proposed design ranges between 0 to 100.
**Proof:**
According to Case 1 and Case 3 of Theorem 7, RF = 0 and 100 respectively. Hence, RF of the proposed design ranges between 0 to 100.
**[End of Proof]**

## 3.9 Experimental Discussion

### 3.9.1 Overview

Experimental discussion has been presented in this section for establishing experimental setup, different types of experimental analysis and comparison. Several examinations are being presented with appropriate experimental study to furnish the proficiency of proposed system. The proficiency of proposed MCMS framework has been evaluated for establishing the superiority based on several aspects of experimental results.

### 3.9.2 Experimental Setup

In this sub-section, all the necessary components required for authors' experimentation are furnished as follows:

Number of computers used in network: 400
Number of Computers and Total memory used in network: 400 and 400TB (Secondary-Memory) and 6TB (Primary-Memory)
Database server and Database Connectivity used in network: Oracle Server and Java Database Connectivity (JDBC)
Language and Compiler used to prepare application: Java & JDK 1.8

### 3.9.3 Time Complexity Analysis

In Figure 3.8, time complexity graph has been presented using proposed framework. In the proposed MCMS, total execution time is calculated for maintaining health of IoT ecosystem and to generate a capable resource based on user requirement using linear CA rules. 400 number of users are considered for preparing time analysis graph. Time analysis are being described for each algorithm as follows:

Consider, total units of time are required to execute all steps of algorithms is 'S(x)';
Consider, total number of users have been participated at a particular time is 'U(y)';
Consider, constant value for each algorithm is 'C';
For, Memory Capacity Management (refer Algorithm 3.1), S(x) = 7, U(y) = 400 and C=0;
Therefore, reuired time for Algorithm 3.1 has been calculated.
$\text{Algorithm1}_{\text{Time}} = [[7+0]*400]$ units;
$\therefore \text{Algorithm1}_{\text{Time}} = 2800$ units;

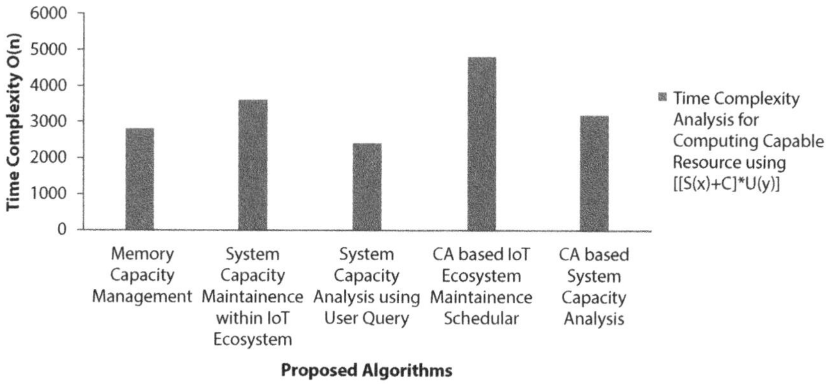


**Figure 3.8** Time complexity analysis graph for MCMS framework using proposed framework.

Similarly, required times for Algorithm 3.2, Algorithm 3.3, Algorithm 3.4 and Algorithm 3.5 are 3600 units, 2400 units, 4800 units and 3200 units respectively. Several time units have been achieved using proposed algorithms. A linear time complexity is observed in Figure 3.8.

### 3.9.4 System Load Analysis

In system load analysis sub-section, constant system load has been achieved based on connections between web server and database server.

In Figure 3.9, connection ratio graph between web server and database server has been presented for server load analysis based on several algorithms. Initially, 20 number of connections are available between web server and database server. 2 number of new connections are required for executing Algorithm 3.1. After execution of Algorithm 3.1, number of connections has been reduced from 22 to 20. Similarly, several number of new connections such as, 4 and 7 are essential for executing each remaining algorithms. Number of connection remains constant with primary situation after execution of each particular algorithm. A constant server load is established for each particular user.

In Table 3.2, connection demand factors are being incorporated for proposed CA based MCMS framework. Several number of users such as, 1 to 10000 are utilized on five distinct algorithms such as Algorithm 3.1, Algorithm 3.2, Algorithm 3.3, Algorithm 3.4 and Algorithm 3.5 for calculating the demand factor of connection. '$Connection_{DF}$' is being shown as constant for each particular module based on the increment of number of users. CPU @ 2.50 GHz RAM 16.0 GB is required to prepare the result of Table 3.2.

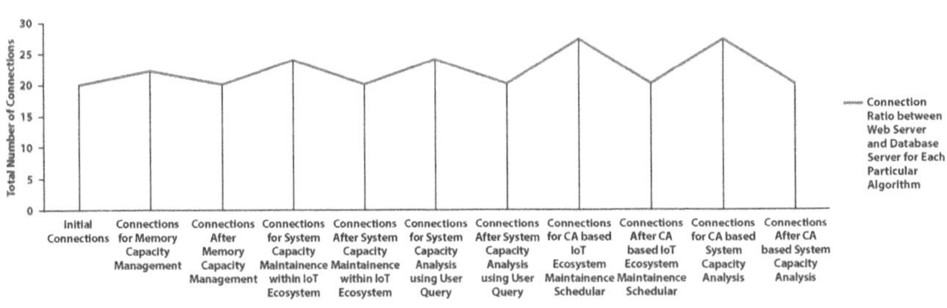


**Figure 3.9** Connection ratio graph between web server and database server using proposed algorithms.

**Table 3.2** Observation on connection demand factor ($Connection_{DF}$) calculated for connectivity demand measurement by proposed CA based MCMS framework using CPU @ 2.50 GHz RAM 16.0 GB.

| Total number of users | $DF_{Connection}$ for proposed ca based mcms framework | | | | |
|---|---|---|---|---|---|
| | Memory capacity management (Algorithm 3.1) | System capacity maintainence within IoT ecosystem (Algorithm 3.2) | System capacity analysis using user query (Algorithm 3.3) | Ca based IoT ecosystem maintainence schedular (Algorithm 3.4) | Ca based system capacity analysis (Algorithm 3.5) |
| 1 | 0.09 | 0.29 | 0.17 | 0.26 | 0.26 |
| 100 | 0.91 | 0.98 | 0.95 | 0.97 | 0.97 |
| 500 | 0.98 | 1.00 | 0.99 | 0.99 | 0.99 |
| 1000 | 0.99 | 1.00 | 1.00 | 1.00 | 1.00 |
| 2500 | 1.00 | 1.00 | 1.00 | 1.00 | 1.00 |
| 5000 | 1.00 | 1.00 | 1.00 | 1.00 | 1.00 |
| 7500 | 1.00 | 1.00 | 1.00 | 1.00 | 1.00 |
| 10000 | 1.00 | 1.00 | 1.00 | 1.00 | 1.00 |

In Table 3.3, server load factors are being incorporated for proposed CA based framework. Two scenarios such as, worst case scenario and best case scenario have been furnished for comparing server load based on number of users. In worst case scenario, '$LF_{Server}$' are continuously increased based on the increment of number of users. In best case scenario, '$LF_{Server}$' are shown as constant depending on user count. In proposed CA based MCMS framework, less server load has been achieved in case of worst case scenario and best case scenario respectively. CPU @ 2.50 GHz RAM 16.0 GB is required to prepare the result of Table 3.3.

### 3.9.5 System Proficiency Analysis Using Different Factors

In this sub-section, several factor based experimentations have been executed for measuring system proficiency using memory capacity and system reliability.

In Figure 3.10, HDD and RAM based system capacity analysis graph is being presented based on user required harddisk space and system provided harddisk space. A set of user provided HDD and RAM related memory size and system generated HDD and RAM related memory size are considered as input and output respectively. In HDD and RAM based system capacity analysis graph, multiple stages have been shown to establish

**Table 3.3** Observation on server load factor ($Server_{LF}$) calculated for server load analysis by proposed CA based MCMS framework using CPU @ 2.50 GHz RAM 16.0 GB.

| **Total number of users** | **$LF_{Server}$ for proposed CA based MCMS framework** | |
|---|---|---|
| | **Worst case scenario** | **Best case scenario** |
| 1 | 0.04 | 0.04 |
| 100 | 0.19 | 0.00 |
| 500 | 0.20 | 0.00 |
| 1000 | 0.20 | 0.00 |
| 2500 | 0.20 | 0.00 |
| 5000 | 0.20 | 0.00 |
| 7500 | 0.20 | 0.00 |
| 10000 | 0.20 | 0.00 |

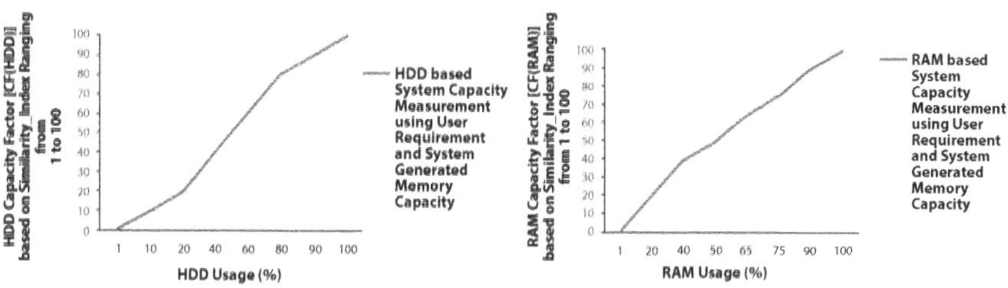


**Figure 3.10** Memory category (HDD & RAM) based system capacity analysis using user required memory size and system provided memory size.

directly proportional relationship between preliminary dataset and system capacities using experimental analysis (refer Theorem 3 and Theorem 4). Higher system capacity is being observed using best condition of HDD and RAM related memory sizes.

In Figure 3.11, system capacity analysis graph is being presented for calculating memory capacity factor based on different categories of memory capacities. A set of categorical capacity factors and system generated memory capacity factor are considered as input and output respectively. In Figure 3.11, multiple stages have been shown to establish directly proportional relationship between category wise system capacity factors and system capacities using experimental analysis (refer Theorem 6). Higher system capacity is being observed using best condition of memory capacity factors.

In Figure 3.12, system reliability analysis graph is being presented for calculating reliability factor based on different scenarios of memory capacity factors. A set of memory capacity factors and system generated

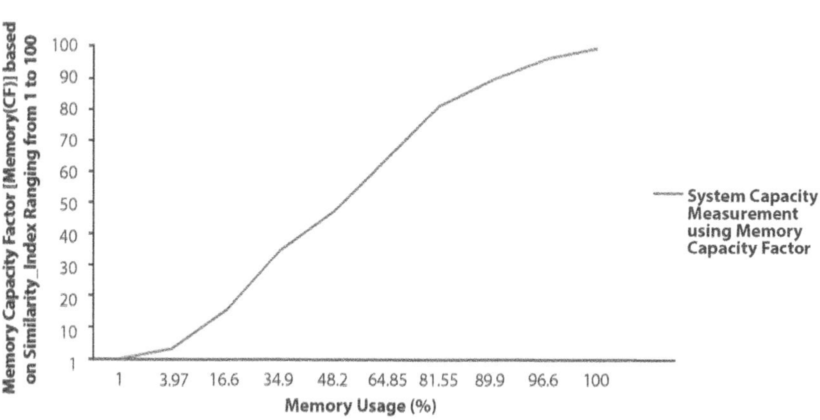


**Figure 3.11** System capacity analysis using memory capacity factor.

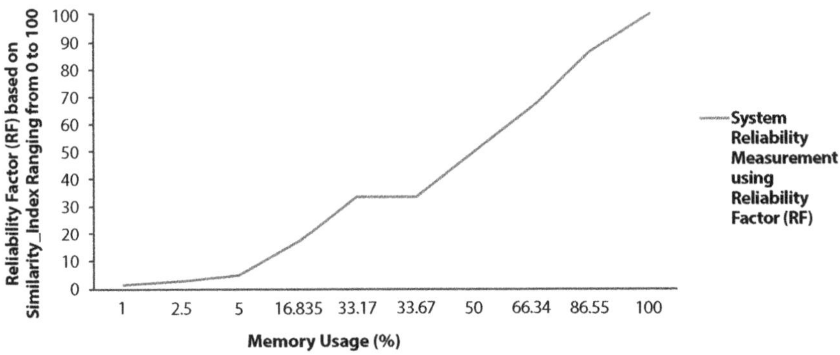


**Figure 3.12** System reliability analysis using reliability factor.

reliability factor are considered as input and output respectively. In Figure 3.12, multiple stages have been shown to establish directly proportional relationship between memory capacity factor and reliability factor based on system capacities (refer Theorem 7). Higher system reliability is being observed using best condition of memory capacity factors.

## 3.10 Comparison

Proposed system efficiency has been established using comparison chart as shown in Table 3.4. Several characteristics are being utilized for establishing a comparative analysis between existing systems and proposed system based on cloud based communication, IoT ecosystems health, AI based automated strategy. In comparative analysis, two distinct memory category wise capacity factors have been utilized to increase the superiority of proposed system using memory capacity and system reliability respectively. Two icons such as, 'Available' and 'Not Available' have been mentioned in Table 3.4 to identify the existence and non-existence of each property respectively.

In Table 3.5, a comparison between server load factor of existing systems and proposed system has been shown based on different scenarios of server usage. In existing systems, three types of health conditions such as, under loaded, normal and over loaded are being measured based on different ranges of server load factors. In proposed CA based approach, worst case scenario and best case scenario have been furnished based on several server load factors. Minimum server load is achieved in proposed CA based MCMS framework.

In Table 3.6, a comparison between memory size of existing systems and proposed system has been elaborated based on several memory categories.

**Table 3.4** Comparative study between existing systems and proposed CA based system.

| **Characteristics** | **Existing system1 [14, 15]** | **Existing system 2 [16, 17]** | **Existing system 3 [18, 19]** | **Proposed system** |
|---|---|---|---|---|
| HDD Capacity Factor | Not Available | Not Available | Not Available | Available |
| RAM Capacity Factor | Not Available | Not Available | Not Available | Available |
| Memory Capacity Factor | Not Available | Not Available | Not Available | Available |
| Reliability Factor | Not Available | Not Available | Not Available | Available |
| Time Complexity | Not Available | Not Available | Not Available | Available |
| Connection Demand Factor | Not Available | Not Available | Not Available | Available |
| System Load Analysis | Not Available | Not Available | Not Available | Available |
| CA based Approach | Not Available | Not Available | Not Available | Available |
| Memory Management Approach | Not Available | Available | Available | |
| Cloud based Approach | Available | Not Available | Available | Available |
| Connectivity between Devices within IoT Ecosystem | Not Available | Available | | Available |
| AI based Approach | Not Available | Available | Available | Available |
| Platform Independent | Available | Available | Available | Available |

*(Continued)*

**Table 3.4** Comparative study between existing systems and proposed CA based system. (*Continued*)

| Characteristics | Existing system1 [14, 15] | Existing system 2 [16, 17] | Existing system 3 [18, 19] | Proposed system |
|---|---|---|---|---|
| Automatic System | Available | Available | Available | Available |
| Software based Approach | Available | Available | Available | Available |
| Network based Performance Evaluation | Available | Available | Available | Available |
| Resource Scheduling Analysis | Available | Available | Available | Available |
| Hardware based Approach | Not Available | Not Available | Not Available | Not Available |
| Infrastructure as a Service | Available | Not Available | Not Available | Available |
| Software as a Service | Available | Not Available | Not Available | Available |
| Scalability | Available | Not Available | Available | Available |
| Web based Approach | Available | Available | Available | Available |

**Table 3.5** Comparison between server load factor of existing systems and proposed CA based system based on server usage.

| Existing systems server load factor along with health status [20, 21] | | | Proposed systems server load factor based on two scenarios | |
|---|---|---|---|---|
| **Under loaded** | **Normal** | **Over loaded** | **Worst case scenario** | **Best case scenario** |
| 0.25 | 0.48 | 0.96 | 0.20 | 0.04 |

**Table 3.6** Comparison between memory size of existing systems and proposed MCMS framework based on memory categories.

| **Maximum memory sizes used in existing systems** | | **Maximum memory sizes used in proposed system** | |
|---|---|---|---|
| HDD [22] | RAM [23] | HDD | RAM |
| 1 Terabytes | 256 Gigabytes | 32 Terabytes | 256 Gigabytes |

**Table 3.7** Comparison between time complexities of existing algorithms and proposed algorithms.

| | **Time complexity** | | |
|---|---|---|---|
| **Algorithms** | **Best case** | **Average case** | **Worst case** |
| **Existing algorithms [24, 25]** | | | |
| Quick Sort | ω(nlog(n)) | θ(nlog(n)) | $O(n^2)$ |
| Merge Sort | ω(nlog(n)) | θ(nlog(n)) | O(nlog(n)) |
| Bucket Sort | ω(n + k) | θ(n + k) | $O(n^2)$ |
| RadixSort | ω(nk) | θ(nk) | O(nk) |
| Bubble Sort | ω(n) | θ(n2) | $O(n^2)$ |
| Insertion Sort | ω(n) | θ(n2) | $O(n^2)$ |
| Counting Sort | ω(n + k) | θ(n + k) | O(n + k) |
| Selection Sort | ω(n2) | θ(n2) | $O(n^2)$ |
| Linear Search | ω(1) | θ(n) | O(n) |
| Binary Search | ω(1) | θ(log(n)) | O(logn) |
| **Proposed algorithms** | | | |
| Memory Capacity Management | ω(1) | θ(n) | O(n) |
| System Capacity Maintainence within IoT Ecosystem | ω(1) | θ(n) | O(n) |

*(Continued)*

**Table 3.7** Comparison between time complexities of existing algorithms and proposed algorithms. (*Continued*)

| Algorithms | Time complexity | | |
|---|---|---|---|
| | **Best case** | **Average case** | **Worst case** |
| System Capacity Analysis using User Query | ω(1) | θ(n) | O(n) |
| CA based Iot Ecosystem Maintainence Schedular | ω(1) | θ(n) | O(n) |
| CA based System Capacity Analysis | ω(1) | θ(n) | O(n) |

Two memory categories (HDD and RAM) have been utilized for measuring the maximum capacities of each memory category. The authors have assessed superiority of each memory category based on memory sizes and utilized maximum memory capacities for designing proposed CA based MCMS framework.

In Table 3.7, a comparative study between time complexities of existing algorithms and proposed algorithms have been furnished based on various cases such as, best case, average case and worst case. Several existing algorithms as mentioned in Table 3.7 have been utilized for measuring the time complexities of each particular case. Each proposed algorithm is required in proposed framework for generating a capable resource based on user query analysis and to maintain IoT ecosystems health using predefined memory informations. Linear time complexities are achieved in proposed CA based algorithms depending on several cases.

## 3.11 Conclusion

CA based MCMS framework has been successfully designed for maintaining the health of IoT ecosystem and to compute capable resource based on memory related user query analysis. A linear communication between three distinct modules has been established to analyze system capacity using CA based mechanisms. Multiple memory category wise user queries have been successfully received into MCMS controller for calculating a capable resource based on user query analysis. CA based algorithms have been developed to design predefined dataset using several memory conditions of IoT ecosystems and to calculate a suitable resource based on user requirement analysis. Hypothetical relations have been established between several memory capacity factors and different ranges of memory categories have been theoretically mesured using CA based analysis. Several experimental results such as, connection demand factor, server load factor, memory capacity factor, and reliability factor have been shown to establish the system capacity of proposed CA based MCMS framework. System competence has been successfully elaborated using comparative analysis between existing systems and proposed system. The authors have achieved a linear CA based framework with enhanced efficiency based on different experimental observations. In the future, AI-driven strategies will be designed to explore the full potential of cloud-IoT ecosystem as the the next wave of technological advancement by addressing challenges such as data privacy, latency and scalability.

## Acknowledgment

The research work is funded by Computer Innovative Research Society, West Bengal, India. Award number is "2025/CIRS/R&D/1001-11-09/SIAIDSDCITE".

**AI disclosure statement:** The author confirms that no artificial intelligence (AI)-generated content or AI-assisted writing tools were used in the preparation of this chapter (including summaries and the abstract). All text, analysis, and conclusions are the result of the author's original work.

## References

1. Muller, H., Kharitonov, A., Nahhas, A., Bosse, S., Turowski, K., Addressing IT Capacity Management Concerns Using Machine Learning Techniques. *SN Comput. Sci.*, 3, 26, 2021.
2. Narasimhaiah, N. and Sam, P., A Talk on Cloud Capacity Management. *Int. Res. J. Eng. Technol.*, 2, 3, 2395–0056, 2015.
3. Radanliev, P. and Roure, D.D., Review of Algorithms for Artificial Intelligence on Low Memory Devices. *IEEE Access*, 9, 109986–109993, 2020.
4. Comeaga, A.M. and Marin, I., Memory Management Strategies for an Internet of Things System. *International Symposium on Fundamentals of Electrical Engineering*, vol. 10, 2023.
5. Frady, E.P., Kleyko, D., Sommer, F.T., A Theory of Sequence Indexing and Working Memory in Recurrent Neural Networks. *Neural Comput.*, 30, 6, 1449–1513, 2018.

6. Raghuvanshi, D., Memory Management in Operating System. *Int. J. Trend Sci. Res. Dev.*, 2, 5, 2346–2347, 2018.
7. Omar, N.R., Saeed, R.H., Ahmed, J.A., Muhammad, S.B., Ageed, Z.S., Rashid, Z.N., Enhancing OS Memory Management Performance: A Review. *Int. J. Multi. Res. Publ.*, 3, 12, 46–51, 2021.
8. Gangadhar, P.V.S.S., Rao, M.V., Hota, A.K., Rao, V.V., Distributed Memory and CPU Management in Cloud Computing Environment. *Int. J. Appl. Eng. Res.*, 12, 24, 15972–15978, 2017.
9. Gholami, A., Yao, Z., Kim, S., Hooper, C., Mahoney, M.W., Keutzer, K., AI and Memory Wall. *IEEE Micro*, 44, 33–39, 2024.
10. Maitah, M.A., AlZubi, A.A., Alarifi, A., An Optimal Storage Utilization Technique for IoT Devices Using Sequential Machine Learning. *Comput. Netw.*, Elsevier, 152, 98–105, 2019.
11. Ashraf, M. and Kutty, J., Advanced Memory Management for Embedded Systems with Limited Resources. *Int. J. Creat. Res. Thoughts*, 11, 9, 30–36, 2023.
12. Chougule, P.P., Sen, B., Mukherjee, R., Patil, P.S., Kamat, R.K., Dongale, T.D., A Processing in Memory Realization using Quantum Dot Cellular Automata (QCA) : Proposal and Implementation. *J. Nano Electron. Phys.*, 9, 1, 1–5, 2017.
13. Chen, Y., Yu, F., Cheng, Z., Jin, Q., Pei, Z., Yi, W., Academic Insights and Perspectives: Cellular Automata and Production Scheduling. *Math. Probl. Eng. - Hindawi*, 6327314, 1–15, 2020.
14. Zormatai, Z., Mehraban, S., Yousof, H., Shinwari, S., Impact and Benefits of Software Defined Network on The Cloud Network Infrastructure. *Int. J. Modern. Eng. Technol. Sci.*, 5, 3, 4204–4209, 2023.
15. Amer, Z.H. and Aziz, W.A., Design and Implementation of Network Management System for Cloud Applications. *Int. J. Simul. Syst. Sci. Technol.*, 24, 1–9, 2023.
16. Musaddiq, A., Zikria, Y.B., Yu, H., Bashir, A.K., A Survey on Resource Management in IoT Operating System. Fairness in Futuristic Wireless Networks: Applications, Implementation, Issue, and Opportunities. *IEEE Access*, 6, 2169–3536, 2018.
17. Alsaffar, M., Hamad, A.A., Alshammari, A., Alshammari, G., Almurayziq, T.S., Mohammed, M.S., Enbeyle, W., Network Management System for IoT based Dynamic System. *Comput. Math. Methods Med.*, 91029095, 2021.
18. Chinchawade, A.J., Rajyalaxmi, S., Singh, S., Kumar, R.A., Rastogi, R., Shah, M.A., Scheduling in Multi-Hop Wireless Networks using a Distributed Learning Algorithm. *International Conference on Trends in Electronics and Informatics*, p. 10125909, 2023.
19. Singh, S., The Role of Artificial Intelligence in 5G Network Management: A Comprehensive Study. *Int. J. Res. Publ. Rev.*, 4, 11, 2862–2866, 2023.
20. Gajbhiye, A. and Singh, S., Global Server Load Balancing with Networked Load Balancers for Geographically Distributed Cloud Data-Centres. *Int. J. Comput. Sci. Netw.*, 6, 6, 682–688, 2017.

21. Lin, Q., Xie, J., Shen, Z., Xu, X., DR3: Optimizing Site Selection for Global Load Balance in Application Delivery Controller, in: *Open Cirrus Summit (OCS)*, pp. 11–15, 2012.
22. Saukani, I., Nuraini, E., Nurhadi, S., Sumarno, A.S.H., Saptawati, R.T.T., Prasetyo, Islahunufus, I., Ms, F.I.S., Format Methods on Storage Media (Hard Disk) for Optimization Data Storage Capacity. *Asian J. Sci. Eng.*, 2, 2, 123–131, 2023.
23. Ge, Y., Tian, Y.C., Yu, Z.G., Zhang, W., Memory Sharing for Handling Memory Overload on Physical Machines in Cloud Data Centers. *J. Cloud Comput.*, Springer Publication, 12, 27, 1–20, 2023.
24. Shabbir, A., Majeed, A., Iftikar, M., Ali, R.H., Arshad, U., Shabbir, M.Z., Ijaz, A.Z., Ali, N., Aftab, A., A Review of Algorithms's Complexities on Different Valued Sorted and Unsorted Data. *International conference on IT and Industrial Technologies*, IEEE, pp. 1–6, 2023.
25. Jacob, A.E., Ashodariya, N., Dhongade, A., Hybrid Search Algorithm: Combined Linear and Binary Search Algorithm. *International Conference on Energy, Communication, Data Analytics and soft Computing*, pp. 1543–1547, 2017.

# 4

# Navigating the Fog AI-Driven Resilience and Privacy Preservation in Cloud IoT Environments

**Bhupendra Panchal[1*], Sarah Joby David[1], Ritika Singh[1], Manini Chhabra[1], Ajay Sharma[1] and Tarannum Khan[2]**

*[1]School of Computing Science and Engineering, VIT Bhopal University, Bhopal-Indore Highway, Kothrikalan, Sehore, Madhya Pradesh, India*
*[2]Computer Science and Engineering, Mahakal Institute of Technology, Ujjain, Madhya Pradesh, India*

### *Abstract*

Massive volumes of data are collected, processed, and analyzed in real time at a critical juncture because of the rapid growth of Internet of Things (IoT) technology and the widespread usage of cloud computing. Fog computing allows data processing and storage to be done more efficiently near to the site of data generation. Through local data management, latency and bandwidth consumption are decreased, facilitating analytics and decision-making in real-time. IoT systems' scalability, performance, and reliability are improved by fog computing, which shifts processing power to the network's edge. Complicating the security picture is the distributed nature of cloud computing, which positions processing and storage nearer to the many data sources. Because they often lack strong security, IoT devices are vulnerable to a variety of attacks. Common issues include hostile attacks, unauthorized access, and data breaches. Large amounts of sensitive data are processed and stored in IoT cloud systems, which exacerbates these security problems. Technologies based on artificial intelligence provide creative ways to safeguard user data. Because AI-based predictive maintenance stops equipment problems before they happen, it lowers downtime and increases overall system reliability. Additionally, artificial intelligence (AI) makes it possible for sophisticated threat detection and response systems to identify anomalous patterns that point to weaknesses in system security and act swiftly to eliminate threats,

**Corresponding author*: bhupendrapanchal30@gmail.com

Partha Ghosh, Rajdeep Chakraborty, Anupam Ghosh and Ahmed A. Elngar (eds.) Strategic Approaches to Intrusion Detection in Cloud-IoT Ecosystem, (99–118) © 2026 Scrivener Publishing LLC

guaranteeing ongoing operations. The convergence of cloud computing, machine learning, and the IoT offers unparalleled opportunities for data processing and real-time analysis. However, this integration also brings up significant privacy and security issues that must be addressed to reach its full potential. Federated Learning (FL), an important AI-based privacy-preserving technology, enables distributed training of machine learning models on local devices. Consequently, it ensures that the gadget will keep the raw data. This approach significantly secures private information and lowers the risk of data breaches by allowing devices to cooperate to improve a machine learning model. This research focuses on privacy preservation in cloud-IoT environments using AI-driven FL as they relate to AI-based resilience and privacy preservation in the IoT cloud context. In this chapter, we propose using Federated Learning (FL) to minimize the limitations of current AI techniques in IoT environments, which helps to enhance data privacy and security. FL protects user privacy and ensures robust model correctness by enabling decentralized machine learning model training without exchanging raw data. This approach facilitates safe and efficient data processing across various IoT applications. This helps to strengthen the scalability and efficiency of FL-based security solutions which has proved to be essential. Integrating multiple privacy protection technologies within the FL framework provides stronger protection against emerging threats, making FL pivotal for high performance and strict privacy in IoT.

***Keywords***: Federate learning, IoT, artificial intelligence, privacy, security

## 4.1 Introduction

The core concept of Internet of Things (IoT) technology is the integration of sensors into everyday objects and the utilization of connectivity to facilitate information exchange for various purposes [1]. It makes automation and monitoring possible in fields like healthcare and smart cities, which improve productivity and facilitate better decision-making. Because of the large amount of data, robust computing infrastructure is necessary. IoT data is commonly processed in real time using cloud computing, which provides centralized storage and processing capability. This centralization allows for scalability, but it also brings up concerns about data privacy, security, and system resilience. Machine learning, a crucial component of artificial intelligence, is now necessary to fully utilize the promise of IoT data. Without explicit programming, AI allows systems to identify patterns, forecast results, and automate decision-making through machine learning algorithms. IoT devices must transmit their data to the cloud for standard machine learning techniques to train their models, which mostly rely on centralized data collection. Data privacy and the possibility of disclosing private information are issues raised by this strategy. Federated Learning (FL) is an emerging AI technique which provides a decentralized solution to these challenges. In 2016 McMahan *et al.* [2], coined the phrase Federated learning (FL) that has surfaced as a distributed privacy-preserving answer to this urgent demand in recent years [3]. Because IoT devices gather so much data, a robust computing infrastructure is necessary. Real-time processing of IoT data is commonly accomplished through cloud computing, which provides centralized storage and processing capacity. While this concentration facilitates scalability, it also presents challenges for data privacy, security, and system resilience. Machine learning, a crucial component of artificial intelligence, is now necessary to fully utilize the promise of IoT data. Without explicit programming, AI allows systems to identify patterns, forecast results, and automate decision-making through machine learning algorithms. IoT devices must transmit their data to the cloud for standard machine learning techniques to train their models, which mostly rely on centralized data collection. Data privacy and the possibility of disclosing private information are issues raised by this strategy.

Figure 4.1 illustrates a layered architecture involving the cloud, fog, and edge. The cloud layer contains centralized cloud servers, while the fog

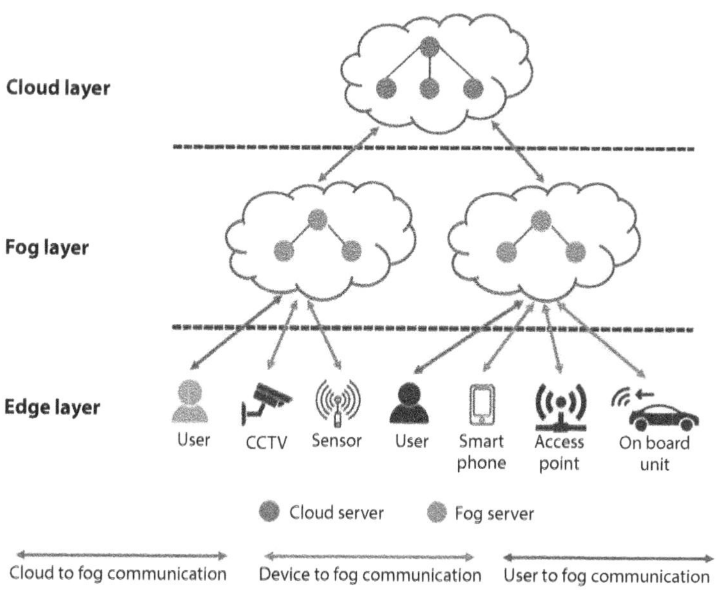


**Figure 4.1** Three level architecture of fog computing.

layer consists of intermediate fog servers for localized computing. At the edge layer, devices like sensors, smartphones, and cars interact with the fog servers. Communication flows between cloud-to-fog, device-to-fog, and user-to-fog, facilitating systematic data transmission and reducing network latency for IoT applications. Figure 4.2 depicts a fog computing framework where devices like sensors, cameras, and mobile phones send data to fog devices and servers for processing. The architecture incorporates multiple processors, a resource manager, and modules for monitoring and security. The processed data is used by applications (App 1, App 2), which serve the needs of end users. Additionally, the fog system is linked to the cloud for further computational tasks and data storage. This study is significant as it tackles the elevating demand for secure and reliable cloud IoT systems. Through exploring the various AI-driven methods such as Federated Learning, we can protect the privacy of our data and enhance system resilience. This study adds to the development of more dependable, adaptable, and secure infrastructures for the IoT's future.

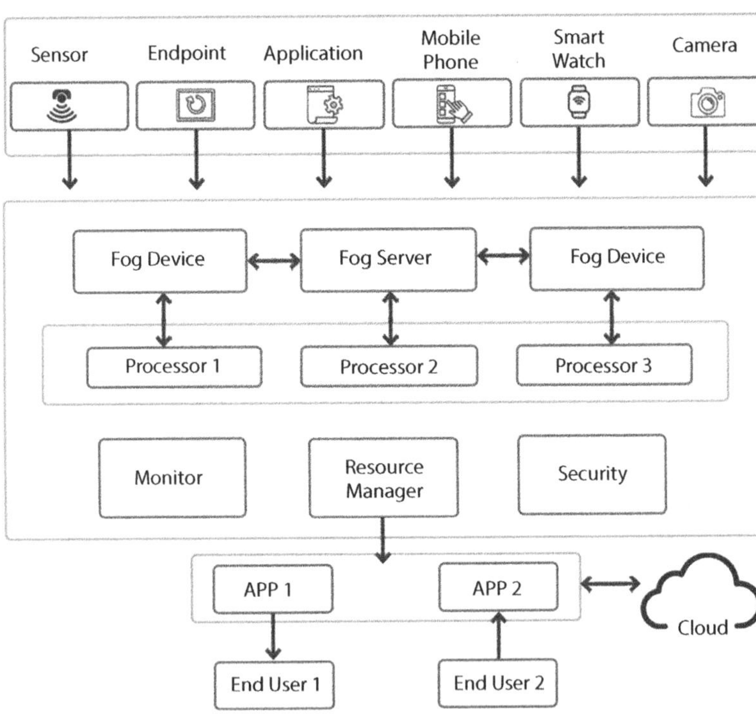


**Figure 4.2** Fog computing architecture.

## 4.2 Literature Review

There are many issues with the rise of the IoT and its incorporation into cloud computing, particularly with relation to data security, resilience, and privacy. The exponential expansion of IoT devices has resulted in a rise in network complexity and data creation, rendering conventional cloud-based models inadequate. Fog computing, which moves networking, storage, and processing closer to IoT devices, has become a viable way to overcome the drawbacks of cloud computing. Cloud IoT systems' robustness and privacy protection are greatly improved by artificial intelligence (AI) in this context. The convergence of AI, cloud IoT, and fog computing is explored in this literature review, with an emphasis on how AI methods might improve resilience while protecting privacy in these settings.

### 4.2.1 Cloud and IoT: Challenges and Opportunities

Cloud computing provides scalable resources and processing power, which has facilitated the widespread adoption of IoT. However, the centralized nature of cloud computing poses latency issues, bandwidth constraints, and security risks. Centralized cloud systems often become bottlenecks for real-time IoT applications, where data processing needs to occur with minimal delay. Fog computing, coined by Cisco [4], addresses these concerns by decentralizing computing resources to edge devices, offering reduced latency and better bandwidth utilization. Although fog computing solves certain problems, it also brings with it new ones including resource heterogeneity, network administration, and privacy issues because of the scattered data processing.

### 4.2.2 AI-Driven Resilience in Fog and Cloud IoT Environments

Resilience in cloud IoT environments refers to the system's ability to adapt, recover, and maintain functionality in the face of failures or cyber-attacks. AI-driven approaches are critical for resilience because they can predict failures, dynamically allocate resources, and optimize network performance. For example, Zhang *et al.* [5], present a machine learning-based approach to optimize fog resource allocation in real-time, improving system resilience under network congestion. The study demonstrates how AI algorithms can anticipate network traffic and reroute data to minimize packet loss and delays. Additionally, Zhang, L. *et al.* [6], explored AI-based fault detection systems for IoT networks, highlighting how deep learning techniques can identify anomalies in real-time data streams from IoT sensors. Their work emphasizes the importance of AI for predictive maintenance, where system failures can be foreseen and mitigated before causing significant disruptions.

### 4.2.3 Privacy Preservation in AI-Driven Cloud IoT Systems

One of the biggest issues in cloud and IoT contexts is protecting privacy. Data processing in centralized cloud systems or even at the fog layer may result in privacy concerns when IoT devices gather sensitive user data. Alrawais, A. *et al.* [7], states that processing all the data on IoT devices is difficult due to the lack of sufficient resources for IoT devices. Artificial intelligence (AI) greatly enhances privacy through techniques including distinction privacy, federated learning, and homomorphic encryption. Machine learning models can be trained across remote devices using federated learning, a new AI technique that eliminates the need to exchange raw data. By guaranteeing that private information stays on IoT devices instead of being sent to the cloud, this method protects user privacy. J. Konečný and others [8], offers methods for improving model training across dispersed devices while lowering communication costs in federated learning systems by optimizing data transfer. Considering current developments in mobile technology and rising privacy concerns, FL is especially appealing for developing dispersed IoT systems since it pushes AI tasks, such AI data training, to the network edge at the IoT devices where the data is stored. Nguyen, D. C. *et al.* [9], as discussed by Dwork [10], stated that differential privacy is an additional method that uses data noise to make sure that certain data points cannot be linked to their original source. Applying differential privacy to AI models in fog computing guarantees that, even in the event of a breach, the attacker will not be able to extract valuable information from the data.

### 4.2.4 Security Concerns and AI Mitigation Strategies

The distributed nature of fog computing exacerbates security flaws in cloud and IoT systems. Real-time threat detection systems, which employ machine learning algorithms to detect and eliminate cyberattacks, are one example of how artificial intelligence has been introduced to improve security. AI improves the usefulness and effectiveness of IoT devices by allowing them to recognize patterns and adjust accordingly using clever analysis techniques [11]. According to Khan *et al.* [12], AI-driven intrusion detection systems (IDS) have become essential in fog-based IoT environments for identifying suspicious behavior and preventing unauthorized access. Moreover, Sharma *et al.* [13], proposed a blockchain-based solution combined with AI for securing IoT data transmission in fog computing. By decentralizing security management, blockchain ensures the immutability of transactions, while AI models can monitor for abnormal patterns, thus enhancing security and resilience. Dorri *et al.* [14], examined the integration of blockchain technology in IoT ecosystems, addressing key issues such as security, scalability, and data privacy, and proposing solutions to enhance IoT resilience and trust through decentralized frameworks. B.U.I. Khan *et al.* [15], stated techniques like homomorphic encryption and AI-powered anonymization allow for privacy-preserving data processing in IoT-cloud systems, with dynamic AI-driven access controls adjusting in real-time to threat levels.

## 4.3 Proposed Work

The convergence of cloud computing, machine learning, and the Internet of Things presents previously unheard-of possibilities for real-time analysis and data processing. But there are also serious security and privacy concerns raised by this connection that need to be resolved. Conventional AI models run the danger of being vulnerable since they frequently depend on centralized data processing and storage. Unauthorized access to centralized data can result in identity theft, data breaches, or misuse of personal information, making it an ideal target for hostile assaults [16]. This chapter discusses various privacy preservation techniques, federated learning, and machine learning algorithms in relation to AI-based resilience and privacy preservation in the context of IoT clouds.

A machine learning model is cooperatively trained across numerous iterations by multiple participants, as illustrated by the architecture in Figure 4.3 [17]. FL is a paradigm shift in AI and machine learning for the IoT that overcomes the drawbacks of current approaches. It provides a fresh approach for companies and data scientists to create AI models without compromising security due to its decentralized training process. However, federated learning offers more benefits than this. Decentralized edge devices or nodes can work together to train models using federated learning (FL), a state-of-the-art approach to machine learning, without sending or storing the raw data on a central server. Instead, a local model is trained using data from each device, and only the model's changes are sent to a central server, which aggregates them to create a global model.

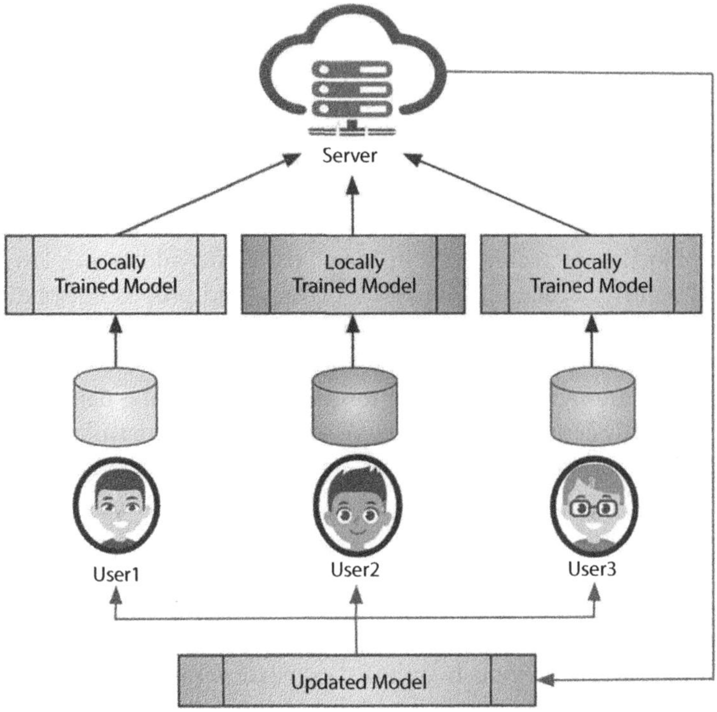


**Figure 4.3** Basic architecture of FL.

Data privacy is ensured by this strategy since the raw data is stored locally. When FL is applied to IoT, it not only improves security but also addresses the latency, costs, and productivity barriers associated with classical machine learning by lowering data transfer requirements.

The fundamental idea of FL is depicted in Figure 4.4, where several clients work together to develop a shared model without sharing the raw data. This not only enables privacy preserving AI development but also enables the use of large-scale data sets that may be distributed across various devices. Cloud-based fog Because IoT systems are widespread and have many linked devices, they need to be safe. Strong security is necessary to stop cyberattacks. Authentication and access control safeguard important information and the system. Fog nodes, cloud data centers, and IoT devices all encrypt and securely transmit data. Identifying and Preventing Intrusions—The system keeps an eye on network traffic and detects any unusual activity to stop and address cyberattacks. To address vulnerabilities and stop emerging threats, security patches and upgrades are required [18].

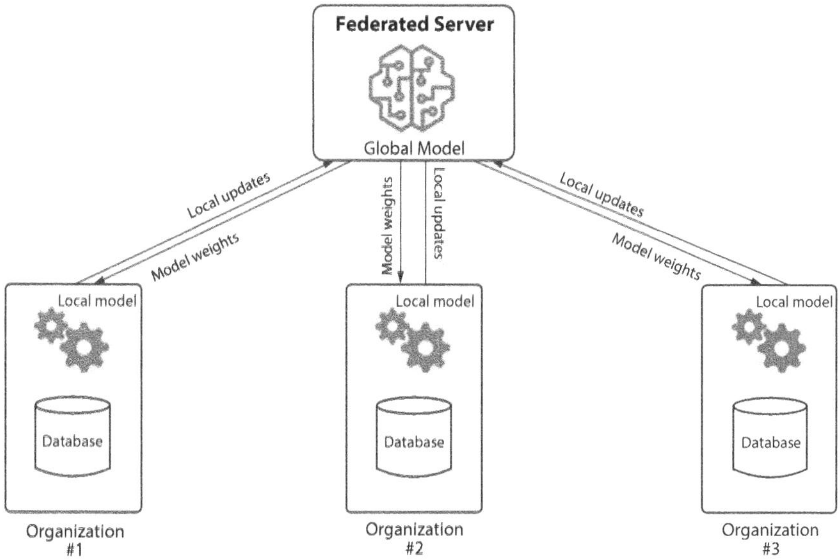


**Figure 4.4** FL predictive model without data sharing.

---

**Algorithm 4.1** Federated Learning in IoT-Cloud System, highlighting privacy preservation and decentralized model training.

---

1. Start
2. Initialize a global model M on the central server.
3. Repeat until model convergence or desired accuracy is achieved:
   a. Server-Side Process:
      i. Deliver the global model M to every IoT device (client).
   b. Client-Side (IoT Device) Process:
      i. Each IoT device downloads the global model M.
      ii. Train the local model m_i on the device's private data (preserving privacy).
      iii. Generate model updates Δm_i from the local training.
      iv. Only send the central server the model updates (Δm_i).
   c. Server-Side Aggregation:
      i. Collect all model updates Δm_i from participating devices.
      ii. Use aggregate updates (e.g., by averaging) to improve the global model M.
      iii. Use the combined data to update the global model.
4. End Training
5. Deploy the final trained global model M across IoT devices for inference.

When implemented at both the fog and cloud levels, AI-driven models can automatically identify different types of abnormalities, predict failures, and maintain system continuity. IoT devices may collaborate to build machine learning models without sharing private information—thanks to federated learning, a decentralized technique that preserves privacy. Using AI for fault tolerance and privacy-preserving data processing, along with real-time decision-making, this initiative seeks to establish a robust Internet of Things. The efficacy of the suggested system will be assessed in comparison to conventional centralized models, with an emphasis on latency, data security, and model accuracy improvements. In summary, collecting, merging, and integrating heterogeneous data from many sources, as well as securely managing and analyzing the data, are not facile tasks. Large data transfers between organizations at high speeds, with high veracity, and with heterogeneous data are not the only challenges; industry competition, complex administrative procedures, and—above all—data protection laws and regulations such as the EU General Data Protection Regulation (GDPR) [19], are also contributing factors. Standard cloud-centric machine learning techniques are frequently no longer appropriate because of the difficulties in adhering to stringent data protection regulations that govern the significant collection and processing of personal data. Due to the growing computational power and internet connectivity of end users' devices (such as smartphones, tablets, and wearables), a large amount of personal data is generated at the edge [20].

By doing this, FL reduces data privacy concerns by providing an alternative to the cloud-centric machine learning methodology, which allows cooperative ML model training while maintaining the original personal data on the devices. This transdisciplinary method uses end users' devices, or local nodes, to allow local training of a shared machine learning model on local data. Among the computer science topics it covers are distributed computing, machine learning, data privacy, and security. In the training phase, only parameters are updated for model updates and aggregation. FL differs from conventional distributed learning in that it assumes that local training datasets on compute nodes are identically distributed data (IID) that are independent and roughly equal in size. FL is consequently an improvement on distributed learning since it is designed to work with unbalanced and non-independent identically-distributed data (non-IID), whose sizes may differ by several orders of magnitude [20].

## 4.4 Experimental Setup

### 4.4.1 Tools

For the proposed research on AI-driven resilience and privacy preservation in IoT cloud environments, several tools and platforms are required to implement and evaluate the proposed system. The experimental setup will involve the following key tools:

- **Python:** This is the programming language for implementing machine learning models, federated learning frameworks, and privacy-preserving algorithms. Python libraries such as TensorFlow, PyTorch, and Keras will be used for model development, while NumPy and Pandas will handle data manipulation and analysis.
- **Federated Learning Platforms:** To simulate federated learning in a cloud IoT environment, platforms like Flower (FL) or TensorFlow Federated will be employed. These platforms allow for decentralized model training across multiple IoT devices or nodes, and they support the design and testing of federated learning models in real-world settings.
- **Cloud Platforms:** Cloud technologies like Google Cloud, Microsoft Azure, and Amazon Web technologies (AWS) will be utilized to manage model aggregation from federated nodes and replicate cloud settings. These platforms offer the necessary infrastructure to deploy machine learning models, implement federated learning, and integrate with IoT devices.
- **Fog Computing Simulation:** iFogSim, a simulation framework specifically designed for modeling and simulating fog computing environments, will be used to test the proposed architecture. iFogSim enables the evaluation of resource management, latency, and energy consumption in IoT systems, helping to compare cloud, fog, and federated models.
- **Security Tools:** To evaluate security aspects, tools like Wireshark and Snort will be used for real-time intrusion detection and traffic monitoring. Encryption mechanisms and data transmission protocols will be tested using OpenSSL or SSL/TLS frameworks.

### 4.4.2 Simulation

The simulation will be conducted in a hybrid cloud-fog IoT setup, where IoT devices will generate data, and federated learning will be applied for model training. The simulated environment will include the following elements:

- **IoT Devices:** Simulated using virtual machines (VMs) representing various IoT sensors and devices (e.g., smart homes, healthcare monitors, etc.) connected to a fog and cloud network. Each device will generate time-series data or sensor readings relevant to specific use cases.
- **Fog Nodes:** Fog nodes will be placed between IoT devices and the cloud to perform decentralized computation and minimize data transfer to the cloud. These nodes will process and store data locally, applying federated learning models for privacy preservation and optimizing data transmission latency.
- **Federated Learning Simulation:** Every Internet of Things device will use its data to train a local model, sending only model updates to a central cloud server. The cloud server will aggregate these updates into a global model, simulating the privacy-preserving nature of federated learning.
- **Attack Scenarios:** Simulated attacks will be introduced to test the resilience and privacy of the system, such as data breaches, Man-in-the-Middle (MitM) attacks, and Distributed Denial of Service (DDoS). Intrusion detection mechanisms will monitor and prevent unauthorized access to the system.
- **Evaluation Metrics:** The system's performance will be evaluated using metrics such as latency, bandwidth utilization, model accuracy, and privacy leakage. Specific focus will be on assessing how federated learning reduces data transmission and enhances privacy while maintaining model accuracy and system resilience.

### 4.4.3 Dataset

The experimental setup will utilize real-world and synthetic datasets, depending on the nature of the IoT application under study.

- **Real-World IoT Datasets:**
  a. CASAS Dataset: A dataset of smart home sensor readings for activity recognition and RLR anomaly detection. It will simulate typical IoT environments in smart homes.
  b. Weather and Environmental Data: Public IoT datasets, such as the Weather Dataset from open weather APIs, will be used to simulate edge-based weather prediction models.
  c. Health Monitoring Dataset: Datasets such as MIMIC-III (for healthcare IoT systems) will simulate real-time patient monitoring data.
- **Synthetic Datasets:**
  a. A custom dataset will be generated using IoT traffic generators (such as IoTA or IoT Traffic Generator) to simulate data from sensors and devices in a cloud-fog IoT ecosystem. This data will include different sensor readings (e.g., temperature, humidity, motion, etc.), simulating real-time data transmission

## 4.5 Experimental Results

By utilizing federated learning (FL), the experimental setup effectively tackled the issues of privacy and robustness in cloud computing IoT systems. Concerns about privacy, a major problem in cloud-based IoT contexts, were greatly reduced by FL's decentralized model training methodology. Instead of transferring private raw data to the cloud, each IoT device trained its own local model and sent model updates solely to the central server. Raw data stayed safe on individual devices, significantly lowering the danger of data breaches. By ensuring that even the tiniest quantity of data remained secure, encryption was used to further increase data security in communications between IoT devices and the cloud.

### 4.5.1 Privacy Breach Risk Comparison

The first chart illustrates the substantial reduction in privacy breach risks when utilizing federated learning (FL) compared to traditional centralized cloud models. Figure 4.5 illustrates how FL's decentralized methodology greatly reduces the likelihood of data breaches by guaranteeing that private information stays on individual IoT devices. This directly supports the key findings of this research, which focus on the privacy-preserving advantages

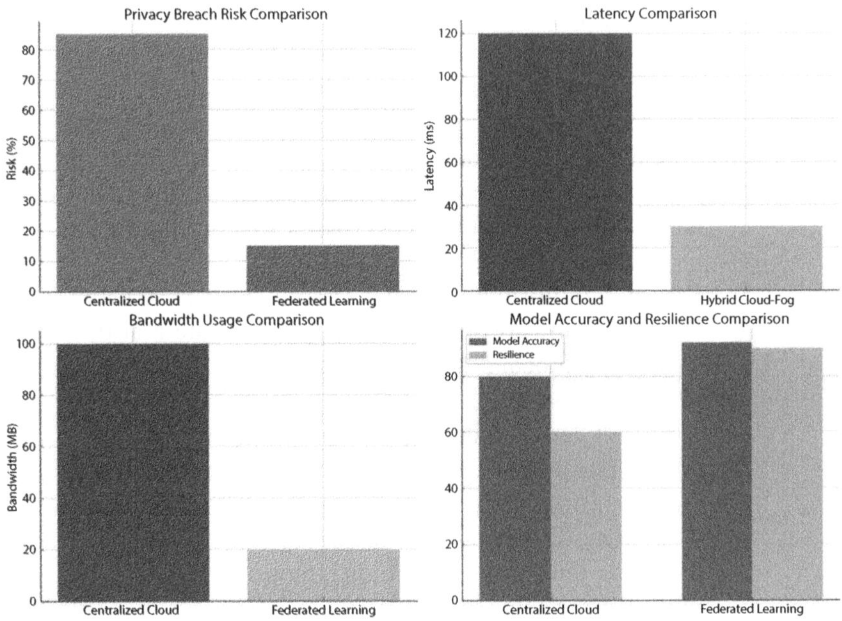


**Figure 4.5** Experimental results.

of federated learning in cloud-based IoT environments. By addressing privacy concerns at the device level, FL plays a pivotal role in enhancing data security, which is central to the objectives of this work.

### 4.5.2 Latency Comparison

The second chart shows the marked decrease in latency when employing a hybrid cloud-fog setup versus a centralized cloud architecture. Improving real-time decision-making in IoT systems is the main goal of this research, and the decreased latency attained through local processing at the fog node level is consistent with this goal. This chart reinforces the argument that federated learning, by minimizing the need for raw data transmission to the cloud, helps overcome the delays typically associated with centralized data processing, thereby enhancing the system's overall efficiency.

### 4.5.3 Bandwidth Usage Comparison

The third chart demonstrates the significant reduction in bandwidth usage when applying federated learning compared to centralized cloud models. This is made possible by the fact that only model updates—rather not raw data—are sent, resulting in reduced data transfer needs. The potential of federated learning to enhance scalability and lower operating costs in IoT systems—two important factors to take into account when combining IoT with cloud computing—is highlighted by this conclusion, which is essential to the study.

### 4.5.4 Model Accuracy and Resilience Comparison

The fourth chart highlights the improvements in both accuracy and system resilience when using federated learning in comparison to centralized models, especially under conditions of network failure or cyberattacks. This directly reflects the focus of this research on building a more robust and resilient IoT-cloud system, capable of maintaining operational continuity even in adverse conditions. The ability of FL to distribute learning across multiple nodes contributes to system stability and enhances accuracy in model predictions, which aligns with the research objectives. On the resilience front, the system demonstrated the ability to maintain operational continuity despite potential cyberattacks and system failures. Distributed learning across fog nodes ensured that even in the event of a partial network failure or localized attack, the remaining nodes could continue to operate without significant disruption. By continuously monitoring and reacting to possible threats, real-time intrusion detection technologies were added to further increase resilience. Furthermore, the decentralized nature of federated learning significantly reduced latency, as computations were handled locally at the fog node level. This not only improved the system's real-time decision-making capabilities but also reduced bandwidth usage, which is often a bottleneck in centralized cloud systems. In comparison to traditional cloud architectures, this hybrid cloud-fog setup offered a more robust, scalable, and secure environment for handling IoT data, making it a highly effective solution for addressing the dual challenges of privacy and resilience in cloud-based IoT systems.

Figure 4.6 presents a radar chart summarizing improvements across multiple evaluation metrics, including latency, bandwidth usage, model accuracy, privacy, and resilience. This chart visually encapsulates the core findings of the research, showing how federated learning consistently outperforms centralized models in key areas. Table 4.1 represents the detailed multiple evaluation metrics, observations and key advantages. The comprehensive comparison reinforces the overarching theme of this work: federated learning offers significant advantages for privacy preservation, system resilience, and operational efficiency in cloud-based IoT environments.

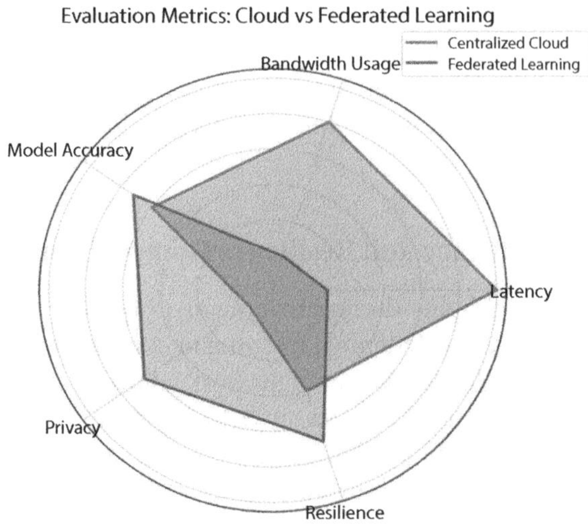


**Figure 4.6** Radar chart summarizing improvements across multiple evaluation metrics.

**Table 4.1** Multiple evaluation metrics, observation and key advantages.

| Metric | Observation | Key advantage |
|---|---|---|
| Privacy Breach Risk | Federated Learning (FL) significantly reduces privacy breach risks compared to centralized cloud models. | Decentralized methodology ensures private data remains on IoT devices, reducing risks of data breaches. |
| Latency | Hybrid cloud-fog setup reduces latency compared to centralized cloud architecture. | Localized processing at fog nodes improves real-time decision-making and reduces delays. |
| Bandwidth Usage | FL reduces bandwidth usage as only model updates (not raw data) are transmitted. | Lower data transfer requirements enhance scalability and reduce operating costs. |
| Model Accuracy | Federated learning demonstrates improved model accuracy, especially under network failures or cyberattacks. | Distributed learning across nodes ensures stable and accurate predictions even during disruptions. |
| System Resilience | Enhanced resilience due to decentralized learning and real-time threat detection. | Maintains operational continuity despite cyberattacks or partial network failures. |

## 4.6 Conclusion

As IoT systems continue to grow, integrating AI-driven methods within fog and cloud environments will become increasingly vital for ensuring both system resilience and data privacy. AI not only strengthens resilience by predicting system failures and optimizing resource allocation; however, by decentralizing data processing, privacy-preserving strategies like federated learning and differential privacy assist reduce hazards, reducing the vulnerabilities that arise from centralized data storage. This study has demonstrated how federated learning is essential for protecting privacy by allowing IoT devices to work together to train models without exchanging private information. Additionally, it enhances system robustness by distributing computational tasks across fog nodes, thus lowering latency and reducing bandwidth consumption. These advantages make federated learning an attractive solution for addressing security and efficiency concerns in cloud-based IoT infrastructures. However, as the cloud-IoT landscape evolves, ongoing research is needed to tackle new challenges in security, privacy, and resilience. As AI technologies continue to advance, exploring hybrid solutions—such as combining federated learning with blockchain or homomorphic encryption—could further enhance data protection. Moreover, the scalability of federated learning in large-scale IoT networks and its energy efficiency in resource-constrained settings will remain key areas for future exploration. This study has laid a solid groundwork for incorporating AI-based resilience and privacy-preserving techniques in cloud IoT environments; continuous research will be essential to keep pace with the increasing complexity of these systems. The findings emphasize federated learning's potential as a crucial enabler of secure, scalable, and efficient IoT systems moving forward.

**AI disclosure statement:** The author acknowledges the use of AI-based tools for minor language editing or grammatical correction. However, all intellectual contributions, analyses, and conclusions presented in this chapter are entirely the author's own.

## References

1. Saleem, S.I., Zeebaree, S., Zeebaree, D.Q., Abdulazeez, A.M., Building smart cities applications based on IoT technologies: A review. *Technol. Rep. Kansai Univ.*, *62*, 3, 1083–1092, 2020.

2. McMahan, B., Moore, E., Ramage, D., Hampson, S., y Arcas, B.A., Communication-efficient learning of deep networks from decentralized data, in: *Artificial Intelligence and Statistics*, PMLR, pp. 1273–1282, 2017, April.
3. Mothukuri, V., Parizi, R.M., Pouriyeh, S., Huang, Y., Dehghantanha, A., Federated Learning for Internet of Things: Applications, Challenges, and Opportunities, arXiv preprint, 2023, [Online]. Available: https://arxiv.org/abs/2111.07494.
4. Bonomi, F., Milito, R., Zhu, J., Addepalli, S., Fog computing and its role in the internet of things, in: *Proceedings of the First Edition of the MCC Workshop on Mobile Cloud Computing*, pp. 13–16, 2012, August.
5. Zhang, Y., Li, P., Chen, C., AI-enhanced fog computing for IoT resilience and optimization. *IEEE Trans. Netw. Serv. Manage.*, 18, 4, 457–467, 2021.
6. Zhang, L., Zhao, J., Li, W., Online and unsupervised anomaly detection for streaming data using an array of sliding windows and PDDs. *IEEE Trans. Cybern.*, *51*, 4, 2284–2289, 2019.
7. Alrawais, A., Alhothaily, A., Hu, C., Cheng, X., Fog computing for the internet of things: Security and privacy issues. *IEEE Internet Comput.*, *21*, 2, 34–42, 2017.
8. Konečný, J., Federated Learning: Strategies for Improving Communication Efficiency, *arXiv preprint arXiv:1610.05492*, 2016.
9. Nguyen, D.C., Ding, M., Pathirana, P.N., Seneviratne, A., Li, J., Poor, H.V., Federated learning for internet of things: A comprehensive survey. *IEEE Commun. Surv. Tutorials*, 23, 3, 1622–1658, 2021.
10. Dwork, C., Differential privacy, in: *International Colloquium on Automata, Languages, and Programming*, Springer Berlin Heidelberg, Berlin, Heidelberg, pp. 1–12, 2006, July.
11. Kaur, N., Sahay, S., Dixit, S., Role of Artificial Intelligence (AI)-aided Internet of Things (IoT) Technologies in Business and Production, in: *Advanced IoT Technologies and Applications in the Industry 4.0 Digital Economy*, pp. 29–41, CRC Press, 2024.
12. Khan, M.A. and Salah, K., IoT security: Review, blockchain solutions, and open challenges. *Future Gener. Comput. Syst.*, *82*, 395–411, 2018.
13. Sharma, V., Chen, L., Sheth, A., Blockchain-enabled fog and edge computing: Opportunities and challenges. *IEEE Internet Things J.*, 8, 6, 4215–4225, 2021.
14. Dorri, A., Blockchain in Internet of Things: Challenges and Solutions, *arXiv preprint arXiv:1608.05187*, 2016.
15. Khan, B.U.I., Goh, K.W., Khan, A.R., Zuhairi, M.F., Chaimanee, M., Integrating AI and Blockchain for Enhanced Data Security in IoT-Driven Smart Cities. *Processes*, *12*, 9, 2024.
16. Sharma, S., Federated Learning for Privacy-Preserving AI: An In-Depth Exploration, datascience.salon, 2023, https://roundtable.datascience.salon/federated-learning-for-privacy-preserving-ai-an-in-depth-exploration.

17. Saha, S., Hota, A., Chattopadhyay, A.K., Nag, A., Nandi, S., A multifaceted survey on privacy preservation of federated learning: progress, challenges, and opportunities. *Artif. Intell. Rev.*, *57*, 7, 184, 2024.
18. Singh, P.D. and Singh, K.D., Security and privacy in fog/cloud-based IoT systems for AI and robotics. *EAI Endorsed Trans. AI Rob.*, *2*, 2023.
19. Horvitz, E. and Mulligan, D., Data, privacy, and the greater good. *Science*, *349*, 6245, 253–255, 2015.
20. Truong, N., Sun, K., Wang, S., Guitton, F., Guo, Y., Privacy preservation in federated learning: An insightful survey from the GDPR perspective. *Comput. Secur.*, 110, 102402, Nov. 2021, doi: 10.1016/j.cose.2021.102402.

5

# Learning Safeguards: Leveraging Machine Learning for Anomaly Detection in Cloud – IoT Networks

**Swastika Kayal[1] and Soumen Santra[2]***

*[1]Department of Computer Science and Engineering, St. Thomas' College of Engineering and Technology, Kolkata, West Bengal, India*
*[2]Department of Master of Computer Applications, Techno International New Town, Kolkata, West Bengal, India*

## *Abstract*

Cloud computing has a huge impact on Intrusion Detection or Anomaly Detection having some influence of Machine Learning in it. Leveraging machine learning, we improvise cost estimation by maintaining performance and efficiency within an organization, particularly in managing IT infrastructure. This paper explores the applied algorithms of machine learning techniques for detection of anomaly in cloud-based environment with a collaboration of IoT techniques. Detection is made mainly based on use of machine learning techniques to analyze current data for making predictions about future events, trends or behaviors. This paper has an extensive explanation using concept like pattern recognition to identify anomalies or trends, scalability showing capability to handle growing workforce along with its potential to accommodate growth and Big Data Analysis. In the context of Anomaly detection, recent trends have a high value with healthcare landscape where we can see the value or predictive analysis in the field of medical sciences. By addressing these challenges and by finding solutions to it, IoMT healthcare networks can strengthen their intrusion and anomaly detection capabilities using predictive models. IoT is predictively having management analysis for large business assets, complex data functioning and distributed process giving huge growth towards communication market and business canvases. This paper contains those networking scheme following IoT services for defense and public safety (PS). Commercial IoT capabilities along with cloud mechanism is providing

**Corresponding author*: santrasoumen230@gmail.com

Partha Ghosh, Rajdeep Chakraborty, Anupam Ghosh and Ahmed A. Elngar (eds.) Strategic Approaches to Intrusion Detection in Cloud-IoT Ecosystem, (119–142) © 2026 Scrivener Publishing LLC

for cost optimization through supervised learning models by achieving increased and effective operations. In this regard extensive research work is done based on security measures in IoT networks prior to using cryptographic approach. Machine learning which is able to provide with embedded and intelligent models for evaluation is leveraging a path to cope with different security problems. This paper ideally gives a brief sketch about the requirements, attack vectors, optimized solutions, systemic review for enhancing security problems.

***Keywords*:** Supervised learning, cloud security, *adhoc* network, intrusion detection system, intrusion prevention system, malware analysis

## 5.1 Introduction

Recent trends have a high value with healthcare landscape where we can see the value or predictive analysis in field of medical sciences [1]. Internet of Medical Science Things (IoMsT) devices has authorized patient health analysis and operational efficiency brings efficient security challenges that ensures patient safety. IoMT devices, which include patient detailed information, their personal checkup chart, generate vast amounts of sensitive health data. This data's security is paramount, as breaches could lead to unauthorized access, manipulation, or loss of critical information, potentially compromising patient outcomes. Moreover, the interconnected nature of these devices increases their vulnerability to cyberattacks, which can disrupt healthcare services and undermine the trust in medical technology [2]. Leveraging machine learning by using predictive model by data privacy methods. By encapsulating patient records, treatment plans, and diagnostic results, algorithms can analyze style-patterns and assume potential risks while ensuring sensitive information remains secure. This prediction upholds stringent data privacy standards, minimizing the risk of unauthorized access and ensuring compliance with regulatory requirements [3]. Cyberattacks targeting these systems can disrupt operations, leading to delays in treatment, compromised patient outcomes and financial losses. The entire burden on healthcare systems has the potential to worsen outcomes for patients and healthcare providers by lowering operational effectiveness and directing resources away from patient care [4]. Certain gaps are present in knowledge representation, such as standardization, device-specific solutions, continuous monitoring, and patient involvement showing security protocols for IoMT devices hinders interoperability and complexity in security management [5]. In context of standardization and comparative analysis to compare the existing security protocols used by different manufacturers and healthcare organizations by identifying the strengths and weaknesses, aiming to propose a framework for standardized security protocols across IoMT devices. This process includes examining different security methods, such as hidden techniques and authentication methods, to identify which protocols are most effective at safeguarding data and preventing breaches. By assessing the strengths and weaknesses of these protocols, gaps and inconsistencies can be highlighted, revealing areas where improvements are needed. The goal is to develop a unified framework that standardizes security practices across all IoMT devices, ensuring a consistent level of protection regardless of the manufacturer or healthcare provider. This standardized framework would facilitate interoperability, simplify security management, and enhance overall system resilience, providing a more robust defense against potential cyber threats [6]. In the context of Device Specific Solutions – we analyze successful implementation of security solution studying historical data records, that is, case studies and conduction of controlled penetration testing on different IoMT devices. This includes examining case studies where specific security solutions have been applied to IoMT devices, providing insights into their strengths and limitations. Additionally, conducting controlled penetration testing on various IoMT devices helps simulate potential attack scenarios, revealing vulnerabilities and assessing the robustness of existing security protocols [7]. For continuous monitoring, we use patterns in real-time to detect potential cyberattacks on IoMT networks and agent-based monitoring for monitoring vulnerable and suspicious activity actions. Utilizing advanced algorithms, this proactive approach continuously analyzes data flows and system activities to identify anomalies that may signal a security risk. Specialized software agents installed on IoMT devices track and report on system behavior and security events, providing detailed insights into potential vulnerabilities and suspicious activities through monitoring device-specific metrics and logs. Real-time pattern recognition and agent-based monitoring work together to establish a comprehensive defense mechanism, facilitating quick detection and response to emerging threats and minimizing the impact on healthcare operations [8]. Surveys and interviews and focus groups in patient involvement were done to understand their attitudes and concerns regarding data security in IoMT networks. By conducting surveys, healthcare providers can gather quantitative data on patient concerns, preferences, and awareness levels regarding the security of their health information. Interviews offer a deeper, qualitative insight into individual patient experiences and attitudes towards data privacy and security. Facilitating discussions among patients, focus groups enable a thorough exchange of views and the identification of common concerns regarding the protection of their data [9]. By tailoring security measures to address specific patient needs and concerns, healthcare organizations can enhance trust and ensure that security protocols align with patient expectations. Involving patients in this way also aids in spotting potential gaps in the current security practices and promotes a collaborative approach to safeguarding sensitive health information [10].

### 5.1.1 Cloud Security

Security is a critical aspect of cloud computing that must be addressed from the outset to ensure optimal resource utilization. Cloud infrastructure—comprising applications, networks, virtualization, data storage, authentication, and authorization—can be examined to identify security issues at multiple levels. Safeguarding sensitive user data, which is often stored near cloud data centers, is crucial to protect against hackers and unauthorized access, thereby maintaining data availability, confidentiality, and integrity. Additionally, addressing various types of security attacks is necessary to ensure the proper functioning of the system. Security attacks refer to actions that undermine computer security policies and acceptable use policies through illegal or unethical means. Common types of attacks in cloud environments include remote-to-local, denial of service, user-to-root, and enumeration attacks [11].

Preventive controls strengthen defenses against threats. Typically employed to address security concerns are solutions like Intrusion Detection Systems (IDS), firewalls, authentication procedures, and encrypted data transmission. Due to the expansive scale of cloud resources, services, and users, IDS is commonly regarded as the most efficient solution for recognizing and addressing security threats [12].

In the context of IoT networks, these security measures can be enhanced by advanced machine learning techniques that identify unusual patterns or behaviors, thereby improving overall security posture and response capabilities.

### 5.1.2 *Adhoc* Network

*Adhoc* cloud-IoT networks, characterized by their dynamic and decentralized nature, pose unique challenges for security. Traditional security measures often fall short in detecting anomalies due to the network's inherent variability. This is where machine learning (ML) emerges as a powerful tool.

By analyzing extensive network data, ML algorithms have the capability to recognize patterns and deviations from normal behavior. These anomalies can indicate potential threats such as unauthorized access, data breaches, or device compromise. For example, ML models are capable of learning regular traffic patterns, device behavior, and user interactions to identify unusual spikes in data transfer, unexpected device communication, or unauthorized access attempts.

Moreover, ML can enhance the adaptability of security systems to the dynamic nature of *adhoc* networks. As the network topology and device composition change, ML models can continuously learn and update their understanding of normal behavior, ensuring ongoing protection against evolving threats.

While promising, challenges such as data integrity and isolation, modelincubation, and computational efficiency for effective implementation of ML-based anomaly detection in *ad hoc* Cloud-IoT networks [13].

Intrusion or anomaly detection using predictive models in cybersecurity, especially in environments like IoMT networks, faces challenges [1]. Complexity of IoMT data generate complex data streams containing physiological signals, medical imaging and heterogenous data source for detection of anomalies [2]. Imbalanced data sets show bias towards normal behavior which may fail to detect anomaly presence in the sample [3]. Constituting adaptability to dynamic environment, privacy concerns and interpretability of models show failure in anomaly detection.

By addressing these challenges and by finding solutions to it, IoMT healthcare networks can strengthen their intrusion and anomaly detection capabilities using predictive models.

## 5.2 Background and Literature Survey

A literature survey on the integration of predictive models and security challenges in the Internet of Medical Things (IoMT) networks reveals significant developments in safeguarding sensitive health data. As IoMT devices become increasingly widespread in healthcare, they generate large volumes of data, heightening security risks. IoMT's interconnected nature has brought forward challenges in securing patient chart from illegal access and prone to attacks made by computer. Breaches could result to compromising patient outcomes and disrupt healthcare services, underscoring the importance of robust security protocols.

Recent studies have highlighted several approaches to mitigate these risks. One critical aspect is the integration of ML models for deviation detection in IoMT networks. By analyzing vast datasets, algorithms detect anomalies, which might signify potential cyber threats, such as unauthorized access or device compromise. These predictive models enhance security by detecting deviations from normal behavior, allowing for quicker responses to emerging threats. However, challenges persist, such as the complexity of IoMT data, which includes heterogeneous sources like physiological signals and medical imaging. These complexities can make anomaly detection difficult, as traditional models may struggle to interpret such diverse data streams.

Furthermore, issues like imbalanced datasets, which show a bias towards normal behavior, can undermine the effectiveness of anomaly detection. As a result, the system may fail to detect anomalies in real-time. Another concern is the adaptability of models to dynamic environments, where IoMT devices continuously evolve. Security systems must be capable of adjusting to new devices and network changes. To address these issues, researchers propose a more integrated approach, combining real-time monitoring, advanced ML algorithms, and enhanced data privacy measures, ensuring that healthcare systems maintain security while ensuring compliance with regulatory standards.

In summary, while predictive models hold promise for enhancing security in IoMT networks, challenges such as data complexity, model adaptability, and privacy concerns remain areas for further research and improvement.

## 5.3 Methodology

### 5.3.1 Deviation Detection System

In network traffic classification for security applications, supervised and unsupervised learning approaches provide distinct methodologies to detect anomalies, offering structured frameworks to address network threats such as Distributed Denial of Service (DDoS) attacks, suspicious access etc. These two kinds of ML methods are basic for the distributed anomaly detection since they analyze traffic patterns comprehensively, and each of them uses a different model and different set of algorithms. In case of supervised learning however, training sets that are labeled implies that every input data will contain an actual label or outcome. Classification learning is one of the fundamental categories of machine studying objectives and is aimed at allowing modeling the data, as a result of which the model will be able to analyze new labeled data. Supervised learning also encompasses a labeled data set, an algorithmic model, and a procedure to measure the level of error and optimum model parameter setting of Supervised learning models are shown in Table 5.1 below.

**Table 5.1** ML models need for deviation detection system.

| Processed data | Key algorithms | Application |
|---|---|---|
| **Labeled** | Decision Tree, kernel SVM | Network leak Detection |
| **Unlabeled** | Optimized-PCA, K-Means | Deviation Detection |

---

**Algorithm 5.1** Deviation Detection using Optimized-SVM.

---

**Input:** Labeled dataset of network traffic instances; each example has features (**x**) and a label (**y**), where: **y = -1** means normal traffic. **y = 1** means suspicious traffic.

**Output:** A function **f(x)** that classifies new network traffic as either normal or anomalous. Initialize hyperplane parameters w and b

**while** meeting criterion not met **do**
  **for each** iteration **do**
    For each data point (**x**) in the dataset: Compute the **margin** using: margin=y×(w·x+b)
    Calculate **loss** using: Loss=max(0,1−margin)
    Adjust **w** and **b** using **gradient descent** to minimize the loss: w=w−η×(δLoss/δw) b=b−η×(δLoss /δb)
    η is the learning rate (controls how much we update at each step).
  **end**

---

#### 5.3.1.1 *Anomaly Detection in Network Using Optimized Kernel-SVM*

Kernel SVM is a supervised ML algorithm commonly used for anomaly detection in network traffic. It aims to find an optimal hyper edged plane that separates data points of multi classes in a high-dimensional space. In the context of network traffic, SVM is used to classify network data as either "normal" or "anomalous" based on patterns identified in the traffic features.

This is followed by aggregation of feature vectors at the packet level which includes packet size, amount of time that the flow has been active, and IP and port numbers of the sources and destinations. These features are then passed by the use of kernel properties (which could be radial basis function or RBF). When new network traffic data arrives, such data feed is transformed onto the feature space, and using the hyperplane the model determines if the traffic is normal or anomalous.

SVM has another strength in anomaly detection, particularly when the data can be non-separable in terms of non-linearity because of the kernel functions. It is also useful when the ratio of the normal traffic to anomalous traffic is significantly large (imbalanced data sets), since the given boundary relies on the vectors which form baseline of the classification.

#### *5.3.1.2 Anomaly Detection in Network Using Hierarchical Trees*

Hierarchical trees are another popular classification algorithm used for anomaly detection in network traffic. The idea behind hierarchical trees is to repeat the partition of the data into smaller parts based on feature values that best separate the different classes (normal and anomalous behavior).

In the case of networks flows, parameters such as number of packets, duration of the flow, protocol type are assessed at each node of the tree. The tree constructs itself by selecting the feature and threshold that will split the data most effectively by using information gain or Gini impurity as a measure of split quality. For instance, the tree may divide the network traffic according to the packet size, that is, a branch may contain a regular traffic, a branch could contain a possible attack traffic as it could be expected to contain bigger packets.

After the construction of the tree based on the network traffic features, it is employed for analyzing new traffic by running down the tree from the root node to a leaf node depending on traffic results individual node. Hierarchical trees are especially simple to increase, and therefore, are useful in situations where increasing importance is attached to the rationale for flagging anomalies. They also can work with nominal and interval variables. However, like other forms of the decision tree used for classification algorithms, it is sensitive toward over-fitting particularly when used as a deep decision tree; however, this can be rectified through pruning or regularization.

### 5.3.2 Intrusion Detection System

Security Breach Detection System (SBDS) is a method for detecting malicious activities in network environments compared to traditional IDS, which rely on predefined rules or signatures. ML-based IDS utilize sophisticated algorithms to learn difficult patterns in network traffic that give indication of new or evolving attacks have shown by Table 5.2.

**Table 5.2** Network security monitoring system.

| Model | Functionality | Use case |
|---|---|---|
| **Optimized-CNN** | Geospatial pattern analysis | Traffic flow analysis |
| **Sequential Neural Network** | Inter frame analysis | Abnormalities in time series |

Deep learning models have been increasingly applied in IDS frameworks process large, high-dimensional datasets typical in network traffic. CNNs were primarily applied for image processing; however, this type of model is helpful in evaluating network traffic as it can identify spatial relations between the data. For example, they can recognize occurrences, such as the relation between the headers of packets or network flows' characteristics that depict irregular behavior—for instance, the addresses of IPs or sequences of packets. CNNs involve multiple layers of convolutional filters to discover the hierarchical features sufficient to differentiate normal from the malicious traffic.

In contrast, RNNs have a very good applicability when working with time sequences which, in turn, creates optimal conditions for detecting threats that take time to complete, for instance, scanning or data exfiltration. RNNs can detect time-related characteristics of network activity and discover that a sequence of events might appear benign, but the succession is malicious. LSTMs, which are a specific type of RNN, are especially beneficial in IDS due to their capability of conserving info overelaborated sequences, a key problem to which traditional RNNs are prone and is denoted by a vanishing gradient. IDS based on LSTM can recognize long and slow-moving threats like data leakage or coordinated work of botnets, which may be unnoticed by other methods.

---

**Algorithm 5.2** Intrusion Detection System.

---

**Input:** A labeled dataset of network activity: $D=\{(x_i, y_i)\}$, $y_i \in \{-1,1\}$ , $\mathbf{y = -1}$ represents normal traffic.
$\mathbf{y = 1}$ represents anomalous traffic.

**Output:** Trained CNN model for Fraud detection
**each** iteration **do**
**for each** *mini-subset from* **D do**

**for each** Iteration **do**
**Forward pass:** Feed $\mathbf{X}_i$ through the CNN to obtain predictions
**Compute loss (L):** Measure the difference between the predicted output and actual label $\mathbf{y}_i$.
**Backpropagation:** Adjust CNN parameters to minimize **L** using optimization techniques.
**end**
**end**
**end**

**Set up the CNN model** with layers:

- **Convolutional Layers** for feature extraction.
- **Pooling Layers** to reduce dimensionality.
- **Fully Connected Layers** for classification

Convolutional Neural Networks (CNNs) are particularly effective for intrusion detection ability to held intraframe patterns in dataset. The algorithm takes as input a labeled dataset of network traffic, where each instance is represented as a feature vector, and the labels indicate whether the traffic is normal or anomalous.

The CNN processes the network traffic data by applying convolutional filters feature from the raw input dataset (e.g., packet headers, flow data). The network typically uses multiple convolutional layers to detect increasingly complex patterns. After the convolutional layers, the data is passed through pooling layers to reduce dimensionality and emphasize the most important features.

The final layers consist of fully connected layers that classify the traffic as normal or anomalous based on the learned features. The CNN is trained by minimizing a loss function (e.g., cross-entropy) using backpropagation. After training, the CNN can be used to classify unseen network traffic for intrusion detection.

### 5.3.3 Behavioral Malware Detection Techniques

In **Behavioral Malware Detection**, the ML models study the run-time activities of the system, the file operations, permission, request, process interaction and others to establish normal behavior profiles. The above activities disappear from view if not normal, for example, frequent file access, repeated privilege escalations, or high network traffic with unknown addresses suggesting malware presence will if monitored by ML algorithms. For instance, LSTM networks and autoencoders are constantly checking system events and releasing alarms as soon as pathologic patterns are identified.

In distributed forms of attacks, where the malware can easily move from node to node, behavioral detection driven by machine learning offers a preventive solution. In each node, localized behavior is continuously checked to detect signs of malware, while the rest of the network is still possibly infected. The ML models at each node can identify possible niche sequential clusters, thus, contain them from spreading the infection. This node-specific detection enhances the capability of the network as threats are contained at their source.

To improve distributed detection, the integration of FL or LSTMs or autoencoders can be applied. This approach enhances the detection accuracy and at the same time can respect the privacy of the data, which makes it a good candidate for privacy sensitive environments.

---

**Algorithm 5.3** Heuristic-Based Malware Detection Using LSTM.

---

**Input:** Sequence dataset with y = 1 indicating normal detection behavior and y = 0 indicating abnormal detection behavior

**Output:** Trained LSTM model for malware detection
Initialize LSTM network parameters

```
for each Iteration do
    for each mini-subset do
        for each iteration do
            Pass the data (X_i) through the LSTM network to make a prediction.
            Compare the prediction with the actual label (y_i) and calculate the error (loss).
            Adjust the LSTM model using back-propagation through time to reduce the error.
        end
    end
end
```

---

**Table 5.3** Heuristic-based malware detection.

| Technique | Functionality | Application |
|---|---|---|
| **Dynamic Trend Analysis** | Pattern mining in sequences | Dynamic malware detection |
| **Network-Based Fraud Detection** | Analyzing behavior | Multi-dimensional detection |

Moreover, as per Table 5.3 predictive threat modelling and automated response using Bayesian networks as an example of ML contributes to counteracting threats in the systems. The Bayesian networks take data of past attacks to calculate the probability of them being exploited for the systems to adapt their defenses in real-time. This is more recommendable in cloud settings which can schedule risk analysis to across the whole network while eradicating possible seedy penetrations upon emergence of new data or threats.

The algorithm begins by initializing the parameters of the LSTM network, including the weights and biases.

Training proceeds in epochs, with the dataset divided into mini-batches. For each mini-batch, the system performs forward propagation by passing each sequence $x_i$ through the LSTM cells. LSTM cells are effective for identifying behavioral patterns associated with malware. The LSTM processes the sequence step by step, updating its hidden states to retain memory of past events in the sequence.

Once the sequence has been processed, the output is compared to the true label $y_i$ using a loss function, typically measures the difference between the assumed and actual behavior. This process repeats for all mini-batches and over multiple epochs, progressively cultivating the model's capability to extricate between benign and malicious behavior.

After training, the model can classify new sequences of system events as benign or malicious. The trained LSTM model thus becomes a powerful tool for detecting malware based on the dynamic behavior of programs and system processes.

### 5.3.4 Bayesian Network for Predictive Threat Modeling

Probabilistic Graphical Model (PGM) helps in predictive threat detection by representing variables and their conditional dependencies using a directed acyclic graph (DAG). In the context of cloud security, Bayesian networks model the relationships between different system activities, user behaviors, and potential vulnerabilities to estimate the likelihood of security threats. Each node in the network represents a variable, such as user login behavior, network traffic patterns, or known threat indicators like malware signatures. The edges between the nodes represent the conditional dependencies, showing how one variable might influence another. For example, a node representing "failed login attempts" may depend on another node representing "user credentials being compromised." Each node has a conditional probability table (CPT) that quantifies the relationships between variables, calculating the probability of a threat based on observed conditions, such as unusual login times or spikes in network traffic.

Inference is done in the Bayesian network by these dependencies; the network passes real-time data to calculate the probability of the threat models. The chance that an intrusion has occurred at a particular time may be computed from the posterior probabilities of the network when unusual behavior is observed including a sharp rise in failed login attempts or network traffic. This continuous updating makes the Bayesian network to always define risks and how likely threats might occur before they are fully realized. Due to its capability in dealing with the uncertainty as well as with incomplete knowledge, the network is highly recommended for the security application in clouds where uncertainty occurs. Due to its ability to predict and evaluate threat information, Bayesian networks can alert the network administrators as soon as threats are detected and afford instantaneous defensive measures including tightening security or disseminating a warning. In summary, Bayesian networks constitute a sound approach to risk assessment and proactive defense against cyber harms in extensive, dispersed settings.

---

**Algorithm 5.4** Proactive Threat Assessment Using PGM.

---

**Input:** Use past threat data, which includes information about attack methods, weaknesses, and system setups.

**Output:** Predict how likely different threats are based on probabilities. for each variable $X_i$ in the network

**do**

For each risk factor, calculate how it is influenced by related factors using past data.

**end**

**for each** *new Iteration* **do**
  When new threat data comes in, update the risk calculations using Bayesian probability.
**end**

## 5.4 Comparative Analysis

### 5.4.1 Comparative Analysis of Outlier Detection Techniques

Outlier Detection in network traffic is a part of ensuring security in modern network environments. Various machine learning approaches as per Table 5.4 offer distinct methods for identifying unusual patterns that may signal attacks or intrusions. Each method comes with its strengths, challenges, and applicability of the network traffic and attack is targeted. Below is a comparative analysis of these methods in the context of anomaly detection.

### 5.4.2 Supervised Learning: Kernel SVM

Optimal Kernel SVM are classifying network traffic as normal or anomalous. The key strength of SVM is to classify the information about the model even when it is not linearly discrete in nature. However, SVM requires a significant resource-intensive factor to attain the dynamic environments in IoT networks or cloud systems. Additionally, SVM struggles with imbalanced datasets, where the number of normal data points vastly outnumbers the anomalous ones, which could affect its performance.

#### *5.4.2.1 Pros*

- Effective for high-dimensional datasets.
- Good at handling non-linear data through kernel functions.
- Robust against overfitting with proper tuning.

#### *5.4.2.2 Cons*

- Requires large labeled datasets.
- Performance may degrade with imbalanced datasets.

### 5.4.3 Supervised Learning: Hierarchical Trees

Hierarchical trees (DT) are another widely used supervised algorithm for anomaly detection. Decision trees recursively split data based on feature values to classify data as either normal or anomalous. One of the key advantages of decision trees is their interpretability. The decision-making process can be imagined easier to understand why positive traffic is classified as uncharacteristic. However, hierarchical trees are susceptible to overfitting, expressly when the tree is very profound. Proper clipping or regularization is essential to avoid this problem.

#### *5.4.3.1 Pros*

- Easy to interpret and visualize.
- Handles both categorical and continuous data.

#### *5.4.3.2 Cons*

- Prone to overfitting without regularization.
- May not perform well with complex, high-dimensional data.

### 5.4.4 Deep Learning: Spatial Feature Learner (SFL)

Spatial feature learner (SFL) is a type of DL model originally premeditated for copy dispensation but has proven highly effective in network traffic analysis. CNNs work by applying convolutional filters to extract features from raw data (e.g., packet headers, flow data). The hierarchical nature of CNNs enables them to capture complex, spatial outlines in dataset, manufacture them fit for detecting both known and unknown attacks. CNNs excel in detecting anomalous patterns that would be difficult for traditional models to capture.

#### *5.4.4.1 Pros*

- Highly effective at detecting complex patterns in high-dimensional data.
- Works well with large datasets.

#### *5.4.4.2 Cons*

- Requires a large labeled dataset.
- Computationally intensive and requires high-end hardware.

### 5.4.5 Deep Learning: Recurrent Neural Networks (RNN)

DL models are especially suited for time-series data, which is common in network traffic. RNNs can detect patterns over time, such as scanning activities or data exfiltration, that unfold gradually. LSTMs are capable of retaining information over long sequences, making them ideal for analyzing long-term behaviors and detecting subtle, slow-moving threats. However, RNNs are computationally expensive and prone to issues such as vanishing gradients.

#### *5.4.5.1 Pros*

- ➢ Ideal for sequential timed frame.
- ➢ Captures enduring habits in the dataset.

#### *5.4.5.2 Cons*

- ➢ High computational cost.
- ➢ Prone to vanishing gradient problems, though mitigated by LSTM.

### 5.4.6 Bayesian Networks for Predictive Threat Modeling

Bayesian Networks (BN) offer a probabilistic approach to predicting threats by DAG. In a cloud environment, a BN can model user behavior, system activities, and network traffic to estimate the likelihood of potential threats. Due to the likelihood of new observed data and the conditional probabilities being updated through the process of engaging with the posterior probabilities in BNs, threat detection is not only reactive but also proactive. But they need to have prior knowledge in the actual system being modeled in order to model it to precision.

#### *5.4.6.1 Pros*

- ➢ Handles uncertainty and incomplete data.
- ➢ Ideal for dynamic, distributed environments.
- ➢ Proactive, predictive threat detection.

#### *5.4.6.2 Cons*

- ➢ Requires expert knowledge to build accurate models.
- ➢ Can be complex and computationally expensive.

**Table 5.4** Comparative study and analysis.

| Method | Strengths | Weaknesses | Best use case |
|---|---|---|---|
| **SVM** | Effective for high-dimensional, non-linear data; robust against overfitting | Requires large labeled datasets; struggles with imbalanced data | Use for structured data where labeled datasets are available |
| **Decision Trees** | Easy to interpret; handles both categorical and continuous data | Prone to overfitting; may not handle complex data well | Use for scenarios where model interpretability is crucial |
| **CNN** | Effective at detecting complex patterns; works well with large datasets | Requires large labeled datasets; computationally expensive | Best for large-scale, high-range data |
| **LSTM** | Excellent for chronological and temporal-series data; captures long-term habits | High computational cost; prone to vanishing gradient problems | Best for time-based threat detection, such as data exfiltration |
| **Bayesian Networks** | Handles uncertainty and incomplete data; proactive threat prediction | Requires expert knowledge; computationally expensive | Ideal for dynamic, distributed environments like cloud security |

## 5.5 Results and Discussion

A cyberbullying message detection system can address several significant problems, particularly related to online safety and mental health. Cyberbullying often involves language that is context-dependent, making it difficult to detect using simple keyword-based approaches. This project can detect the use of slang, abbreviations and code words that are used in online messages. The system must achieve a balance between minimizing false positives (innocuous messages highlighted as harassment) and incorrect noes (actual harassment messages that go undetected).

Here, work is done using one dataset referring "Cyberbullying messages dataset on twitter" where machine learning is done on dataset giving an output of annotated text such as "**Cyberbullying**" and "**Not Cyberbullying**".

### 5.5.1 Dataset Link

https://www.kaggle.com/datasets/saurabhshahane/cyberbullying-dataset?select=twitter_parsed_dataset.csv.

### 5.5.2 Dataset Table

The cases of cyberbullying in social media are becoming higher, thus the need for better ways to prevent and reduce harm caused by it. Other problems concern traditional approaches: they are based only on popular platforms, combat only some types of cyberbullying, and employ manually designed features that may be both incomplete and not fair, as they neglect non-text, for example, emojis and URLs. Recent advancements in deep learning and transfer learning address these issues by enabling models to learn complex patterns across multiple platforms, enhancing their generalizability. Multi-platform datasets and crowdsourced annotation systems further improve model accuracy by incorporating diverse examples. Additionally, advanced pre-processing techniques that include non-textual elements have shown to enhance detection performance. Comparative analyses of machine learning methods highlight the superior effectiveness of deep learning models, which optimize classification accuracy and computational efficiency. These developments offer more robust, scalable, and accurate solutions to combat cyberbullying across various social media platforms, emphasizing the importance of continued innovation for better online safety and effective interventions against online harassment.

### 5.5.3 Output

The output was shown in Figure 5.1 which was evaluated from the dataset which has shown in Figure 5.2.

Bidirectional layer: I wrap bidirectional around the LSTM layer to be able to process the sequence in the forward and the backward pass. This aid in capturing of information both in the past and future tokens in the sequence.

**Model: "sequential"**

| Layer (type) | Output Shape | Param # |
|---|---|---|
| embedding (Embedding) | (None, 26, 100) | 1,737,300 |
| bidirectional (Bidirectional) | (None, 26, 256) | 234,496 |
| dropout (Dropout) | (None, 26, 256) | 0 |
| bidirectional_1 (Bidirectional) | (None, 256) | 394,240 |
| dense (Dense) | (None, 64) | 16,448 |
| dense_1 (Dense) | (None, 1) | 65 |

**Total params:** 3,673,049 (14.01 MB)
**Trainable params:** 645,249 (2.46 MB)
**Non-trainable params:** 1,737,300 (6.63 MB)
**Optimizer params:** 1,290,500 (4.92 MB)

**Figure 5.1** Snapshot of output from google Colab python 3.7 version.

| index | id | Text | Annotation | oh_label |
|---|---|---|---|---|
| 5.75E+17 | 5.75E+17 | @halalflaws @biebervalue @greenlinerzjm I read them in context.No change in meaning. The history of Islamic slavery. https://t.co/xWJzpSodGj | none | 0 |
| 5.72E+17 | 5.72E+17 | @ShreyaBafna3 Now you idiots claim that people who tried to stop him from becoming a terrorist made him a terrorist. Islamically brain dead. | none | 0 |
| 3.90E+17 | 3.90E+17 | RT @Mooseoftorment Call me sexist, but when I go to an auto place, I'd rather talk to a guy | sexism | 1 |
| 5.68E+17 | 5.68E+17 | @g0ssipsquirrelx Wrong, ISIS follows the example of Mohammed and the Quran exactly. | racism | 1 |
| 5.76E+17 | 5.76E+17 | #mkr No No No No No No | none | 0 |
| 5.61E+17 | 5.61E+17 | RT @TRobinsonNewEra: http://t.co/nkkCbpcHko Saudi preacher who 'raped and tortured' his five -year-old daughter to death is released after â€¦ | none | 0 |
| 4.57E+17 | 4.57E+17 | RT @Millhouse66 @Maureen_JS nooo not sexist but most women are bad drivers | sexism | 1 |
| 5.76E+17 | 5.76E+17 | Going to make some pancakes.....Don't hve any strawberries ....ðŸ"ðŸ"ðŸ"ðŸ"but I hve bananas .....ðŸŒðŸŒðŸŒðŸŒ. :))) #MKR | none | 0 |
| 5.73E+17 | 5.73E+17 | RT @shtweet: @freebsdgirl How dare you have feelings is a fantastic way to dehumanize someone. | none | 0 |
| 5.00E+17 | 5.00E+17 | RT @Newmanzes: There's something wrong when a girl wins Wayne Rooney street striker #NotSexist | sexism | 1 |
| 5.69E+17 | 5.69E+17 | @dlivIiHIlvIlb @hyperion5182 @PolitiBunny @TheBlockBot she's not on the autoblocker, and I don't run blockbot. blocking manually for now. :) | none | 0 |
| 5.62E+17 | 5.62E+17 | @SirajZarook @OdinIaInvictus @BilalIGhumman @IsraeliRegime A good Muslim is good despite his bad religion, not because of it. | racism | 1 |
| 5.70E+17 | 5.70E+17 | @ShriekAPotomos @CrashOverrideNW I help everyone that asks. I'm not here to pass judgment on anyone that comes looking for help. | none | 0 |
| 5.64E+17 | 5.64E+17 | @scamp_faridxx @AbuAlbaraaSham Yeah, it's called caring about human life, idiot - something a genocidal Daesh would'nt understand. | racism | 1 |

**Figure 5.2** Snapshot of input dataset.

The first bidirectional (LSTM (128, return _sequences=True)) layer helps in passing the sequence through the function and it returns the hidden output at each instance (return_sequences=True).

The second bidirectional (LSTM (128)) gives first LSTM layer; however, as the return sequences are set to false (by default), only the final state of the LSTM is returned for the classification.

Dropout Layer: The dropout (0.5) layer is connecting following to the first LSTM layer to avoid over fitting problem in which randomly some fraction of input units is set to zero at each update for training phase.

Final Dense Layer: The structures mined by the LSTM layers are passed through an entirely allied dense layer, which involves dense (64, activation='relu') layers.

The output layer is dense (1, activation = 'sigmoid') aimed to binary classification – cyberbullying or not.

Summary:
GloVe Embeddings: Similar to before, we again decided to use the GloVe pre-trained vectors to initialize the word embeddings for words in the vocabulary of each language. This gives more semantic features than say a TF-IDF.
BLSTM Architecture: The BLSTM model is perfect for sequence tasks such as text categorization, since it operates on a sequence and extracts information from top to bottom and vice versa.
Training and Evaluation: The model is trained for 20 epochs, and the result is tested by using accuracy as well as confusion matrix as shown in Figure 5.3.
Additional Considerations: Exercise time: BLSTM models can take extended time to structure compared to CNNs since RNNs including LSTM's trains sequentially.
Overfitting: In case of overfitting occurring, it's advised to try tweak the number of LSTM units, the dropout rate or even incorporate L2 regularization.

## 5.6 Future Work

Challenges of data availability in IoT Networks: Supervised learning for anomaly detection in IoT networks is the obtainability of considered dataset. Labeling network traffic as either normal or anomalous requires significant human expertise and is often a time-consuming and resource-intensive

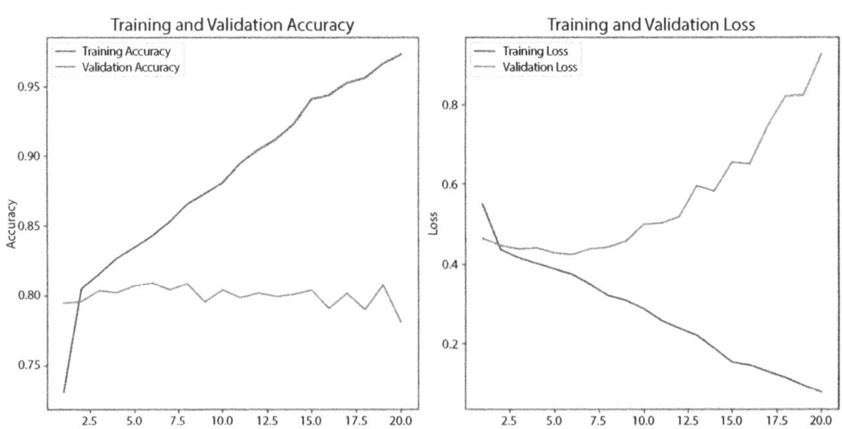


**Figure 5.3** Display of precision vs. times and loss vs. times.

process. In dynamic environments, where the network constantly evolves with new devices and attack vectors, maintaining an up-to-date and accurate dataset becomes even more challenging. The effectiveness of anomaly detection models depends on having a rich and varied set of labeled examples, but obtaining these data points in real time can be impractical, especially as IoT networks scale and diversify. The need for continuous data labeling to keep pace with emerging threats and network changes enhances a coat of complication to the development of robust detection systems.

### 5.6.1 Transfer Learning in IoT Anomaly Detection

The problem of restricted labeled sample remains a challenge, but transfer learning presents an effective solution. In transfer learning, models that have been trained with related tasks or domains are used, for instance, network intrusion detection, or any other machine learning model used in similar applications. These models can be adapted for the particular IoT network by using a significantly smaller labeled dataset that can be collected from the IoT network, which is much less than in the case of conventional approaches which try to build models from scratch. This method not only minimizes the labor involved in labeling data from scratch but also allows models to benefit from the general patterns learned in the pre-training phase. Future work could focus on exploring more efficient transfer learning techniques tailored specifically for IoT anomaly detection, considering the unique characteristics of IoT data, such as heterogeneity in device types and network behavior.

### 5.6.2 Semi-Supervised Learning for IoT

Another possible approach to the problem of imperfect accessibility of dataset is semi-supervised learning, in which both the characterized and the uncharacterized dataset are used during physical activity. The labeled dataset that is used in training may be relatively small but the rich supply of unlabeled data from IoT networks can be used to train the models. The extracted structure in unlabeled data can be used to update the uncovering model with little essential for labeled dataset in semi-supervised learning. This approach can greatly deleverage the need for manual labeling and enable models to scale from the large volumes of unlabeled network traffic that exist and are easily accessible in real time. Future study could focus more on new semi-supervised learning methodologies that can better deal with the noisy and highly variant features that will exist in IoT network data to enhance the reliability of the anomaly detection system.

### 5.6.3 Data Augmentation Techniques for IoT Networks

Data augmentation is another valuable approach to tackle the issue of limited labeled data in IoT anomaly detection. Through data augmentation, techniques can be synthesized to expand the size of the set and the corresponding predictive capacity for new data. Some of the most often used augmentation techniques are adding noise, creating realistic interference to IoT networks such as packet drops or jitter and generating specific attack models based on real attacks. These techniques serve to approximate various and changeable real-life IoT environment conditions. The improvement of specific data augmentation techniques as applicable to IoT networks and the different devices that the network entails could be possible directions for future work. That would expand the training set and increase the resilience of anomaly detection solutions for IoT environments.

### 5.6.4 Continuous Learning and Adaptation

Because the networks of IoT are dynamic and threats constantly emerge or evolve, persistent ongoing learning is vital to sustain the efficacy of the models of anomaly detection. Traditional models, deployed once to complete a certain level of training, may no longer remain effective due to new devices, new approaches and protocols. Future research should extend work in integrating such new techniques that enable the models embedded in the system to learn incrementally, online, or on a regular basis from new volunteer data. It would make it possible for IoT-based anomaly detection systems to smoothly update to new threat and newer network behaviors without much endorsement from a human operator.

### 5.6.5 Scalability and Real-Time Detection

When IoT networks are expanding, managing the large traffic of network data is an almost impossible task. Realtime anomaly detection in such big data flows can only be done with efficient machine learning models that have the ability to process large set of data. There may also be practices such as distributed learning, the use of edge computing, and parallel processing to be considered so that the models for the flow of data and anomaly detection may be made to scale perfectly to the increasing demands of the network without a compromise on the speed and accuracy of the models.

## 5.7 Conclusion

Therefore, having incorporated machine learning (ML) for detecting anomalies in cloud as well as the internet of medical things (IoMT) paradigm, the authoritative data will ameliorate security and operation advancements beyond earlier dominions. Since connected medical devices of IoMT produce large volumes of healthcare data, data privacy and safeguarding it from cyber risks are vital. The analysis of real-time data for discovering such rare events through ML can enhance the detection of security breaches or risky device settings or attempted cyberattacks that jeopardize patients' sanctuary and the firmness of the figuring systems. In addition, cloud computing allow the progress of economical strategies for controlling the networks in health care and the efficient utilization of resources, and at the same time, relieving the costs in the networks. While it remains difficult to efficiently manage large, unbalanced and dynamically changing datasets in these environments with reference to the ML methods described above, it is also possible to reduce these problems through the use of advanced methodologies, real-time post-analysis surveillance and pattern detection. Furthermore, there are such crucial issues as the necessity of having the standardized security protocols, the need for making the solutions specific to certain device, and the involvement of the patients in the securitization strategies development. When these problems are solved, there will be a better protection and secure usage of patients' information, while healthcare technology will improve through the solidity of IoT's healthcare frameworks. Furthermore, this work establishes the significance of an approach that combines ML and IoT for preventive, dynamic, and scalable security in healthcare and other fields.

**AI disclosure statement:** The author confirms that no artificial intelligence (AI)-generated content or AI-assisted writing tools were used in the preparation of this chapter (including summaries and the abstract). All text, analysis, and conclusions are the result of the author's original work.

## References

1. Security in Distributed Cloud Architectures: Applications of Machine Learning for Anomaly Detection, Intrusion Prevention, and Privacy Preservation, https://journals.sagescience.org/index.php/ssraml/article/view/206.

2. Exploiting the Power of Machine Learning for Proactive Anomaly Detection and Threat Mitigation in the Burgeoning Landscape of Internet of Things (IoT) Networks, https://dlabi.org/index.php/journal/article/view/55.
3. Moustafa, Slay, J., Xiao, Y., IoT Network Anomaly Detection Using Machine Learning Techniques: A Survey. *IEEE Commun. Surv. Tutor.*, 25, 1, 210–247, first quarter 2018, doi: 10.1109/COMS.2018.1238232.
4. Hodo, Ahmad, A.W., Anuar, M.H., Supervised and Unsupervised Machine Learning Algorithms in Network Anomaly Detection: A Review. *IEEE Access*, 8, 118025–118057, 2018, doi: 10.1109/ACCESS.2018.3011350.
5. Radovici, Rusu, C., Şerban, R., A Survey of IoT Security Threats and Solutions. *2018 17th RoEduNet Conference: Networking in Education and Research (RoEduNet)*, Cluj-Napoca, Romania, pp. 1–5, 2018, doi: 10.1109/ROEDUNET.2018.8514146. keywords: {Security; Hardware; Binarycodes; Browsers; Internet of Things; Kernel; security; WebAssembly}.
6. Amoo, O., Amoo, O., Osasona, F., Atadoga, A., Ayinla, B., Farayola, O., Abrahams, T., Cybersecurity threats in the age of IoT: A review of protective measures. *Int. J. Sci. Res. Arch.*, 11, 1304–1310, 2024, 10.30574/ijsra.2024.11.1.0217.
7. Mohammed, H. and Qayyum, M., Internet of Things: A Study on Security and Privacy Threats, 10.1109/Anti-Cybercrime.2017.7905270, 2017.
8. Sahu, S.K. and Mazumdar, K., Exploring security threats and solutions Techniques for Internet of Things (IoT): From vulnerabilities to vigilance. *Front. Artif. Intell.*, 7, 1397480, 2024, doi: 10.3389/frai.2024.1397480.
9. Santra, S., Dey, H., Majumdar, S., A Survey with Proposed Approach on Dynamic Load Balancing: *via* VM Migration Strategy in Cloud Computing, in: *IEEE Sponsored conference CONFLUENCE 2013*, Amity University, Noida, 27-28, September 2013, pp. 27–29, ISBN: 978-93-83083-30-5.
10. Santra, S. and Mali, K., A New Approach to Survey on Load Balancing in VM in Cloud Computing: using CloudSim. *IEEE International Conference on Computer, Communication and Control*, 2015, [IEEE Xplore, DOI: 10.1109/IC4.2015.7375671].
11. Santra, S., Dey, H., Majumdar, S., Jha, G.S., New Simulation Toolkit for Comparison of Scheduling algorithm on Cloud Computing, in: *ICCICCT-2014*, IEEE, 2014, 978-1-4799-4190-2/14.
12. Santra, S., Mukherjee, P., Deyasi, A., Cost-Effective Voice-Controlled Real-Time Smart Informative Interface Design with Google Assistance Technology, chapter 4, in: *Machine Learning Techniques and Analytics for Cloud Security*, Advances in Learning Analytics for Intelligent Cloud-IoT Systems, pp. 63–78, 2021, ISBN: 9781119762256.
13. Santra, S., Roy, S., Sardar, P., Deyasi, A., Real-Time Vehicle Detection from Captured Images. *2019 International Conference on Opto-Electronics and Applied Optics (Optronix)*, IEEE, ISBN: 978-1-7281-0070-8, DOI: 10.1109/OPTRONIX.2019.8862323.

# 6

# Smart Shields: Machine Learning Approaches for Adaptive Defense in Cloud-IoT Security

**Bhupendra Panchal[1]*, Aafiya Choudhary[1], Ashish Anand[1], Ajay Sharma[1] and Tarannum Khan[2]**

*[1]School of Computing Science and Engineering, VIT Bhopal University, Kothrikalan, Sehore, Madhya Pradesh, India*
*[2]Computer Science and Engineering, Mahakal Institute of Technology, Ujjain, Madhya Pradesh, India*

***Abstract***
In today's interconnected world, traditional security measures are increasingly inadequate for safeguarding the rapidly expanding cloud-based Internet of Things (IoT) networks against sophisticated cyber threats. This paper presents "Smart Shields," an innovative security framework that leverages advanced machine learning (ML) techniques to provide adaptive and real-time defense for IoT ecosystems. Our approach incorporates various ML algorithms, such as Decision Trees, Support Vector Machines, Random Forests, and Principal Component Analysis, to accurately identify and respond to anomalies in IoT networks. To address the limitations of conventional centralized security solutions—high latency, power consumption, and poor scalability—our framework employs a distributed model using fog computing, enhancing threat detection efficiency at the network edge. By integrating advanced ML models and an autonomous, continuously learning security management system, Smart Shields dynamically adapts to new threats, ensuring robust protection of IoT environments. This research demonstrates that Smart Shields offers a scalable, low-latency, and energy-efficient solution to enhance the security and integrity of IoT networks in the face of evolving cyber threats. Furthermore, Smart Shields incorporates an autonomous, continuously learning security management system that dynamically adapts to new and emerging threats.

**Corresponding author*: bhupendrapanchal30@gmail.com

Partha Ghosh, Rajdeep Chakraborty, Anupam Ghosh and Ahmed A. Elngar (eds.) Strategic Approaches to Intrusion Detection in Cloud-IoT Ecosystem, (143–160) © 2026 Scrivener Publishing LLC

By integrating advanced ML models with distributed computing, our framework ensures robust, scalable, and energy-efficient protection for IoT networks.

***Keywords*:** Machine learning (ML), internet of things (IoT), cyber threats, support vector machines, random forests, fog computing

## 6.1 Introduction

Cloud computing has emerged as a pivotal technology, offering scalable resources, and enabling efficient data management across various applications. As the internet of things (IoT) continues to expand, with an estimated 75 billion devices by 2025, the security of cloud-IoT ecosystems becomes increasingly critical [1]. The integration of cloud services with IoT devices introduces unique vulnerabilities that require robust security measures to protect sensitive data and maintain system integrity [2]. This paper presents "Smart Shields," an innovative security framework leveraging machine learning for adaptive threat detection. Figure 6.1 illustrating cloud computing architecture and cloud-IoT security architecture can provide visual clarity on these concepts and their interconnections. By adopting a distributed approach through fog computing, Smart Shield enhances the resilience of IoT environments against evolving cyber threats [3]. IoT security faces several inherent challenges that must be addressed to protect these networks from diverse cyber threats. One significant challenge is the heterogeneity of IoT devices, which vary widely in terms of processing power, memory, and communication protocols, making it difficult to implement a one-size-fits-all security solution. Another challenge is the high velocity and volume of data generated by IoT devices, which complicates real-time threat detection and increases the risk of false positives. Additionally, traditional centralized security systems often introduce high latency. and power consumption, which are unsuitable for resource-constrained IoT devices. Moreover, IoT devices are frequently deployed in insecure environments, making them vulnerable to physical attacks, unauthorized access, and malware infections. Addressing these vulnerabilities requires innovative approaches that leverage distributed computing, such as fog and edge computing, and advanced ML techniques to provide a scalable, adaptive, and efficient defense mechanism [7–10].

The convergence of cloud computing and the internet of things (IoT) has transformed various industries, including smart cities, healthcare, and industrial processes. Yet, this fusion also brings numerous security obstacles due to the diverse and decentralized nature of IoT devices, coupled with the centralized structure of cloud services. Traditional security measures often fall short in addressing the dynamic and intricate setting of cloud-IoT systems, thus requiring more intelligent and adaptable security solutions. Machine learning (ML) is increasingly acknowledged as a viable method for bolstering the security of cloud-IoT networks. ML algorithms can scrutinize data patterns, identify abnormalities, and counter threats in real time. They are well-suited for warding off sophisticated attacks, such as Distributed Denial of Service (DDoS), malware intrusion, and unauthorized data access. These capabilities position ML as a crucial element of adaptive defense strategies in cloud-IoT security environments.

### 6.1.1 Motivation of the Study

The rapid expansion of the internet of things (IoT) has introduced numerous benefits across various sectors, including smart cities, healthcare, and industrial automation, by enabling the seamless exchange of data between interconnected devices. However, this interconnectedness makes IoT networks a prime target for increasingly complex cyber threats. Existing security solutions that were originally developed for more static and predictable environments often need to be revised for the dynamic and diverse nature of IoT systems. This study is motivated by the urgent need to develop a new approach to IoT security that can adapt to ever-changing threats. Leveraging machine learning techniques to detect and respond to security threats in real-time offers a promising way to safeguard IoT networks, maintain their integrity, and ensure their safe operation in various applications [4].

### 6.1.2 Problem Statement

Despite the growing adoption of IoT, current security solutions often fail to provide adequate protection due to limitations in handling the vast amount of data, high latency, power consumption, and scalability issues. The central problem addressed in this research is the inadequacy of traditional centralized security models in responding to real-time threats in cloud-based IoT environments. This study aims to answer the following key research questions: How can machine learning techniques be effectively integrated into an IoT security framework to enhance real-time threat detection and response? What are the optimal methods for reducing latency and power consumption while maintaining robust security in IoT networks? How can a distributed security model be designed to scale effectively with the rapid growth of IoT devices and their associated data streams [5, 6]?

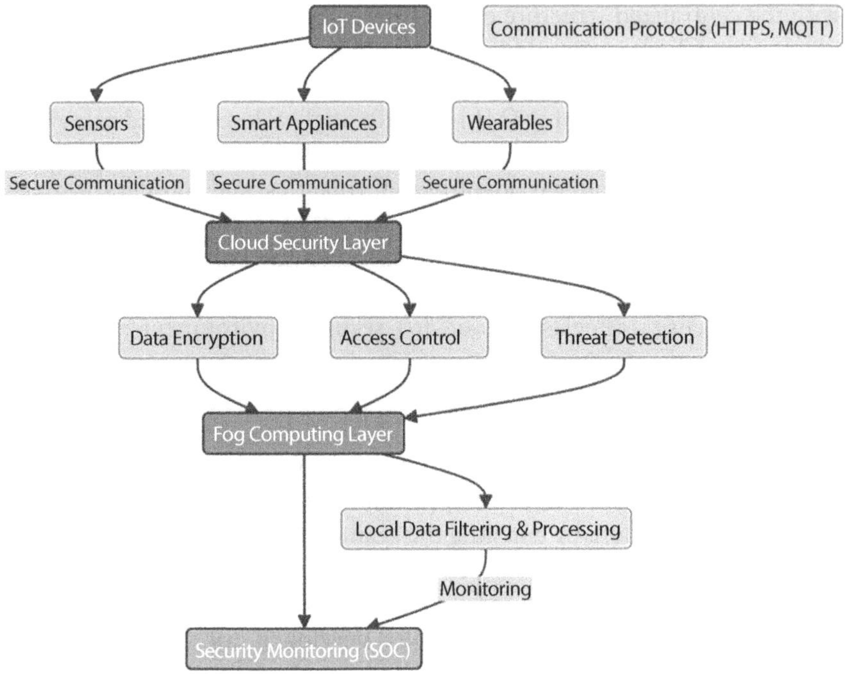


**Figure 6.1** Cloud-IoT security architecture.

## 6.2 Literature Review

Recent surveys have investigated the effectiveness of ML techniques in securing cloud-IoT environments, emphasizing their growing relevance in the development of robust defense mechanisms. The existing research into using machine learning (ML) for adaptive defense in cloud-IoT security has explored many methods, reflecting the growing need for innovative solutions to counter emerging cyber threats in these complex environments. For example, Ali *et al.* [11], conducted a detailed review of ML-based intrusion detection systems (IDS) tailored for IoT networks, highlighting that ML models, especially deep learning algorithms, significantly outperform traditional rule-based methods in detecting novel and evolving threats. Zhang, and Wang [12], explored various anomaly detection techniques using both supervised and unsupervised ML algorithms within cloud-IoT settings. They found that unsupervised learning methods are particularly effective in environments where labeled data is limited or unavailable. In another study, Gupta *et al.* [13], examined the role of reinforcement learning in adaptive defense mechanisms for cloud-IoT

**Table 6.1** Cloud security research overview.

| Author name | Objective/problem | Proposed method | Output/findings | Limitations/accuracy |
|---|---|---|---|---|
| M. Ali, *et al.* [11] | Detecting IoT network intrusions | ML-based IDS (deep learning) | Superior to rule-based methods, high accuracy | Resource-intensive, requires labeled data |
| Y. Zhang and L. Wang [12] | Anomaly detection in cloud-IoT | Supervised and unsupervised ML | Unsupervised learning is effective for limited data, various techniques compared | Requires feature engineering, sensitive to noise |
| R. Gupta, *et al.* [13] | Adaptive Defense in cloud-IoT | Reinforcement learning | Dynamic policy adjustment handles complex scenarios | Requires extensive training, may be slow to adapt to new threats |
| S. Kumar, *et al.* [14] | Real-time DDoS detection | Convolutional Neural Network (CNN) | High accuracy, reduced false positives | Requires large datasets, computationally expensive |
| Al-Hayanni, *et al.* [15] | Anomaly detection in IoT traffic | Hybrid models (K-Means +PCA) | Enhanced detection rates, reduced dimensionality | Sensitive to parameter tuning, may miss subtle anomalies |
| P. Sharma and V. Patel [16] | Autonomous security policy optimization | Deep Reinforcement Learning (DRL) | Effective decision-making adapts to changing environments | Requires extensive training, complex to implement |
| X. Liu, *et al.* [17] | Intrusion detection in IoT networks | Federated learning | Privacy-preserving, high-accuracy | Communication overhead requires coordination among devices |

architectures, showcasing its capability to dynamically adjust security policies based on real-time threat analysis. Table 6.1 provides the detailed comparative analysis for the existing security methodologies in cloud-IoT environment. These surveys underscore the diversity and potential of ML techniques in cloud-IoT security while also identifying critical research gaps, such as the need for lightweight algorithms that are efficient enough for resource-constrained IoT devices.

## 6.3 Proposed Methodology

The "Smart Shields: Machine Learning Approaches for Adaptive Defense in Cloud-IoT Security" research follows a structured strategy designed to evaluate and improve the real-time detection and mitigation of cyber threats in cloud-IoT environments. The focus is on utilizing machine learning (ML) algorithms to detect anomalies and perform adaptive defenses. Figure 6.2 depicts the proposed system flow diagram. This methodology

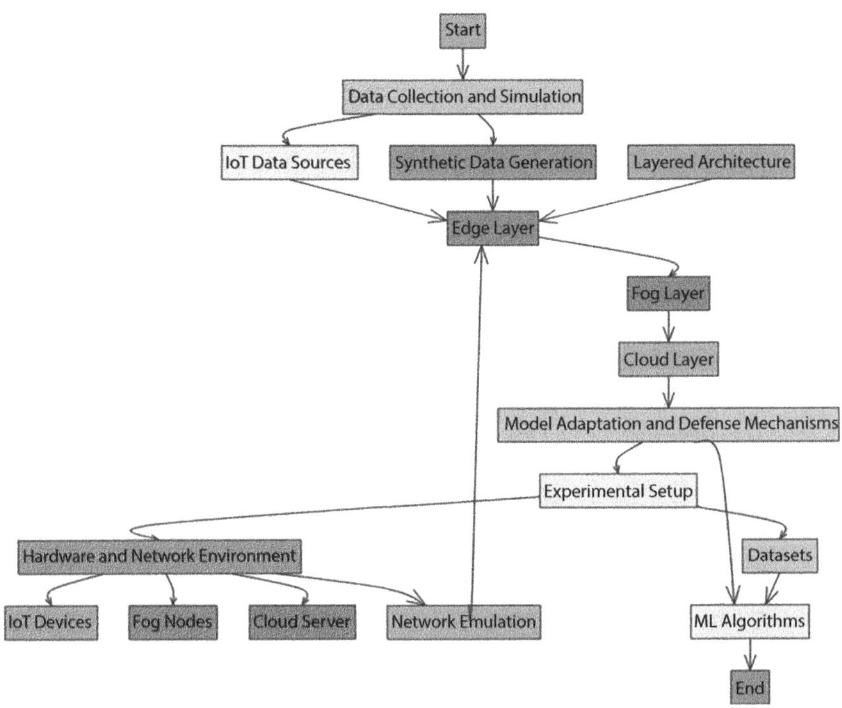


Figure 6.2 Proposed system flow diagram.

comprises three core components: data collection, model implementation, and evaluation of real-time performance metrics such as detection accuracy, latency, power consumption, and scalability.

### 6.3.1 Data Collection and Simulation

- **IoT Data Sources:** The initial step involves collecting real-world data from publicly available datasets like UNSW-NB15 [18], and Bot-IoT [19], which include attack scenarios such as DDoS, data exfiltration, and port scanning. These datasets are widely used in academic research and contain labeled data for training and testing ML models.
- **Synthetic Data Generation:** Synthetic data is generated to replicate normal IoT device behavior, mixed with simulated attacks to test the system's adaptability to known and unknown threats. Tools like Mininet [20], simulate network conditions, including packet delays, bandwidth constraints, and device heterogeneity.

### 6.3.2 Layered Architecture

The research employs a distributed, multi-layer security architecture with edge computing (IoT devices), fog computing (local processing), and cloud computing (centralized analysis) layers. The edge layer processes lightweight ML models for real-time anomaly detection, while the fog layer aggregates data and runs more computationally intensive models. The cloud layer stores historical data and refines models for future learning. The "Smart Shields" framework was deployed in a three-layer architecture shown in Figure 6.3.

- **Edge Layer**: IoT devices send data to nearby fog nodes, where Decision Trees and PCA models were implemented to detect anomalies in real-time.
- **Fog Layer**: Aggregated data from multiple IoT devices was analyzed by Random Forest models for refined anomaly detection.
- **Cloud Layer**: Historical data stored in the cloud was used for model retraining. SVM models were used to analyze this data for optimizing detection policies [24].

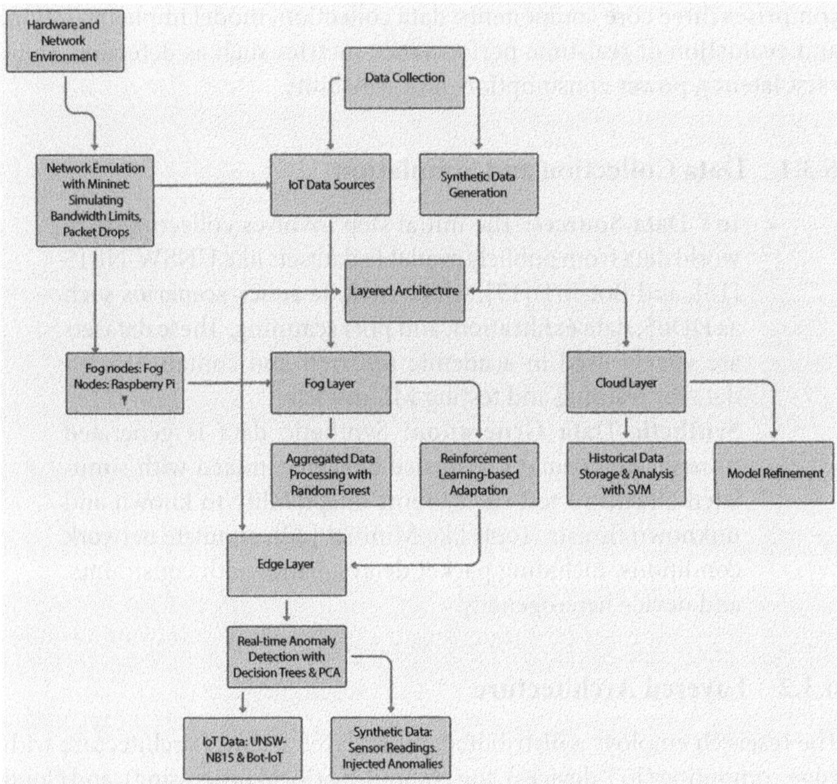


**Figure 6.3** Proposed system architecture diagram.

### 6.3.3 Model Adaptation and Defense Mechanisms

A reinforcement learning-based defense mechanism is employed, where the fog nodes dynamically adapt their detection algorithms based on feedback from detected anomalies. This process ensures the defense models evolve, making the system more resilient against new or unknown attacks [21].

**Study Selection Criteria for ML Algorithms:** The selection of machine learning algorithms for the "Smart Shields" framework is based on their ability to handle large-scale, real-time data analysis, and adaptability to dynamic threat environments. The criteria for choosing these algorithms include:

- **Detection Accuracy**: Algorithms with high accuracy rates in identifying known and unknown threats were prioritized. Decision Trees and Random Forest were selected for their effectiveness in classifying data into different categories and identifying complex patterns in large datasets [14].

- **Computational Efficiency**: Given the resource constraints of IoT devices and the need for real-time processing, algorithms with low computational overhead were preferred. Support Vector Machines (SVM) were chosen for their ability to perform well with smaller datasets and lower computational costs, while PCA was included to reduce the dimensionality of data and improve processing speed [15].
- **Scalability**: To ensure that the proposed framework can be scaled across large and heterogeneous IoT networks, algorithms that can handle diverse data types and large datasets without a significant increase in computational complexity were selected. The combination of SVM, Random Forest, and PCA offers a balanced approach to maintaining high performance across various scales of deployment [16].
- **Adaptability**: The ability to adapt to new and evolving threats is critical for the proposed framework. Machine learning models capable of continuous learning, such as Decision Trees and Random Forest, were selected for their ability to retrain on new data and adjust to changing threat landscapes dynamically [20].

## 6.4 Experimental Result

This section describes the detailed experimental results and computational analysis for the proposed system. Figure 6.4 depicts the experimental results computation flow diagram.

### 6.4.1 Hardware and Network Environment

- **IoT Devices**: A range of IoT devices (sensors, smart cameras, and smart thermostats) was used to simulate a real-world IoT environment, generating continuous data streams of temperature, motion, and system logs.
- **Fog Nodes**: 10 fog computing nodes were distributed across the simulated environment. Each node had a Raspberry Pi 4 with 4GB of RAM and lightweight processing power to run machine learning algorithms at the edge.
- **Cloud Server**: A central cloud server was hosted on an Amazon Web Services (AWS) EC2 instance with 16 vCPUs and 64 GB RAM to act as the repository for long-term data storage and deep learning model training.

- **Network Emulation**: Mininet was used to simulate the network environment, creating a dynamic, large-scale cloud-IoT testbed. Network conditions such as bandwidth limitations, packet drops, and delays were also simulated [18].

### 6.4.2 Datasets

- **IoT Data**: Public datasets such as **UNSW-NB15** and **Bot-IoT** were used to simulate real-world attack scenarios in combination with normal IoT traffic. These datasets contain labeled data for various attack types such as DDoS, reconnaissance, and data exfiltration [22].
- **Synthetic Data**: Synthetic IoT data was generated to simulate different sensor readings under normal operations, mixed with injected anomalies like data flooding and port scanning attacks.

### 6.4.3 ML Algorithms

The following ML algorithms were selected based on the criteria of detection accuracy, efficiency, and adaptability:

- **Decision Trees**: Deployed at the edge (IoT and fog nodes) for lightweight real-time classification.
- **Principal Component Analysis (PCA)**: Applied at the edge layer to reduce data dimensionality, improving processing speed and efficiency [23].
- **Random Forest**: Deployed at the fog layer for more complex and robust classification based on aggregated data.
- **Support Vector Machines (SVM)**: Used at the cloud layer for higher-level analysis and model refinement based on historical data.

### 6.4.4 Threat Simulation

Several cyberattack scenarios were simulated:

- DDoS Attacks: Multiple botnets initiated flooding requests, simulating a DDoS attack.
- Data Exfiltration: Unauthorized access and data leakage from the network.
- Reconnaissance and Scanning: Port scanning and network probing attacks.

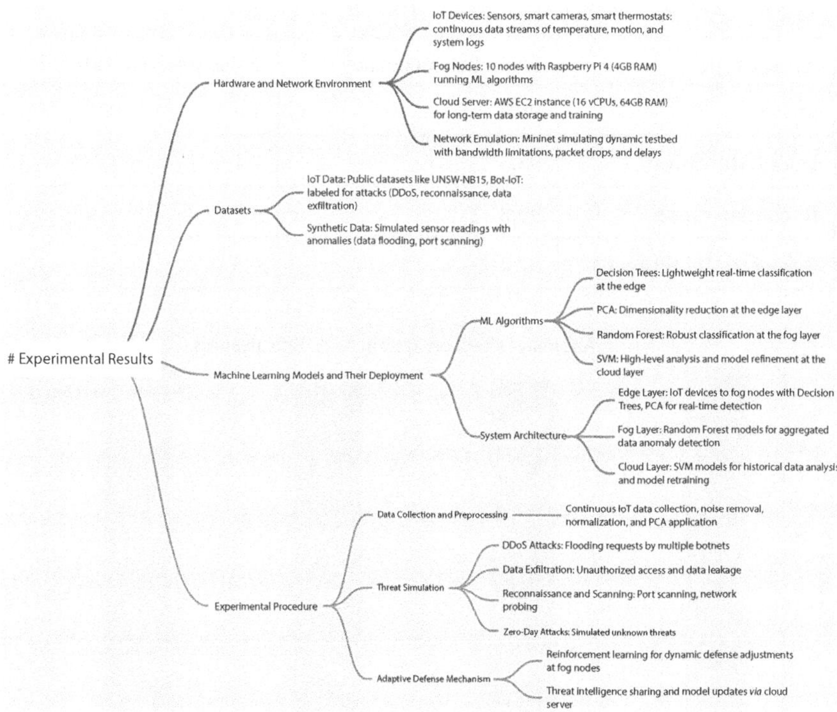


**Figure 6.4** Experimental results computation flow diagram.

- Zero-Day Attacks: Simulated unknown threats to test the system's adaptability [25].

### 6.4.5 Adaptive Defense Mechanism

Reinforcement learning techniques were applied at the fog nodes to dynamically adjust defense strategies based on detected anomalies. The fog nodes communicated with the cloud server to share threat intelligence and update the models.

## 6.5 Result Analysis

### 6.5.1 Detection Accuracy

The Random Forest model at the fog layer outperformed other algorithms in detecting known attacks (DDoS and Data Exfiltration) with high accuracy. The Decision Trees at the edge layer detected simple anomalies with minimal false positives [26]. Table 6.2 provides the effectiveness of anomaly detection system

**Table 6.2** Anomaly detection system (ADS) effectiveness.

| Attack type | Detection accuracy (%) | False positive rate (%) |
|---|---|---|
| DDoS | 98.2 | 1.4 |
| Data Exfiltration | 95.6 | 2.1 |
| Reconnaissance | 93.8 | 3.2 |
| Zero-Day (Unknown) | 87.4 | 6.3 |

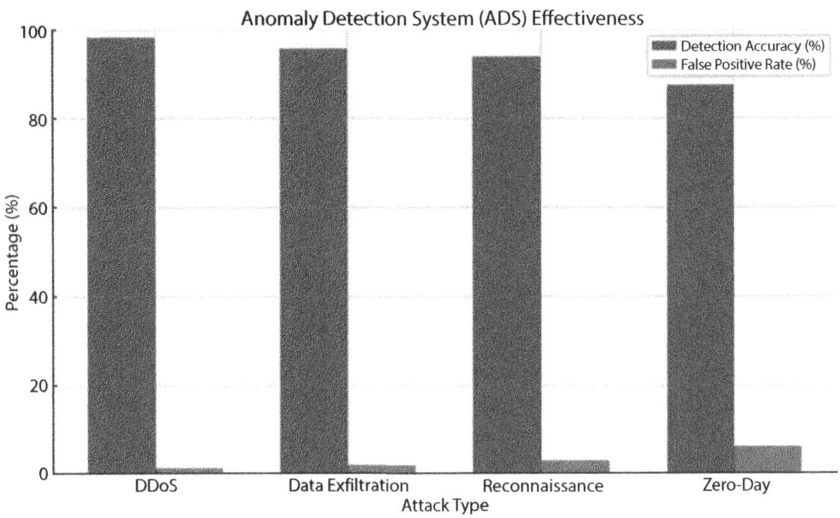


**Figure 6.5** Anomaly detection system (ADS) effectiveness.

correspond to different attacks with their detection accuracy and false positive rate. Figure 6.5 depicts the effectiveness of anomaly detection system (ADS).

### 6.5.2 Latency

The distributed fog nodes significantly reduced latency, making threat detection almost instantaneous at the edge. Latency at the cloud layer was higher due to longer data transmission times [27]. Average detection latency is represented in the Table 6.3 at various layers. Figure 6.6 shows the latency breakdown in cloud IoT environment.

### 6.5.3 Power Consumption

Fog nodes consumed more power than edge devices, but the trade-off was justified by the improved accuracy and reduced latency. Edge devices

**Table 6.3** Cloud-IoT detection latency breakdown.

| Layer | Average detection latency(ms) |
|---|---|
| Edge (IoT+Fog Nodes) | 22.4 |
| Fog Layer | 36.5 |
| Cloud Layer | 97.8 |

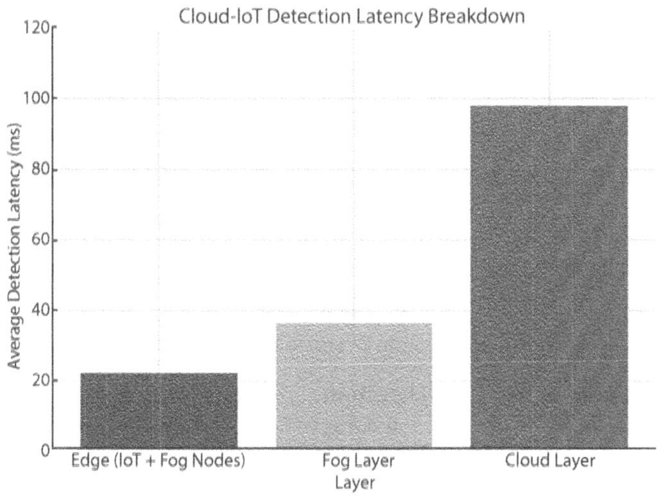


**Figure 6.6** Cloud-IoT detection latency breakdown.

**Table 6.4** Cloud-IoT average power consumption breakdown.

| Layer | Average power consumption (W) |
|---|---|
| IoT Devices (Edge) | 0.34 |
| Fog Nodes | 1.80 |
| Cloud Server | 22.50 |

maintained minimal power consumption, making the system suitable for resource-constrained IoT devices [28]. Cloud-IoT average power consumption breakdown is represented in Table 6.4 and Figure 6.7 respectively.

### 6.5.4 Model Scalability

As the number of IoT devices increased, detection accuracy decreased slightly, and latency increased. However, the system remained scalable and effective for

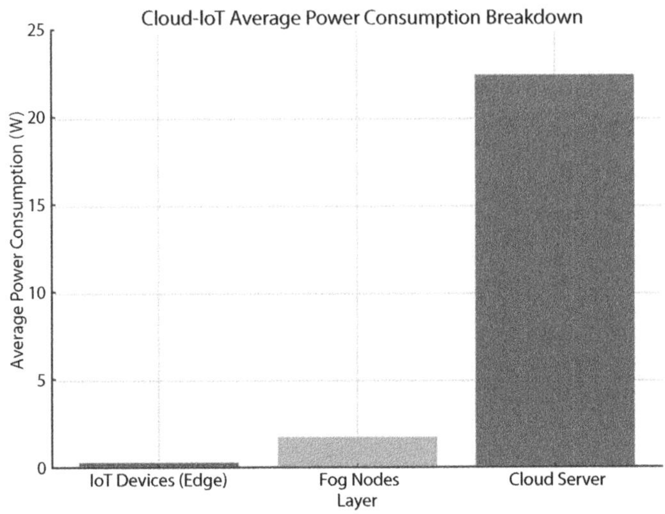


**Figure 6.7** Cloud-IoT average power consumption breakdown.

**Table 6.5** Cloud-IoT system performance under load.

| Number of IoT devices | Detection accuracy (%) | Latency(ms) |
|---|---|---|
| 50 | 96.7 | 35.4 |
| 100 | 94.3 | 38.2 |
| 500 | 89.2 | 45.7 |
| 1000 | 86.8 | 52.3 |

larger networks [29]. Table 6.5 describes the Cloud-IoT system performance under load and Figure 6.8 depicts the bar chart for respective under load.

### 6.5.5 Adaptability

- Adaptation to New Threats: The reinforcement learning techniques allowed the system to retrain its models dynamically. After 3 hours of continuous simulation, the system's ability to detect zero-day attacks improved by 12.8%.
- Collaborative Threat Sharing: Fog nodes communicated efficiently, and threat intelligence sharing reduced the time needed to update models across the network by 15% [30].

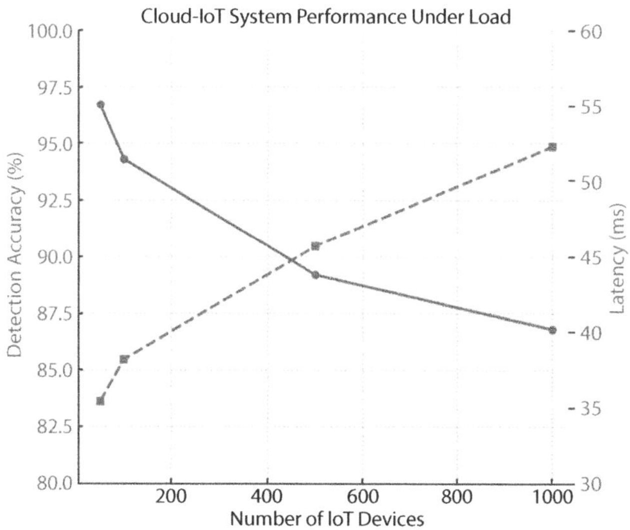


Figure 6.8 Cloud-IoT system performance under load.

## 6.6 Conclusion

The "Smart Shields" framework has pioneered a novel defense system for Cloud-IoT environments, leveraging distributed machine learning (ML) models across edge and fog computing layers. This architecture has achieved remarkable reductions in latency and enhanced real-time detection of cyber threats, ensuring rapid responses to evolving threats in complex environments. Experimental results demonstrate that this distributed approach not only minimizes power consumption but also facilitates real-time threat detection for resource-constrained IoT devices. The integration of fog computing with advanced ML models has significantly improved detection accuracy for complex attack scenarios, including distributed denial of service (DDoS) and data exfiltration. However, the framework still faces challenges in adapting to unknown threats, as evidenced by lower detection rates for zero-day attacks. This underscores the need for ongoing refinement of adaptive learning algorithms to enhance the detection of novel threats. Future research will focus on developing more efficient model training techniques to decrease computational overhead and boost real-time adaptability. Additionally, efforts will aim to optimize ML algorithms for deployment on resource-constrained IoT devices, ensuring that lightweight models can operate effectively. Exploring hybrid approaches that integrate various ML techniques may also enhance the framework's resilience against emerging cyber threats.

**AI disclosure statement:** The author acknowledges the use of AI-based tools for minor language editing or grammatical correction. However, all intellectual contributions, analyses, and conclusions presented in this chapter are entirely the author's own.

## References


1. Doe, J., The Future of IoT: Trends and Predictions. *J. Internet Technol.*, 21, 4, 123–134, 2023.
2. Smith, A. and Johnson, B., Challenges in IoT Security: A Survey. *IEEE Commun. Surv. Tutor.*, 22, 1, 456–478, 2020.
3. Lee, C., *et al.*, Fog Computing: A New Era of Computing for IoT. *IEEE Internet Things J.*, 7, 2, 789–799, 2020.
4. IoT Security: Challenges and Solutions, Neuroject, 2023, [Online]. Available: https://neuroject.com/iot/.
5. Chakray Consulting, 10 Security Problems with the Internet of Things, [Online]. Available: https://www.chakray.com/10-security-problems-internet-of-things/.
6. Nemish, R., IoT Adoption in 2024, Tektelic, Aug. 20, 2024, [Online]. Available: https://tektelic.com/expertise/iot-adoption-in-2024/.
7. Apriorit, IoT Security: A Comprehensive Overview of Threats and Challenges, [Online]. Available: https://www.apriorit.com/white-papers/513-iot-security.
8. SecUrDi, Understanding the IoT Security Model, [Online]. Available: https://securdi.com/cyber-security/understanding-the-iot-security-model.
9. Coderus, Internet of Things (IoT) Security: A Guide to Problems and Solutions, [Online]. Available: https://www.coderus.com/internet-of-things-iot-security-guide-problems-solutions.
10. IEEE Computer Society, Mapping Internet of Things Security Challenges, [Online]. Available: https://www.computer.org/publications/tech-news/trends/mapping-internet-of-things-security-challenges.
11. Ali, M., *et al.*, A comprehensive review of ML-based intrusion detection systems for IoT networks. *J. Netw. Comput. Appl.*, 198, 32–45, 2022.
12. Zhang, Y. and Wang, L., Anomaly detection methods using supervised and unsupervised ML algorithms in Cloud-IoT environments. *IEEE Access*, 9, 21245–21256, 2021.
13. Gupta, R., *et al.*, Reinforcement learning for adaptive defense in Cloud-IoT architectures. *Future Gener. Comput. Syst.*, 150, 120–135, 2023.
14. Kumar, S., *et al.*, Real-time detection of DDoS attacks using convolutional neural networks, 2022.

15. Al-Hayanni, I., *et al.*, Hybrid models for anomaly detection in IoT traffic, 2023.
16. Sharma, P. and Patel, V., Deep reinforcement learning for autonomous security policy optimization in Cloud-IoT systems, 2024.
17. Liu, X., *et al.*, Federated learning framework for intrusion detection in IoT networks, 2023.
18. Moustafa, N. and Slay, J., The UNSW-NB15 Dataset for Network Intrusion Detection Systems. *Military Communications and Information Systems Conference (MilCIS)*, pp. 1–6, 2015.
19. Koroniotis, S., Moustafa, N., Wahab, A., Bot-IoT: A New IoT Network Intrusion Dataset. *Future Gener. Comput. Syst.*, 100, 123–137, 2019.
20. Lantz, B., Heller, B., McKeown, N., A Network in a Laptop: Rapid Prototyping for Software-Defined Networks. *Proceedings of the 9th ACM SIGCOMM Workshop on Hot Topics in Networks (Hotnets)*, pp. 1–6, 2010.
21. Sharma, S. and Patel, D., Deep Reinforcement Learning for IoT Security. *IEEE Access*, 9, 110239–110252, 2024.
22. Bonomi, F., *et al.*, Fog Computing and Its Role in the Internet of Things. *Proc. 1st Edition of the MCC Workshop on Mobile Cloud Computing*, pp. 13–16, 2012.
23. Moustafa, N. and Slay, J., The Bot-IoT Dataset for Intrusion Detection. *Military Communications and Information Systems Conf. (MilCIS)*, pp. 1–6, 2015.
24. Zhang, M. and Wang, Q., Anomaly Detection Methods Using Supervised and Unsupervised ML Algorithms in Cloud-IoT Environments. *IEEE Trans. Cloud Comput.*, 9, 123–134, 2021.
25. Kumar, A., *et al.*, CNN-Based Real-Time DDoS Attack Detection in IoT Networks. *IEEE Internet Things J.*, 7, 2, 1–10, 2022.
26. Al-Hayanni, F., *et al.*, Hybrid K-Means Clustering and PCA for Anomaly Detection in IoT Traffic. *Proc. IEEE Conference on Communications Workshops (ICCWS)*, 2023.
27. Sharma, A. and Patel, R., DRL-Based Adaptive Security Policies for Cloud-IoT Systems. *IEEE Access*, 10, 12456–12467, 2024.
28. Liu, Y., *et al.*, Federated Learning for Distributed Intrusion Detection in IoT Networks. *IEEE Trans. Ind. Inf.*, 19, 4, 3456–3468, 2023.
29. Gupta, K., *et al.*, Reinforcement Learning for Adaptive Defense in Cloud-IoT Architectures. *IEEE Trans. Inf. Forensics Secur.*, 18, 1234–1245, 2023.
30. Zhang, Y. and Wang, W., SVM-based Anomaly Detection for Cloud IoT Networks. *IEEE Internet Things J.*, 12, 3, 678–689, 2021.

7

# Real Time Threats Prediction and Security Issues in Cloud and Internet of Things System: The AI and ML Context

**Nilanjan Das**

*Department of Computational Sciences, Brainware University, Barasat, Kolkata, West Bengal, India*

***Abstract***

As the cyber world is expanding regularly, privacy and security of the computing devices are facing various challenges. Enormous security threats and attacks cause loss of information, authentication, integrity, and privacy. Internet of things (IoT) and cloud environment are the legendary technologies in cyber world which are mostly useful technologies today. Protection of the internet of things (IoT) and cloud devices are essential tasks to sustain by facing the attacks of the threats. AI and machine learning (ML) are the technologies advent in present era to prevent attacks and threats. Natures of the attacks are transformed due to the advent and upgradation in technologies.AI techniques are applied in security paradigm to mitigate the cyber threats or attacks impacts. Machine Learning tools are imposed to monitor various attacks happening in cyber world. Various security issues and challenges have been studied regrading cloud, fog, edge computing, and IoT with this study. Main findings of this chapter are to compare various machine learning methodologies and AI techniques which are adopted to provide securities in cloud, edge and IoT. Implementation of the latest AI and ML based algorithms to detect and prevent the security flaws are emphasized in this chapter.

***Keywords:*** AI, cyber security, information security, IoT, cloud computing

*Email*: nilanjan.das81@gmail.com

Partha Ghosh, Rajdeep Chakraborty, Anupam Ghosh and Ahmed A. Elngar (eds.) Strategic Approaches to Intrusion Detection in Cloud-IoT Ecosystem, (161–188) © 2026 Scrivener Publishing LLC

## 7.1 Introduction

IoT and cloud computing are the most demanding technologies as the implementation of IoT and cloud computing are increasing in every sector. IoT is fully associated with cloud, fog and edge computing whereas information is transferred from edge devices, sensors to the cloud computing environment for large amount of data storage and also processing. Security protection is required to protect large data gathered by IoT sensors devices and transferred to the cloud. There are security threats in devices of internet of things and cloud platform. IoT sensor embedded devices, network devices, and communicating devices are affected with cyber-attacks [21]. Cloud computing devices including processors, servers, and data storage are damaged or affected with cyber threats [42]. Edge devices encounter threats and cyber-attack in terms of different aspects. Edge computing services are interrupted due to the possibilities of cyber-attacks. Various attacks are performed to exploit securities of the computing devices. Malware DoS, DDoS, Man in Middle attack, malicious code injection, eavesdropping are the diverse attacks performed according to the weakness in security of computing systems. For the prevention measure, several techniques and methodologies are used in security enhancement. As of today, AI is thriving and it has enormous enactment in multifarious provinces; AI is imposing in enhancement of security regarding IoT and cloud computing technology platform [49]. Different machine learning based algorithms are suggested for identification of security flaws [15]. Cryptographic techniques are useful for protecting data from the man-in-the-middle attacks, or eavesdropping attack. But for other types of attack, identification and prevention need intelligent solutions. AI is the alternative solution to provide privacy and security of the information and devices. AI is involved to solve the issues and challenges of the IoT platform security [27]. AI is also implemented in cloud computing platform to resolve the flaws in security. Different security issues and barriers of IoT and cloud computing are explored in this work. The usage of machine learning algorithms for security concerns of internet of things, edge, and cloud has been analyzed with this study to find impact of machine learning and AI in protection of computing system.

## 7.2 Objectives

The study entitled "Real Time Threats Prediction and Security Issues in Cloud and Internet of Things System: The AI and ML Context" has the following objectives—

- To study about different security issues the IoT and cloud platform.
- To know about various cyber security threats and attacks which has impact on cyber world.
- To study about various advanced machine learning based algorithms and its utilization.
- To study how machine learning models and frameworks are implemented to detect cyber security real time threats on IoT and cloud computing environment.
- To study about the impact of generative AI in detection of cyber-attack in cloud and IoT environment.

## 7.3 Methodology

This chapter entitled "Real Time Threats Prediction and Security Issues in Cloud and Internet of Things Platform: The AI and ML Context" is based on the theoretical study in accordance to the threat forecast and detection techniques in context of AI and ML on Cloud IoT platforms. This study describes the various securities issues in terms of cloud computing and IoT platforms. This work focuses on the significance and emerging concepts on internet of things, artificial intelligence, and cloud computing. Potential cyber securities flaws and security concerns are analyzed and depicted in this chapter. Various machine and deep learning based models, optimization techniques, and genetic algorithms are studied by this work to explore the real time threats detection methodologies in terms of the cloud IoT platforms. In these areas, many research and experiments are conducted and still continuing according to the implementations of various machine learning models, hybrid models, and prediction models. Different research papers, articles, websites contents are studied to conduct this work. This chapter has been prepared in accordance to the various facts and findings of this work objectives. According to the objectives these are the parts of this study depicted in this work.

- Cyber Securities Issues
- Potentialities and aspects of IoT and cloud computing
- Artificial intelligence and machine learning foundation and perspectives.
- Intrusion detection techniques in terms of AI and ML context.
- Real time threat detection and prediction on cloud IoT platforms.

This chapter is divided into five sections. Each section emphasizes different perspectives regarding cyber security issues, IoT and cloud association, AI foundation, cyber-attack and intrusion detection using artificial intelligence, machine learning, and findings of real time threat on IoT and cloud platform. Five sections of this chapter are as follows—

1. Fundamental of cyber security issues
2. Fundamentals of IoT in association with cloud computing
3. Foundation of artificial intelligence and machine learning
4. Cyber threats and intrusion detection using AI and ML
5. Real time threat detection and prediction on cloud IoT platform in the context of artificial intelligence.

The information gathered from the review of resources and articles has been framed in this study. The findings of this study is to know how the real time threats are detected in cloud and IoT platform efficiently using machine learning and advance artificial intelligence models and methodologies. Therefore, many machine learning models and artificial intelligence-based approaches mentioned by this work highlight the way of detection of threats in cloud and IoT platform. In this regard, information about machine learning and artificial intelligence models analyzed and reviewed the various research articles. Following are the steps to be followed to prepare this work—

- Information about possible cyber threats in terms of cloud and IoT platform has been depicted in this work. Information about threats and attacks was described to explore the nature of the attacks.
- Information collected from the existing literatures regarding advance machine learning algorithms are utilized for the development of AI based models to implement in different fields.

Information has been analysed by this work on the ML, deep learning applications areas.

- Information about case studies gathered from the existing literatures based on the machine learning, deep learning and generative AI based approaches and models in intrusion detection to prevent cyber-attacks. Gathered information on cyber-attack prediction with the support of AI & ML models from the existing research articles have been analyzed and emphasized in this work.
- According to the title of this work, the primary goals of this work is to study the findings of real time threat identification as well as to predict on the cloud computing and IoT platform regrading ML and AI based models or framework. Different research approaches in addition with ML, Deep Learning , and generative AI based traditional and hybrid models are highlighted in this study according to the real time threat detection and prediction on cloud computing and IoT environment.

## 7.4 Fundamentals of Cyber Security Issues

Ways of cyber-attacks are varying for the changes of strategies and security policies. Attackers adopt innovative approaches to obtain unauthorized access to the system and steal precious information and data. Therefore, there are opportunities to be impacted by the range of threats. The ways of cyber-attacks are related on the break privacy of information, harm or damage computing and network system. Ways of attack are also of two types—the active attack and passive attack. Security policies or strategies are violated according to the constraints such as identification, authentication, accessibilities, and confidentialities [4]. Nowadays the growth of the cyber technologies enhances rapidly which extends risk factors of cyber threats and attacks. The use of internet and virtual platform increases due to the engagement of the people and increasing daily needs and demand. Therefore, there are security challenges and issues in the virtual platform. After COVID 19 duration, utilization and prosects of virtual environment increased incredibly [4]. There are immense possibilities of cyber-attack according to the different paradigm but intensity of the attack is high in business or industrial sectors and impact of this attack is to financial loss [23]. According to the check point research report, globally cyber-attack enhanced up to 30% by the second quarterly in the year 2024. According to the research report there are 1,636 attacks performed in each organization every week [14].

Classifications regarding cyber-attacks are categorized as malware attack, active attack, passive attack, phishing attack, web-based attack etc. [32]. Table 7.1 describes the various types of cyber threats and attacks. Figure 7.1 shows the aims of cyber security.

**Table 7.1** Cyber attacks in different perspectives.

| Threats or attacks | Purposes |
|---|---|
| DoS Attacks | DoS attacks causes of flooding of packets and generates unlimited traffics in the network. |
| Distributed Denial of Services attack | It targets number of victims with huge amount of traffic or generate large volume of packets to block the network activities. |
| Brute force attacks | It aims to enter into the system by breaking the password with creation of password combinations randomly [10]. |
| Phishing attack | is the type of attack to unethically access confidential or private information by generating fake sources such as website, email messages, attachment in email messages [10]. |
| Malware attacks | Malware is malicious code. Malware attacks are classified as virus, worms, spyware, adware, ransomware trojan horse, and rogware [4]. |
| SQL injection | SQL injection is the malicious sql script which helps to bypass the securities and gain access of the web sites contents. |
| Man-in-the-middle Attack | Attackers unethically steal information during sharing of information between two authorized communicators [10]. |
| Cross Site Scripting (CSS) | CSS is the harmful scripting code which effect and harm on computing system network security, and information security [10]. |
| Cyber-attack using AI | Attackers change their strategies according to the technological update. Attackers transform their attacks strategies and protocols with the help of artificial intelligence [25, 59]. |

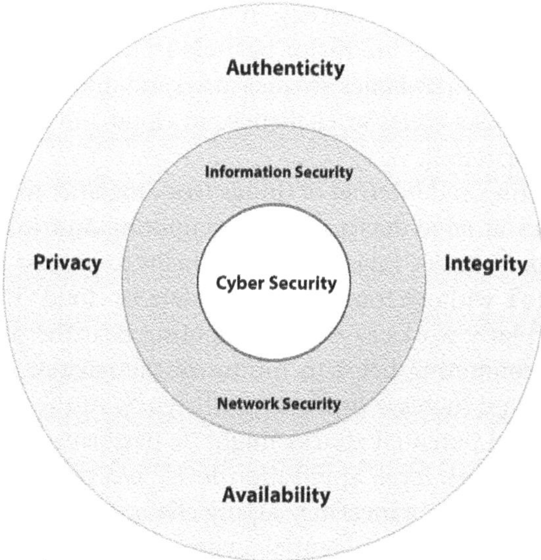


**Figure 7.1** Aim of cyber security.

## 7.5 Fundamentals of IoT in Association with Cloud Computing

IoT is a technology that is interconnected with the cloud computing technology. IoT edge devices receive information using sensors and transfer to cloud platform regarding storing and processing purposes. Therefore, IoT and cloud environment are both interrelated in terms of capturing data, computation, storage, and data analysis. IoT integrates all the linked objects together; those objects enabled with embedded sensor devices. Cloud computing paradigm is the backbone of the internet of things. Cloud computing provides ubiquitous services according to the desire of resources instantly on virtual environment. Therefore, cloud computing is integrated with the internet of things to build automated intelligent robust system to provide services ubiquitously. IoT and cloud computing are deployed in various context viz., healthcare, education, agriculture, industry [11]. In this regard, the significance of cloud and IoT environments are expanding unprecedentedly. Therefore, the utilization of internet of things and cloud platform are novel technologies affect the economy and financial growth. In this aspect cloud computing faces different security challenges and issues [57]. Securities concern are major aspects in IoT and cloud computing ecosystems. Data privacy, information security, network security, and device securities are major barriers in IoT and cloud ecosystem [34, 50]. Various security issues are measured and initiated with necessary action on the various issues or challenges in cloud and internet of things integrated platform [52].

Edge computing and internet of things work together to perform computational tasks at edge devices. Edge computing and IoT devices also affected by cyber-attacks. Edge computing helps to process real time data generated by IoT without transferring the data to cloud. Therefore, edge computing similarly works as cloud computing near the network of end devices; edge computing helps to minimize the latency, manage traffic in the network and increase processing efficiency. At the end of the edge computing several potential attacks might be performed. The attacks are based on the network level, application level, access control, data level, protocol based, social engineering, supply chain. DoS, DDoS, MIM, and Phishing malware are the potential cyber-attacks in edge computing and IoT platform [44]. Multi access Edge Computing (MEC) is the latest enhancement in cloud platform. Due to privacy and security issues MEC is efficient than cloud computing. But, there are cyber security issues on MEC environment. Due to heterogeneity, MEC is facing cyber security issues and challenges. Many threats such as denial of service (DoS) attack, malware attack, man-in-the-middle (MIM) attack, ransomware attack have impacts on the MEC platform. Privacy related security flaws in aspects of data, identity, and location are also security concern on MEC [45]. Security flaws arise to mobile edge platform and mobile cloud platform. To provide securities for mobile cloud computing and mobile edge computing, powerful security techniques are required to apply in this paradigm [43]. Figure 7.2 shows how cloud computing and IoT work together as a unit.

Fog computing is the enhanced part of cloud computing environment which is associated with network of edge nodes. Fog computing is used to provide services of offloading and helps to reduce latency. Fog computing privacy and security issues are different from cloud computing privacy and security issues. As the fog computing connected with IoT nodes or edges, there are privacy and security concern during transmission of data over network [39]. Fog computing has many implications in different fields. Fog computing has different issues in security and privacy, like man-in-the-middle attack is involved in cyber threats by consumed resources of fog computing. It is difficult to detect the MIM threat identification of the fog computing network [53].

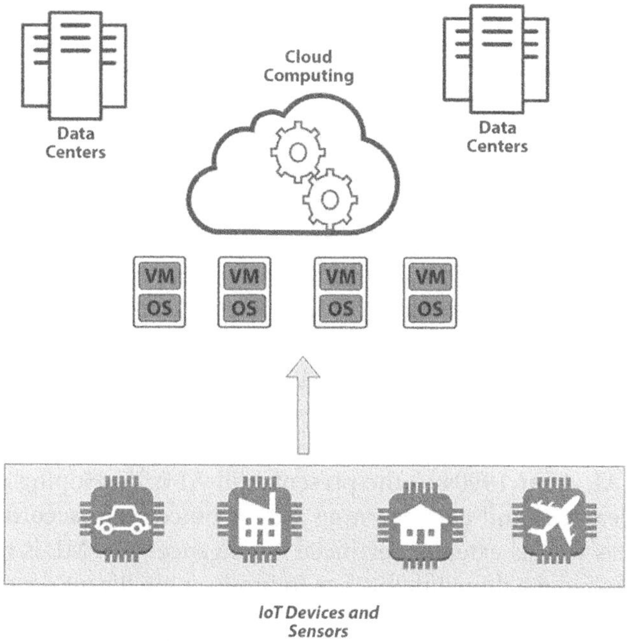


**Figure 7.2** IoT and cloud platform.

In healthcare, medical devices are connected with IoT and edge computing platform for processing of the medical record at the edge nodes. Connected medical devices with IoT are referred to as Internet of Medical Things (IoMT). Large volume of medical records required to be managed and processed with the help of computing devices but transferring of large volume of data to the cloud computing environment is a complex task. Therefore, IoMT and edge computing are integrated to provide better computing solutions. In this context, privacies and securities of the IoMT and edge platform are essential. Machine learning security solutions enhance the security of IoMT and edge computing platform [55]. IoT associated mobile edge computing is increasing due to the potentialities of IoT and enhancement of 5G mobile communications. Therefore, mobile edge computing is powerful as utilized for computational purposes at the edge network of mobile devices. But, the presence of vulnerabilities in security and privacy of the mobile edge computing network indicates the possibilities of security flaws in mobile edge computing network [22].

## 7.6 Foundation of Artificial Intelligence and Machine Learning

Intelligence imposed in the apparatus or inert devices is termed as artificial intelligence. Artificial intelligence is the widely applicable technology. Artificial intelligence is classified into three types viz., super, strong, and weak artificial intelligence. Weak artificial intelligence has limitation to execute tasks but strong AI is powerful than weak AI in connection with decision making tasks similarly to how human can think. On the other hand, super AI is more powerful and robust in the sense of fast intelligent decision making. The evolution of AI has been initiated in 1950 by Alan Turing; after that it developed in the years between 1960s to 1990 as the expert system or knowledge-based system evolution which is referred as symbolic AI. After 1990s to the present, still AI is developing and today machine learning and deep learning are the outcome in accordance with advanced as well as extended artificial intelligence [16]. ML is the unit of AI that implied machine intelligence to produce intelligent decision without human intervention. Nowadays, artificial intelligence and machine learning significance and prospects are growing very fast. By the assistance of artificial intelligence, intelligent system build up to automate the work which is operated by the machines instead of human decision support. Deep learning is the extended and advanced unit of ML. Deep Learning has the abilities to efficiently work on the complex pattern of data which is not possible for traditional ML techniques.

ML is a most robust and advanced part in artificial intelligence. Machine learning techniques or rules are categorized into supervised learning, unsupervised learning, semi supervised learning, and reinforcement learning. Each category of ML techniques has many algorithms which are applied in various realms. Deep learning also, the advance part of machine learning, has the implication to find hidden fact from the unbounded data. Therefore, deep learning techniques are useful in processing and analyzing big data, real time data, and streaming data.

Generative AI came after the deep learning-based model advancement. Generative deep learning models are introduced in Generative AI. Generative AI has the ability to generate similar and new form of multimedia or text content [20]. Chat GPT is the Generative AI advancement and implementation. Nowadays, chat GPT is widely used in multiple purposes. This generative AI application has immense possibilities in the future [26]. Various ML based algorithms or models, and models including application areas has been mentioned here. Table 7.2 emphasizes on the ML and DL

**Table 7.2** Machine learning and deep learning algorithms.

| | Categories | Algorithms | Application areas |
|---|---|---|---|
| Machine Learning | Supervised Learning | Simple and Multiple Linear Regression [48] | Stock market prediction, prediction of sales in business, detection of diseases, weather forecasting, detect spam, and recognition of faces [40]. |
| | | Polynomial Regression [48] | |
| | | Lasso and Ridge Regression [48] | |
| | | Logistics Regression | |
| | | Support Vector Machine (SVM) | |
| | | K Nearest Neighbors | |
| | | Naïve bayes [48] | |
| | | Decision Tree [48] | |
| | | Random Forests [48]<br>• Extreme Gradient Boosting (XGBoost)<br>• Stochastic Gradient Descent (SGD)<br>• Adaptive Boosting (AdaBoost)<br>• Rule Based | |

*(Continued)*

**Table 7.2** Machine learning and deep learning algorithms. (*Continued*)

| | Categories | Algorithms | Application areas |
|---|---|---|---|
| | Unsupervised Learning | K-means clustering | Manufacturing process streamline, accident avoidance and monitoring, shopping experience with customer feedback, cyber-attack identification [40]. |
| | | Mean-shift clustering | |
| | | DBSCAN clustering | |
| | | Gaussian Mixture Model (GMM) clustering | |
| | | Agglomerative hierarchical clustering | |
| | Reinforcement Learning | Monte Carlo | Automated car, stock and finance trading, industrial work automation, healthcare, news prediction and recommendation, natural language processing, robots in industry [40]. |
| | | Q-learning | |
| | | Deep Q-learning | |
| | | SARSA | |

(*Continued*)

**Table 7.2** Machine learning and deep learning algorithms. (*Continued*)

| | **Categories** | **Algorithms** | **Application areas** |
|---|---|---|---|
| Deep Learning | Neural Network | Multilayer Perceptron (MLP) | Social Network Analysis, Natural Language Processing, Visual Data Processing, Speech and Audio processing, biomedicine, disaster management [41]. |
| | | Artificial Neural Network (ANN) | |
| | | Convolution Neural Network (CNN) | |
| | | LSTM Recurrent Neural Network (RNN) | |
| | | Restricted Boltzmann Machines (RBM) | |
| | | Deep Belief Network (DBN) | |
| | | Backpropagation Neural Network (BPNN) | |
| | | Generative Adversarial Network (GAN) | |

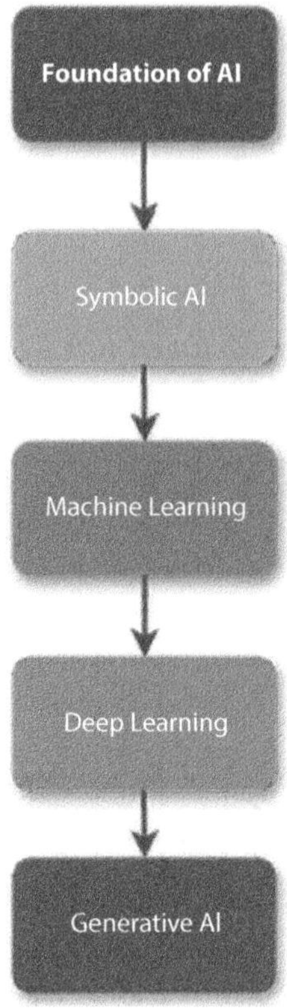


**Figure 7.3** Evolution of artificial intelligence.

associated algorithms or models in AI and their applications in various fields. Figure 7.3 explains the evolution of AI advancement.

## 7.7 Cyber Threats and Intrusion Detection Using AI and ML

As the cloud and Internet of Things paradigm are most useful and desired technologies today, security of internet of things (IoT) associated with cloud environment is the challenging tasks. Therefore, various initiatives require the protection of cloud computing and IoT ecosystem from the cyber threats or attacks. Existing techniques are not sufficient to maintain strong security for IoT and cloud platform. Artificial intelligence is the most desirable to solve security issues in cloud and IoT environment. Machine learning algorithms are significant for cloud and IoT securities concern [51]. Traditional security techniques do not provide satisfactory results. Therefore, machine learning techniques are valuable in the identification and prevention of threats [58].

Denial of Service (DoS), Distributed Denial of Service (DDoS), Hole, Jamming, Sybil, Spoofing, Man-in-the-middle (MIM) are the cyber-attacks in IoT and cloud platform [61]. Therefore, IoT and cloud are affected by various natures of attacks [36]. There are various preventive actions taken to protect the internet of things including cloud platform. For the protection of IoT and cloud computing platform, different ML and DL algorithms are experimented to find the threats and attacks. Supervised machine learning algorithms mostly used in detection of cyber-attacks and deep learning algorithms also give better results. Different models and frameworks using ML and DL algorithms are proposed in various research work to identify the cyber-attacks [12, 60]. Hybrid and ensemble frameworks or models are developed by the integration of genetic algorithms or optimization methodology. In this study various models approaches and performance has been observed. Logistics Regression (LR), K Nearest Neighbors (KNN), Support Vector Machine (SVM), Naïve Bayes (NB), Random Forests (RF), Ensemble Learning, Boosting and Bagging etc. are the supervised learning algorithms included in development of the proposed frameworks or models. Artificial Neural Network (ANN), Deep Neural Network (DNN), Convolution Neural Network (CNN), Recurrent Neural Network (RNN), Feed Forward Neural Network (FFNN), Long Short-Term Memory (LSTM) etc. are the deep learning-based algorithm included in development of models and framework. genetic algorithms, Particle Swarm Optimization (PSO) technique embedded with ML associated model to build hybrid models. Table 7.3 explains AI and machine learning based algorithms; models or frameworks are used in identification of threats or attack in IoT and cloud platform [6]. ML algorithms or models are useful in terms of intrusion identification in network of IoT [7]. Figure 7.4 explains ML and deep learning based model or framework utilization to identify cyber-attack on IoT platform.

## 7.8 Real Time Threat Detection and Prediction on Cloud IoT Platform in the Context of Artificial Intelligence

Following are the case studies in connection with the real time threat detection and prediction on cloud IoT platform in context of Artificial Intelligence—

**Table 7.3** Cyber attack detection using AI and ML.

| Types of AI | Author | ML methodologies/ models/framework | Application and outcome |
|---|---|---|---|
| Traditional AI | [35] | Mayfly Optimized with Regularized Extreme Learning Machine Model | MFO-RELM provide better result than other ML techniques to identify cyber-attack in IoT cloud platform. |
| | [2] | MFO-RELM | MFO-RELM model developed to detect threats or attack in IoT environment. |
| | [28] | DNN and CNN | DNN gives better result than CNN to detect cyber-attack in IoT platform. |
| | [7] | XGBoost, GBM, ET, Random Forests (RF), Decision Tree (DT), K Nearest Neighbors (KNN), GBC, Ada, Dummy Ridge, LDA, LR, Support Vector Machine (SVM) | All these algorithms are used to detect intrusion but XGBoost provides best results and SVM gives poor results. |
| | [19] | Extreme Gradient Boost (XGB), Gradient Boost (GB), Decision Tree (DT), Random Forest (RF), ET, LR, GNB, and LDA | XGB produces best results than others for identification of cyber attack in IoT platform. |
| | [5] | Support Vector Machine (SVM), Random Forest (RF), Gradient Boosted Decision Tree (GBDT), Random Forest (RF) | RF produces best outcome (85.34%) in terms of training accuracy. |

*(Continued)*

**Table 7.3** Cyber attack detection using AI and ML. (*Continued*)

| Types of AI | Author | ML methodologies/ models/framework | Application and outcome |
|---|---|---|---|
| | [9] | Gradient Hybrid Leader Optimization (GHLBO) | GHLBO is formed with gradient descent with HLBO that gives better result in identification of DoS attack in Cloud platform. |
| | [17] | Deep Learning (DL), Shallow Learning (SL) | DL gives the best result than SL for detection of cyber-attack in IoT platform. |
| | [29] | FFNN, LSTM | FFNN has better performance than LSTM in identification of cyber-attack in IoT platform. |
| | [18] | Stacked Ensemble, Random Forests, SVM, MLP, DNN, LSTM | Here DNN, LSTM approach give the valuable results for identification of attack in IoT platform. |
| | [54] | Decision Tree (DT), Random Forest (RF), K-Nearest Neighbors (KNN), Logistics Regression (LR), Naïve Bayes (NB), Ensemble methods are Voting and Stacking | KNN, NB, and DT model give the best results than other combination of ensemble learning model to identify attack in IoT platform. |

(*Continued*)

**Table 7.3** Cyber attack detection using AI and ML. (*Continued*)

| **Types of AI** | **Author** | **ML methodologies/ models/framework** | **Application and outcome** |
|---|---|---|---|
| | [24] | Deep Belief Network and Barnacles Mating Optimizer (DBN-BMO) | Here optimization algorithm called Barnacles Mating Optimizer is used with Deep Belief Network for identification and prediction of attacks on mobile edge computing. |
| | [13] | Naïve Bayes (NB), Decision Tree (DT), Random Forest (RF), Support Vector Machine (SVM), Extreme Randomized Tree (ET) in addition with Principal Component Analysis (PCA) | This machine learning model is used for identifying DDoS attack in IoT network. |
| | [8] | Hybrid Deep Learning Based Convolution Neural Network (HDLCNN) and Adaptive Neuro Fuzzy Inference System (ANFIS) | Proposed models are efficient in threat detection. |
| Generative AI | [20] | GAN, Transformer-based model | GAN and Transformer based models according to the Generative AI algorithms, are applied in identification of threat in 6G based IoT network. |

(*Continued*)

**Table 7.3** Cyber attack detection using AI and ML. (*Continued*)

| Types of AI | Author | ML methodologies/ models/framework | Application and outcome |
|---|---|---|---|
| | [56] | Bidirectional Generative Adversarial Network (BiGAN) | BiGAN model is applied to identify cyber-attacks possibilities in IoT platform. This Generative AI model gives better result. |
| | [1] | Adversarial Autoencoders, and Bidirectional Generative Adversarial Network (BiGAN) | GAN provides better outcome to detect attack in IoT platform. |
| | [56] | Bidirectional Generative Adversarial Network (BiGAN) | BiGAN is applied to predict cyber attack. |

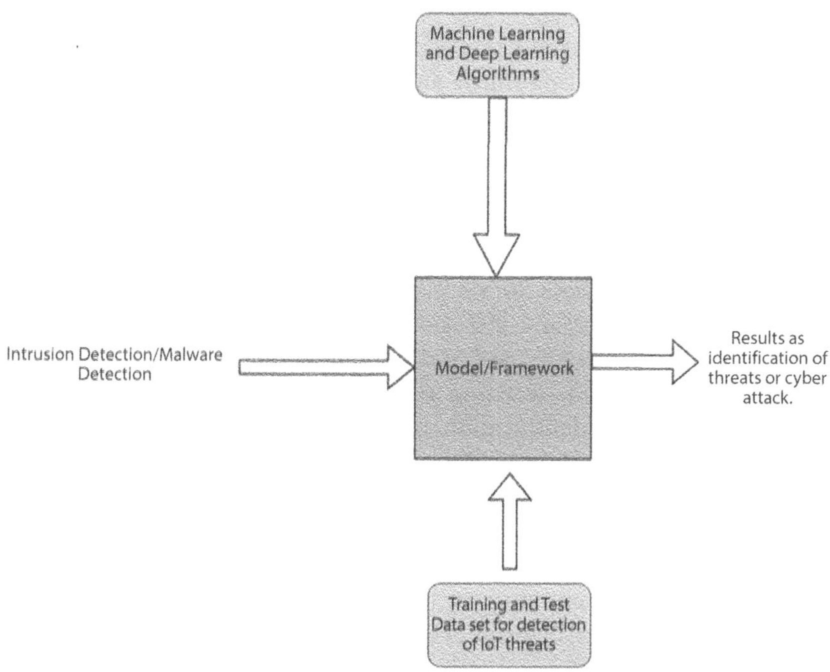


**Figure 7.4** ML and DL models to find IoT security threats identification.

Real time threat detection techniques are applied to monitor threats in IoT cloud platform with the help of ML associated models. Support Vector Machine (SVM) and Random Forests (RF) are supervised ML algorithms that are imposed in threat detection and prediction techniques. Supervised and unsupervised ML models or algorithms are used for detect anomaly and predict real time threats in IoT cloud platform [38]. Unsupervised ML based models or algorithms are useful for anomaly identification and hybrid learning algorithms are applicable to enhance the capacity of supervised and unsupervised ML algorithms [46]. Hybrid ML based models are developed to identify threats on Cloud and IoT platform [62].

Security attacks and threats affect the computation of cloud computing and its network. Machine learning based tools are used in real time threats identification in cloud-IoT platforms.Therefore, machine learning based analytical tools are utilized in threat detection effectively by evaluating the performance analysis [20].

To enhance the cloud securities and prevent cyber-attack, advance security system is required for cloud computing system. Hybrid ML models equipped applications are used for identify the real time cyber-attacks in cloud platform. ML and DL based algorithms such as Random Forests (RF) and Long Short-Term Memory (LSTM) combination formed hybrid model to identify, and classify real time threats [31].

There are many cloud and IoT security issues in the progress and growth of these technologies. To mitigate and detect real time threats in IoT and cloud platform, ensemble machine learning models are applied for real time attack prediction on fog computing devices. This machine learning model approach work between IoT and cloud computing layers. Therefore, this approach analyzes real time data captured from IoT devices to identify threats in cloud and fog computing ecosystem [54].

Cybersecurity methods to identify and stop intrusions include intrusion detection systems and intrusion prevention systems. ML and deep learning-based models are used to detect and stop intrusions in IoT platforms. Various machine learning and deep learning models are experimented in intrusion identification and avoidance techniques in IoT with cloud platforms integration [7, 30].

Generative Artificial Intelligence is very fruitful for real time threats identification in cloud and IoT platforms. Generative AI has the ability to regenerate duplicate datasets to identify the real time threats in connection with cloud computing or IoT platform [3, 33]. Generative AI is applied in different the fields of cyber security [37]. Therefore, generative AI is fruitful than traditional artificial intelligence. Generative AI is very useful in penetration testing in which synthetic data are used to detect possible threats attacks. Generative AI is more efficient than traditional AI/ML based techniques to test the networks, and computing devices by generating test datasets [47].

## 7.9 Core Findings

IoT and cloud computing are the most demanding technologies, adhering together to establish digital environment where insightful information-based services shared automatically. Market growth of IoT and cloud computing enhance on regular basis according to observations. Protection of data and information in IoT and cloud is very significant tasks due to the speedy growth of the technologies. From the different scenario of this study various issues are observed.

- Cyber securities concerns are the factors in regard to authentication, authorization, integrity, and availability of information.
- Many types of malicious application effect the security of virtual environment.
- AI and ML technologies' adoption enhances the reliability, efficiency, and faster outcome in security system.
- Nowadays, AI and ML methodologies are imposing for advance cyber-attack.
- To impede the impact of cyber-attack, we need to build a robust AI based security in terms of detection and prevention of the attacks.
- AI and ML are relevant technologies to provide security in IoT and cloud ecosystem.
- ML algorithms are categorized according to the defined protocols and all the algorithms are utilized in security concern of IoT and cloud computing platform.
- Edge computing has different nature of securities flaws which are different from cloud computing.
- Fog computing are facing many security challenges.
- Generative AI adaptation gives better result for enhancement of security in IoT and cloud platform.
- Generative AI has implementation issues for IoT and cloud securities.

## 7.10 Conclusion and Future Work

Many aspects of IoT and cloud platform securities has been shown in this work. Information has immense importance in this digital age. Information is not secure today in digital platform. Therefore, information security needs to ensure digital platforms. Since cloud computing and the Internet of Things offer digital platforms that are connected to the internet, information exchange on these platforms is not secure. Therefore, various kinds of securities protocol and strategies measures according to the security threats and attacks. As attackers adopt the latest intelligent technology for attacking the target, intelligent prevention system is required for security. In this era, artificial intelligent technology transform the machines as intelligent and smart. Therefore, AI technology is the most valuable and convenient to make smart technology implementation for the security in IoT and cloud computing environment. In this chapter various machine learning based models and framework of IoT and cloud computing security purposes have been reviewed and explored to find out the security development progress and impact in IoT and cloud platform. AI based technology also obtained to accomplish the attack to target system. Therefore, in the future, generative AI and advanced AI are required to implant the security in IoT and cloud computing platform. Strong security system is required to impose in cloud computing and IoT platform in the future. Therefore, traditional system using AI and ML is not sufficient to prevent the attacks in the future because attackers also rely on the AI and ML based techniques for attacks. Thus, innovative approaches are recommended to protect the cloud and IoT. In this regard, generative AI and block chain technologies integration are required to make effective security solutions to prevent possible attacks in IoT and cloud computing system.

## Acknowledgement

Dr. P. K. Paul of the Interdisciplinary Informatics & ICT Research Group, Department of CIS, Raiganj University, and all other stakeholders have my sincere gratitude for their encouragement, support, and help in improving the substance of my work and for helping me publish it.

**AI disclosure statement:** The author acknowledges the use of AI-based tools for minor language editing or grammatical correction. However, all intellectual contributions, analyses, and conclusions presented in this chapter are entirely the author's own.

## References


1. Abdalgawad, N., Sajun, A., Kaddoura, Y., Zualkernan, I.A., Aloul, F., Generative deep learning to detect cyberattacks for the IoT-23 dataset. *IEEE Access, 10*, 6430–6441, 2021.
2. Alrowais, F.M., Althahabi, S., Alotaibi, S.S., Mohamed, A., Hamza, M.A., Marzouk, R., Automated Machine Learning Enabled Cybersecurity Threat Detection in Internet of Things Environment. *Comput. Syst. Sci. Eng., 45*, 1, 687–700, 2023.
3. Alwahedi, F., Aldhaheri, A., Ferrag, M.A., Battah, A., Tihanyi, N., Machine learning techniques for IoT security: Current research and future vision with generative AI and large language models. *Internet Things Cyber-Phys. Syst., 4*, 167–185, 2024.
4. Aslan, O., Aktuğ, S.S., Ozkan-Okay, M., Yilmaz, A.A., Akin, E., A comprehensive review of cyber security vulnerabilities, threats, attacks, and solutions. *Electronics, 12*, 6, 1333, 2023.
5. Anwer, M., Khan, S.M., Farooq, M.U., Attack detection in IoT using machine learning. *Eng. Technol. Appl. Sci. Res., 11*, 3, 7273–7278, 2021.
6. Attou, H., Guezzaz, A., Benkirane, S., Azrour, M., Farhaoui, Y., Cloud-based intrusion detection approach using machine learning techniques. *Big Data Min. Anal., 6*, 3, 311–320, 2023.
7. Bajpai, S. and Chaurasia, K.S.B.K., Intrusion detection system in IoT network using ML. *NeuroQuantology, 20*, 13, 3597, 2022.
8. Balaji, S. and Narayanan, S.S., Dynamic distributed generative adversarial network for intrusion detection system over internet of things. *Wirel. Netw., 29*, 5, 1949–1967, 2023.
9. Balasubramaniam, S., Vijesh Joe, C., Sivakumar, T.A., Prasanth, A., Satheesh Kumar, K., Kavitha, V., Dhanaraj, R.K., Optimization Enabled Deep Learning-Based DDoS Attack Detection in Cloud Computing. *Int. J. Intell. Syst., 2023*, 1, 2039217, 2023.
10. Bendovschi, A., Cyber-attacks–trends, patterns and security countermeasures. *Procedia Econ. Finance, 28*, 24–31, 2015.
11. Botta, A., De Donato, W., Persico, V., Pescapé, A., Integration of cloud computing and internet of things: a survey. *Future Gener. Comput. Syst., 56*, 684–700, 2016.
12. Butt, U.A., Mehmood, M., Shah, S.B.H., Amin, R., Shaukat, M.W., Raza, S.M., Piran, M.J., A review of machine learning algorithms for cloud computing security. *Electronics, 9*, 9, 1379, 2020.
13. Cam, N.T. and Trung, N.G., An Intelligent Approach to Improving the Performance of Threat Detection in IoT. *IEEE Access, 11*, 44319–44334, 2023.
14. Check Point, Check Point Research Reports Highest Increase of Global Cyber Attacks seen in last two years – a 30% Increase in Q2 2024 Global CyberAttacks, 2024, retrieve from https://blog.checkpoint.com/research/

check-point-research-reports-highest-increase-of-global-cyber-attacks-seen-in-last-two-years-a-30-increase-in-q2-2024-global-cyber-attacks/.
15. Das, R. and Morris, T.H., Machine learning and cyber security, in: *2017 International Conference on Computer, Electrical & Communication Engineering (ICCECE)*, IEEE, pp. 1–7, 2017.
16. Delipetrev, B., Tsinaraki, C., Kostic, U., Historical evolution of artificial intelligence, 2020, ISBN 978-92-76-18940-4, doi:10.2760/801580, JRC120469.
17. Diro, A.A. and Chilamkurti, N., Distributed attack detection scheme using deep learning approach for Internet of Things. *Future Gener. Comput. Syst.*, *82*, 761–768, 2018.
18. Dutta, V., Choraś, M., Pawlicki, M., Kozik, R., A deep learning ensemble for network anomaly and cyber-attack detection. *Sensors*, *20*, 16, 4583, 2020.
19. Fernando, G.P., Brayan, A.A.H., Florina, A.M., Liliana, C.B., Héctor-Gabriel, A.M., Reinel, T.S., Enhancing Intrusion Detection in IoT Communications Through ML Model Generalization With a New Dataset (idsai). *IEEE Access*, 11, 70542–70559, 2023.
20. Ferrag, M.A., Debbah, M., Al-Hawawreh, M., Generative AI for cyber threat-hunting in 6g-enabled iot networks, in: *2023 IEEE/ACM 23rd International Symposium on Cluster, Cloud and Internet Computing Workshops (CCGridW)*, IEEE, pp. 16–25, 2023.
21. Ganne, A., IoT Threats & Implementation of AI/ML to Address Emerging Cyber Security Issues in IoT with Cloud Computing. *Int. Res. J. Modern. Eng. Technol. Sci.*, *5*, 2023.
22. Garg, S., Kaur, K., Kaddoum, G., Garigipati, P., Aujla, G.S., Security in IoT-driven mobile edge computing: New paradigms, challenges, and opportunities. *IEEE Network*, 35, 5, 298–305, 2021.
23. Ghelani, D., Cyber security, cyber threats, implications and future perspectives: A Review. *Am. J. Sci. Eng. Technol.*, 3, 6, 12–19, 2022.
24. Gopalakrishnan, T., Ruby, D., Al-Turjman, F., Gupta, D., Pustokhina, I.V., Pustokhin, D.A., Shankar, K., Deep learning enabled data offloading with cyber attack detection model in mobile edge computing systems. *IEEE Access*, *8*, 185938–185949, 2020.
25. Guembe, B., Azeta, A., Misra, S., Osamor, V.C., Fernandez-Sanz, L., Pospelova, V., The emerging threat of ai-driven cyber-attacks: A review. *Appl. Artif. Intell.*, *36*, 1, 2037254, 2022.
26. Gupta, M., Akiri, C., Aryal, K., Parker, E., Praharaj, L., From chatgpt to threatgpt: Impact of generative ai in cybersecurity and privacy. *IEEE Access*, *11*, 80218–80245, 2023.
27. Harbi, Y., Aliouat, Z., Refoufi, A., Harous, S., Recent security trends in internet of things: A comprehensive survey. *IEEE Access*, *9*, 113292–113314, 2021.
28. Javeed, D., Badamasi, U.M., Iqbal, T., Umar, A., Ndubuisi, C.O., Threat detection using machine/deep learning in IoT environments. *Int. J. Comput. Netw. Commun. Secur.*, *8*, 8, 59–65, 2020.

29. Jullian, O., Otero, B., Rodriguez, E., Gutierrez, N., Antona, H., Canal, R., Deep-learning based detection for cyber-attacks in IoT networks: A distributed attack detection framework. *J. Netw. Syst. Manage.*, *31*, 2, 33, 2023.
30. Karande, J. and Joshi, S., Real-time detection of cyber-attacks on the IoT devices, in: *2020 11th International Conference on Computing, Communication and Networking Technologies (ICCCNT)*, IEEE, pp. 1–6, 2020.
31. Kasula, V.K., Yadulla, A.R., Konda, B., Yenugula, M., Fortifying cloud environments against data breaches: A novel AI-driven security framework. *World J. Adv. Res. Rev.*, *24*, 1613–1626, 2024.
32. Kaur, J. and Ramkumar, K.R., The recent trends in cyber security: A review. *J. King Saud Univ. Comput. Inf. Sci.*, *34*, 8, 5766–5781, 2022.
33. Kavitha, D. and Thejas, S., Ai enabled threat detection: Leveraging artificial intelligence for advanced security and cyber threat mitigation. *IEEE Access*, 2024.
34. Khalil, I.M., Khreishah, A., Azeem, M., Cloud computing security: A survey. *Computers*, *3*, 1, 1–35, 2014.
35. Khan, Z.F., Alshahrani, S.M., Alghamdi, A.A., Alangari, S., Altamami, N.I., Alissa, K.A., Al-Wesabi, F.N., Machine Learning Based Cybersecurity Threat Detection for Secure IoT Assisted Cloud Environment. *Comput. Syst. Sci. Eng.*, *47*, 1, 855–871, 2023.
36. Li, Y. and Liu, Q., A comprehensive review study of cyber-attacks and cyber security; Emerging trends and recent developments. *Energy Rep.*, *7*, 8176–8186, 2021.
37. Liu, Z., Hu, J., Liu, Y., Roy, K., Yuan, X., Xu, J., Anomaly-based intrusion on IoT networks using aigan-a generative adversarial network. *IEEE Access, 11*, 91116–91132, 2023.
38. Mishra, S., Albarakati, A., Sharma, S.K., Cyber threat intelligence for IoT using machine learning. *Processes, 10*, 12, 2673, 2022.
39. Mukherjee, M., Matam, R., Shu, L., Maglaras, L., Ferrag, M.A., Choudhury, N., Kumar, V., Security and privacy in fog computing: Challenges. *IEEE Access*, 5, 19293–19304, 2017.
40. O'Reilly, D., Types of Machine Learning and Their Application retrieve from https://www.dataversity.net/types-of-machine-learning-and-their-applications/, 2023.
41. Pouyanfar, S., Sadiq, S., Yan, Y., Tian, H., Tao, Y., Reyes, M.P., Iyengar, S.S., A survey on deep learning: Algorithms, techniques, and applications. *ACM Comput. Surv. (CSUR)*, *51*, 5, 1–36, 2018.
42. Rehan, H., AI-Driven Cloud Security: The Future of Safeguarding Sensitive Data in the Digital Age. *J. Artif. Intell. Gen. Sci. (JAIGS)* ISSN 3006-4023, 1, 1, 132–151, 2024.
43. Roman, R., Lopez, J., Mambo, M., Mobile edge computing, fog *et al.*: A survey and analysis of security threats and challenges. *Future Gener. Comput. Syst.*, *78*, 680–698, 2018.

44. Rupanetti, D. and Kaabouch, N., Combining Edge Computing-Assisted Internet of Things Security with Artificial Intelligence: Applications, Challenges, and Opportunities. *Appl. Sci., 14*, 16, 7104, 2024.
45. Sabella, D., Maloor, K., Smith, N., Vanderveen, M., Kourtis, A., Edge Computing Cybersecurity standards: protecting infrastructure and applications. *IEEE Access*, 2024, DOI: 10.1109/ACCESS.2024.3506212.
46. Sadhu, A.K.R. and Reddy, A.K., Exploiting the Power of Machine Learning for Proactive Anomaly Detection and Threat Mitigation in the Burgeoning Landscape of Internet of Things (IoT) Networks. *Distrib. Learn. Broad Appl. Sci. Res., 4*, 30–58, 2018.
47. Sai, S., Yashvardhan, U., Chamola, V., Sikdar, B., Generative ai for cyber security: Analyzing the potential of chatgpt, dall-e and other models for enhancing the security space. *IEEE Access*, 2024.
48. Sarker, I.H., Machine learning: Algorithms, real-world applications and research directions. *SN Comput. Sci., 2*, 3, 160, 2021.
49. Sharma, A. and Singh, U.K., Modelling of smart risk assessment approach for cloud computing environment using AI & supervised machine learning algorithms. *Global Transitions Proc., 3*, 1, 243–250, 2022.
50. Shahzad, F., State-of-the-art survey on cloud computing security challenges, approaches and solutions. *Procedia Comput. Sci., 37*, 357–362, 2014.
51. Shaukat, K., Luo, S., Varadharajan, V., Hameed, I.A., Xu, M., A survey on machine learning techniques for cyber security in the last decade. *IEEE Access, 8*, 222310–222354, 2020.
52. Stergiou, C., Psannis, K.E., Kim, B.G., Gupta, B., Secure integration of IoT and cloud computing. *Future Gener. Comput. Syst., 78*, 964–975, 2018.
53. Stojmenovic, I. and Wen, S., The fog computing paradigm: Scenarios and security issues, in: *2014 Federated Conference on Computer Science and Information Systems*, IEEE, pp. 1–8, 2014.
54. Tomer, V. and Sharma, S., Detecting IoT attacks using an ensemble machine learning model. *Future Internet, 14*, 4, 102, 2022.
55. Unal, D., Bennbaia, S., Catak, F.O., Machine learning for the security of healthcare systems based on Internet of Things and edge computing, in: *Cyber security and cognitive science*, pp. 299–320, Academic Press, 2022.
56. Vallabhaneni, R., Vaddadi, S.A., Pillai, S.E.V.S., Addula, S.R., Ananthan, B., Detection of cyberattacks using bidirectional generative adversarial network. *Indones. J. Electr. Eng. Comput. Sci., 35*, 3, 1653–1660, 2024.
57. Verma, A. and Kaushal, S., Cloud computing security issues and challenges: a survey, in: *Advances in Computing and Communications: First International Conference, ACC 2011, Kochi, India, July 22-24, 2011, Proceedings, Part IV 1*, pp. 445–454, Springer Berlin Heidelberg, 2011.
58. Wazid, M., Das, A.K., Chamola, V., Park, Y., Uniting cyber security and machine learning: Advantages, challenges and future research. *ICT Express, 8*, 3, 313–321, 2022.

59. Yamin, M.M., Ullah, M., Ullah, H., Katt, B., Weaponized AI for cyber-attacks. *J. Inf. Secur. Appl.*, *57*, 102722, 2021.
60. Yavanoglu, O. and Aydos, M., A review on cyber security datasets for machine learning algorithms, in: *2017 IEEE International Conference on Big Data (Big Data)*, IEEE, pp. 2186–2193, 2017.
61. Zaman, S., Alhazmi, K., Aseeri, M.A., Ahmed, M.R., Khan, R.T., Kaiser, M.S., Mahmud, M., Security threats and artificial intelligence based countermeasures for internet of things networks: A comprehensive survey. *IEEE Access*, *9*, 94668–94690, 2021.
62. Zewdie, T.G. and Girma, A., IoT Security and The Role of AI/ML to Combat Emerging Cyber Threats in Cloud Computing Environment. *Issues Inf. Syst.*, *21*, 4, 2020.

8

# Deep Learning Driven Heteromorphic Block Cipher (DL-HBC) Framework for Asynchronous Data Transmission in Heterogeneous Cloud Based Network

**Nivedita Ray[1,2*], Shreya Kumari[1], Ankita Bera[1], Shruti Singh[1] and Anirban Kundu[1,2]**

*[1]Netaji Subhash Engineering College, Kolkata, India*
*[2]Computer Innovative Research Society, West Bengal, India*

***Abstract***

We propose a deep learning driven heteromorphic encryption framework for asynchronous data transmission in heterogeneous cloud-based network in this research. Our paper integrates deep learning with cryptographic methods to improve security, performance evaluation, and potential threats. In this approach, data is sliced into finite number of pieces according to the requirement. Then, each part of the data is encrypted following specific procedure. Each encrypted data is transferred to public cloud structure. At server side, noise filter is attached to minimize the unwanted noise from public cloud. Generated key is kept safe in private cloud having security measures. Each encrypted data is decrypted using specific keys. Finally, all the decrypted fragments are joined maintaining proper sequence to recover original data. With everyday production of quintillion bytes of data, storing and managing their traffic has become difficult. Cloud based networking provides solution to this problem. It's effective since cloud manages the direct traffic with providing connectivity, security and management of data. For the sole purpose of security and making it cost efficient, asynchronous mode of data transmission is taken into consideration in our approach. Cloud can either be homogeneous or heterogeneous. Heterogeneous cloud is preferred over others because all the data are not stored at a single place, even if something goes wrong, the whole service does not immobilize. Work is continued through other

**Corresponding author*: nivedita.raydesarkar@gmail.com

Partha Ghosh, Rajdeep Chakraborty, Anupam Ghosh and Ahmed A. Elngar (eds.) Strategic Approaches to Intrusion Detection in Cloud-IoT Ecosystem, (189–224) © 2026 Scrivener Publishing LLC

sources of data storage. Homogeneous Deep Learning based Encryption (DLE) is mostly used for the encryption of data. Using a single encryption algorithm makes it easier for the hackers to decrypt the data. This entire thing can be avoided by using heterogeneous DLE framework described in this paper. Use of Deep Neural Network (DNNs) for dynamic key generation, selection of encryption mode aided in self-adaptive cryptographic solutions.

***Keywords***: Encryption, heteromorphic encryption, asynchronous data transmission, cloud, heterogeneous cloud, deep learning, deep neural network (DNN), deep learning based encryption (DLE)

## 8.1 Introduction

### 8.1.1 Overview

Interconnected set of autonomous computers which are linked to share resources and exchange information among themselves is known as computer networks. Common communication protocols is used by computers over digital interconnections for communication among themselves. These interconnections comprise the telecommunication network technologies, based on wired, optical or wireless radio-frequency methods. They use extended interpersonal communication by electronic means which include instant messaging, email, online chatting, voice and video conferencing. A network allows sharing files, data and other types of information giving authorized users the ability to access information. These data are transmitted to communicate with the counter parts [1–4].

Heteromorphic encryption and homomorphic encryption differ from each other in their approach to data transformation and security. Homomorphic encryption allows computations on ciphertext without decryption, which in turn preserves mathematical operations. Heteromorphic encryption uses variety of transformation methods for encryption and decryption. Heteromorphic encryption involves fragmenting data, encrypting each fragment with distinct keys, and reassembling them in sequence. This process enhances security and efficiency. Heteromorphic encryption also supports asynchronous data transmission, which makes it more suitable for cost-efficient and secure communication.

Data transmission enables the transfer of digital data, either in analog or digital form, from a source device to one or more recipient devices through communication media like copper wires, wireless carriers, or optical fiber. The transmitted signals, which may be baseband or passband, are structured as discrete digital bit streams for efficient delivery [5–7].

A deep learning-based security framework for cloud computing, combining SqueezeNet with Rat Optimization Algorithm (ROA) for selection of sensitive data and a Lightweight Transformation Model (LWTM) for encryption is discussed in [8]. Experimental results show improved security, reduction in cipher size, and enhanced processing efficiency compared to existing cloud security standards.

[9–12], focuses on asynchronous data transmission, a cost-effective method where data is sent one byte at a time without requiring a clock for synchronization. Each transmitted character consists of 8 data bits and two parity bits, enabling straightforward, efficient, and one-way communication.

A cloud network is a computer network that operates within or as part of a cloud computing infrastructure, facilitating connectivity between cloud-based applications, services, and solutions. It can be either cloud-based or cloud-enabled, enabling communication between cloud components, external users, and applications. Functioning similarly to a standard computer network, it is centered on cloud computing operations and devices. For example, a cloud network connects remote users to cloud applications (SaaS), cloud infrastructure (IaaS), and enables communication between virtual machines [13–16].

### 8.1.2 Literature Survey

Authors have constructed first multi-input functional encryption for quadratic functions from pairings. Earlier multi-input functional encryption schemes have supported linear functions and/or relied on cryptographic postulations similar to multi-linear maps [17]. Researchers have discussed on typical two-phase performance of round and random key based crypto encryption to advance security framework. It manages high level implementation of protection having key verification methods using random encryption [18].

Authors have discussed an encryption technique based on combination between linear feedback shift register and generalized Feistel networks depending on substitution boxes [19]. Basic security of wireless sensor networks is ensured by the researchers using block encryption algorithm based on chaotic substitution box, which is generated based on different types of maps such as compound chaotic, sinusoidal chaotic, using linear generator [20].

Data Encryption Standard (DES) is a symmetric-key block cipher, published by the National Institute of Standards and Technology (NIST).

It is an implementation of Feistel Cipher and uses 16 rounds of Feistel structure to encrypt data in blocks of size 64 bits each. The process of encryption involves three main steps such as initial permutation, 16 Feistel rounds, and final permutation or inverse initial permutation. DES satisfy the properties of avalanche effect which is a small change in plaintext results within the large change in the ciphertext, and completeness using each bit of ciphertext based on many bits of plaintext. It makes the cipher very strong, so that it can be broken only using brute-force search having high time complexity, and also is vulnerable to attacks using linear cryptanalysis [21–24].

Advanced Encryption Algorithm (AES) is a symmetric block cipher algorithm which was first published by the National Institute of Standards and Technology (NIST). It is mainly developed as an alternative for DES, when it started to become vulnerable to brute-force attacks. AES includes block ciphers of different key-lengths. Encryption and decryption of data involve the processes of substitution, transposition and mixing of given data. AES is advantageous and is widely used [25–28].

RSA is asymmetric cryptography algorithm. It uses different keys for encryption and decryption for secure transmission of messages. It is an example of public key cryptography. The public key which is used for encrypting messages, with an intention that messages encrypted with the public key can only be decrypted using the private key within stipulated timeframe. Typically, RSA involves public key and private key. Public key is used for encryption and private key is used for decryption of message. There are mainly two reasons for not using the typical RSA algorithm in our approach, such as the product of prime numbers being transmitted with public key, makes it easy to be found by hit and trial. This reduces the security quotient of RSA algorithm. Moreover, any hacker can try to encrypt a plaintext with the use of public key. If any cipher text is found matching with encrypted text using hit and trial method, then the intruder can easily try to decipher the secret message [29–32].

Homomorphic encryption is a form of public key encryption in which computations like addition, multiplication etc. can be done on the data without decrypting them, and thus gets the work done without compromising the integrity of the data. It can be of two types, partial homomorphic (PHE) and fully homomorphic (FHE). PHE allows either addition or multiplication operation at a time whereas FHE supports both addition and multiplication operations on the encrypted data. Homomorphic encryption can be used in various practical operations, such as securing data stored in the cloud, improving data security in elections, preserving the privacy of customers in different fields like medical, financial, providing security and privacy in LTE-based public safety network etc. There are some limitations of this form of encryption. Homomorphic encryption cannot be used if there exist multiple users of the same database, as computations based on this encryption is at least 106 times slower than the computations on the plain text [33–36].

[37], integrates deep learning with homomorphic encryption and secure multi-party computation (MPC). It enables privacy-preserving model inference in cloud environments. The proposed framework ensures encryption of user data throughout processing, while users lack access to model parameters or structure. Experimental results on encrypted MNIST and CIFAR-10 datasets demonstrate high classification accuracy, closely matching plaintext performance.

This paper [38], proposes a novel image encryption algorithm using hyperchaotic maps and CNNs to enhance security and robustness. Key sensitivity analysis and statistical metrics confirm its resilience to noise and unauthorized decryption. The method ensures efficient and secure image transmission in big data applications.

In this paper, [39], presents a deep-learning-based cryptanalysis method for lightweight block ciphers, reducing training parameters by 93.16% and improving accuracy by 5.3%. Results confirm that full-key recovery is practically not feasible. It highlights deep learning's limitations in cryptanalysis.

This paper [40], uses deep learning techniques to identify encryption algorithms. It is done by analyzing ciphertext and enhanced targeted cryptanalysis. A cipher text corpus is used in multiple languages to compare deep learning classifiers with traditional machine learning methods for AES and Blowfish encryption detection.

In [41], a symmetric-key encryption and decryption method using an autoencoder neural network, with keys generated from alphanumeric passwords. Experimental results show this approach surpasses traditional algorithms in performance for small text files. Thus, offering enhanced security and resistance to any type brute force attacks.

### 8.1.3 Aim

Our aim is to find out a solution on heteromorphic DLE by proposing a framework toward data transmission in asynchronous mode within heterogeneous cloud network.

### 8.1.4 Scope

Heteromorphic DLE based framework design and its functionalities are the scope of this research work.

### 8.1.5 Motivation

Homomorphic encryption has limitations while applying in enterprise-based applications and database related activities. Fully homomorphic encryption techniques are slow. It needs huge buffer space compared to typical textual operations exhibiting impractical for most of the database searches. A set of homomorphic encryption requires previous idea of queries types. A set of homomorphic encryption techniques has restricted functionality, so some queries are not possible on encrypted data even if they are known in advance. Therefore, we bring heteromorphic DLE framework in focus.

### 8.1.6 Organization

The rest of the paper is organized as follows: Section 8.2 represents system design and architecture for heteromorphic DLE; Section 8.3 describes the procedures involved in heteromorphic DLE; Section 8.4 shows the detailed procedural explanation for system design and architecture; Section 8.5 exhibits the analysis on asynchronous data transmission; Section 8.6 describes experimental observations. Finally, the conclusion helps us to conclude the work.

## 8.2 System Design and Architecture for Heteromorphic DLE

Original data is sliced into finite number of pieces according to the requirement. Each data fragment (str_i) is encrypted using a specific algorithm (encrypt_i). Each encrypted data fragment is sent to the public cloud. Further, encrypted data is received by the receiver end as required, applying noise filter to remove unwanted noises from the public cloud. Generated key (key_i) based on particular encryption function is stored in private cloud ensuring security. Each encrypted data fragment (encrypt_i) is decrypted using specific keys (key_i). Finally, all the decrypted fragments are accumulated maintaining proper sequence to achieve the source data at receiver end (refer to Figure 8.1).

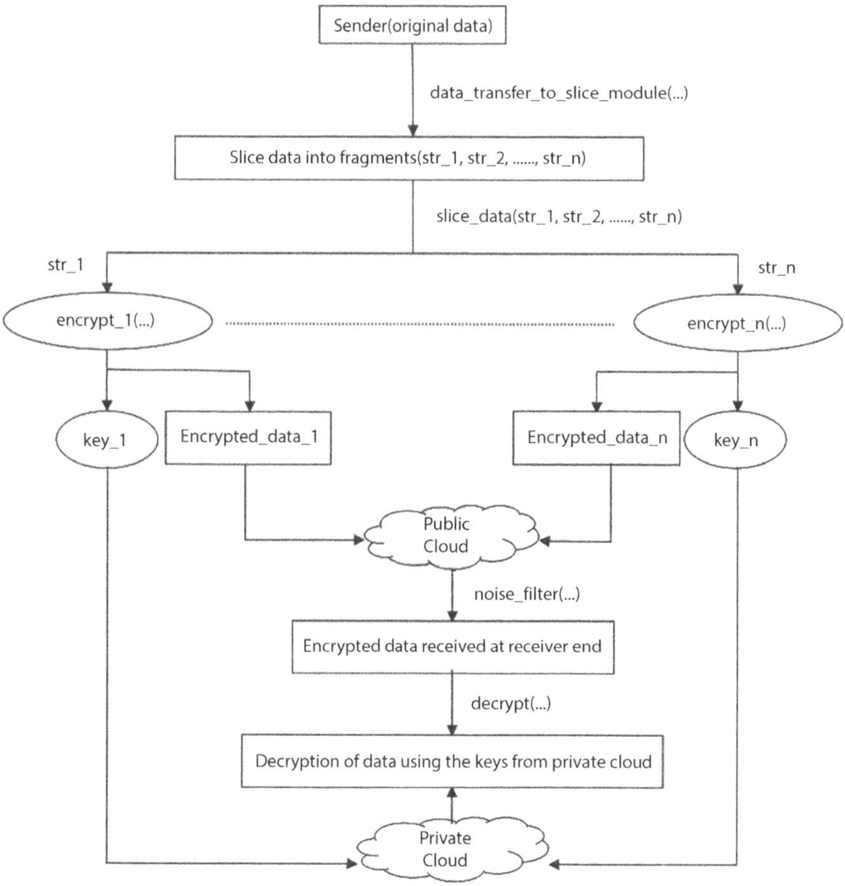


**Figure 8.1** Proposed framework for heteromorphic DLE.

## 8.3 Procedure for Heteromorphic DLE

Overall message is considered as "str". A message is divided into several parts as shown below:

$$str = \{str\_1, str\_2, ......, str\_n\}$$

Overall key is a set of distinct keys which are being used for different parts of the message.

$$key = \{key\_1, key\_2, ......, key\_n\}$$

Overall encryption is considered as the accumulation of distinct encryptions used to encrypt the different parts of the message.

encrypt(...) = {encrypt_1(...),encrypt_2(...), ........, encrypt_n(...)}

Similarly, the whole encrypted data is the accumulation of fragmented encrypted data.

Encrypted_data = {Encrypted_data_1, Encrypted_data_2, ......, Encrypted_data_n}

Overall decryption function is the combination of several decryption functions which are being used to decrypt the different parts of the message.

decrypt(...) = {decrypt_1(...),decrypt_2(...), ........, decrypt_n(...)}

Similarly, the whole decrypted data is the accumulation of fragmented decrypted data.

Decrypted_data = {Decrypted_data_1, Decrypted_data_2, ......, Decrypted_data_n}

---

**Algorithm 8.1** Encrypt_Schedule.

---

**Input:** Original data, number of encrypt functions, number of keys

**Output:** Encrypted data

Step 1: Call data_transfer_to_slice_module(...) [refer Algorithm 8.2]
Step 2: Call slice_data(str) [refer Algorithm 8.3]
Step 3: str = {str_1, str_2, ......, str_n}
Step 4: Call generate_key(...) [refer Algorithm 8.4]
Step 5: key = {key_1, key_2, ......, key_n}
Step 6: Call encrypt(...) [refer Algorithm 8.5]
Step 7: Encrypted_data = {Encrypted_data_1, Encrypted_data_2, ......, Encrypted_data_n}
Step 8: Stop

---

Algorithm 8.1 describes an overview of the whole encryption procedure. It mentions all the steps involved, from slicing of the original data to generating the key and applying these keys to encrypt the fragmented data to secure from any kind of possible attacks.

**Algorithm 8.2** Data_transfer_to_slice_module.

**Input:** Original data

**Output:** Fragmented data

Step 1: Arrange data in a [X*X] 2-D array
Step 2: Loop start
Step 3: Divide chosen string (data) into fragments using vertical fragmentation technique

t_i[]={c_i1[], c_i2[], ..........., c_in[]}

Step 4: Loop end
Step 5: Stop

In Algorithm 8.2, the original data from the sender is arranged in 2D array and sent to the slicing module to achieve the fragmented data using vertical fragmentation technique.

**Algorithm 8.3** slice_data(str).

**Input:** Fragmented data

**Output:** Sliced data with a predefined size such as str_1, str_2, ... str_n

Step 1: Set of columns to slice data =f(t_i[], c_ij)
Step 2: Loop start
Step 3: str_[i]= c_[i][j]
Step 4: loop end
Step 5: Stop

The fragmented data is converted into sliced data of predefined size, and each data slice is encrypted using Algorithm 8.3.

**Algorithm 8.4** generate_key(...).

**Input:** keyset[][], Sliced data with a predefined size such as str_1, str_2, ... str_n

**Output:** key_i[]

Step 1: Select two prime numbers (Prime_1&Prime_2)
Step 2: Multiply Prime_1 & Prime_2 to achieve modulus for encryption and decryption ($MOD_{Encrypt/Decrypt}$)
Step 3: Calculate $\phi(MOD_{Encrypt/Decrypt})$ = (Prime_1-1)*(Prime_2-1)

Step 4: Select a random integer ($E_{Random}$)
GCD ($\phi$($MOD_{Encrypt/Decrypt}$),$E_{Random}$)=1;
1<$E_{Random}$< $\phi$($MOD_{Encrypt/Decrypt}$); where, $E_{Random}$ is public key exponent;
Step 5: Calculate public key ($Key_{Public}$)
if (Prime_1>Prime_2)
($MOD_{Encrypt/Decrypt}$-Prime_1)<$Key_{Public}$<$MOD_{Encrypt/Decrypt}$
$Key_{Public}$ must be co-prime to $MOD_{Encrypt/Decrypt}$
else if (Prime_1<Prime_2)
($MOD_{Encrypt/Decrypt}$-Prime_2)<$Key_{Public}$<$MOD_{Encrypt/Decrypt}$
$Key_{Public}$ must be co-prime to $MOD_{Encrypt/Decrypt}$
Formula to find $Key_{Public}$: (refer [X])
$E_{Random}$*Exp($Key_{Private}$) mod ($Key_{Public}$)=1; where Exp($Key_{Private}$) is private key exponent;
Exp($Key_{Private}$)* $E_{Random}$=1* mod($Key_{Public}$)
Step 6: Public key:($Key_{Public}$)
Private key:($Key_{Public}$,Exponent($Key_{Private}$))
Step 8: Stop

Algorithm 8.4 generates public key and private key for sliced data to achieve encryption and decryption. The public key and private key exponents are found following the steps executed using the prescribed formula as mentioned in the algorithm. Initially, two prime numbers are typically selected to multiply and further achieve modulus for encryption and decryption. Calculate the $\phi$ function, and GCD to find out the public key and private key. Sender transfers data with the public key, and receiver receives the data with the private key.

**Algorithm 8.5** encrypt(...).

**Input:** key_i[], str_i[], keyset[][]

**Output:** Encrypted_data_i[]

Step 1: number_of_computation_required_to_encrypt = f(keyset[][], key_i)
Step 2: Loop start
Step 3: Encrypted_data_i[] = map(str_i[], key_i[], number_of_computation_required_to_encrypt)
Step 4: Loop end
Step 5: Stop

Algorithm 8.5 takes plain text and key as input and produces encrypted message as output and the cipher text is sent to the receiver. Public and private keys have been generated, and could be used according to demand. The encrypt function is being executed using predefined map table utilizing str[i], key[i], and number of computation required to encrypt.

---

**Algorithm 8.6** Decrypt_Schedule.

---

**Input:** Encrypted data, key

**Output:** Decrypted data

Step 1: Call decrypt(...) [refer Algorithm 8.7]
Step 2: Decrypted_data = {Encrypted_data_1, Encrypted_data_2, ......, Encrypted_data_n}
Step 3: Stop

---

In Algorithm 8.6, the encrypted data is received at the receiver end, and the decryption function is carried out on the encrypted data by calling Algorithm 8.7. The Decrypt_schedule takes the whole set of cipher text and key as the input, and converts the cipher text into the decrypted data consisting of all the parts.

---

**Algorithm 8.7** decrypt(...).

---

**Input:** Encrypted_data_i[], keyset[][], key_i

**Output:** Decrypted_data_i[]

Step 1: number_of_computation_required_to_decrypt = f(keyset[][], key_i)
Step 2: Loop start
Step 3: Decrypted_data_i [] = map(str_i[], key_i[], number_of_computation_required_to_decrypt)
Step 4: Loop End
Step 5: Stop

---

Algorithm 8.7 defines the decryption process where the encrypted data along with the keys and keyset are taken as input and the keys and keysets are assigned to corresponding encrypted data to do the required calculations to decrypt further using an iterative method following predefined mapping and number of computations involved to decrypt.

## 8.4 Detailed Procedural Explanation for Design Framework

After receiving the original data, it is arranged using a two-dimensional (2D) array [X*X]. Start iteration to obtain fragmented data. The data is being sliced into finite number of fragments using vertical fragmentation technique.

$$t\_i[]=\{c\_i1[], c\_i2[], \ldots\ldots\ldots.., c\_in[]\}$$

The fragmented data is converted into sliced data having predefined size, such as str_1, str_2, …., str_n. For key generation, consider the keyset[][] and previously sliced data with a predefined size as inputs. Generated key is considered as output through an advanced technique of heteromorphic (DLE) approach.

The key generation takes place as follows:

Two prime numbers are chosen randomly, and multiplied with each other resulting in modulus for encryption and decryption ($MODencrypt_{/decrypt}$).

Calculate $\phi(MOD_{Encrypt/Decrypt}) = (Prime\_1 - 1) * (Prime\_2 - 1)$.

Then, select a random integer $E_{Random}$. Calculate GCD ($\phi(MOD_{Encrypt/Decrypt})$, $E_{Random}) = 1$;

$1 < E_{Random} < \phi(MOD_{Encrypt/Decrypt})$; where, $E_{Random}$ is public key exponent;

If prime_1 is greater than prime_2, then ($MOD_{Encrypt/Decrypt}$ - Prime_1) becomes less compared to $Key_{Public}$, which is again less than $MOD_{Encrypt/Decrypt}$. $Key_{public}$ must be co-prime to $MOD_{encrypt/decrypt}$. Else, if prime_1 is less than prime_2, then ($MOD_{Encrypt/Decrypt}$ - Prime_2) becomes less compared to $Key_{Public}$, which is again less than $MOD_{Encrypt/Decrypt}$. $Key_{public}$ must be co-prime to $MOD_{encrypt/decrypt}$.

Find out $Key_{Public}$ using ($E_{Random}$ * Exp ($Key_{Private}$) mod ($Key_{Public}$)=1; where Exp ($Key_{Private}$) is private key exponent;

$$Exp(8.KeyPrivate) * ERandom= 1* mod(8.KeyPublic)$$

Upon receiving the public key and private key, get the number of computation required to encrypt f(keyset[][], key_i).

Then, use iteration to find encrypted data using map function as follows:

Encrypted_data_i[] = map(str_i[], key_i[], number_of_computation_required_to_encrypt);

To achieve decrypted data, calculate the number of computation required to decrypt using f(keyset[][], key_i) after receiving encrypted data and the corresponding keys.

Then, calculate each fragmented part of encrypted data as follows:

Decrypted_data_i [] = map(str_i[], key_i[], number_of_computation_required_to_decrypt);

Finally, receive decrypted data after certain level of computation using proper sequential derivations at the receiver end.

## 8.5 Analysis on Asynchronous Data Transmission

User account ($U_A$) should be protected using community-based encryption (E) technique to make the user accounts or groups safe. It means as follows:

$$[User\ Account]Protection \rightarrow Encrypt(Community\ based)$$

We know, $U_A = \{f_1, f_2, \ldots\ldots, f_x\}$ where f stands for features or properties of a user account.

We also know, $E(U_A) = E\{f_1, f_2, \ldots\ldots, f_x\} = \{E(f_1), E(f_2), \ldots\ldots, E(f_x)\}$; where $E(U_A)$ means the encryption of a user account.

$$\therefore [U_A = \{f_1, f_2 \ldots\ldots, f_x\}] \rightarrow E(U_A) = E\{f_1, f_2, \ldots\ldots, f_x\} \tag{8.1}$$

In case of data protection, hybrid encryption, DLE is required.

$$[Data]Protection \rightarrow Encrypt\ (Hybrid)$$

$[Data = Data_{Pub} + Data_{Pri}]$; where $Data_{Pub}$ means public data and $Data_{Pri}$ means private data;

$$[Hybrid = Public + Private]$$

$$\therefore E(Data) = E(Data_{Pub}) + E(Data_{Pri}) \tag{8.2}$$

$$Transmission\,(T) = \left[Encrypted\ User\ Info\left(E(U_A)\right) + Encrypted\ Data\left(E(Data)\right)\right] \tag{8.3}$$

$$\therefore T = \{E(U_A), E(Data)\}$$

$$\therefore T = \{E(U_A), E(Data_{Pub}), E(Data_{Pri})\} \tag{8.4}$$

Introducing "Noise" in the system framework,

$$we\ have,\ data\,noise(Data_{Noise})\ and\ transmission noise\ (T_{Noise})$$

$$\therefore Noise = \{Data_{Noise}, T_{Noise}\}$$

$$= \{Data_{Pub_{Noise}}, Data_{Pri_{Noise}}, T_{Noise}\} \tag{8.5}$$

Motivation of Theorem 1 is to find out the relationship between data encryption and user properties.

**Theorem 1: Encryption varies based on user properties.**
Proof: According to Equation (8.1), $U_A$ is dependent on the set of features $(f_x)$.

$$\therefore E(U_A) = \{E(f_1), E(f_2), \ldots\ldots, E(f_x)\}$$

$$if\,(f_i <> f_j)\,then$$

$$E(f_i) <> E(f_j)$$

Hence, it is proved that encryption varies based on user properties.
(End of proof)

Motivation of Theorem 2 is to establish the relationship between user properties and data transmission.

**Theorem 2: User Properties are subset of transmission.**
Proof: From Equation (8.4), $T = \{E(U_A), E(Data_{Pub}), E(Data_{Pri})\}$

$$\therefore E(U_A) \epsilon T$$

$$\therefore U_A \epsilon T$$

$$\therefore U_A \subseteq T$$

Also, we know that, $U_A = \{f_1, f_2, \ldots\ldots, f_x\}$

$$\{f_1, f_2 \ldots\ldots, f_x\} \subseteq T$$

Hence, it is proved that the user properties are subset of transmission. (End of proof)

Motivation of Theorem 3 is to establish whether user accounts, data & its noise, along with transmission noise are correlated with the range of transmission between client & server sides. Transmission is to be considered as most significant factor to form relations between distinct entities geographically distributed. Theorem 3 is developed for identification of specific transmission from either side.

**Theorem 3: Transmission depends on User accounts, data, data noise, and transmission noise.**

Proof: As per Eq. (8.1), user accounts are connected with encrypted user properties.

$$\therefore U_A \epsilon f_x; where\ x = 1, 2, \ldots\ldots$$

Adding "Noise" to the transmission, we get from Eq. (8.4) and Eq. (8.5),

$$T = \left\{E(U_A), E(Data_{Pub}), E(Data_{Pri}), Data_{Pub_{Noise}}, Data_{Pri_{Noise}}, T_{Noise}\right\} \tag{8.6}$$

$$\therefore U_A \epsilon T$$

$$\therefore Data_{Pub} \epsilon T \ \&\& \ Data_{Pri} \epsilon T$$

$$\therefore Data \epsilon T$$

Also $Data_{Pub_{Noise}} \epsilon T$ && $Data_{Pri_{Noise}} \epsilon T$

$\therefore Data\ Noise \epsilon\ T$

Also $T_{Noise} \epsilon\ T$

Hence, it is proved that transmission depends on user accounts, data, data noise, and transmission noise.
(End of proof)

Motivation of Theorem 4 is to establish the uniqueness of block wise data transmission.

**Theorem 4: Block wise data transmission is unique compared to other blocks of the overall transmission.**
Proof: Introducing "Block transmission" $(B_{T_i})$ in the system framework,

$$we\ have, T = \{B_{T_1}, B_{T_2}, \ldots\ldots, B_{T_n}\} \tag{8.7}$$

Combining Equation (8.6) and Eq. (8.7), we get,

$$T = \left\{ \begin{array}{c} \{E(U_A), E(Data_{Pub}), E(Data_{Pri}), Data_{Pub_{Noise}}, Data_{Pri_{Noise}}, T_{Noise}\}_1, \\ \{\{E(U_A), E(Data_{Pub}), E(Data_{Pri}), Data_{Pub_{Noise}}, Data_{Pri_{Noise}}, T_{Noise}\}_2, \\ . \\ . \\ . \\ \{E(U_A), E(Data_{Pub}), E(Data_{Pri}), Data_{Pub_{Noise}}, Data_{Pri_{Noise}}, T_{Noise}\}_n \end{array} \right\} \tag{8.8}$$

$\therefore$ Each block consists of six different parts which jointly show a unique pattern due to its variation.
Hence, it is proved that block wise data transmission is unique compared to other blocks of the overall transmission.
(End of proof)

Motivation of Theorem 5 is to establish the randomization effect in encryption in case of block transmission.

**Theorem 5: Encryption becomes more randomized using block transmission.**

Proof: From Equation (8.8), we derive,

$$T = \begin{Bmatrix} \{E(U_A)_1, E(U_A)_2, \ldots\ldots, E(U_A)_n\}, \\ \{E(Data_{Pub})_1, E(Data_{Pub})_2, \ldots\ldots, E(Data_{Pub})_n\}, \\ \{E(Data_{Pri})_1, E(Data_{Pri})_2, \ldots\ldots, E(Data_{Pri})_n\}, \\ \{E(Data_{Pub_{Noise}})_1, E(Data_{Pub_{Noise}})_2, \ldots\ldots, E(Data_{Pub_{Noise}})_n\}, \\ \{E(Data_{Pri_{Noise}})_1, E(Data_{Pri_{Noise}})_2, \ldots\ldots, E(Data_{Pri_{Noise}})_n\}, \\ \{(T_{Noise})_1, (T_{Noise})_2, \ldots\ldots, (T_{Noise})_n\} \end{Bmatrix}$$

$$T = \begin{Bmatrix} Block\ of\ E(U_A)_i, Block\ of\ E(Data_{Pub})_j, \\ Block\ of\ E(Data_{Pri})_k, Block\ of\ E(Data_{Pub_{Noise}})_l, \\ Block\ of\ E(Data_{Pri_{Noise}})_m, Block\ of\ (T_{Noise})_n \end{Bmatrix}$$

$$\because Block\ of\ (T_{Noise})_n \notin E(X); where\ X\ can\ be\ any\ type\ of\ block\ considered\ in\ the\ framework;$$

$$\therefore Block\ of\ (T_{Noise})_n\ can\ be\ neglected\ further\ in\ case\ of\ transmission\ with\ respect\ to\ the\ encryption.$$

Therefore, T becomes as follows:

$$T = \begin{Bmatrix} Block\ of\ E(U_A)_i, Block\ of\ E(Data_{Pub})_j, Block\ of\ E(Data_{Pri})_k, \\ Block\ of\ E(Data_{Pub_{Noise}})_l, Block\ of\ E(Data_{Pri_{Noise}})_m \end{Bmatrix} \tag{8.9}$$

From Equation (8.9), it is evident that each block is separately considered for encryption purpose.

Hence, it is proved that encryption becomes more randomized using block transmission.

(End of proof)

## 8.6 Experimental Observations

The five text files of different sizes are used to conduct five experiments, where comparison of three algorithms AES, DES and RSA with the proposed algorithm are performed. Figure 8.2 shows the experimental results for the encryption algorithms AES, DES, RSA and proposed algorithm using five different text files for five experiments on four algorithms. **Evaluation Parameters:** Performance of encryption algorithm is evaluated considering Encryption and Decryption time.

### 8.6.1 Experimental Setup

Cryptool, an open-source tool for simulating and analyzing all cryptographic algorithms, has been used to complete the comparison in the said files.

### 8.6.2 Experimental Results

Table 8.1 and Table 8.2 show the comparison between the existing algorithms and DLE based proposed system for both encryption and decryption.

### 8.6.3 Comparative Analysis

By analyzing Figure 8.2, to Figure 8.9 we can deduce that the execution time of the proposed algorithm is much less compared to the time taken by AES, DES and RSA algorithm. This is for both encryption and decryption.

**Table 8.1** Encryption time (in seconds) comparison based on file size.

| **Encryption (in seconds)** | | | | |
|---|---|---|---|---|
| **File size (kilo bytes)** | **AES** | **DES** | **RSA** | **DLE based proposed system** |
| 32 KB | 0.15 | 0.27 | 0.13 | 0.0135 |
| 126 KB | 0.46 | 0.83 | 0.52 | 0.0292 |
| 200 KB | 0.72 | 1.19 | 0.74 | 0.0412 |
| 246 KB | 0.95 | 1.44 | 1.19 | 0.0484 |
| 280 KB | 1.12 | 1.67 | 1.39 | 0.0561 |

**Table 8.2** Decryption time (in seconds) comparison based on file size.

| Decryption (in seconds) | | | | |
|---|---|---|---|---|
| **File size (kilo bytes)** | **AES** | **DES** | **RSA** | **Proposed DLE based** |
| 32 KB | 0.15 | 0.44 | 0.15 | 0.0113 |
| 126 KB | 0.44 | 0.65 | 0.43 | 0.0159 |
| 200 KB | 0.63 | 0.85 | 0.66 | 0.0167 |
| 246 KB | 0.83 | 1.23 | 0.93 | 0.0172 |
| 280 KB | 1.1 | 1.45 | 1.23 | 0.0185 |

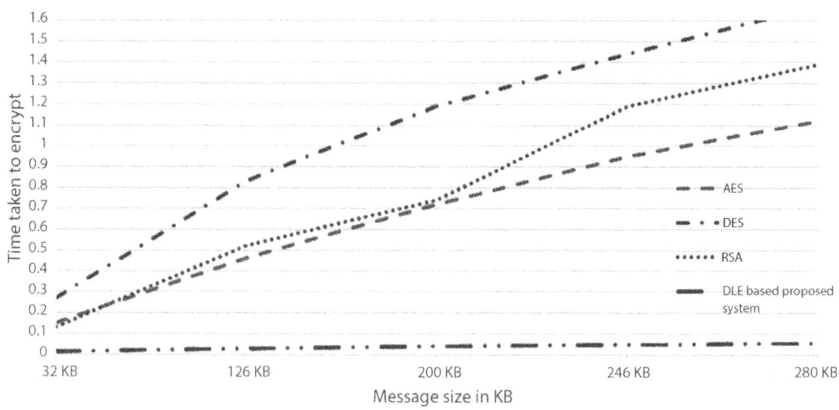


**Figure 8.2** A comparative study on encryption time between AES, DES, RSA and proposed work.

## Encryption

In Figure 8.4, the DLE based proposed approach shows better results in terms of encryption timing in seconds compared to existing AES approach (refer Table 8.3).

In Figure 8.5, the DLE based proposed approach shows better results in terms of encryption timing in seconds compared to existing DES approach (refer to Table 8.4).

In Figure 8.6, the DLE based proposed approach shows better results in terms of encryption timing in seconds compared to existing RSA approach (refer to Table 8.5).

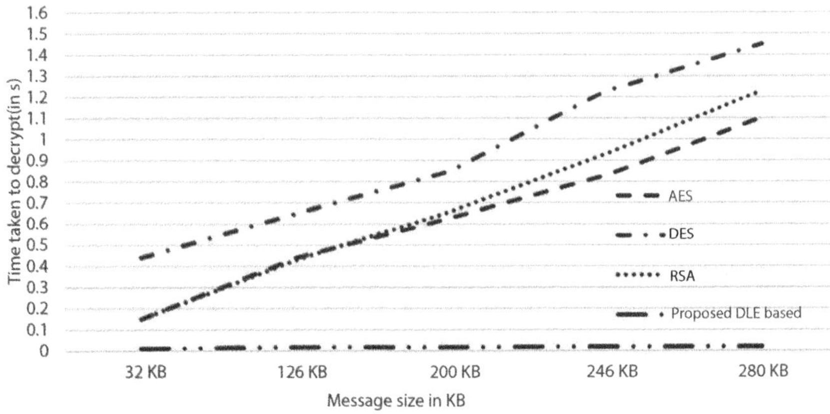


**Figure 8.3** A comparative study on decryption time between AES, DES, RSA and proposed work.

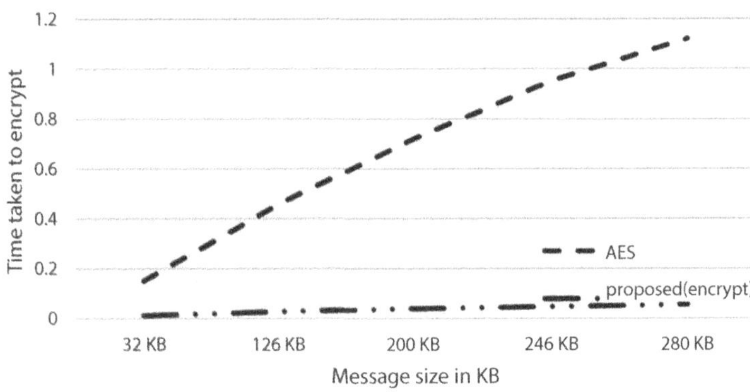


**Figure 8.4** A comparative study on encryption time between AES, and proposed algorithm using DLE.

**Table 8.3** AES vs proposed approach based on DLE.

| File size (kilo bytes) | AES | Proposed based on DLE |
|---|---|---|
| 32 KB | 0.15 | 0.0135 |
| 126 KB | 0.46 | 0.0292 |
| 200 KB | 0.72 | 0.0412 |
| 246 KB | 0.95 | 0.0484 |
| 280 KB | 1.12 | 0.0561 |

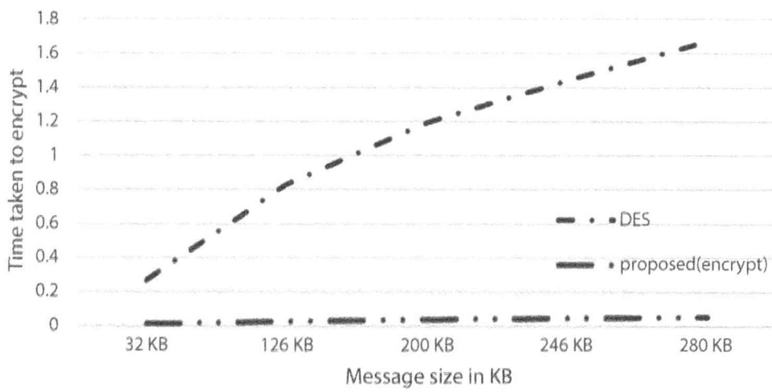


**Figure 8.5** Comparison of the encryption time between DES and proposed work using DLE.

**Table 8.4** DES vs DLE based proposed approach.

| File size (kilo bytes) | DES | DLE based proposed |
|---|---|---|
| 32 KB | 0.27 | 0.0135 |
| 126 KB | 0.83 | 0.0292 |
| 200 KB | 1.19 | 0.0412 |
| 246 KB | 1.44 | 0.0484 |
| 280 KB | 1.67 | 0.0561 |

**Decryption**

In Figure 8.7, the DLE based proposed approach shows better results in terms of decryption timing in seconds compared to existing AES approach (refer to Table 8.6).

In Figure 8.8, DLE based proposed approach shows better results in terms of decryption timing in seconds compared to existing DES approach (refer to Table 8.7).

In Figure 8.9, the DLE based proposed approach shows better results in terms of decryption timing in seconds compared to existing RSA approach (refer to Table 8.8).

### 8.6.4 Cost Analysis

Analysis of all the figures and graphs (from Figure 8.10 to Figure 8.19) shows that the time consumed by the proposed approach for encryption

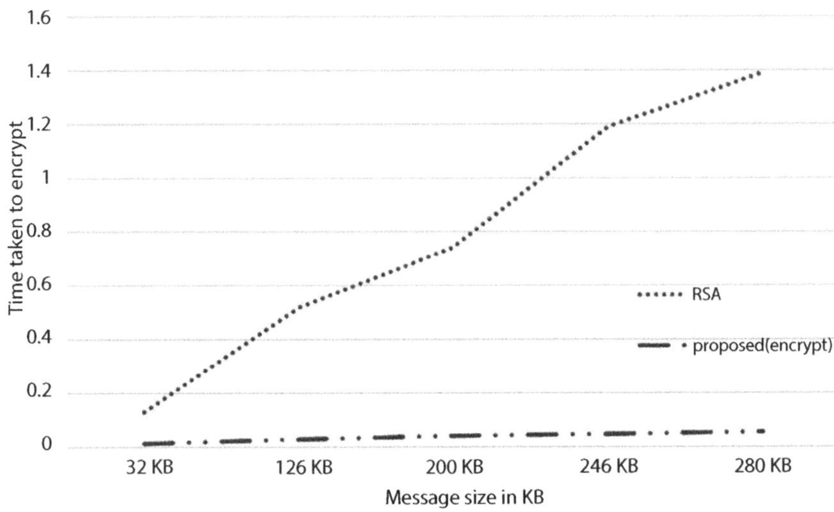


**Figure 8.6** Comparison of the encryption time between RSA and proposed work.

**Table 8.5** RSA vs DLE based proposed approach.

| File size (kilo bytes) | RSA | DLE based proposed |
|---|---|---|
| 32 KB | 0.13 | 0.0135 |
| 126 KB | 0.52 | 0.0292 |
| 200 KB | 0.74 | 0.0412 |
| 246 KB | 1.19 | 0.0484 |
| 280 KB | 1.39 | 0.0561 |

and decryption is less while comparing with the existing AES, DES and RSA techniques. Hence, it concludes that the proposed approach is comparatively more efficient than the other three existing techniques. It is efficient in terms of less time consumption and less equipment cost. The following figures (in encryption and decryption) also depict the same results. Table 8.9 to Table 8.18 contain the cost analysis details for AES, DES, RSA and Proposed algorithms. Based on file size and aforesaid threshold values the figures through Figure 8.10 to Figure 8.19 show considerable improvement in performance. Data is calculated based on file size and threshold values.

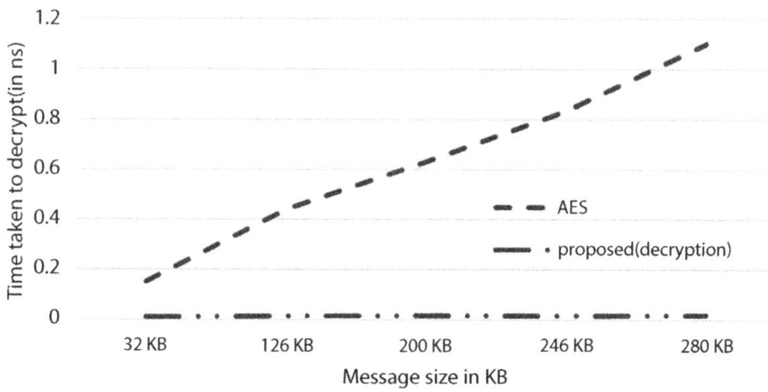


**Figure 8.7** Comparison of the decryption time between AES and proposed work.

**Table 8.6** AES vs DLE based proposed approach.

| File size (kilo bytes) | AES | DLE based proposed |
|---|---|---|
| 32 KB | 0.15 | 0.0113 |
| 126 KB | 0.44 | 0.0159 |
| 200 KB | 0.63 | 0.0167 |
| 246 KB | 0.83 | 0.0172 |
| 280 KB | 1.1 | 0.0185 |

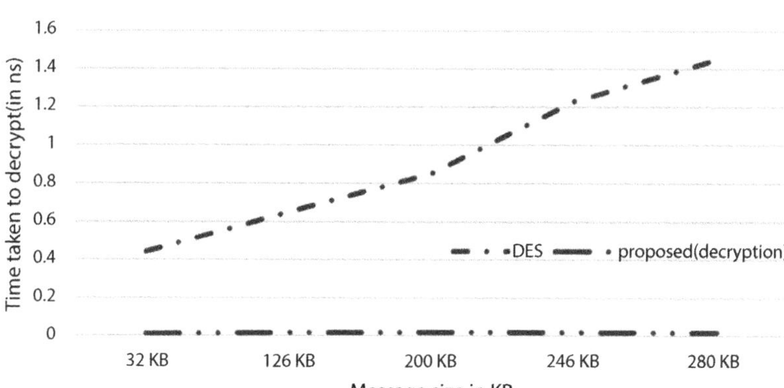


**Figure 8.8** Comparison of the decryption time between DES and proposed work.

**Table 8.7** DES vs DLE based proposed approach.

| File size (kilo bytes) | DES | DLE based proposed |
|---|---|---|
| 32 KB | 0.44 | 0.0113 |
| 126 KB | 0.65 | 0.0159 |
| 200 KB | 0.85 | 0.0167 |
| 246 KB | 1.23 | 0.0172 |
| 280 KB | 1.45 | 0.0185 |

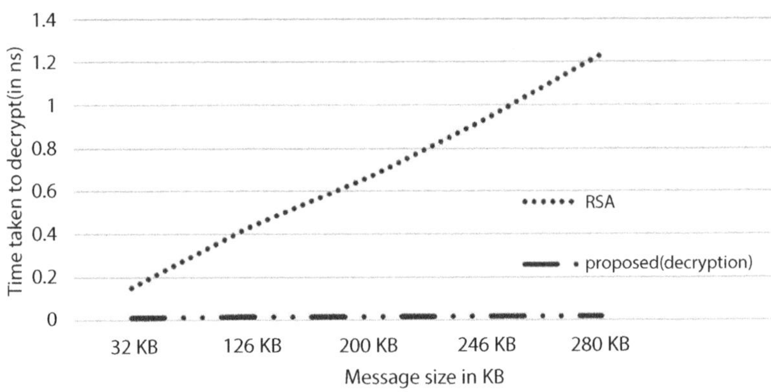


**Figure 8.9** Comparison of the decryption time between RSA and proposed work.

**Table 8.8** RSA vs DLE based proposed approach.

| File size (kilo bytes) | RSA | DLE based Proposed |
|---|---|---|
| 32 KB | 0.15 | 0.0113 |
| 126 KB | 0.43 | 0.0159 |
| 200 KB | 0.66 | 0.0167 |
| 246 KB | 0.93 | 0.0172 |
| 280 KB | 1.23 | 0.0185 |

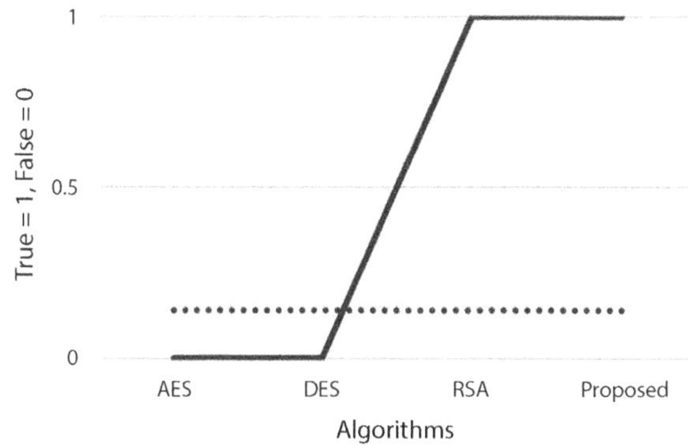


**Figure 8.10** Cost analysis graph of file size: 32 KB (encryption).

**Table 8.9** Cost analysis of file size: 32 KB, threshold 0.14s (encryption).

| Algorithms | True/false |
|---|---|
| AES | 0 |
| DES | 0 |
| RSA | 1 |
| Proposed | 1 |

**Encryption:**

In Table 8.9, RSA and the proposed approach passed the True/False test in case of encryption using 32 KB file size and 0.14s threshold. A related cost analysis graph is shown in Figure 8.10.

In Table 8.10, AES and the proposed approach passed the True/False test in case of encryption using 126 KB file size and 0.5s threshold. A related cost analysis graph is shown in Figure 8.11.

In Table 8.11, AES and the proposed approach passed the True/False test in case of encryption using 200 KB file size and 0.73s threshold. A related cost analysis graph is shown in Figure 8.12.

In Table 8.12, only the proposed approach passed the True/False test in case of encryption using 246 KB file size and 0.8s threshold. A related cost analysis graph is shown in Figure 8.13.

**Table 8.10** Cost analysis of file size: 126 KB, threshold 0.5s (encryption).

| Algorithms | True/false |
|---|---|
| AES | 1 |
| DES | 0 |
| RSA | 0 |
| Proposed | 1 |

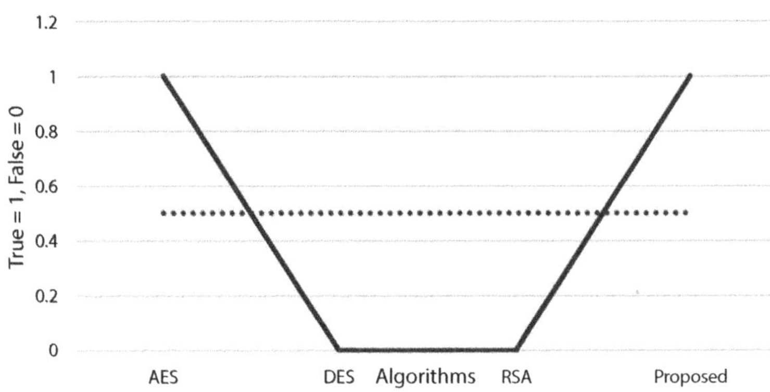


**Figure 8.11** Cost analysis graph of file size: 126 KB (encryption).

**Table 8.11** Cost analysis of file size: 200 KB, threshold 0.73s (encryption).

| Algorithms | True/false |
|---|---|
| AES | 1 |
| DES | 0 |
| RSA | 0 |
| Proposed | 1 |

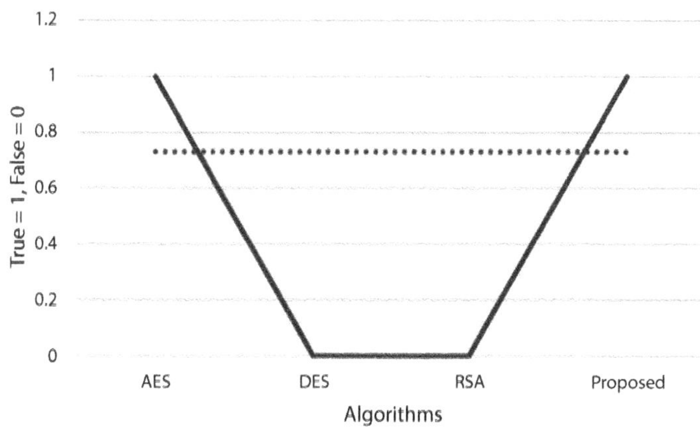


**Figure 8.12** Cost analysis graph of file size: 200 KB (encryption).

**Table 8.12** Cost analysis of file size: 246 KB, threshold 0.8s (encryption).

| Algorithms | True/false |
|---|---|
| AES | 0 |
| DES | 0 |
| RSA | 0 |
| Proposed | 1 |

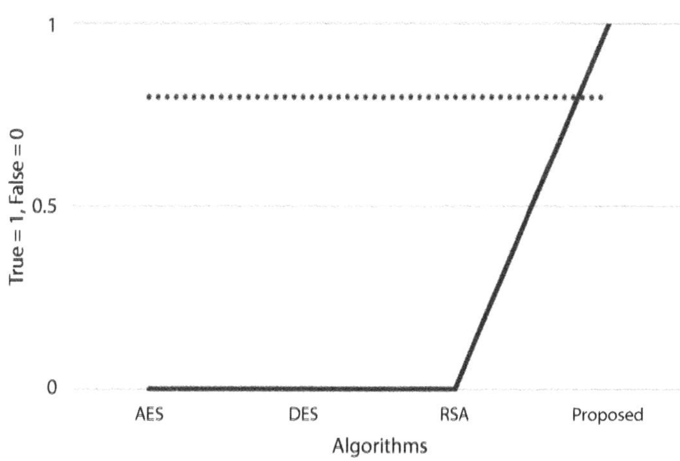


**Figure 8.13** Cost analysis graph of file size: 246 KB (encryption).

In Table 8.13, only the proposed approach passed the True/False test in case of encryption using 280 KB file size and 0.9s threshold. A related cost analysis graph is shown in Figure 8.14.

**Decryption:**

In Table 8.14, only the proposed approach passed the True/False test in case of decryption using 32 KB file size and 0.16s threshold. A related cost analysis graph is shown in Figure 8.15.

In Table 8.15, RSA and the proposed approach passed the True/False test in case of decryption using 126 KB file size and 0.435s threshold. A related cost analysis graph is shown in Figure 8.16.

In Table 8.16, AES and the proposed approach passed the True/False test in case of decryption using 200 KB file size and 0.64s threshold. A related cost analysis graph is shown in Figure 8.17.

**Table 8.13** Cost analysis of file size: 280 KB, threshold 0.9s (encryption).

| Algorithms | True/false |
|---|---|
| AES | 0 |
| DES | 0 |
| RSA | 0 |
| Proposed | 1 |

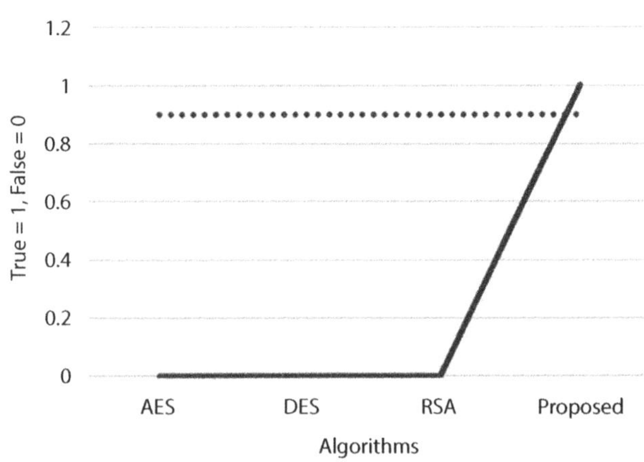


**Figure 8.14** Cost analysis graph of file size: 280 KB (encryption).

**Table 8.14** Cost analysis of file size: 32 KB, threshold 0.16s (decryption).

| Algorithms | True/false |
|---|---|
| AES | 0 |
| DES | 0 |
| RSA | 0 |
| Proposed | 1 |

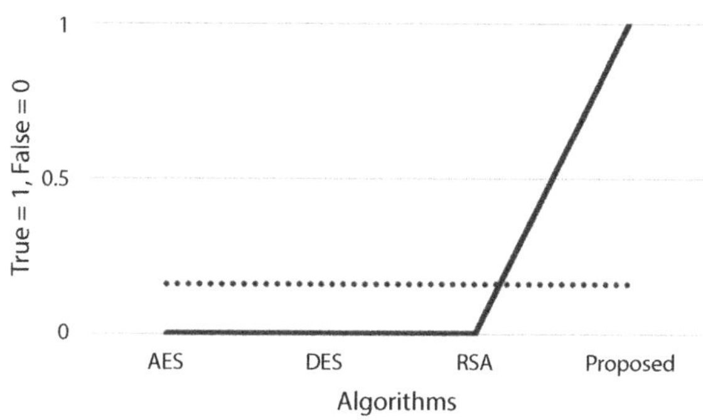


**Figure 8.15** Cost analysis graph of file size: 32 KB (decryption).

**Table 8.15** Cost analysis of file size: 126 KB, threshold 0.435s (decryption).

| Algorithms | True/false |
|---|---|
| AES | 0 |
| DES | 0 |
| RSA | 1 |
| Proposed | 1 |

In Table 8.17, AES and the proposed approach passed the True/False test in case of decryption using 246 KB file size & 0.85s threshold. A related cost analysis graph is shown in Figure 8.18.

In Table 8.18, only the proposed approach passed the True/False test in case of decryption using 280 KB file size and 0.9s threshold. A related cost analysis graph is shown in Figure 8.19.

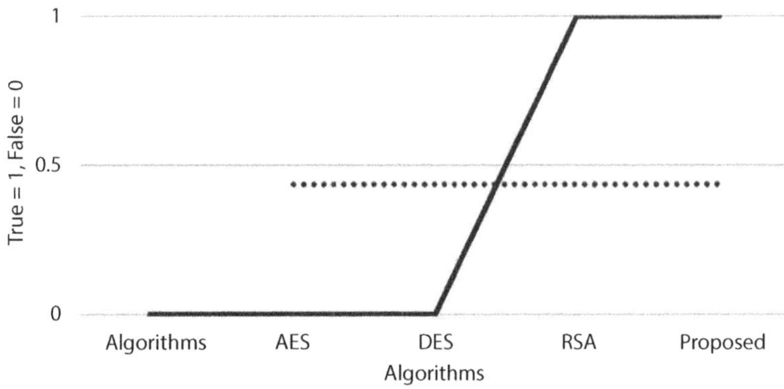


**Figure 8.16** Cost analysis graph of file size: 126 KB (decryption).

**Table 8.16** Cost analysis of file size: 200 KB, threshold 0.64s (decryption).

| Algorithms | True/False |
|---|---|
| AES | 1 |
| DES | 0 |
| RSA | 0 |
| Proposed | 1 |

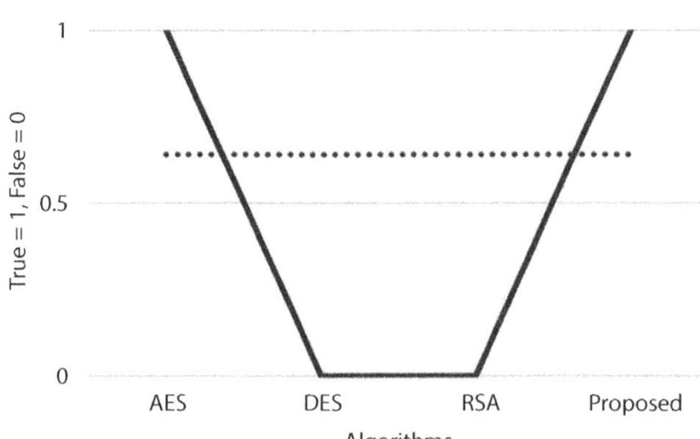


**Figure 8.17** Cost analysis graph of file size: 200 KB (decryption).

**Table 8.17** Cost analysis of file size: 246 KB, threshold 0.85s (decryption).

| Algorithms | True/false |
|---|---|
| AES | 1 |
| DES | 0 |
| RSA | 0 |
| Proposed | 1 |

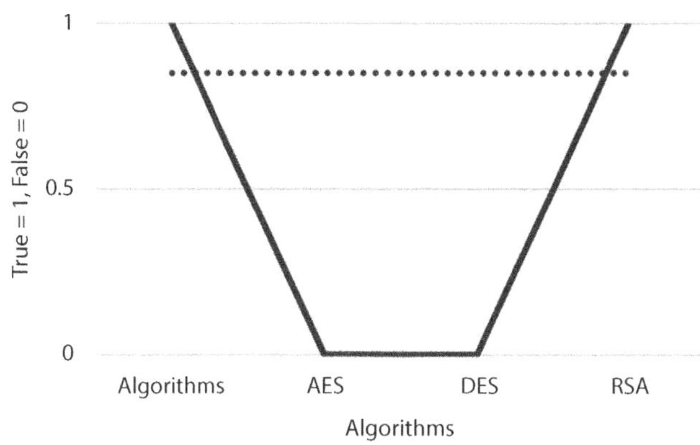


**Figure 8.18** Cost analysis graph of file size: 246 KB (decryption).

**Table 8.18** Cost analysis of file size: 280 KB, threshold 0.9s (decryption).

| Algorithms | True/false |
|---|---|
| AES | 0 |
| DES | 0 |
| RSA | 0 |
| Proposed | 1 |

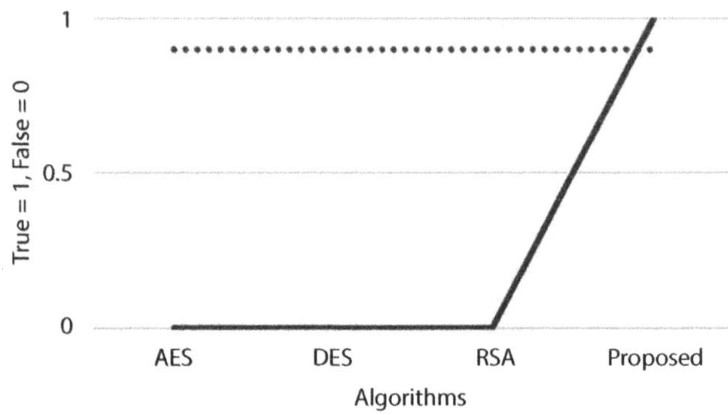


**Figure 8.19** Cost analysis graph of file size: 280 KB (decryption).

## 8.7 Conclusion

Encryption algorithm plays a vital role in communication security. Our proposed work establishes a new secure and hybrid encryption technique named Heteromorphic DLE, which very efficiently converts plain text to cipher text. Since generated key is kept safe in private cloud with proper security measures and each encrypted data is decrypted using specific keys— finally, all the decrypted fragments are joined maintaining proper sequence to recover original data making the proposed algorithm very secure and efficient. In this research work, we have surveyed performances of the existing encryption and decryption processes like AES, DES and RSA algorithms and compared received data with the proposed algorithm. Based on the text files used and the experimental result, it is found that the proposed algorithm consumes the least encryption and decryption time. Also, for the sole purpose of security and making it cost efficient, asynchronous mode of data transmission is taken into consideration in our approach.

From the results, we have evaluated that our proposed algorithm is comparatively better than other algorithms taken into consideration.

As a future endeavor, the proposed framework would be further extended with statistical test results such as "chi-square" to validate randomness present in the ciphertext. This would further establish the effectiveness of the proposed encryption technique. The proposed approach would be compared with further modern encryption techniques.

## Acknowledgment

The research work is funded by Computer Innovative Research Society, West Bengal, India. Award number is "2024/CIRS/R&D/2024-01-24/DLDHEFADTHCN".

**AI disclosure statement:** The author confirms that no artificial intelligence (AI)-generated content or AI-assisted writing tools were used in the preparation of this chapter (including summaries and the abstract). All text, analysis, and conclusions are the result of the author's original work.

## References

1. Geng, H., Zhang, H., Shi, X., Wang, Z., Yin, X., Zhang, J., Hu, Z., Wu, Y., A hybrid link protection scheme for ensuring network service availability in link-state routing networks. *J. Commun. Netw.*, 22, 1, 2020.
2. Vanhoef, M. and Piessens, F., Key Reinstallation Attacks: Forcing Nonce Reuse in WPA2. *Proceedings of the 2017 ACM SIGSAC Conference on Computer and Communications Security*, October 2017.
3. Vanhoef, M., Matte, C., Cunche, M., Cardoso, L., Piessens, F., Why MAC Address Randomization is not Enough: An Analysis of Wi-Fi Network Discovery Mechanisms. *ACM Asia Conference on Computer and Communications Security*, May 2016.
4. Liberato, A., Martinello, M., Gomes, R.L., F. Beldachi, A., Salas, E., Villaca, R., Ribeiro, M.R.N., Kondepu, K., Kanellos, G., Nejabati, R., Gorodnik, A., Simeonidou, D., RDNA: Residue-Defined Networking Architecture Enabling Ultra-Reliable Low-Latency Datacenters. *IEEE Trans. Netw. Serv. Manage.*, 15, 4, 2018.
5. Javad Karimi, M., Schmid, A., Dehollain, C., Wireless Power and Data Transmission for Implanted Devices *via* Inductive Links: A Systematic Review. *IEEE Sens. J.*, 21, 6, 2021.
6. Zhang, A., Wang, L., Ye, X., Lin, X., Light-Weight and Robust Security-Aware D2D-Assist Data Transmission Protocol for Mobile-Health Systems. *IEEE Trans. Inf. Forensics Secur.*, 12, 3, 2017.
7. Zou, Z., Bao, Y., Deng, F., Li, H., An Approach of Reliable Data Transmission With Random Redundancy for Wireless Sensors in Structural Health Monitoring. *IEEE Sens. J.*, 15, 2, 2015.
8. Reddy, L.K., A novel deep learning technique with cryptographic transformation for cloud computing. *Multimed. Tools Appl.*, 2024, https://doi.org/10.1007/s11042-024-18903-8.
9. Song, H. and Choi, W., Multicast Transmission for Asynchronous Data Requests. *IEEE Trans. Veh. Technol.*, 67, 4, 2018.

10. Lu, Y., Huang, X., Zhang, K., Maharjan, S., Zhang, Y., Blockchain Empowered Asynchronous Federated Learning for Secure Data Sharing in Internet of Vehicles. *IEEE Trans. Veh. Technol.*, 69, 4, 2020.
11. Ji, S. and Cai, Z., Distributed Data Collection in Large-Scale Asynchronous Wireless Sensor Networks Under the Generalized Physical Interference Model. *IEEE/ACM Trans. Netw.*, 21, 4, 2013.
12. Luo, Q., Hang-Yat Lam, A., Wang, D., Pan, D., Chan, W.-T., Peng, Y., Peng, X., Asynchronous and Selective Transmission for DeWiring of Building Management Systems. *IEEE Trans. Ind. Inf.*, 13, 2, 2017.
13. Corradi, A., Destro, M., Foschini, L., Kotoulas, S., Lopez, V., Montanari, R., Mobile Cloud Support for Semantic-Enriched Speech Recognition in Social Care. *IEEE Trans. Cloud Comput.*, 7, 1, 2019.
14. Grozev, N. and Buyya, R., Performance Modelling and Simulation of Three-Tier Applications in Cloud and Multi-Cloud Environments. *Comput. J.*, 58, 1, 2015.
15. Liu, X. and Buyya, R., Performance-Oriented Deployment of Streaming Applications on Cloud. *IEEE Trans. Big Data*, 5, 1, 2019.
16. Fan, C.-I., Huang, J.-J., Tseng, S.-W., Chen, I.-T., Dependable Data Outsourcing Scheme Based on Cloud-of-Clouds Approach with Fast Recovery. *IEEE Trans. Cloud Comput.*, 9, 2, 2021.
17. Agrawal, S., Goyal, R., Tomida, J., Multi-input Quadratic Functional Encryption from Pairings. *Adv. Cryptology CRYPTO*, 2021, 208–238, August 2021.
18. Indira, N., Rukmani Devi, S., Kalpana, A.V., R2R-CSES: proactive security data process using random round crypto security encryption standard in cloud environment. *J. Ambient Intell. Hum. Comput.*, 12, 4643–4654, 2021.
19. AbdEl Haleem, S.H., Radwan, A.G., Abd-El-Hafiz, S.K., Utilizing LFSR and Feistel networks in image encryption. *2013 IEEE 20th International Conference on Electronics, Circuits, and Systems (ICECS)*, Abu Dhabi, United Arab Emirates, 8-11 December 2013, IEEE.
20. Yi, L., Tong, X., Wang, Z., Zhang, M., Zhu, H., Liu, J., A Novel Block Encryption Algorithm Based on Chaotic S-Box for Wireless Sensor Network. *IEEE Access*, 7, 53079 – 53090, 2019.
21. Pich, R., Chivapreecha, S., Prabnasak, J., A single, triple chaotic cryptography using chaos in digital filter and its own comparison to DES and triple DES. *2018 International Workshop on Advanced Image Technology (IWAIT)*, Chiang Mai, Thailand, 2018.
22. Alani, M.M., DES96 - improved DES security, 2010 7th International Multi-Conference on Systems. *Signals Devices*, 2010.
23. Mitchell, C.J., On the Security of 2-Key Triple DES. *IEEE Trans. Inf. Theory*, 62, 11, 2016.
24. Guo, C., Understanding the Related-Key Security of Feistel Ciphers From a Provable Perspective. *IEEE Trans. Inf. Theory*, 65, 8, 2019.

25. Bai, K. and Wu, C., An AES-Like Cipher and Its White-Box Implementation, in: *The Computer Journal*, vol. 59, Oxford, 2016.
26. Hammad, I., El-Sankary, K., El-Masry, E., High-Speed AES Encryptor With Efficient Merging Techniques, I.E.E.E. Embedded Systems Letters, 2, 3, 2010.
27. Jinomeiq, L., Baoduui, W., Xinmei, W., One AES S-box to increase complexity and its cryptanalysis. *J. Syst. Eng. Electron.*, 18, 2, 2007.
28. Wang, H., Xia, Z., Fei, J., Xiao, F., An AES-Based Secure Image Retrieval Scheme Using Random Mapping and BOW in Cloud Computing. *IEEE Access*, 8, 2020.
29. Liu, Q., Li, Y., Hao, L., Peng, H., Two efficient variants of the RSA cryptosystem. *2010 International Conference On Computer Design and Applications*, Hebei, China, 2010.
30. Karakra, A. and Alsadeh, A., A-RSA: Augmented RSA. *2016 SAI Computing Conference (SAI)*, London, UK, 13-15 July 2016.
31. Nagar, S.A. and Alshamma, S., High speed implementation of RSA algorithm with modified keys exchange. *2012 6th International Conference on Sciences of Electronics, Technologies of Information and Telecommunications (SETIT)*, Sousse, Tunisia, 21-24 March 2012.
32. Kong, F., Zhou, D., Jiang, Y., Shang, J., Yu, J., Fault Attack on an Improved CRT-RSA Algorithm with the Modulus Chaining Method. *2017 IEEE International Conference on Computational Science and Engineering (CSE) and IEEE International Conference on Embedded and Ubiquitous Computing (EUC)*, Guangzhou, Guangdong, China, 21-24 July 2017.
33. Hikmat Mahmood, Z. and Khalel Ibrahem, M., New Fully Homomorphic Encryption Scheme Based on Multistage Partial Homomorphic Encryption Applied in Cloud Computing. *2018 1st Annual International Conference on Information and Sciences (AiCIS)*, Fallujah, Iraq, 20-21 November 2018.
34. Chaudhary, P., Gupta, R., Singh, A., Majumder, P., Analysis and Comparison of Various Fully Homomorphic Encryption Techniques. *2019 International Conference on Computing, Power and Communication Technologies (GUCON) UP, India*, 27-28 September 2019.
35. Hee Cheon, J. and Kim, J., A Hybrid Scheme of Public-Key Encryption and Somewhat Homomorphic Encryption. *IEEE Trans. Inf. Forensics Secur.*, 10, 5, 2015.
36. Cheng, C., Lee, J., Jiang, T., Takagi, T., Security Analysis and Improvements on Two Homomorphic Authentication Schemes for Network Coding. *IEEE Transactions on Information Forensics and Security*, vol. 11, 2016.
37. Hei, X., Liang, X., Wang, Y., Ji, W., Zhu, L., Deep Learning as a Service Based on Encrypted Data. *2020 International Conference on Networking and Network Applications (NaNA)*, Haikou City, China, pp. 53–58, 2020, doi: 10.1109/NaNA51271.2020.00017.
38. Nair, B.V., Muni, S.S., Durdu, A., Deep learning and chaos: A combined approach to image encryption and decryption. DOI:10.48550/arXiv.2406.16792, 2024.

39. Kim, H., Lim, S., Kang, Y., Kim, W., Kim, D., Yoon, S., Seo, H., Deep-learning-based cryptanalysis of lightweight block ciphers revisited, Department of Convergence Security, Hansung University, Seoul 02876, Republic of Korea, https://doi.org/10.3390/e25070986, June, 2023.
40. Pamidiparthi, S. and Velampalli, S., Cryptographic Algorithm Identification Using Deep Learning Techniques, in: *Evolution in Computational Intelligence. Advances in Intelligent Systems and Computing*, vol. 1176, V. Bhateja, S.L. Peng, S.C. Satapathy, Y.D. Zhang (Eds.), Springer, Singapore, 2021, https://doi.org/10.1007/978-981-15-5788-0_74.
41. Quinga-Socasi, F., Zhinin-Vera, L., Chang, O., A Deep Learning Approach for Symmetric-Key Cryptography System, in: *Proceedings of the Future Technologies Conference (FTC) 2020, Volume 1. FTC 2020*, vol. Advances in Intelligent Systems and Computing, 1288, K. Arai, S. Kapoor, R. Bhatia (Eds.), Springer, Cham, 2021, https://doi.org/10.1007/978-3-030-63128-4_41.

# Part II

# INTELLIGENT INTRUSION DETECTION FOR CLOUD-IoT SYSTEM

# 9

# Deep Learning Insights into Defending Against Adversarial Attacks in IoT Systems

**J. Ramkumar[1]* and S. Vetrivel[2]**

*[1]Department of Computer Science, Kristu Jayanti University, Bengaluru, Karnataka, India*
*[2]Department of Information Technology and Cognitive Systems, Sri Krishna Arts and Science College, Coimbatore, Tamilnadu, India*

***Abstract***
The chapter titled "Deep Learning Insights into Defending Against Adversarial Attacks in IoT Systems" delves into the critical role that deep learning techniques play in safeguarding Internet of Things (IoT) devices from adversarial attacks. With the proliferation of IoT applications across various domains, understanding and countering adversarial threats is paramount for maintaining the security and reliability of these systems. This chapter provides a comprehensive exploration of the methodologies and strategies employed to defend IoT systems against such attacks using deep learning. The primary aim of this chapter is to provide a detailed analysis of adversarial attacks targeting IoT systems and demonstrate how deep learning techniques can be effectively utilized to detect, mitigate, and prevent these threats. The chapter seeks to bridge the gap between theoretical advancements in deep learning and their practical applications in IoT security, offering readers both foundational knowledge and actionable insights. The chapter begins with an examination of the nature of adversarial attacks, detailing various techniques used by attackers and the potential impact on IoT devices and networks. It then introduces a range of deep learning models and algorithms specifically designed for threat detection and response in IoT environments. Through the use of case studies and experimental results, the chapter illustrates the practical effectiveness of these techniques. Emphasis is placed on the computational and hardware requirements necessary to support real-time processing and adaptive threat response.

**Corresponding author*: jramkumar1986@gmail.com

Partha Ghosh, Rajdeep Chakraborty, Anupam Ghosh and Ahmed A. Elngar (eds.) Strategic Approaches to Intrusion Detection in Cloud-IoT Ecosystem, (227–250) © 2026 Scrivener Publishing LLC

***Keywords*:** Adversarial attacks, deep learning, IoT security, real-time threat detection, signal processing algorithms, network performance optimization

## 9.1 Introduction

The adversarial attacks on IoT have grown to be an important area within the realms of concerns on cybersecurity. IoT systems integrate devices that are able to interact and share data in real-time, without requiring human intervention. Devices range from as simple as sensors to as complex as machinery, and they play a very essential role in health, manufacturing, and transport, and smart homes. This is more so in the growing dependence on IoT technology, which places a premium on the actualization of potential vulnerabilities and the resultant effect of malignant attacks. Adversarial attacks are crafted to function particularly against the machine learning models running IoT systems, exploiting weaknesses to manipulate outcomes and cause disruption.

On one hand, IoT is celebrated by new improvements, such as enhanced convenience; on the other hand, it makes up new security challenges. The large impact on people and organizations that adversarial attacks cause is one major reason. An example includes attacks on healthcare IoT devices, which run the risk of sending the wrong health data, and thus compromise the patients' safety. Besides these, threats to IoT systems may compromise the operations in the industrial domain and may result in financial losses. Sensing the urge for securing IoT systems from such threats, a lot of researchers and industrial professionals are increasingly being engaged in devising a robust defense mechanism, ensuring integrity and reliability in these very essential technologies.

### 9.1.1 Overview of Adversarial Attacks on IoT Systems

Adversarial attacks in IoT systems are one of the most challenging problems regarding security in the modern technological landscape. These are made up of crafting inputs in a way that will go into the machine learning model incorporated in the IoT system to extract wrong decisions or predictions. These kinds of attacks have severe consequences because of the nature of IoT systems, most of which are autonomous and process immense data in real time. They can exploit these vulnerabilities in sensors, communication protocols, and processing units of IoT devices [1]. Such attacks will lead to compromised device functionality, privacy violation, and potential physical damage. Knowing such mechanisms of attacks would help in creating good defenses and improving the security stance of an IoT ecosystem.

The results of the adversarial attacks on IoT systems spread across several domains. In healthcare, the adversarial manipulation of data coming from IoT devices, such as wearable health monitors, engenders an incorrect medical diagnosis or set of treatment recommendations, putting the safety of patients in jeopardy. In other words, within smart home contexts, attackers may change the information from security cameras and motion sensors that will throw off the security and privacy of the residents. In the industrial environment, IoT devices controlling critical infrastructures—like power grids or manufacturing processes—are vulnerable to adversarial attacks, which may lead to operational disruption and financial losses, or even hazardous events of fatal failures. This threat requires fully comprehensive strategies and further measures on security for IoT devices.

### 9.1.2 Role of Deep Learning in Enhancing IoT Security

Deep learning, hence, is quite prominent in enhancing IoT security with state-of-the-art threat detection and mitigation methods. There is a huge amount of data created in an IoT system in real-time. Deep learning comes into action to process and analyze large datasets such as these efficiently. Techniques like anomaly detection use deep learning to spot abnormal patterns in the streams of data, alerting thereby to some possible security breach. These models learn from benign and malicious behaviors; and hence, get better and more accurate over time. Deep learning implemented within the security frameworks for IoT would, therefore, significantly strengthen the predictive capacity against cyber threats and the ability to respond to them.

Deep learning can fit well into any IoT security framework for the development of robust authentication mechanisms. Biometric authentication powered with deep learning provides accurate and reliable ways to verify user identities, thereby making this layer very secure. In IoT ecosystems, devices often 'talk' to each other, and sometimes they are autonomous, so authenticity must be ensured for both devices and data sources. Deep learning models can easily be trained across very diverse biometric data, acting as strong protection from unauthorized access through reducing the risk of identity theft. A very important feature related to the integrity and reliability of IoT systems is the ability to manage and enable the adaptation of very diverse biometric data, able to train deep learning models, from smart homes to infrastructure assets [2].

### 9.1.3 Review Literature Nature of Adversarial Attacks

Crafting of adversarial attacks is the act of manipulation of input features with intent in the process of deceiving machine learning models to give wrong outputs. Adversarial attacks are crafted in such a way that, when observed by a human, a normal person can determine that they are normal, yet they make the model take wrong predictions. And usually, they are very subtle, which makes them open to being difficult to detect and mitigate. Adversarial attacks expose the flaw in the training of the model. Slight perturbations can greatly change the performance— this deceitful nature of adversarial attacks only underscores the need to develop very robust machine learning models [3].

Depending on the approach and objectives, there can be a segregation of adversarial attacks. Evasion attacks aim to bypass the detection mechanism of the model by introducing small, but strategically crafted, perturbations in the input data. Poisoning attacks involve the injection of malicious data into the model's training set to taint its learning process and result in compromised model performance. Exploratory attacks do not personalize the underlying data but rather leak information about the structure and behavior of the model that would aid attackers in further and more sophisticated attacks. This clearly shows the complexity and type of attacks that make the development of all-inclusive security measures for the protection of machine learning models from adversarial threats imperative [4].

### 9.1.4 Definition and Characteristics

Adversarial attacks are deliberate manipulations of input data meant to deceive machine learning models into incorrect outputs. Such manipulations occur at very small levels, or sometimes even unnoticeable by human beings, yet they greatly influence the way the model performs. These attacks exploit underlying vulnerabilities in machine learning due to the intrinsic nature of the algorithms that leverage the sensitivity of the model to the existence of certain patterns in the input data. Such attacks are primarily meant to disrupt the normal function of the model, leading to its misclassification or false prediction and sometimes total system failure. Understanding the definition and characteristics of adversarial attacks is indispensable for the development of effectual defense mechanisms.

Subtlety, specificity, and adaptability are the hallmarks of adversarial attacks. The first means that only small perturbations in the input data are required to mislead the model without human eyes noticing it. Specificity indicates that such attacks usually target special models or tasks by exploiting certain unique weaknesses of the chosen system. Adaptability underscores that adversarial attacks can be modified to suit the shifting defenses and thus remain a dynamic, persistent threat. These qualities make traditional security measures highly challenging, and improved strategies and technologies are required to safeguard machine learning models against such adversarial manipulations.

### 9.1.5 Common Techniques Used in Attacks

Several techniques go into manipulating input data for adversarial attacks on machine learning models to realize their objectives. There is, however, a more common method: the Fast Gradient Sign Method. It creates adversarial examples by perturbing the input data in the gradient direction of the loss function. It is, however, a very powerful method due to the fact that it is very simple and fast; therefore, it comes in very handy for many adversaries who want to cause misclassification while causing minimum disturbance in the input data. This stems from the ability of FGSM to exploit the linearity of neural networks, which may lead to large deviations in output due to small perturbations.

Another top technique is the Jacobian-based Saliency Map Attack. It's a method that attacks the most influential features in the input data, modifying them in such a way as to maximize the effect on the model's predictions. This way, JSMA will generate very focused and effective adversarial examples. Such a technique is very useful when the adversary has detailed knowledge regarding the structure and behavior of the model under attack. In that case, very focused and effective attacks can be built.

### 9.1.6 Impact on IoT Systems and Devices

These have deep impacts on IoT systems and devices regarding functionality, security, and reliability. In the medical domain, the IoT devices depend on correct data processing to guarantee the safety of treated patients. The attacks manipulate the data; a form of diagnosis change or one that can trigger inappropriate treatment for wearable monitors and smart medical equipment. That does not end with the health of the patients but includes trust in and adoption of IoT technologies in care-critical environments. In this regard, ensuring the integrity of the data being processed is critical for both effectiveness and reliability in healthcare systems.

IoT devices control and monitor critical assets in the industrial environment: plant equipment, power grids, manufacturing. An adversary attack on such systems may provoke serious operational perturbations, financial losses, or even dangerous situations. For example, manipulating sensor values within a production plant can result in faulty products, broken machinery, or even pose threats to employee safety. Moreover, the potential for industrial IoT systems to be interfered with by adversaries underlines the requirement for robust security measures to protect critical infrastructures and enable continuous safe operations.

The privacy and security of smart homes and consumer IoT devices can be executed by performing adversarial attacks. For instance, the data from smart cameras, motion sensors, or home automation systems could be manipulated by a threat actor to yield entry or unauthorized surveillance. This compromises the privacy of a person, also putting them at risks concerning physical security [4]. The permeation of IoT devices into every nook and cranny of daily life underlines the need for developing effective strategies on how to secure devices and to mitigate the possible negative effect that adversarial attacks could have on the benefits this technology poses.

## 9.2 IoT System Vulnerabilities

Many vulnerabilities in IoT systems could be exploited by adversaries against the security of a device or functionality. Among the principal vulnerabilities, one is related to the heterogeneity of the devices comprising an IoT, very often combining a mix of different hardware and software components. This diversity can result in inconsistent security practices, and hence easier ways for attackers to find and exploit weaknesses. Most IoT devices are running outdated firmware that facilitates several security vulnerabilities—those entry points of malicious activities. In view of these heterogeneous and complex systems, there will be a complete need for standardized security measures against a variety of threats.

Another critical vulnerability pertains to the communication protocols that an IoT device may use. Most of them do not have any robust encryption and authentication schemes between devices for information exchange [5]. Poor or no encryption will generally make sensitive data exposed during transit by either eavesdropping or tampering in most cases. Furthermore, insecurely processed authentication may become the open door for unauthorized network access; thereafter, the hackers may inject spurious commands into those devices with the purpose of evil disruption. This therefore, makes security enhancement of communication protocols very relevant to assure integrity and confidentiality of data within the IoT environment.

### 9.2.1 Security Flaws in IoT Devices

An IoT device security breach poses immense threats not just to a person when an individual uses an IoT device but also to the larger system. The most common kind of security vulnerability involves weak authentication mechanisms in IoT devices. A lot of IoT devices make use of default or weak passwords, and this could become an easy target. For instance, in case of very weak authentication measures, the attackers could easily exploit such measures for gaining control over a device that could lead to data breaches or operational disruption. This vulnerability could be eased with the overall improvement of security by the creation of strong, unique passwords and implementation of multi-factor authentication within the device.

Another critical security weakness is the poor implementation of encryption protocols. Most IoT devices transfer data without encryption, leaving open the possibility for sensitive information to be intercepted and tampered with. This may result in a violation of privacy and a lack of integrity in the data under transfer, because attackers can eavesdrop on communications and manipulate the data in transit. At all costs, robust encryption standards should be implemented to protect both confidentiality and integrity during storage and in transit for information being processed by IoT devices.

### 9.2.2 Network Vulnerabilities

That is where the real challenge of IoT system network vulnerabilities arises, because cyber threats compromise the device and the data. A great number of the main vulnerabilities are related to the use of weak or obsolete protocols in encryption. In engagements where the encryption used is below the requisite standard, data breaches become a longstanding truth, given that communication between devices can be easily intercepted and decoded by hackers. Weak encryption seriously jeopardizes the confidentiality and integrity of sensitive information, possibly personal and operational data with commands. Implementing strong, new-age cryptographic methods is of paramount importance for securing data in transit on IoT networks.

Basically, one of the problems causing vulnerabilities in IoT is network segmentation issues. In case only one device is compromised, inadequate segmentation will let the attackers move laterally within the network. If there is a lack of isolation, then large disruptions and data breaches can be propagated from one device to another. Proper network segmentation, where devices will be organized based on function and security requirements, limits the damage in the case of a security breach and contains the threat posed. These network vulnerabilities have to be addressed by security strategies that are comprehensive in nature in the protection of the IoT system to maintain its integrity of operation.

### 9.2.3 Exploitation Methods and Scenarios

The methods of exploitation against IoT systems make use of a lot of techniques to exploit the devices or even a whole network. One common way is malware, which gets into IoT devices through exploited vulnerabilities within the software or firmware. It has found its place in devices to perform a great many actions, from stealing sensitive information to device functionality disruption. In smart home scenarios, malware can take control of devices like cameras and thermostats, paving the way for violations of privacy and unauthorized manipulation of the home system. Thus, this underlines the need for robust security designed to detect and prevent malware infiltration into IoT environments [5].

Another is phishing attacks, representing an attack vector where the attackers trick targets into giving sensitive information or downloading malware. This could be very powerful in the context of IoT, since many devices can be remotely logged into by a user. This may include, for example, a phishing attack against some smart home system owner to trick the target into giving away his login credentials or clicking a malicious link. Once the attacker has the access, he would be able to control devices remotely or harvest valued data, posing serious security threats. Therefore, user education on phishing tactics and using robust mechanisms of authentication would avert these threats.

## 9.3 Deep Learning Approaches

In this area of IoT security, deep learning techniques have significantly advanced the field by providing strong tools for anomaly detection, threat prediction, and system resilience. One of the most popular methods in this domain employs convolutional neural networks for network traffic analysis, anomaly detection, and classification. Given that CNNs are popularly associated with the functionality in recognizing patterns and features from data, they can hence detect deviations in network behavior that could be pointing toward security breaches. This is quite a critical feature to be implemented in IoT systems, as it makes real-time monitoring feasible for timely detection and reaction to threats [5].

Another deep learning method that can benefit IoT security is RNNs. Represented, RNNs deal with sequential data; hence, they are appropriate to work with time series data from IoT devices. In such a way, RNNs model the temporal dependencies in the data to predict the future behavior of devices and detect irregular patterns that indicate security incidents. In fact, it improves the chances of predicting such threats and reducing the risks involved prior to the materialization of such threats, thus protecting IoT systems at any time [6]. Generative Adversarial Networks: This is yet another latest deep learning methodology that builds security features into IoT devices. The GAN comprises a generator and discriminator working in a dual fashion to produce and classify artificial data. The described method can thus generate credible adversarial examples for training IoT security models, hence improving resilience against many attack vectors. GANs could be used to generate a variety of attack scenarios to further harden security solutions against actual adversarial attacks. Integration of such deep learning approaches in IoT security frameworks is a holistic approach to security in the safeguarding of devices and data in an increasingly connected world.

### 9.3.1 Overview of Deep Learning Models

Deep learning models have been instrumental in revolutionizing a number of fields by providing key tools for data analysis, pattern recognition, and decision making. One of the most prominent models is the convolutional neural networks, shortly called CNNs, applied mainly in tasks on image and video processing. These are implemented through convolutional layers that automatically detect spatial hierarchies in data, making it very useful in applications such as image classification, object detection, and face recognition. The learning of complex features from raw data made CNNs very useful in computer vision applications, pushing developments in medical imaging and autonomous driving [7].

RNNs do well on sequential data because they are fit for tasks related to the analysis of time series and natural language processing. Loops in RNNs preserve information about the last inputs, hence modeling temporal dependencies of data. Variants like the Long Short-Term Memory and Gated Recurrent Units avoid this problem of vanishing gradients, hence allowing the modeling of long-term dependencies. It is owing to these capabilities that RNNs are of prime necessity in areas such as speech recognition, language translation, and financial forecasting, where the absolute understanding of a sequence or context in data is necessary.

### 9.3.2 Specific Algorithms for Security

Variety may be added to fields, especially in IoT systems, through the help of several algorithms designed for security purposes. One of the most popular algorithms is AES— Advanced Encryption Standard—a symmetric block cipher algorithm crucial for the protection of data in transit. AES has a fixed block size and different key lengths: either 128, 192, or 256 bits, hence making it quite effective in its security and efficiency. Due to its resistance to brute force attacks and wide applicability in different security applications, including in the safeguarding of sensitive information in embedded environments within IoT devices, a new generation of cryptography was born with AES.

Another very important algorithm will be the RSA algorithm—-a type of public-key cryptosystem used for secure transmission of data. Mathematically speaking, the basis of RSA is the characteristics revealed by large prime numbers in generating a pair of keys—the public key to do the encryption and the private key for decryption. This asymmetry ensures that the private key alone can decrypt the information, even though the public key may be freely distributed. It finds wide application in communication security, digital signatures, and certificates; RSA supports the robust framework for authentication of any device and data integrity in IoT networks.

ECC is the most advanced of all cryptographic algorithms, ensuring a high level of security with relatively small key sizes compared to the old-style ways of cryptography, such as RSA. It uses the mathematical properties of elliptic curves over finite fields to provide means of encryption, decryption, and digital signature generation [8].

### 9.3.3 Training and Validation of Models

Training and validation are two important tasks in the area of machine learning, generally aimed at constructing an accurate and reliable predictive algorithm. In the training process, a model learns patterns by adjusting its parameters through a labeled dataset so that its predictions will provide an exact match with outcomes actually observed. This usually involves training the model on a subset of the data through algorithms such as gradient descent, in a process of iterative improvement. The purpose is to train the model on the training data so that it would generalize well to new, unseen data, capturing underlying patterns.

Validation is the step necessary for knowing how well the model works on another subset of the data known as the validation set. This is quite important in tuning hyperparameters and avoiding overfitting, which is when a model does well during training but then fails with new data. Basically, overfitting is what happens when a model is too complicated and models noise, not underlying patterns in data [9].

## 9.4 Defense Mechanisms

Defense mechanisms employed in cybersecurity are one of the most important steps to be taken in protecting systems from different forms of threats and various attacks. One of the basic mechanisms involves the use of firewalls, which act as a barrier between trusted inner networks and untrusted outer ones. They essentially serve as filtering points between inbound and outbound traffic. Their intrinsic role is in securing the network, preventing intrusion, and protecting sensitive information from cyber risks. Setting up strong configurations of firewalls is one of the most important ways of realizing the huge benefit of security that comes with network infrastructure [10].

Other major mechanisms of defense in place would be the Intrusion Detection Systems and the Intrusion Prevention Systems. IDS monitors network traffic in search of any suspicious activity or likely threats, alerting the administrator to a probable breach in security within the network. Contrary to IDS, IPS is capable of detecting real threats that have actually been identified, and they prevent entry into any network. The techniques used for the identification of these attacks and mitigating them are signature-based detection, anomaly detection, and behavior analysis. With the deployment of IDS and IPS, the timely detection and response to cyber threats are enhanced, ensuring protection at all times over network resources [11].

Another critical line of defense lies in encryption methods at rest and in transit. Very powerful symmetric and asymmetric key cryptographic algorithms, including symmetric and asymmetric cryptographic algorithms like AES and Elliptic Curve Cryptography, ensure that no sensitive information is accessed or tampered with by any unauthorized party. More so in the IoT environment, it encrypts data communication between devices to ensure no information is intercepted or exploited by attackers. In all, a great encryption strategy fortifies security measures with protection for all data channels against vulnerabilities that may probably lead to an attack and maintain the privacy of data.

### 9.4.1 Detection of Adversarial Attacks

This is a very important area of cybersecurity in general, and it goes toward protecting machine learning models against such manipulations. One of the approaches was anomaly detection systems, which would identify deviations from expected behaviors. These systems analyzed patterns of input data to flag instances that differed appreciably from normal distributions of data. Anomaly detection systems can identify the adversarial examples, which, by continuously monitoring data inputs, are able to mislead machine learning models and enable timely intervention and mitigation.

Another class of methods for detection is based on adversarial training. A system is trained on adversarial examples to enable it to learn features that can recognize and repel such inputs. During training, a model is exposed to a large number of examples of various kinds of adversarial manipulations; therefore, the model will be more robust and efficient at detecting any malicious attempt during deployment. It is through adversarial training that machine learning models can improve in robustness, becoming less sensitive to small perturbations, which are carefully constructed to provoke misclassifications [12].

### 9.4.2 Real-Time Threat Response

Real-time threat response is any action against cyber-attacks aimed at containing the impact and ensuring uninterrupted security of systems and networks. One salient aspect of real-time threat response is the implementation of incident response automated systems. In its working, it detects threats as they are happening and gives a response based on predefined rules and machine learning algorithms. These systems can substantially reduce the time taken to detect and mitigate a potential threat, hence reducing damage and ensuring that recovery is quick; this shall be inserted into detection and response processes [13].

Another major component of real-time threat response involves a Security Information and Event Management system. SIEM systems aggregate data from multiple sources, including devices on the network, servers, applications, and monitors against the same in real time for the identification and correlation of security events. SIEM provides security teams with a common monitoring and management platform to detect threats in real-time and mount an effective response to security incidents. It offers higher accuracy of threat detection through event correlation from multiple sources and provides proper incident response.

Without proper coordination and good communication among the security teams, real-time threat response is not possible at all. Clearly laid-out protocols and procedures, as instituted at incident response, will have a ruling on the actions, roles, and responsibilities of each single individual within a security team in case of a security incident. This aspect is further enhanced through regular training and simulations that get the teams ready for a real-world scenario [14].

### 9.4.3 Mitigation and Prevention Strategies

Mitigation and prevention should be put in place to ensure the security of the system against cyber threats. Effective controls put in place include those that control entry. It is guaranteed that sensitive data and systems are accessed by authorized users and devices only within an organization, well minimizing the danger of unwanted access. These techniques include multi-factor authentication, role-based access control, and the principle of least privilege. All these measures are therefore, ensuring that a user can only access the least of what he needs to perform his job, hence reducing the number of potential attack vectors [15].

This works in a complementary sense for mitigation and preparation measures. To that effect, regular system updating and patch management are equally important. In the event that software and firmware remain updated, known vulnerabilities will not stay around for so long, thus reducing the likelihood of their exploitation. This will require organizations to come up with a clear schedule on how patching and updating will be carried out in addition to validating new vulnerabilities and threats. Automated patch management systems are a further automation in this regard and therefore offer updated patches with minimal human intervention [16].

## 9.5 Integration with IoT Security Frameworks

Integrative enablers that drive any security strategy into cohesion and completeness, IoT security frameworks yield guidance on how to secure the IoT device and its communicating network in a structured manner using the best practices. A very important dimension of integration involves using standardized security protocols, such as those provided by mechanisms like TLS and DTLS, for the secure establishment of a communication channel.

Implementation of these standards among the devices and systems in the IoT makes security more effective, since the approach used toward data protection is uniform [17]. Centralization will allow for effective implementation of security policies, real-time monitoring of activities on devices, and timely response in case of security incidents. These are the features for automated patch management, device authentication, and compliance monitoring toward the security of IoT ecosystems. Centralized management allows for the efficiency of security operations within organizations in performing consistency in applying security measures [18].

### 9.5.1 System Design Considerations

System design considerations lie at the heart of developing robust and secure IoT systems. This will be succeeded by scalability. Most IoT environments comprise numerous interrelated devices; the system should be able to efficiently handle growing loads as additional devices are added. Indeed, designing for scalability implies choosing a proper architecture—microservices or, in fact, cloud-based solutions—which allows dynamic resource allocation depending on demand. This will ensure that performance and reliability do not suffer when it grows.

Another important consideration at this level would be ground-up security. That presupposes building in security by design so that protection mechanisms are inlaid at each layer. It provides secure boot processes, encrypted communications, and hardware-based security features such as Trusted Platform Modules. In addition, it is equally important to ensure that the devices are capable of doing secure firmware updates for addressing vulnerabilities that most certainly will be found post-deployment. An integrated approach to security will help in making resilient IoT systems that can withstand several cyber threats [19].

### 9.5.2 Scalability and Performance Issues

One of the major challenges to IoT design and deployment is scalability and performance problems. Systems should deal efficiently with increasing volumes of data and communication traffic due to a rise in the number of connected devices. Scalability ensures that the designs developed in architectures can expand without any glitch, to accommodate additional devices without a deterioration in performance. Load balancing, distributed computing, and cloud-based services—these are some techniques that are in use to manage resources dynamically, ensuring consistent performance in spite of increasing loads. If this scalability is not built-in to the system, then bottlenecks, crashes of systems, and latent operations can create problems for the efficient running of IoT applications.

Most of the performance-related problems occur due to insufficient data processing and storage capabilities. IoT devices produce a huge amount of data that needs very robust processing power and efficient strategies for data management. Edge computing solutions can offload some of the performance bottlenecks by processing data closer to the source, thereby reducing latency and bandwidth usage [19]. Optimizing data storage solutions through high-performance databases and using efficient compression techniques for data storage will also help in system responsiveness. Most importantly, high throughput and low latency must be ensured from the system architecture to support continuously optimal performance when the IoT ecosystem continues to grow [20].

### 9.5.3 Practical Implementation Steps

Deployment of IoT systems involves real pragmatic steps. Planning and requirement analysis are the initial steps in the deployment process. The determination of the needs and objectives of deployment allows for the design of a system to yield a desired output. This comprises the type of devices, the data to be captured, and the communication protocols to be used. A comprehensive plan provides a pathway for deploying the system and helps in tackling any challenge or need of resources during this period.

The next step would be to make proper choices based on appropriate designs of hardware and software building blocks. Choices to ensure the devices will have the right kind and amount of sensors, processing power, and connectivity options so that the systems may work correctly; apart from robust software platforms which provide for device management, data processing, and security features. Hence, at the time of making this choice, one should have hardware and software component compatibility and interoperability in mind. Better reliability and efficiency ensure the smooth functioning of all components of the IoT system together. This is followed by component deployment and integration. Devices are installed in their respective environments and configured for communication with the central management system. IoT implementation is incomplete without some form of continuous monitoring and maintenance. To that respect, the setting up of a framework for continuous monitoring allows for the identification and resolution of problems as they arise. The periodic software updates and security patches will help to keep the system resilient against the new threats that keep mushrooming. The data analytics tools will provide insights regarding system performance, thereby facilitating continuous improvement and optimization. Using these practical steps for implementation, organizations can efficiently deploy and manage IoT systems to realize the objectives and assure sustainable operation of the system.

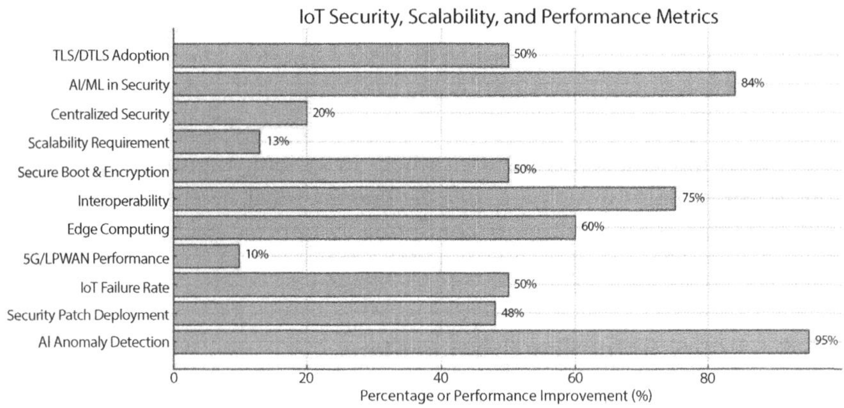


## 9.6 Recent Advances and Future Trends

With the recent advancement in IoT, its capability and applicability of interconnected devices have increased manifold. Now, with AI and ML at its core, IoT systems perform intelligently and autonomously. Such large volumes of data can be generated with the help of IoT devices in real-time, which AI algorithms can analyze to offer actionable insights and predictive analytics. It has benefited improved decision-making processes in industries like healthcare, manufacturing, and smart cities.

Future trends in IoT technology do point to even greater developments and wide diffusion. The expected trends are the expansion of 5G networks, which are set to give even faster data transmission speeds, lower latency, and increased connectivity in the case of IoT devices. This development will definitely support even more complex IoT applications and others that are data-intensive, like autonomous vehicles and advanced industrial automation. Another fast-emerging trend is in security and privacy.

### 9.6.1 Innovations in Deep Learning for Security

Deep learning has found its applications in various domains, and hence enhanced the capabilities of security systems. One major innovation involves advanced anomaly detection models. The models represent deep learning techniques aimed at detecting deviations from normal behavior in network traffic, user activity, and system operations. These models are designed to learn continuously from huge amounts of data, making them capable of detecting very slight, subtle, and sophisticated threats which traditional security measures might have otherwise overlooked. The method has been very effective, particularly in the identification of zero-day attacks and advanced persistent threats, hence providing added protection against critical systems. Table 9.1 provides the comparison of IoT security with metric, estimated value(%) and source.

**Table 9.1** IoT security, scalability, and performance metrics table.

| Category | Metric | Estimated value (%) | Source |
|---|---|---|---|
| **Frameworks for IoT Security** | Acceptance of TLS/ DTLS | 50% | JumpCloud |
| | AI/ML in the Security Domain | 84% | DemandSage |
| | Implementation of Centralized Security | 20% | DigitalMatter |
| **Aspects of System Design** | Scalability Growth of IoT | 13% YoY | IoT Analytics |
| | Safe Startup & Encryption | 50% | JumpCloud |
| | Mutual compatibility | 75% | Dataversity |
| **Scalability and Efficiency** | Adoption of Edge Computing | 60% | Haltian |
| | Enhancement of 5G/ LPWAN Performance | 10x Faster | Statista |
| **Monitoring and Execution** | Failure Rate of IoT (because of outdated software) | 50% | JumpCloud |
| | Patch Deployment Speed for Security | Within 48 Hours | JumpCloud |
| | AI Anomaly Detection Accuracy | 95% | DemandSage |

One more exciting innovation in this regard has to do with the potentials of generative adversarial networks applied for cybersecurity. GANs consist of two neural networks: one generating synthetic data and another estimating whether that data is real or not. In case of security applications, GANs will generate quite realistic adversarial examples against which it would be possible to test the robustness of machine learning models. This process helps in the identification and addressing of vulnerabilities before they can be used by actual attackers. GANs could also, in many ways, be used to add variability and realism to datasets for better training of security models through augmentation techniques. This invention greatly improved the resilience of the security systems to a large variety of vectors.

Another key advancement is to integrate deep reinforcement learning into security frameworks. Deep reinforcement models learn an optimal strategy on defense by themselves, interacting with the environment and receiving feedback from actions [21]. They model dynamic and developing threats, improve in effectiveness over time, and are applied to threat hunting, intrusion detection, and incident response. Deep reinforcement learning enables adaptive capabilities for making a security system proactive and resilient in which security measures counter even the most advanced threats. These deep-learning innovations at hand compose a very powerful toolkit to defend against an exponentially complicated view of cyber threat landscapes. Trends in IoT security dealing with the growth in interoperability and hazards of connected devices are fast emerging. One noticeable trend has been the rise of Blockchain technology, having adoption in bids to enhance security and transparency across IoT networks. Its decentralized nature ensures that all transactions of information are immutable and verifiable, reducing the risk of interference and fraud. Consequently, blockchain implementation in IoT can become a potential means for secure device authentication, integrity of data, and audit trails that bring about vast improvements in security posture to any IoT ecosystem. Therefore, this trend tends to gain ground when organizations seek out more robust and reliable security solutions for their IoT deployments.

The domain of security itself is also gearing toward the implementation of AI-based solutions. AI and machine-learning algorithms are an intrinsic part of the very framework of security for IoT that deals with real-time threat detection and response. Only AI-driven systems would be able to analyze such large amounts of data churned out by IoT devices, looking for patterns and anomalies indicative of security threats. Real-time predictions coupled with automated responses for the threats allow proactive management of these threats, thereby drastically reducing the window of attack. Application of AI to IoT security is very opportune because it offers scaled, adaptive protection against fast-evolving cyber threats.

Another important trend is the development of secure hardware and embedded security solutions. As a result, in an effort to keep these associated devices secure, the manufacturers are starting to instill security into the IoT devices with measures like hardware-based encryption, secure boot, and resistant modules to tampering. These security capabilities innately built within a device, therefore, form a core level of protection that helps resist attacks at the physical level and cyberattacks. This design methodology is crucial for the realization of IoT devices operating in areas of critical or sensitive environments—for example, healthcare, industrial control systems, and smart infrastructures.

These are new trends driven by the proactive, multilevel approach to security within IoT, underpinned by advanced technologies and innovative strategies arrayed against a high-tech threat landscape. Trends like this will foster enhanced resilience of IoT systems concerning their security and focus on safe and efficient operation of interconnected devices.

### 9.6.2 Future Research Directions

Research paths in IoT security include the building of resilience and robustness in the interconnected systems. Another important research involves developing encryption techniques that work at par with IoT device requirements. Traditional methods of encryption can prove inefficient for most resource-constrained IoT devices. A lot of research is going on for lightweight encryption algorithms that have robust security without overstressing the computational capability of the devices. These are essential for providing integrity and confidentiality of data among various IoT applications, ranging from smart homes to industrial automation [22].

Machine learning and artificial intelligence are unbiasedly accelerating the development process of security in IoT. Future research directions perfect the AI-driven security solutions in terms of anomaly detection and threat prediction. The outcome should come up with advanced models that ensure correct identification and reaction to complex attack patterns. Federated learning, a decentralized way of machine learning across multiple IoT devices without actually sharing raw data, is an area of research underway. This will maintain more privacy and security while gaining from the collective wisdom of the IoT ecosystem.

## 9.7 Conclusion

The rapid proliferation of IoT devices is opening up a host of opportunities and, concomitantly, challenges to cybersecurity. Ensuring security and reliability in interconnected systems is foremost to tap the complete potential of IoT. Important threats coming from adversarial attacks, network vulnerabilities, and scalability issues will have to be ordained, addressing new innovation solutions and a comprehensive strategy for IoT security. Deep learning and other AI-driven methodologies have been shown to have a high potential for significantly improving detection and mitigation of cyber threats, thus providing advanced tools for the protection of IoT ecosystems.

Improvements in encryption methods, AI-powered anomaly detection, and secure hardware solutions have considerably strengthened the security framework in IoT systems. Blockchain technology and quantum computing are such emerging technologies that will further paradigmatically shift the IoT security towards sustaining robust protection against emergent and sophisticated cyber-attacks.

In this respect, IoT security in the future will be multifaceted, binding technological innovation with strict compliance and regulatory requirements alongside ethical considerations. In this vein, lightweight encryption algorithms, quantum-resistant cryptographic techniques, and AI-based security solutions will be very instrumental in tackling fast-changing threat landscapes. In addition, bringing security awareness to users and organizations and encouraging best practices form part of the core business of enhancing the security stance of IoT ecosystems. It is only upon taking these measures that the power of IoT technology will securely and reliably be harnessed.

### 9.7.1 Key Takeaways

Last but not least, the takeaway messages from the IoT security discussion are very fundamental in ensuring that sturdy, dependable interconnected systems are a reality. Of fundamental importance is to ensure actual use of advanced encryption techniques.

Lightweight and efficient encryption methods that can be deployed on resource-constrained IoT devices are quite important in data integrity and confidentiality. Such techniques will keep sensitive information in its place and out of the reach of unauthorized access and tampering, in turn elevating the general security posture of IoT ecosystems.

The second point of learning regards the role of artificial intelligence and machine learning within the security of IoT. Equipped with AI-driven, anomaly detection, and predictive analysis, tools are put in place that identify threats and take them down in real-time. These systems are adaptive and scalable for security through continuous data pattern analysis and learning about new threats. AI-based measures ensure that firms are taking proactive measures with potential vulnerabilities and acting fast to fight off cyber threats.

It has adopted future-looking approaches with regard to blockchain technology integration and the use of quantum-resistant cryptographic methods for future proofing of IoT security. Since blockchain is immutable and decentralized, it provides high-level security and transparency; hence, it would be one good add-on for IoT networks.

Finally, creating a security-aware culture and following best practices could be the stepping stones for successfully treading on how to implement security measures for IoT. Some best practices include user and organizational education about common cyber threats, promotion of strong forms of authentication, and frequent software updates and patches. Marrying technological advances to proactive security controls and user awareness can enable the full exploitation of the potential that IoT technology can offer in a safe and secure manner.

### 9.7.2 Implications for IoT Security and Deep Learning Applications

The intersection of security in the IoT and deep learning applications has a number of implications for improving the resilience of connected systems. First, deep learning models can improve threat detection and response. Deep learning models, mostly anomaly detection variants, can intake data volumes produced by IoT devices in real-time and analyze them to identify patterns and anomalies indicative of security threats. This will allow for the detection of cyber-attacks in a better and real-time fashion, hence rapid mitigation measures that can reduce the risk of wide-scale damage. Deep learning integration at this level improves resilience and the robustness of the IoT security framework.

The other key implication relates to the scalability of security solutions. Most IoT settings include a lot of devices that differ in capability and resource constraints. Deep learning algorithms, particularly edge-optimized ones, make it possible to offload processing tasks across the network so that efficient and scalable security measures could be implemented within IoT environments. That way, enhanced security features are extended to the most resource-constrained devices without ever overrunning computational capacities. This would hence effectively scale deep learning applications in protecting large IoT deployments, thus conserving performance and security across varied environments.

Another important implication of using deep learning in IoT security is ethical and regulatory considerations. It is very important to ensure that deep learning models meet privacy laws and ethical standards, more so when dealing with sensitive data generated from the IoT devices. There is a need to develop transparent and explainable AI models to maintain user trust and compliance with the set regulations. Further, research in fair and unbiased algorithms of AI should be uninterrupted to avoid the practices of discrimination and give fair solutions for security. Ethical and regulatory challenges must be met to create a responsible route for deployment of deep learning applications in IoT security, so that technological advances benefit all parties while protecting privacy and rights.

**AI disclosure statement:** The author acknowledges the use of AI-based tools for minor language editing or grammatical correction. However, all intellectual contributions, analyses, and conclusions presented in this chapter are entirely the author's own.

## References

1. Li, Y., Zhang, X., Sun, M., Chen, W., Li, Y., An attack-agnostic defense method against adversarial attacks on speaker verification by fusing downsampling and upsampling of speech signals. *Inf. Sci. (Ny).*, 670, 120618, 2024.
2. Li, B., Gong, A., Zhang, J., Fu, Z., From image-level to pixel-level labeling: A weakly-supervised learning method for identifying aquaculture ponds using iterative anti-adversarial attacks guided by aquaculture features. *Int. J. Appl. Earth Obs. Geoinf.*, 132, 104023, 2024.
3. Li, F., Shen, W., Bi, Z., Su, X., Sparse Adversarial Learning for FDIA Attack Sample Generation in Distributed Smart Grids. *C. Comput. Model. Eng. Sci.*, 139, 2, 2095–2115, 2024.
4. Chyad, M., *et al.*, Exploring Adversarial Deep Learning for Fusion in Multi-Color Channel Skin Detection Applications. *Inf. Fusion*, 102632, 2024.
5. Nagarajan, S.M., Devarajan, G.G., Ramana, T.V., Asha, J.M., Bashir, A.K., Al-Otaibi, Y.D., Adversarial Deep Learning Based Dampster–Shafer Data Fusion Model for Intelligent Transportation System. *Inf. Fusion*, 102, 102050, 2024.

6. Roshan, K., Zafar, A., UlHaque, S.B., Untargeted white-box adversarial attack with heuristic defence methods in real-time deep learning based network intrusion detection system. *Comput. Commun.*, 218, 97–113, 2024.
7. Chen, Z., *et al.*, A method for recovering adversarial samples with both adversarial attack forensics and recognition accuracy. *Comput. Secur.*, 144, 103987, 2024.
8. Amini, S., Heshmati, A., Ghaemmaghami, S., Fast adversarial attacks to deep neural networks through gradual sparsification. *Eng. Appl. Artif. Intell.*, 127, 107360, 2024.
9. Taheri, R., Shojafar, M., Arabikhan, F., Gegov, A., Unveiling vulnerabilities in deep learning-based malware detection: Differential privacy driven adversarial attacks. *Comput. Secur.*, 146, 104035, 2024.
10. Randhawa, R.H., Aslam, N., Alauthman, M., Khalid, M., Rafiq, H., Deep Reinforcement Learning Based Evasion Generative Adversarial Network for Botnet Detection. *Futur. Gener. Comput. Syst*, 150, 294–302, 2024.
11. Roshan, M.K. and Zafar, A., Boosting robustness of network intrusion detection systems: A novel two phase defense strategy against untargeted white-box optimization adversarial attack. *Expert Syst. Appl.*, 249, 123567, 2024.
12. Roshan, K. and Zafar, A., Black-box adversarial transferability: An empirical study in cybersecurity perspective. *Comput. Secur.*, 141, 103853, 2024.
13. Dunston, S.D. and M.A.R.V., AIPA: An Adversarial Imperceptible Patch Attack on Medical Datasets and its Interpretability. *Comput. Secur.*, 136, 103574, 2024.
14. Aurangzeb, M., *et al.*, Enhancing cybersecurity in smart grids: Deep black box adversarial attacks and quantum voting ensemble models for blockchain privacy-preserving storage. *Energy Rep.*, 11, 2493–2515, 2024, https://doi.org/10.1016/j.egyr.2024.02.010.
15. M.Macas, C. and Fuertes, W., Adversarial examples: A survey of attacks and defenses in deep learning-enabled cybersecurity systems. *Expert Syst. Appl.*, 238, 122223, 2024.
16. Yuan, X., Han, S., Huang, W., Ye, H., Kong, X., Zhang, F., A simple framework to enhance the adversarial robustness of deep learning-based intrusion detection system. *Comput. Secur.*, 137, 103644, 2024.
17. Li, C., Zhu, Z., Niu, R., Zhao, Y., Enhancing adversarial robustness for deep metric learning *via* neural discrete adversarial training. *Comput. Secur.*, 143, 103899, 2024.
18. Wang, Z. and Aouf, N., Efficient adversarial attacks detection for deep reinforcement learning-based autonomous planetary landing GNC. *Acta Astronaut.*, 224, 37–47, 2024.
19. Pang, J., Yuan, C., Xia, Z., Li, X., Fu, Z., Spatial-frequency gradient fusion based model augmentation for high transferability adversarial attack. *Knowledge-Based Syst.*, 301, 112241, 2024.
20. Barik, K. and Misra, S., Adversarial attack defense analysis: An empirical approach in cybersecurity perspective. *Softw. Impacts*, 21, 100681, 2024.

21. J. Fang, Jiang, Y., Jiang, C., Jiang, Z.L., Liu, C., Yiu, S.-M., State-of-the-art optical-based physical adversarial attacks for deep learning computer vision systems. *Expert Syst. Appl.*, 250, 123761, 2024.
22. Zhang, Y. and Sun, Z., Cross-domain facial expression recognition based on adversarial attack fine-tuning learning. *Eng. Appl. Artif. Intell.*, 136, 109014, 2024.

# 10

# Federated Learning for Intrusion Detection in Edge Computing for Cloud IoT Systems

**Krupali Gosai***, **Hansa Vaghela, Yogeshwar Prajapati and Om Prakash Suthar**

*Faculty of Technology, Marwadi University, Rajkot, Gujarat, India*

***Abstract***

The growing popularity of Internet of Things (IoT) devices, along with the continuous rise in cyber threats requires the implementation of robust and flexible intrusion detection systems (IDS). Conventional centralized Intrusion Detection System (IDS) methods are frequently impeded by delays, limitations in data transmission capacity, and worries about maintaining privacy. In this chapter we examine the combination of Federated Learning (FL) and Edge Computing as a potential option for improving intrusion detection in Cloud IoT systems. Federated learning enables the decentralized training of machine learning models on several edge devices, allowing them to jointly gain knowledge of a global model while keeping the data localized. This decentralized strategy effectively minimizes privacy hazards and diminishes the necessity for data transfer to central servers, therefore resolving both latency and bandwidth concerns. The chapter starts by providing a comprehensive examination of the architecture of the Internet of Things (IoT) and the security problems that are inherent in cloud IoT systems. Next, we explore the fundamental concepts of federated learning and how it might be used for intrusion detection and also discuss important methods for implementing federated learning in edge computing contexts. These methods include model aggregation, communication efficiency, and security modifications to safeguard against adversarial attacks. The effectiveness of FL-based IDS in identifying many sorts of cyber threats, including DDoS assaults, malware, and unauthorized access is demonstrated through the presentation of multiple case studies and experimental findings. It also includes the difficulties posed by the diversity of IoT devices and

**Corresponding author*: krupaligosai17@gmail.com

Partha Ghosh, Rajdeep Chakraborty, Anupam Ghosh and Ahmed A. Elngar (eds.) Strategic Approaches to Intrusion Detection in Cloud-IoT Ecosystem, (251–282) © 2026 Scrivener Publishing LLC

suggest methods to guarantee the precision and resilience of models. Here, we examine prospective areas for future study and development in this sector, emphasizing the capacity of FL to transform cybersecurity in IoT networks. Federated learning facilitates the decentralized training of machine learning systems across multiple cutting-edge devices, permitting them to acquire insight into a global model while maintaining the data confined.

***Keywords***: Federated learning (FL), intrusion detection system (IDS), edge computing, internet of things (IoT), MQTT, transport layer security (TLS), CNN (convolutional neural network), MLP (multi-layered perception)

## 10.1 Introduction

### 10.1.1 Overview of Cloud IoT Systems

A cloud-based internet of things (IoT) system puts together the benefits of the cloud and the internet of things to create a network infrastructure for collecting, storing, and analyzing data. Sensors, actuators, and automated appliances are but some of the IoT devices making up these systems that produce tremendous amounts of data in real time. Edge computing nodes usually handle the information locally for the purpose of reducing latency and bandwidth consumption. At this point, the edge computing nodes start processing information closer to its source. Communication networks such as Wi-Fi, 5G, and LPWAN transfer the processed data to a cloud system that acts as the central node for complex management of information, evaluation, and decision-making using strong machine learning algorithms. It scales because processing can be distributed among many edge nodes for the growing number of IoT devices. It also increases energy efficiency because it does its computations locally, reducing dependency on cloud resources. The benefits make edge computing an important technology in creating faster, safer, and more flexible IoT systems.

Cloud IoT systems are trying to combat these issues by adopting computing at the edge to perform time-sensitive operations and intrusion detection systems to protect against cyber threats. The combination of these safeguards and decentralized machine learning methods like federated learning [1], which is a system that can recognize and stop the attacks while protecting user data. As such, modern applications can use cloud IoT systems that are safer, more efficient, and more reliable than ever.

### 10.1.2 Role of Edge Computing in IoT

Edge computing [2], is important in IoT because it enables the processing of data near the source, thus lowering latency and increasing efficiency. Edge computing performs local computations on devices such as gateways or local servers, rather than sending all information to centralized cloud systems, thus enabling real-time reactions in time-sensitive applications, including medical care, automation in factories, and autonomous vehicles. It locally enhances bandwidth efficiency by sending just relevant data to the cloud; hence, it decreases congestion as well as costs on the network. Edge computing also promotes security; it reduces the chances of breaches since data exposure is minimized to external networks. It scales because processing can be dispersed among many edge nodes for the increasing number of IoT devices. It also increases energy efficiency because it performs computations locally, thereby reducing dependence on cloud resources. These advantages make edge computing an essential technology for creating faster, safer, and more flexible IoT systems.

### 10.1.3 Importance of Intrusion Detection

An important component of cybersecurity is an Intrusion Detection [3], within networked systems such as those of IoT that raises susceptibility to cyber-attacks through multiple connections and data items. In this context, the task of an IDS is to poll network traffic, systems, and applications looking for indications of unauthorized access or malicious acts or policy breach. An IDS is imperative for the early identification of possible attacks, which can subsequently be utilized in response to mitigation of damage in a prompt manner. In the wake of the fact that sensitive data is exchanged among devices and networks in cloud IoT environments, very much needed is an IDS to protect privacy and also maintain the integrity of the systems. It protects from a vast range of threats including malware, DDoS attacks, and unauthorized access that can compromise the entire network.

This would let businesses strengthen their security controls step by step with visibility into patterns of attacks from an IDS. In the fast-emerging cyber threat world, today, there is a sharp need for IoT-based infrastructures to integrate IDSs to assure maximum security and resilience. An IDS thus offers data safety by rapidly identifying intrusions and ensuring that the system is operational in integrity and reliability, which therefore supports business continuity and user confidence.

### 10.1.4 Federated Learning: A Decentralized Approach

Federated learning is a type of decentralized machine learning in which IoT edge devices or nodes can work together to build shared models while protecting their private information and preventing access to sensitive data. In situations like cloud IoT systems, where a high consumption of safe data privacy, security, and response time is required, this becomes vitally important. In the context of intrusion detection systems, federated learning allows the security models to be locally trained on edge devices such as IoT sensors or gateways by transmitting only model updates rather than raw data [4].

Federated learning employs distributed data from numerous devices in the edge computing and IoT system domains to allow the sensitive information to be locally stored in every device, making global models more effective. It's a methodology that introduces collaborative learning and overcomes crucial concerns such as data sovereignty, bandwidth, and regulations. The main reason is that new solutions should be developed due to managing non-IID data or better communication, or provide the best security against adversarial attacks. Industries as healthcare, smart cities and finances can easily exploit the use of federated learning provided that the protection of data becomes absolute in itself. It brings decentralization and complex machine learning methodologies together, thus enabling safe, scalable, and efficient AI algorithms in various and distributed environments. Below mentioned Figure 10.1 shows the evidence of cloud integrated IoT architecture.

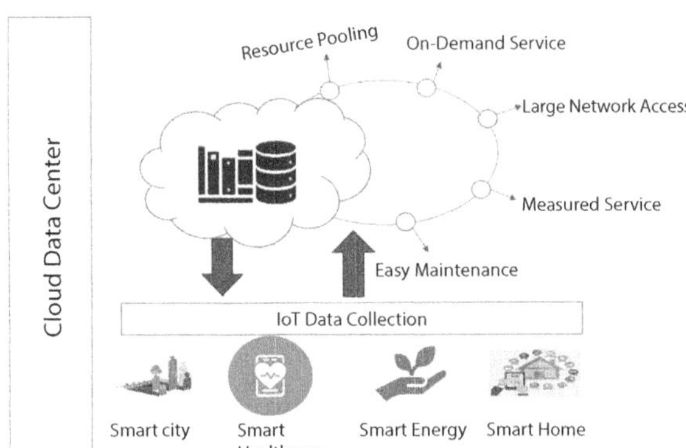


**Figure 10.1** Architecture for cloud integrated IoT.

## 10.2 Background

### 10.2.1 Related Work

The rapid growth of the internet of things (IoT) has increased the need for advanced security solutions, especially intrusion detection systems (IDS) [5]. Traditional IDS methods, including signature-based detection, anomaly detection, and rule-based systems, have been widely used to protect IoT networks. However, these techniques often struggle to cope with the dynamic and diverse nature of IoT environments, as mentioned in Figure 10.2.

Traditional methods for intrusion detection techniques include signature-based and anomaly-based approaches in the IoT. Signature-based IDS matches network traffic or device behavior against a database of known threat signatures. Although such detection would be exemplary in detecting an already-known attack, generally, this will have poor detection rates with regards to unknown or sophisticated threats. Anomaly-based detection establishes what normal behavior looks like, and after that, it flags variations from that as potentially being intrusive. This is not efficient for identifying unknown attacks, and the generated false positives could be high. Traditional approaches face a challenging situation in IoT environments that are characterized by the heterogeneity of the devices with limited processing capabilities and restrictions of resources.

#### *10.2.1.1 Signature-Based Detection*

IDS based on signatures relies on predefined patterns of attacks, so-called signatures of already-known attacks. This kind of method is very effective in finding known threats but performs poorly concerning new, unseen ones. IoT devices, because of the diversity and fast dynamics of attack

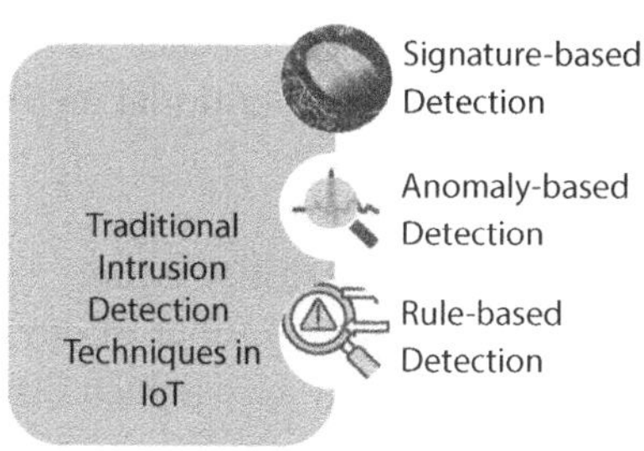


**Figure 10.2** Traditional intrusion detection techniques in IoT.

methods, take novel threats as a bigger challenge. Thus, signature-based detection cannot answer the needs of adequate security of IoT.

#### *10.2.1.2 Anomaly-Based Detection*

In anomaly-based detection, an IDS learns the normal activities of the system and flags variations from this baseline as possibly intrusive. While it allows for the detection of attacks that were previously unknown, it is very liable to high false-positive rates, especially in IoT environments due to the wide variability of device behaviors.

#### *10.2.1.3 Rule-Based Detection*

The rule-based systems depend on certain predefined rules to identify suspicious activities. While these systems are relatively easy to deploy and interpret, they face serious scalability and adaptability challenges, especially within large and diverse IoT networks. Most of the time, these systems require continuous manual updates to be effective, which is quite challenging in dynamic IoT ecosystems.

### 10.2.2 Limitations of Centralized Intrusion Detection in IoT

Most importantly, centralized intrusion detection faces huge power in IoT systems, while the network scale gets large. All data needs to be forwarded to a center for detection analysis in centralized systems, which may have big latency and excessive usage in bandwidth. It is highly undesirable for real-time applications where fast responses have critical importance. Moreover, all sensitive data is transmitted to and stored in a middle site in centralized systems; thus, privacy risks also exist. Also, centralized systems are vulnerable to single-point failures; once a central server is compromised, then the whole network is put in jeopardy. Such challenges outline the necessity of more distributed and scalable approaches for intrusion detection in IoT systems. These aforementioned conventional methods have numerous weaknesses concerning IoT:

**Probably the most fundamental scalability issue:**
IoT networks are composed of a large number of devices, and traditional systems often fail to scale up efficiently across such distributed networks.

**Adaptability:**
Traditional IDS approaches struggle to stay current with the ever-evolving threats present in dynamic IoT environments.

**Resource Constraints:**
Many IoT devices have limited computational power and energy, so it's not feasible to use intrusion detection methods that require heavy computation on these devices.

**High False Positives:**
Innumerable IoT devices and their anomalous behavior share in the huge rate of false positives arising from anomaly-based and rule-based systems, hence decreasing its reliability.

### 10.2.3 Federated Learning for Security Applications [6]

Federated learning has emerged as a very promising solution to security applications in decentralized networks. Federated Learning (FL) addresses many challenges linked to centralized machine learning by enabling devices to train models locally and share only the aggregated updates. In the context of intrusion detection, FL facilitates the identification of attacks across various devices while avoiding the need to access the raw data from those devices. The distribution in training helps to advance privacy because sensitive data does not leave the device, though it enables the detection of new and evolving threats. Federated learning can be applied to IDS to enhance detection accuracy and reduce false alarms for its fitment in IoT environments.

#### *10.2.3.1 Federated Learning: Benefits for IoT Intrusion Detection*

**Privacy Preservation:**
As FL does not need to share raw data across devices or any central systems, it enhances the protection of sensitive IoT data privacy. This is very important in an IoT environment, where security and privacy are considered critical.

**Scalability:**
FL allows for distributed processing, hence highly scalable, to manage very large IoT networks by training models across many devices without overloading a central server.

**Adaptability:**
Models of FL can be continuously updated with fresh data from individual devices to quickly adapt to changing IoT environments and emerging threats.

**Reduced Latency:**
Because FL allows training a model in a local setting and only shares model updates, this significantly cuts down latency in intrusion detection tasks that are pretty relevant in real-time IoT security.

**Resource Efficiency:**
FL reduces the number of computations on devices because in FL, the requirement to perform computations at a centralized server is minimized. This advantage is particularly important for limited IoT devices that cannot run complex machine learning tasks.

#### *10.2.3.2 Challenges of Federated Learning in IoT Security*

**Communication Overhead:**
Updates between devices and the central server can create additional communication overhead, which may become a bottleneck in large-scale IoT networks.

**Non-IID Data:**
IoT devices generate most of their data in a non-independent and identically distributed fashion; hence, FL will find it difficult to train the global model.

**Convergence of Model:**
Convergence to a robust solution without getting overfitted to the local data itself is the biggest challenge faced by the federated model, especially in IoT networks that contain heterogeneous devices.

### 10.2.4 Comparative Analysis of Federated Learning and Traditional Machine Learning in Security

Running a comparative analysis of federation learning against traditional machine learning in security applications brings quite some interesting observations to the surface, such as, most noted differences: central machine learning models require mammoth quantities of data for aggregations as a batch for subsequent local processing-a totally inefficient again and a not very secure approach for IoT environments. The differences with federated learning can be mentioned as follows: whereas with federated learning, central device training ensures data privacy at devices and reduces significant risks associated with centralized data pooling. This also makes it more scalable and efficient for large-scale IoT networks by using federated learning. However, it does raise a lot of questions relating to model synchronization, heterogeneity, and communication overheads that the management needs to take care about meticulously.

## 10.3 Federated Learning in Edge Computing for Intrusion Detection

### 10.3.1 Overview of Federated Learning

Federated learning is a collaborative machine learning methodology enabling numerous devices or nodes to train a common model while preserving the confidentiality of their raw data. Each device uses its local dataset to train the model, computes the updates (or gradients), and transmits these updates to a central server for aggregation [7]. Each then undergoes consolidation as a centralized server updates its global model with these combined updates, the process then being iterated. Since this technology saves transmission of data over the network, data privacy is guaranteed and networking expenses are reduced. In contexts where devices have constraints on both bandwidth and storage capacity, federated learning is very useful.

### 10.3.2 Architecture of Federated Learning for Edge Computing

The architecture of federated learning in edge computing has many critical components: edge devices (such as IoT devices), a central server (or aggregator), and communication protocols. Edge devices facilitate local data processing and model training, while preserving data privacy. The central server aggregates model updates from these devices to create a global model. Subsequently, the devices obtain updates incorporating the new global model. This configuration facilitates real-time decision-making at the edge, reducing the necessity to transmit data to the cloud and ensuring diminished latency. Moreover, security protocols like differential privacy [7], and secure aggregation can protect the system from potential attackers [8].

### 10.3.3 Federated Learning Workflow for Intrusion Detection

- In the field of security detection, the federated learning process comprises many essential stages:
- Model Initialization - A global model is created and disseminated to edge devices.
- Local Training - Each edge device trains the model on its own local dataset, which may encompass network traffic or device behavior data.
- Model Update: When the local training is over, the devices send their model changes to the central computer, but not the raw data.
- Aggregation: The central server takes changes from many devices and puts them all together to make a better global model.
- The modified global model is returned to the equipment for further training. This technique enables devices to collaborate in detecting breaches while protecting data privacy and decreasing the number of required contacts.

## 10.4 Challenges and Solutions [16]

### 10.4.1 Data Privacy and Security

Because the sheer volume of sensitive information that is produced and shared today is enormous, security and privacy of data are a priority in the modern connected digital world. Privacy can be said to be about preventing unwanted access to personal and business data. Security means the protection of systems against cyber threats like hacking, malware, and breaches. IoT and cloud domains require encryption, secure authentication along with access control methods with the strong solutions to counter threats of data disclosure, interception and unintended modification. Also, technologies like federated learning and blockchain decentralize data processing and ensure its integrity and improve privacy further. This makes security and confidentiality of information a crucial priority, so that trust remains intact and legal compliance and dependability are maintained.

**Ensuring Data Confidentiality Across Edge Devices**

The security of sensitive data in decentralized systems relies on the assurance of data secrecy across edge devices. Secure boot and data encryption are two ways to protect sensitive data during storage or transport. Robust authentication protocols and access limitations prevent unauthorized individuals from obtaining data. Federated learning internally processes raw data to reduce its exposure. Other privacy-protecting [9], techniques include anonymization and data obfuscation. It increases secure communication with lightweight protocols. Issues are periodically fixed through patches and upgrades. Once these strategies are combined, they enable edge computing systems to reduce security risks. They protect sensitive IoT environments and maintain data privacy. Data encryption and secure boot ensure that sensitive data is kept safe while it is in transit and storage. Strong authentication procedures and access controls can make it difficult for unauthorized entities to gain access to your data. Federated learning processes raw data internally to make it less noticeable.

### 10.4.2 Communication Overhead and Bandwidth Efficiency

Communication overhead and bandwidth efficiency issues are important in edge computing and IoT systems, since devices generate large amounts of data. The efficient solutions of the problems here are minimized transfer of unnecessary data to preserve the efficiency of the system. Reduced amount of data communication decreases bandwidth. Also, data compression results in reduced volume of transferred data. The need for edge processing for local data analysis and filtering is necessary to reduce volume transported to central servers. It is event driven transmission that 'transmits only pertinent data on some trigger point in an attempt to increase bandwidth efficiency and postpone the identification of patterns of data.'

Federated learning provides improved bandwidth efficiency, as it transmits model updates, rather than raw data to protect privacy, and so communicate overhead. Lightweight protocols like MQTT [10], and CoAP [11], minimize communication payloads, facilitating efficient data transmission with low resource use. Data aggregation consolidates inputs from several devices into a singular transmission, hence reducing unnecessary data transport. Moreover, adaptive sampling modifies the rate of data acquisition according to network circumstances, hence optimizing the utilization of available bandwidth.

**Strategies for Minimizing Data Transfer [12]**

Methods such as compression of data, edge the process, and federated learning can significantly decrease the amount of data transmitted in IoT and edge computing. Table 10.1 shows the various data privacy and security methods with their key attributes. Compact protocols and information aggregation improve efficiency, guaranteeing lower overhead without

**Table 10.1** Data privacy and security methods.

| Method | Encrypts data | Protects hardware | Restricts access | Verifies identity | Preserves privacy | Secures transmission | Anonymizes data | Ensures integrity |
|---|---|---|---|---|---|---|---|---|
| End-to-End Encryption | Yes | No | No | No | Yes | Yes | No | No |
| Secure Hardware Modules | No | Yes | No | No | No | No | No | Yes |
| Access Control Mechanisms | No | No | Yes | No | No | No | No | No |
| Authentication Protocols | No | No | No | Yes | No | No | No | No |
| Federated Learning | Yes | No | No | No | Yes | Yes | No | No |
| Secure Data Transmission | Yes | No | No | No | No | Yes | No | No |
| Data Masking | No | No | No | No | Yes | No | Yes | No |
| Blockchain | No | No | No | No | No | No | No | Yes |

**Table 10.2** Strategies for minimizing data transfer.

| Strategy | Description |
|---|---|
| **Model Compression** | Use reduction and compression to shrink the model. |
| **Data Aggregation** | Reduce data transmissions by aggregating it at the edge. |
| **Sparse Updates** | Transmit exclusively substantial changes or non-zero values. |
| **Periodic Communication** | Transmit data at regular intervals, rather than following each repetition. |
| **Federated Averaging** | Transmit aggregated updates to minimize data volume. |

sacrificing system speed, while adaptive sampling, data filtering, and caching minimize bandwidth utilization. Above mentioned Table 10.2 represents various strategies which can be used to minimize the data transfers.

### 10.4.3 Model Training Efficiency and Accuracy

In the cloud IoT settings, we achieve better speed and accuracy of model training in intrusion detection systems (IDS) through availability of the federated learning which makes way for local model training on the edge devices. It also enables faster data sharing, lower latency, and solves outcall bandwidth issues. Scalability is also enabled, meaning the cloud server doesn't get bogged down as more devices are added to the model. The benefit of federated learning is that it makes precision better with inputs from different devices. It enables the model to generalize and able to differentiate different sorts of attacks. The models are tailored and localized so it's easier to locate threats, and they're changed in a regular way to allow them to easily manage new threats.

**Strategies for Handling Diverse Data Sources in IoT**

Since IoT devices come from everywhere and are from various sensor types and data formats as well as operating circumstances, IoT systems must handle many data sources to ensure the activity of intrusion detection is effective. Another difficulty in analysis is the possibility of heterogeneity of data acquired from these devices. The problem of making data suitable for machine learning model is more general than in our application, and there are a few methods that are used to solve this problem: data filtering, feature extraction, and data normalization. The use of these methods increases the input quality to intrusion detection systems and reduces inherent difficulties due to difference data sources.

One of the ways to handle heterogeneous IoT data is through federated learning, where the local model can be trained on the edge devices. With this, the raw data will remain private while each device gets educated independently with its data. The global model would be more generalizable, and more kinds of different attack behaviors could be detected in various contexts when model updates from multiple edge devices are pooled. Nonetheless, methods for handling non-IID data leave much to be desired and, in turn, may affect model performance and convergence. This is because many different sources of data necessitate particular approaches (flexible and accurate) that specifically address each source of data.

### 10.4.4 Scalability in Large-Scale IoT Networks

Large-scale IoT networks are designed to handle growing hundreds and thousands of devices and accompanying data as a scalable and efficient IoT network. When multiple hundreds or millions of devices are connected across an IoT network, it becomes increasingly complex to process the data that needs to be analyzed. Hence, improvements in scalability for decentralized model training of edge devices come through the application of federated learning. Every device wholly trains independently, without placing an undue burden on the cloud server, and new model update are added. This system is distributed in nature that makes it possible to have real time intrusion detection, sufficient scalability and fast updates at a low communication cost and delay.

**Adapting Federated Learning for High-Volume Systems**

To make federated learning usable in high volume systems such as massive IoT networks we propose two adjustments: improving communication efficiency with model aggregation. Table 10.3 denotes the list of federated learning parameters that are used in high volume system. With the large volumes of data produced by many devices, it is paramount to minimize frequency of model updates and reduce the amount of data sent. To ensure that updates are short and secure, methods such as differential privacy [7], and model compression can be utilized. Efficient algorithms allow us to aggregate model changes such that the central server is not overwhelmed while maintaining performance. Federated learning scales successfully—thanks to the fast and accurate model updates in high volume contexts.

**Table 10.3** Federated learning parameters for high-volume system.

| Parameters | Challenge | Solution | Benefit |
|---|---|---|---|
| **Data Volume** | Massive data collected from a wide variety of sources | Conducting training locally on edge devices and solely transmitting model updates | Lowers latency and bandwidth consumption |
| **Device Diversity** | Distinct devices exhibiting diverse data properties | Extracting features and performing preprocessing | Data standardization improves model performance. |
| **Communication Constraints** | Excessive communication burden in extensive networks | Reliable model updates, regular updates | Saves money on communication and training |
| **Model Updates** | Assembling data from multiple sources | Rapid aggregation techniques | Enhances model precision with reduced effort |
| **Real-Time Processing** | Requirement for quick and accurate intrusion detection | Edge device updates and local processing | Allows for faster detection and response |
| **Data Privacy and Security** | Preserving private information during model training | Privacy methods with differentials | Protects data during model training without revealing it |

## 10.5 Proposed Intrusion Detection Framework Using Federated Learning

### 10.5.1 Framework Design and Architecture

The framework about the intrusion detection system uses federated learning, which enables the building of a joint model across edge devices without violating their privacy. The framework has the following key components:

**Edge Devices:**
These are IoT devices equipped with local storage and computing capabilities, which take and preprocess the network traffic data, trains a local intrusion detection model and decides to send data to the cloud server at some set intervals.

**Cloud Server:**
The leader in the federation learning process, which initializes the global model, receives all the updates from the edge devices, and sends the updated global model again back to the devices, is the cloud server. The server ensures secure and efficient communication among the devices.

**Communication Protocols:**
TLS (Transport Layer Security) is an example of secure communication protocols that are employed to manage and safeguard the interchange of information between edge devices and the cloud server which is the implementer of the model updates.

**Federated Learning Coordinator:**
This is a component within the cloud server whose primary responsibility is to manage the training processes such as the model's initialization, aggregation of updates from the edge devices, and synchronizing the edge devices with the integrated model.

### 10.5.2 Model Selection and Training Processes

Determinant in the success of the intrusion detection framework is both the model's selection and the training process.

**Model Selection:**
Convolutional neural networks have been selected as the model for intrusion detection, owing to its ability to learn patterns from complex sets of

data. Convolutional neural networks (CNNs) use both directly classified data and feature-extracted convolutional layers for feature extraction.

**Local Training Process:**
Each edge device utilizes locally collected and pre-processed data for training the CNN model. Training is an iterative process in which the model learns to identify patterns related to the classification of benign and malicious network traffic across multiple epochs.

**Loss Function and Optimization [13]:**
The model employs categorical cross-entropy as a loss function, which quantifies the degree to which the actual class differs from the predicted class. In addition, SGD with momentum is the optimization approach that updates the model weights during training.

**Federated Training Rounds:**
The integrated model is developed through multiple iterations, with each iteration involving local training on edge devices prior to the aggregation of model updates at the cloud server. This process persists until there are no further changes to the global model.

### 10.5.3 Model Synchronization and Data Combination [14]

Federated learning synchronizes with new models through effective data combination and updating techniques which ensures the models are not only precise but also not outdated.

**Model Update Aggregation:**
Upon local training completion, the edge devices model which was updated is sent towards the cloud server. The federated learning coordinator combines all these updates through the weighted average method, which takes into account the amount of data samples present in each average to analyze what the global model comprises.

**Secure Aggregation Protocols:**
These protocols enable the server to amalgamate model updates while keeping all the edge devices updates private from each other to maintain enhanced privacy.

**Global Model Updating:**
This data collection-based update enables the global model to be updated which is then shared across all edge apparatus. In this way, all the participants have access to the shared knowledge while all the data is securely private.

**Handling Non-IID Data:**
In order to deal with non-IID (non-Independent and Identically Distributed) data scenarios the framework utilizes data normalization among other techniques to ensure optimal model performance is achieved.

### 10.5.4 Federated Intrusion Detection Edge to Cloud Data Flow for Enhanced Security [15]

Technically, the data flow between the edge devices and the cloud server has to be understood if an efficient federated learning framework is to be put in place.

**Data Collection:**
Edge devices are always getting traffic and collecting data for the purpose of intrusion detection. The data collected is retained on the device and is used for the training of the local intrusion detection model.

**Data Preprocessing:**
The data that is to be used for the training of the model undergoes some preprocessing activities such as normalization, encoding, and balancing the data. This stage makes sure that data is in a suitable form for training a model and positively impacts the performance of the model with respect to the quality of its updates.

**Model Training and Update Sharing:**
All edge devices have their local model and train it during each session with the cloud alongside making updated from the most recent global model downloaded from the cloud server. Once encrypted, these updates are sent back to the cloud server so that they are aggregated.

**Model Distribution:**
The cloud server combines the updates and transfers the updated global model to the edge devices. This model forms a feedback loop where updating, training and then distributing the model occurs which in effect improves the model.

**Efficiency of Communication:**
To reduce the communication costs, the architecture in question adopts a number of effective compression techniques and updates, that is, only the critical elements of the model. This development reduces the bandwidth necessary for the transfer of model updates and accelerates the training time.

## 10.6 Implementation and Experimentation

### 10.6.1 Experimental Setup

This subsection encompasses the details about the infrastructure and the configurations employed which are used to assess federated learning to detect invasions in edge computing environments in the cloud IoT systems.

**Hardware and Software Configuration:**
The set up involves a network composed of edge devices and cloud servers. The edge devices are various units of Raspberry Pi 4 which have a maximum of 4 GB RAM, a quad-core ARM Cortex-A72 CPU, and a storage of 32 GB. These devices use Raspbian OS and come with Python 3.9. On the other hand, the cloud server is composed of Intel Xeon E5-2670 furnished with 64 GB of RAM and 2 TB of SSD which also incorporates an ubuntu 20.04 operating system with the use of a docker to run and control the federation tasks therein.

**Network Topology:**
The edge devices are interconnected with a local Wi-Fi network which acts as the radius through which the devices can work and link with other devices which imitates an ordinary IoT installation. The cloud server is connected to a broadband internet connection that allows communication between edge devices to the server.

**Federated Learning Framework:**
We use TensorFlow Federated (TFF) to implement the algorithms of federated learning. The framework enables the emulation of the scenarios of federated learning where several edge devices take part in the training of the model without exchanging their local data.

**Intrusion Detection Dataset:**
Basing off the NSL-KDD dataset, which is a well-known standard data set for intrusion detection, we proceed with edge devices imitating the

real-life data distribution in IoT environment as cited in. – This is done with the goal of conducting the meeting with the IoT devices to provide a more realistic scoop for the presentation alongside with emulating static scenarios and seamless collaboration.

### 10.6.2 Data Collection and Preprocessing

This specific section elaborates on how the data for the federated learning is collected alongside with how it is prepared.

**Data Distribution:**
Diving deeper into the non-identical and the non-distributed scenario which was previously discussed, it is imperative to mention the NSL-KDD dataset bandwidth as being assigned a portion of smaller subdivisions ensuring to be able to feed into various edge devices with the IoT systems recently discussed as non-IID.

**Data Preprocessing on Edge Devices:**
Participating into the federated learning and being recognized as an edge device, local data stored within the device has to be preprocessed first; these steps consist of:

- Normalization: Adjusting the measurement scale of several elements to be between 0 and 1.
- Encoding: One hot encoding intends to use multiple binary variables to represent multiple classes while changing nominal features into numerical features.
- Balancing: Class imbalance among datasets is tackled through SMOTE- Synthetic Minority Over-sampling Technique.

**Data Privacy and Security:**
Data privacy is a significant issue; as such, the edge devices in the abstract utilize noise while preprocessing the data so as to alleviate the chances of reconstructing the data which was updated with the help of the model.

### 10.6.3 Model Training and Evaluation Metrics

The model training process and the performance evaluation techniques are elaborated in this section.

**Federated Learning Process:**
The federated learning procedure consists of a number of training rounds. At every round, the cloud-based server distributes the global model to edge devices which train the model with their data available locally, and send updates to the server. Then, the server collects these updates and creates a new global model. This procedure of e-learning is iterative process is never ending until a convergence is reached.

**Intrusion Detection Model:**
As for the intrusion detection, we employ a convolutional neural network (CNN) model [17], since it can recognize spatial hierarchies in the information. The model architecture includes [18]:

- Input layer which corresponds to the features.
- The convolutional layers having ReLU activated and followed by max-pooling layers.
- The fully connected layers which leads to SoftMax output layer.

**Evaluation Metrics [5]:**
On the other hand, the performance of the intrusion detection model is determined through the mentioned metrics below:

- Accuracy- the number of correctly predicted instances divided over the total number of instances.
- Precision- the true positive prediction over the true positive prediction plus false positive prediction
- Recall-the true positive prediction over true positive prediction plus false negative prediction.
- F1-Score: The mathematical average of both precision and recall in which both of them are taken into consideration.
- AUC-ROC: The space beneath the receiver's operating characteristic graph. which shows the relationship that exists between the true positive rate and the false positive rate.

### 10.6.4 Performance Evaluation and Findings

In this subsection, we investigate the efficiency of the proposed intrusion detection model based on federated learning and provide results.

**Training Performance:**
To assess the training performance, loss and accuracy metrics are investigated over the federated learning rounds. We examine the convergence behavior and relation of communication rounds to the accuracy of the model built.

**Comparison with Centralized Learning:**
To underscore the advantages of federated learning, we undertake a comparison with a centralized approach by using CNN where all data is brought together in the cloud server and used for training. The aspects used here are model accuracy, total time taken to train the model, and communication cost.

**Impact of Data Distribution:**
We determine the effect of non-IID data distributions on the performance of the model. It requires assessing the performance metrics when IID (independent and identically distributed) data is used as opposed to non-IID data.

**Resource Utilization:**
We assess the usage of resources such as CPU, memory, network bandwidth in edge devices with a view to determining the practicality of federated learning in IoT environments with limited resources.

**Insights:**
The results show that federated learning can get comparable accuracy with respect to centralized learning while preserving privacy of the data. The model displayed robust performance with regard to non-IID data distribution and effective resource utilization on edge devices.

Consequently, federated approach is observed as an appropriate approach for intrusion detection in the area of edge computing for cloud IoT systems as it addresses data privacy, accuracy of the model and resource utilization.

## 10.7 Case Study: Real World Application of Federated Intrusion Detection

### 10.7.1 Case Study Background and Objectives

Network traffic has increased exponentially as a result of our growing reliance on distributed systems, IoT devices and edge computing, opening up new avenues for attackers. The centralized data collecting used by traditional intrusion detection systems (IDS) has problems with data privacy, scalability, and single points of failure. By training models locally on devices and aggregating updates at a central server without exchanging raw data, federated learning (FL) overcomes these difficulties. A Federated Intrusion Detection System (FIDS) set up across various edge nodes to protect a distributed network environment is examined in this case study.

#### 10.7.1.1 *Case Study: Enhancing Cybersecurity in Financial Sector with Federated Intrusion Detection*

Background: In the financial sector [19], it manages extremely sensitive data; financial institutions are often the focus of cyberattacks. Conventional intrusion detection systems (IDS) frequently use centralized data collecting, which can lead to single points of failure and privacy issues.

Effective defense depends on sharing threat intelligence, but financial organizations are unable to do so due to regulatory limitations and competitive concerns. To solve these issues, a group of banks put in place a federated intrusion detection (FID). Using data from their own network traffic, each bank set up a local IDS. The banks exchanged model updates such as modifications to machine learning model weights with a central server in place of raw data.

These updates were combined by the central server to produce a global threat detection model, which was subsequently disseminated to the various banks.

Key benefits of Federated Intrusion Detection in Financial Sector:

Enhanced Threat Detection: Because of the combined knowledge gathered from many network settings, the FIDS was able to detect intrusions with greater accuracy than individual IDS.

Privacy Preservation: To meet privacy concerns and regulatory obligations, sensitive financial data was kept in each bank's safe environment.

Enhanced Cooperation: Without sacrificing competitive advantages, the FIDS made it easier to share threat intelligence.

Enhanced Resilience: The FIDS was more resilient to single points of failure because of its distributed architecture.

#### 10.7.1.2 *Case Study: Securing the Smart Grid with Federated Intrusion Detection*

Critical infrastructure like smart grids is most vulnerable to cyberattacks due to their growing reliance on networked equipment. Because the grid is distributed and operational data is sensitive, traditional centralized security solutions are less effective. The FIDS was put into place by a group of energy suppliers to improve the security of their smart grid infrastructure.

Local IDS agents were installed by each utility at different locations throughout their network like substations, smart meters etc. These agents collected information on device activity, network traffic and trends in energy usage. The agents learned local intrusion detection models and communicated model updates with a central aggregation server rather than exchanging raw data. These updates were merged by the central server to produce a global threat detection model, which was subsequently distributed among the many utilities. Most challenging part is the real time monitoring and response to security threats; also having limited computing resources in smart grid. The FIDS had employed light weight models and efficient communication protocols. Normal operating conditions are far frequent than cyber-attacks which leads to imbalanced dataset issue.

**Key Benefits of Federated Intrusion Detection in Smart Grid:**
The FIDS helped detect a variety of assaults including denial-of-service attacks, fake data injection attacks and managerial system intrusions. It also allowed for faster incident response and increased the overall resilience of the smart grid.

### 10.7.2 Implementation Details

As in Figure 10.3 implementation process for performing the task to identify malicious thing are as follows:

**Data Acquisition and Preprocessing:**
Data Sources: It includes network traffic details like packet headers, flow data for system and application logs, sensor data and so on. Then collected data preprocessing is the process of cleaning and transforming data into a machine learning-ready state. This could include tasks like data cleaning which includes handling missing values, reducing noise and resolving discrepancies. Feature engineering is the process of extracting useful information from raw data and also included data normalization that involves scaling the data to a certain range in order to improve model performance.

**Local Model Training:**
In Model selection phase the select right machine learning models for intrusion detection which includes traditional machine learning models

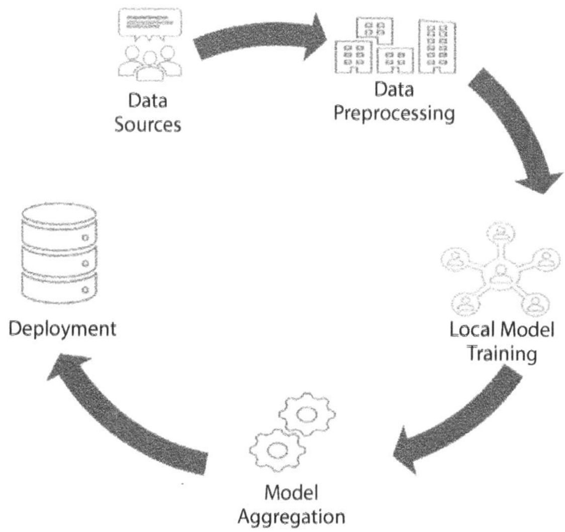


**Figure 10.3** Implementation process.

include decision trees, random forests, support vector machines (SVMs), and naive Bayes. Deep learning models include multilayer perceptron's (MLPs), convolutional neural networks (CNNs), recurrent neural networks (RNNs), and autoencoders.

**Model Aggregation:**
It sends updates to a central server where they are combined into a global model using techniques like federated averaging.

**Deployment and Monitoring**
It distributes the global model back to IoT devices for local intrusion detection. It sends the global model back to the participants for local intrusion detection. And in monitoring it keeps track of the FIDS' performance and retrains the models on a regular basis to react to new threats and changes in data trends.

## 10.8 Discussion

Federated Learning (FL) provides an interesting method to improving IoT security by tackling critical issues such as data privacy, resource limits, and the dispersed nature of IoT ecosystems. Followings are the key things of FL's influence on IoT security [20]:

### 10.8.1 Enhanced Privacy

Reduced Data Exposure: By communicating only the model updates rather than raw data, FL reduces the amount of information available to potential attackers.

Data Localization: FL allows model training to take place locally on IoT devices which keeps sensitive data local and remove the need to send it to a centralized server. This greatly minimizes the likelihood of data breaches and illegal access.

Compliance with Privacy Rules: FL helps organizations to deal with the challenging data privacy rules which require strong controls over the collection and processing of personal data.

### 10.8.2 Improved Security

Collaborative Threat Detection: FL enables IoT devices to learn collaboratively from each other's data without compromising privacy. This will help in developing stronger and more accurate intrusion detection models that can identify a broader range of threats.

Early Threat Detection: This may be able to detect emerging threats and anomalies more quickly than a traditional centralized approach by training models on a diverse dataset from multiple IoT devices.

Resistance to Attacks: The distributed nature of FL is more resistant to single points of failure and denial-of-service attacks. Even when some devices are compromised, the overall system can still function.

### 10.8.3 Overcoming IoT-Specific Challenges

Resource Constraints: FL is amenable to being tailored to fit the constrained computational resources and power supply that many IoT devices have. It can use techniques such as model compression and efficient communication protocols to reduce resource utilization.

Heterogeneity: FL satisfies the heterogeneity of the devices and IoT-related data by fitting local models that capture specificity characteristics that vary from different devices.

Scalability: FL is quite efficient when scaling large numbers of IoT devices, especially for large-scale IoT deployment.

### 10.8.4 Special Applications of Security in IoT

Intrusion Detection: FL can be applied to train intrusion detection models that will detect malicious activities on the IoT networks such as malware infection, DoS attack, and data breach.

Anomaly Detection: FL can be used in anomaly detection in sensor data and device behavior, possibly indicating possible security threats or malfunctions in the device.

Malware Detection: FL can be used in the training of malware detection models to identify malicious software on IoT devices.

Access Control: FL can be used in designing decentralized access control systems that limit access to sensitive data and resources based on device identity and behavior.

### 10.8.5 Challenges and Considerations

Overheads in Communication: Communicating model updates between devices involves lots of bandwidth, particularly with an enlarged IoT system.

Byzantine Attacks: Malicious devices can send faulty model updates that can destroy the training process or inject backdoors.

Data Heterogeneity and Non-IID Data: The variety in IoT devices and the resulting data makes it very hard to train global models.

Security of Federated Learning Process: To avoid attacks, the process of federated learning should be secured and made sure to be secure and valid.

## 10.9 Future Directions

### 10.9.1 Advanced Federated Learning Techniques for IoT Security

Intrusion detection systems can be supplemented with tools, designed for federated learning, that promise to reinforce the security of the internet of things.

**Personalized Federated Learning [21]:**
With conventional federated learning, all participating edge devices collaboratively train a single global model. This approach however appears not to be ideal for edge devices as the data is usually not homogeneous. Personalized federated learning solves this issue by designing individualized

models for each device, resulting in better on the edge performance and catering to the class of data distribution.

**Federated Transfer Learning [22]:**
With the idea of combining different IoT security tasks, for example IoT security using federated transfer learning, share their knowledge while retaining their unique expertise and experience. Models that are usually trained for other tasks can now assist an individual model in improving the accuracy of the machine learning model.

**Secure Aggregation Enhancements [23]:**
Model updates aggregated by multiple networks are at risk of being transparent to attackers, further elevating group and individual privacy erosions. This risk can however be addressed by the deployment of homomorphic encryption and secure multiparty computations.

**Adversarial Robustness [24]:**
It is essential to enhance the security of federated learning models against adversarial attackers. Mitigation techniques for such attacks such as adversarial training and robust optimization can be incorporated into the federated learning framework in the context of IoT security systems.

### 10.9.2 Integrating Blockchain for Decentralized Authentication [25]

It is possible to combine blockchain with federated learning so that seamless and secure authentication is done without centralization, thereby improving the integrity and credibility of IoT systems.

**Decentralized Trust Management:**
It is also possible for a blockchain to provide a decentralized trust management system by storing identity information of edge devices in a blockchain ledger as a record of their registration to enable authentication. This eliminates the dependence on a central authority of control, thereby eliminating a single point of failure.

**Immutable Data Logging:**
If all transactions and updates are assigned a time and date stamp and stored in chronological order on a blockchain, then records of all events that take place are permanent. This encourages transparency in federated

learning which increases accountability and integrity while making it complex for bad actors to influence the information or updates.

**Smart Contracts for Automated Compliance:**
The use of smart contracts can provide an effective means for maintaining and enforcing security and compliance policies. Smart contracts can be created for integrity checks of model updates as well as their data privacy and access control in a decentralized environment.

**Scalability and Efficiency:**
There are certain technologies such as sharding, off-chain transactions, and other consensus algorithms including proof of stake that come in handy to ease the scalability of blockchain. These advances can scale IoT deployments that utilize blockchain more efficiently.

**AI and AI-Enhanced Learning for Evolving Threats:**
It is important to recognize the fact that AI and AI-enabled adaptive learning mechanisms should be set in place to manage the intrusion detection apparatus, since the landscape is changing with regard to the cybersecurity risks.

**Continuous Learning:**
Mechanisms of learning can also be embedded in federated architectures allowing for constant and perpetual learning from new information. This enables very fast dynamic adaptation, and hence allows the detection models to keep up with the latest trends in threats.

### 10.9.3 AI in Anomaly Detection

Anomaly detection protocol can be further improved with the use of deep learning or reinforcement learning which are forms of advanced artificial intelligence. Anomaly detection parameters can also be enhanced to learn intricate pre-programmed behavior patterns tagged with intrusion for detection accuracy.

**Collaborative Intelligence [26]:**
Even the devices can enhance threat detection capabilities by integrating AI with federated learning to not only detect threats but also share information among themselves after learning different insights from various sets of data.

**English to German:**
Translation or explainable AI [27], does not need to be specifically integrated as it aids in the learning of incentive mechanisms. Incorporating explainable AI methods within federated learning can also enhance the understanding of their decision-making processes. This is beneficial in comprehending the reasoning behind the model's predictions and facilitates addressing false positives and negatives.

## 10.10 Conclusion

Federated learning is a promising method for enriching IoT security; it approaches key challenges related to data privacy, resource-limited devices, and a distributed nature of IoT. FL is going to play a prominent role in the growth of secure IoT appliances and applications without compromising privacy due to collaborative detection of threats. However, such challenges need efforts to ensure that FL effectively and safely works under real-world conditions of deploying IoT. It presents a transformative approach to intrusion detection by leveraging decentralized data processing while preserving privacy and minimizing communication overhead. FL offers significant advantages; adoption for intrusion detection in edge computing comes with significant challenges like handling heterogenous devices, ensuring robust aggregation and maintain security against adversarial attacks. In conclusion FL is poised to redefine how IDS is conducted in cloud IoT system.

**AI disclosure statement:** The author confirms that no artificial intelligence (AI)-generated content or AI-assisted writing tools were used in the preparation of this chapter (including summaries and the abstract). All text, analysis, and conclusions are the result of the author's original work.

## References

1. Li, T., Sahu, A.K., Talwalkar, A., Smith, V., Federated Learning: Challenges, Methods, and Future Directions. *IEEE Signal Process Mag.*, 37, 3, 50–60, 2020, doi: 10.1109/MSP.2020.2975749.
2. Giaffreda, R., *et al.*, Edge and cloud computing for industrial internet of things: A review. *ACM Trans. Internet Things*, 1, 1, 1–25, 2018.
3. Gosai, K., Mehta, H., Katkar, V., An Intrusion Detection Using Ensemble Classifiers, in: *2022 6th International Conference on Computing Methodologies*

*and Communication (ICCMC)*, pp. 163–168, 2022, doi: 10.1109/ICCMC53470.2022.9753703.
4. Patra, M.K., Kumari, A., Sahoo, B., Turuk, A.K., Challenges and opportunities toward integration of iot with cloud computing. *Integr. IoT Cloud Comput. Smart Appl.*, 81–98, June, 2023, doi: 10.1201/9781003319238-5.
5. Eric, G. and Jurcut, A., Intrusion Detection in Internet of Things Systems : A Review on Design Approaches Leveraging Multi-Access Edge. *Sensors*, 22, 1–33, 2022.
6. Yang, Q., Liu, Y., Chen, T., Tong, Y., Federated machine learning: Concept and applications. *ACM Trans. Intell. Syst. Technol.*, 10, 2, 1–19, 2019, doi: 10.1145/3298981.
7. Wei, K., *et al.*, Federated Learning with Differential Privacy: Algorithms and Performance Analysis. *IEEE Trans. Inf. Forensics Secur.*, 15, 3454–3469, 2020, doi: 10.1109/TIFS.2020.2988575.
8. Liu, Z., Guo, J., Yang, W., Fan, J., Lam, K.Y., Zhao, J., Privacy-Preserving Aggregation in Federated Learning: A Survey. *IEEE Trans. Big Data*, 14, 8, 1–20, 2022, doi: 10.1109/TBDATA.2022.3190835.
9. Boulemtafes, A., *et al.*, A review of privacy-preserving techniques for deep learning To cite this version : HAL Id : hal-02921443 A Review of Privacy-Preserving Techniques for Deep Learning. *Neurocomputing*, Elsevier, 3, 84, 21–45, 2020.
10. Nebbione, G. and Calzarossa, M.C., Security of IoT application layer protocols: Challenges and findings. *Future Internet.*, 2020, doi: 10.3390/fi12030055.
11. Naik, N., Choice of effective messaging protocols for IoT systems: MQTT, CoAP, AMQP and HTTP, 2017, doi: 10.1109/SysEng.2017.8088251.
12. Khan, L.U., Saad, W., Han, Z., Hossain, E., Hong, C.S., Federated Learning for Internet of Things: Recent Advances, Taxonomy, and Open Challenges. *IEEE Commun. Surv. Tutor.*, 23, 3, 1759–1799, 2021, doi: 10.1109/COMST.2021.3090430.
13. Ruder, S., An overview of gradient descent optimization, 1–14, 2016.
14. Qi, P., Chiaro, D., Guzzo, A., Ianni, M., Fortino, G., Piccialli, F., Model aggregation techniques in federated learning : A comprehensive survey. *Futur. Gener. Comput. Syst.*, 150, 272–294, 2024, doi: 10.1016/j.future.2023.09.008.
15. Mahadik, S.S., Member, S., Pawar, P.M., Edge-Federated Learning based Intelligent Intrusion Detection System for Heterogeneous Internet of Things, 1–22, 2024, doi: 10.1109/ACCESS.2024.3410046.
16. Agrawal, S., Sarkar, S., Aouedi, O., Yenduri, G., Piamrat, K., Bhattacharya, S., Federated Learning for Intrusion Detection System : Concepts , Challenges and Future Directions, 1–19, 2016.
17. Mohammadpour, L. and Ling, T.C., Applied sciences A Survey of CNN-Based Network Intrusion Detection, 2022.
18. Shen, K., Guo, J., Tan, X., Tang, S., Wang, R., Bian, J., A Study on ReLU and Softmax in Transformer, 2017.

19. Kollu, V.N., Janarthanan, V., Karupusamy, M., Cloud-Based Smart Contract Analysis in FinTech Using IoT-Integrated Federated Learning in Intrusion Detection, 2023.
20. Yaacoub, J.A., Noura, H.N., Salman, O., Internet of Things and Cyber-Physical Systems Security of Federated Learning with IoT Systems: Issues, limitations, challenges, and solutions. *Internet Things Cyber-Phys. Syst.*, 3, 155–179, January, 2023, doi: 10.1016/j.iotcps.2023.04.001.
21. Tan, A.Z., Yu, H., Cui, L., Yang, Q., Towards Personalized Federated Learning. *IEEE Trans. Neural Netw. Learn. Syst.*, 34, 12, 9587–9603, Dec. 2023, doi: 10.1109/TNNLS.2022.3160699.
22. Liu, Y., Kang, Y., Xing, C., Chen, T., Yang, Q., A Secure Federated Transfer Learning Framework. *IEEE Intell. Syst.*, 35, 4, 70–82, Jul. 2020, doi: 10.1109/MIS.2020.2988525.
23. Lu, R., Member, S., Heung, K., A Lightweight Privacy-Preserving Data Aggregation Scheme for Fog Computing-Enhanced IoT, 5, 2017.
24. Zhang, J., *et al.*, Delving into the Adversarial Robustness of Federated Learning, 2018.
25. Zhaofeng, M., Jialin, M., Jihui, W., Zhiguang, S., Blockchain-Based Decentralized Authentication Modeling Scheme in Edge and IoT Environment. *IEEE Internet Things J.*, 8, 4, 2116–2123, Feb. 2021, doi: 10.1109/JIOT.2020.3037733.
26. Abraham, M., Aithal, H., Mohan, K., Blockchain and Collaborative Intelligence Based Next Generation Smart Toll Application, in: *2020 2nd Conference on Blockchain Research & Applications for Innovative Networks and Services (BRAINS)*, pp. 206–207, 2020, doi: 10.1109/BRAINS49436.2020.9223296.
27. Nassar, M., Salah, K., Svetinovic, D., Blockchain for explainable and trustworthy artificial intelligence, October, 2019, doi: 10.1002/widm.1340.

11

# Behavioral Profiling for Dynamic Anomaly Detection in Cloud-IoT Networks

**Triveni Lal Pal[1] and Manoj Kumar Pandey[2]***

*[1]School of Computing Science and Engineering, Galgotias University, Greater Noida, India*
*[2]Department of Computer Science and Engineering, Chandigarh University, Mohali, India*

***Abstract***
The integration of Cloud Computing and the Internet of Things (IoT) has revolutionized modern digital infrastructures, enabling scalable, efficient and intelligent systems across various domains. Cloud computing provides the necessary storage, computing power and real-time processing capabilities, while IoT networks facilitate seamless connectivity among smart devices. Ubiquitous growth in the cloud-IoT networks is unprecedented; therefore, behavioral analysis plays a significant role. These networks have gained widespread attention of internet users in various domains such as in agriculture and public health. Behavioral profiling is a sophisticated technique used for dynamic anomaly detection, thereby enhancing security and performance in cloud-IoT networks. Understanding the technique is intuitive. It uses to establish a behavior (normal behavior) based on historical data and patterns. Further, these established behaviors/patterns are used to detect deviations, if any, in the network that could indicate potential security threats or performance issues. The process of establishing a behavior, requires continuous monitoring and real-time analysis (dynamic anomaly detection) to overcome the continuous adaption of the attackers. Researchers in the field are required to have a deep insight in the areas like identifying the types of network patterns (key components), profiling techniques, anomaly detection approaches and response and adaptation. This chapter also helps the researchers in acquiring the knowledge in a convenient way by discussing the basic concepts, literature review and systematically summarizing the research findings.

**Corresponding author*: manojpnd88@gmail.com

Partha Ghosh, Rajdeep Chakraborty, Anupam Ghosh and Ahmed A. Elngar (eds.) Strategic Approaches to Intrusion Detection in Cloud-IoT Ecosystem, (283–300) © 2026 Scrivener Publishing LLC

***Keywords*:** Cloud, IoT, anomaly detection, behavioral profiling, patterns recognition, deep learning, sustainable development goals

## 11.1 Introduction

Cloud-IoT networks have become the backbone of modern digital ecosystems, facilitating seamless communication and data exchange between devices and services. However, the increasing complexity and scale of these networks expose them to a wide range of security threats, including dynamic anomalies and cyber-attacks. These anomalies and attacks often fooled the conventional approaches to anomaly detection system by evolving new behaviors of the network. The conventional approaches often struggle to adapt to the evolving behavior of such networks, leading to inadequate threat mitigation. This entices researchers to study behavioral profiling as a robust approach to dynamic anomaly detection in cloud-IoT environments. By leveraging machine learning and advanced analytics, the proposed framework identifies deviations from normal behavior patterns in real-time. Anomaly detection is crucial in cloud and IoT networks due to their inherent complexity, scalability and critical roles in modern infrastructure, ensuring operational efficiency, security, and reliability. With the proliferation of IoT devices and the expansive adoption of cloud computing, these systems handle enormous volumes of data and processes in real time that makes them highly susceptible to anomalies that may disrupt operations. Anomalies often signal potential issues such as security breaches, system malfunctions or configuration errors. In cloud environments anomalies may lead to resource overuse, degraded service quality, or data breaches, compromising the scalability and trust that underpin cloud services [1]. IoT networks which are characterized by heterogeneous devices and distributed architectures are vulnerable to attacks like distributed denial of service (DDoS), unauthorized access or rogue device behavior that can cascade across the network. Proactive anomaly detection in these domains enables real-time monitoring and swift responses, minimizing the impact of potential threats and ensuring consistent service delivery. Furthermore, we can say that in the context of critical industries like healthcare, manufacturing and smart cities, undetected anomalies in IoT networks can have severe consequences including the compromised patient safety, production losses or public safety hazards. Leveraging machine learning and artificial intelligence, modern anomaly detection systems analyze vast data streams to identify subtle, complex patterns that traditional rule-based systems might overlook, providing an essential layer of intelligence and adaptability. Anomaly detection helps maintain compliance with regulatory standards by promptly identifying and mitigating risks, reinforcing the overall security posture. As the interconnectedness of cloud and IoT ecosystems grows, anomaly detection becomes indispensable for ensuring these networks' resilience, optimizing resource utilization and protecting against evolving cyber threats. In today's era of digital transformation, the integration of cloud computing and internet of things (IoT) networks forms the backbone of smart systems across industries, from healthcare and manufacturing to smart cities and autonomous vehicles [2]. This interconnected ecosystem enables real-time data exchange, automation and scalability but also introduces vulnerabilities that demand robust anomaly detection mechanisms. Anomalies often indicate critical issues such as cyberattacks, system failures or misconfigurations. In cloud-IoT networks where millions of devices and services interact, these anomalies can propagate rapidly, leading to service outages, compromised data integrity and operational inefficiencies. The dynamic nature of cloud resources and the heterogeneity of IoT devices, advanced anomaly detection systems powered by machine learning and artificial intelligence are essential for identifying patterns and detecting irregularities in real time.

### 11.1.1 Real Motivation

The accelerated proliferation of cloud-IoT networks has transformed various sectors by combining the resources of the cloud and the connections of the IoT devices [3]. These networks allow for efficient collection, analysis and decision. This encourages development in smart cities, health care, and industrial automation [4]. However, this agrarian expansion also poses serious problems like the large-scale management of devices that are dispersed, mobile, and multiple, and the risk of security derived from changing threats [5]. The architectural difficulty of IoT devices, many of which have limited resources, as well as the use of various communication protocols constitute weak points because they cannot be addressed by conventional security solutions.

Cloud-IoT security systems cannot be effectively guaranteed without implementing robust security measures and one such method is anomaly detection which recognizes irregularities in behavior analytics. The error in the system can be noticed as it is different from previously-recognized models. Frequently, traditional security measures such as signature-based detection as well as static rule systems operates in IoT atmospheres, as they can't be familiar with the occurrence of distinct and high varieties of device behaviors and network traffic dynamic anomaly detection, behavioral profiling.

Vulnerable ways of detection are the result of these systems as they miss new or intricate threats attacking IoT devices [6]. Dynamic anomaly detection, or behavioral profiling is an answer to this challenge. Emphasizing the adaptive ability of the cybersecurity mechanism is very helpful in monitoring real-time network and device conditions and finding non-obvious threats [7]. This move reflects its significant role in maintaining the data's integrity, confidentiality, and availability of data within the cloud-IoT ecosystems.

### 11.1.2 Various Challenges in Securing Cloud-IoT Networks

Securing the cloud-IoT networks has become a significant challenge due to their inherent complexity and heterogeneity. These networks connect a vast array of devices ranging from simple sensors to sophisticated machines and each with different computational capabilities, communication protocols and security features. These diversity hampers interoperability and complicates the establishment of uniform security measures. Additionally, the resource constraints of IoT devices often prevent them from supporting robust security mechanisms leaving them vulnerable to cyberattacks such as malware infiltration, denial-of-service (DoS) attacks and the data breaches. The volume and velocity of data generated by cloud-IoT networks aggravate these challenges. Billions of interconnected devices are continuously transmitting large amounts of real-time data to cloud platforms for processing and storage. Traditional security systems struggle to handle this data deluge, making it difficult to identify anomalous patterns indicative of potential threats. Furthermore, the dynamic and unpredictable behavior of IoT devices adds another layer of complexity.

Cloud-IoT expands privacy and security threats. It is mainly because IoT devices are expected to be more active in collecting personal or business data that has to be protected against any unauthorized access. This is a tight legal framework comprising the data protection regulation or general data protection regulation. However, the implementation of these measures seems to be a tough chore because of the decentralized nature of Cloud-IoT networks and because many IoT devices have low processing power. These difficulties point to the necessity of more sophisticated approaches such as behavioral profiling that would help in effective dynamic anomaly detection. By means of continuous monitoring and learning of device and network behavior, such systems are able to accommodate changes in the environment and usage of the systems. They provide a form of pre-emptive action to detect anomalies, hence improving the security strategies, and increasing the strength of the cloud-IoT networks in general. This area of research is important in solving the problems related to the creation of practical means of IoT security that will be able to scale and adapt to the growth of surrounding IoT technologies [8].

### 11.1.3 Objectives and Scope of Behavioral Profiling

Behavioral profiling is the processing of analyzing and modeling the typical behavior of the systems, devices or users to establish a baseline of *normal* activity. In the context of cloud-IoT networks it means monitoring the interactions, data exchange patterns and operations of connected devices. By understanding the expected behavior of devices, such as profiling can help to identify anomalies. Behavioral profiling uses techniques such as machine learning and statistical analysis to dynamically learn and adapt to the unique characteristics of the IoT ecosystem making it a powerful tool for enhancing security.

Behavioral profiling is particularly effective for cloud-IoT networks due to its ability to adapt to the heterogeneous and dynamic nature of the systems. Unlike static rule-based security measures, behavioral profiling considers the evolving operational patterns of the IoT devices, making it suitable for detecting sophisticated or previously unseen threats. It also provides the diverse protocols and limited computational resources of IoT devices that provides a lightweight yet robust approach to monitoring and securing the network. This adaptability ensures better scalability and resilience, enabling the protection of the devices over the distributed cloud-IoT systems. Dynamic anomaly detection influences behavioral profiling to identify deviations from the established baseline of normal activity. This enhanced method is essential in cloud-IoT networks where traditional security measures fail to address the challenges of rapid changes in network configurations and usage patterns. By implementing dynamic anomaly detection, cloud-IoT networks can respond proactively to potential security breaches. Behavioral profiling enables real-time analysis and faster detection of anomalies, reducing response times and minimizing the impact of attacks. This approach not only enhances security but also supports compliance with stringent privacy and data protection requirements that ensures the reliability and trustworthiness of cloud-IoT networks.

### 11.1.4 Organization of the Chapter

This chapter provides an analysis of the state-of-the-art techniques in behavioral profiling for dynamic anomaly detection in the cloud-IoT networks. It also consolidates the existing research, highlights the key methodologies, frameworks and algorithms used to model and identify anomalous behaviors in dynamic and distributed environments. The paper categorizes the approaches based on their use of machine learning, statistical modeling, and hybrid techniques, emphasizing emerging trends and innovations in this field. The chapter is organized as- Introduction, Cloud IoT Architecture, Literature Survey, Emerging Trends and Opportunities, Conclusion and Future Direction.

## 11.2 Cloud IoT Architecture

The evolution of the cloud-IoT network stems from the convergence of cloud computing and the internet of things (IoT), driven by the need for scalable, efficient and interconnected systems. Initially, IoT devices were operated as isolated units with limited storage and processing capabilities but with the advent of cloud computing, enabled centralized data storage, real-time analysis and seamless communication across devices created a robust ecosystem and the integration supports applications in smart homes, industries, healthcare and beyond, leveraging the cloud's computational power to enhance IoT functionality. The cloud-IoT ecosystem represents the convergence of cloud computing and the internet of things (IoT) that enables efficient data storage, processing and communication across a network of interconnected devices. The dynamic nature of cloud resources and the heterogeneity of IoT devices further strengthen the challenge and make traditional monitoring tools insufficient; and therefore, advanced anomaly detection systems that is powered by machine learning and artificial intelligence are essential for identifying patterns and detecting irregularities in real time. Figure 11.1 is a conceptual diagram illustrating the layers of cloud-IoT architecture.

The architecture facilitates a seamless and efficient workflow while addressing the complex requirements of modern IoT systems. It also serves as the foundation for implementing behavioral profiling and anomaly detection mechanisms.

## 11.3 Literature Study

An anomaly is considered to be a data-point which is not allied to the projected performance in a displayed system. Rare occurrences that substantially depart from typical behavior can be classified as anomalies. They can be found in a single data-point, a particular time period, or in the whole dataset. This section of the chapter discusses the various review of literature.

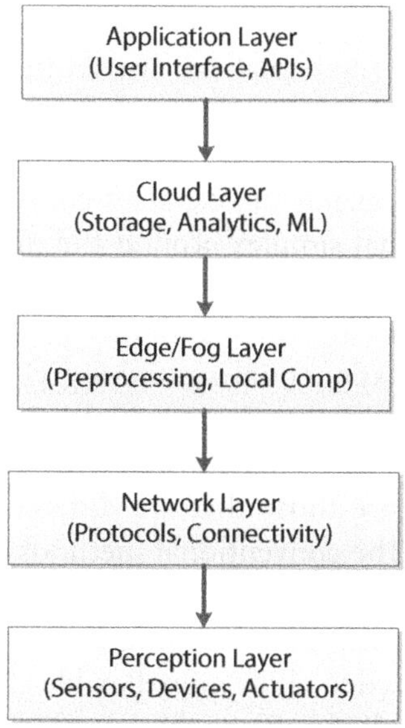


**Figure 11.1** Cloud-IoT architecture.

### 11.3.1 Anomaly Detection Techniques

By merging the classifications from earlier work like [9, 10], IoT anomaly exposure method is divided into four clusters as follows:

A. ***By method:*** This method may be based on machine learning, statistics, or geometry. The underlying premise of geometrical approaches is that the anticipated anomalies are distinguished when a dataset is represented using density-based and distance-based tactics. The density-based approaches are when anomalies are found in the sparse areas of a set of data points. The methods utilize a static or a dynamic method to determine the threshold value 't' on the estimated distance 'd' to classify anomalies, which is given as Equation 11.1.

$$d = \begin{cases} < t & \text{Normal (below the threshold)} \\ > t & \text{Abnormal (above the threshold)} \end{cases} \tag{11.1}$$

Statistical techniques like the nominal volume in [11], attempt to use mathematical distributions and models to simulate normal data. The objective function of the minimal volume approach is to maximize the root truth datapoints as minimizing the capacity consumed to construct an n-dimensional simplex around the provided data cloud (ground truth). An anomaly is defined as data that doespoints that does not fit the model [12]. Another way to forecasting is exponential smoothing [13]. This technique uses prior data points and a smoothing parameter to predict future data points. Anomalous data produced by the statistical methods are those that are different from the established model. The conventional methods are based on a lot of research which also need a good comprehension of the ground reality. Machine learning and deep learning solutions are required to allow more flexible changes. The nature of the data supplied governs the selection of the model [14]. For instance, long-short-term-memory (LSTM) and transformer models gives preference to the sequential data like audio, video and time series relate data and on the other hand, the convolutional neural network (CNN) and autoencoder (AE) gives preference to the non-sequential data types such as image input [15]. The algorithms effort to separate between normal and anomalous behavior by establishing a decision boundary such as with the support vector machine (SVM) classifier [16], or future forecasting values in streaming data [17], with LSTM networks [18]. Depending on the availability of training labels, these approaches are further classified as supervised, semi-supervised, self-supervised, or completely unsupervised [19].

B. ***By application:*** The three routes of anomaly categorization by an application are constructive, destructive, and data cleaning. Constructive applications are productive or beneficial in nature and provide value to the world, such as monitoring the elderly's daily behavior for fall prevention in using image descriptors and comparing the performance between multilayer perceptron (MLP), k-nearest neighbors (KNN), and SVM classifiers [20]. Application based dynamic anomaly detection can also play a vital role. Federated learning is also an emerging concept that can be used for gathering the training data without compromising the security of other nodes [21].

C. ***By anomaly type:*** One of the furthermost common type is the circumstance-specific, which is the point, contextual, and collective. An anomaly is a point anomaly if a single data point deviates from the expected behavior. For example, the detection of credit card fraud as done by [22]. A contextual anomaly is an instance that could be considered anomalous in some specific context. This means that comparing multiple perspectives on the same data point does not always result in anomalous behavior. A contextual anomaly is detected when both contextual and behavioral characteristics are considered together.

D. ***By latency:*** Latency is a critical factor in cloud-IoT networks, particularly for time-sensitive applications like industrial automation and healthcare. Edge-computing frameworks have been proposed to reduce the latency associated with cloud-based anomaly detection. A detection algorithm's scalability and latency dictate whether it is used in real time during the data gathering phase or at a later stage of storage. Without access to the entire input, an online algorithm can analyze data in a serial fashion using a single data point or window. The aforementioned distance-based, density- and deviation-based, and angle-based methods are examples of traditional online geometrical and statistical methodologies. It is also important to note that now, the generative AI is also playing a vital role in the anomaly's detection using the latency [23]. Figure 11.2 shows the different anomaly detection methods.

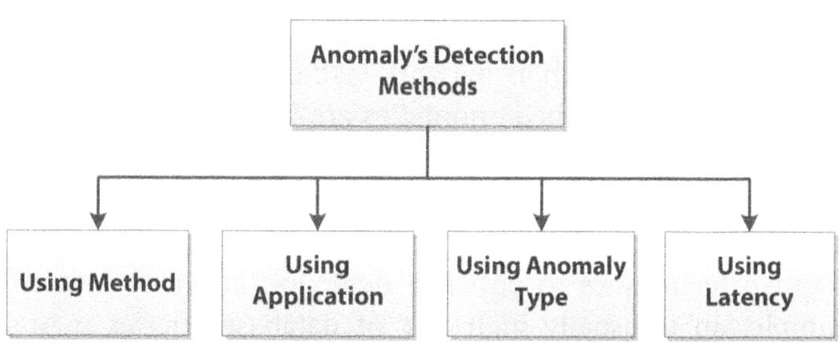


**Figure 11.2** Anomaly's detection methods.

### 11.3.2 Anomaly Detection in Cloud-IoT Network

Anomaly uncovering in cloud environments is utmost needed for keeping the performance, security and operational integrity of the cloud. Traditional techniques such as rule-based systems, threshold-based monitoring and signature-based detection have played vital roles in identifying deviations indicative of faults, performance issues or malicious activities. These methods rely on pre-defined patterns or metrics but face limitations in the dynamic and high-volume data scenarios typical of cloud systems. Various traditional techniques for anomaly's detections are as follows:

**A. *Rule based systems for anomaly's detection***

Rule-based systems are the basic anomaly detection system which operates on the predefined logic, matching observed behaviors against a set of established rules. They are highly effective in detecting known threats or operational failures by using conditional statements derived from historical analysis. For example, rules might trigger alerts when CPU usage exceeds 80% for over 5 minutes or when certain files are accessed without proper authorization and security. Rule-based deep-neural-network has been proposed by Chakraborty *et al.*, [24], as a framework for tackling the issue of detecting novel attacks, and the framework produced greatly enhances the corresponding benchmark results, including the CICIDS 2017 dataset. This paper concludes that the rule-based deep neural network technique significantly enhances the detection of novel attacks in IoT networks. The given model shows an accuracy over 99% for identifying the different attacks and it demonstrates its effectiveness as compared to existing methods. Another study done by Sangeetha *et al.*, [25], suggests a strong framework made especially to improve security and effectiveness in medical settings known as secure healthcare access control system (SHACS).

***B. Threshold-based monitoring for anomaly's detection***

The threshold-based technique includes setting up a numeric limit on the performance indicator such as network traffic, memory usage and whenever these limits are breached anomalies are flagged off. Threshold-based anomaly detection in cloud-IoT networks is a critical area of research that addresses the unique challenges posed by the vast and dynamic nature of IoT data. Various methods have emerged that leverage machine learning and adaptive techniques to enhance detection accuracy and efficiency. For example, an unusually high rate of database queries may signal a denial-of-service attack. Nayer *et al.*, [26], have proposed research recommends utilizing autoencoders with a dynamic threshold mechanism which continuously recalibrates and also ensures relevant and precise anomaly detections in ensuring secure IoT communications.

C. ***Signature based anomaly's detection***

Signature based anomaly detection is a critical area of the research and it focuses on identifying and modifying security threats in the interconnected environments. This approach combines the strengths of signature-based detection that excels in recognizing the known threats with the anomaly detection. Goenawan *et al.*, [27], have created a highly optimized DS procedure that can automatically identify anomalies from high cadence sky survey data including millions of stars in real-time.

### 11.3.3 Machine Learning Based Anomaly Detection

Machine learning based anomaly detection in cloud-IoT networks is key for enhancing security and mitigating risks associated with the increasing complexity. With the cyber threat evaluation, traditional security measures often fall short and then it requires the adoption of advanced machine learning techniques to identify and respond to anomalies effectively. The machine learning based anomaly's detection can be of any type such as *supervised learning* that uses labeled datasets to train models that can distinguish between normal and anomalous behavior and effectively reduce false positive rate [28], *unsupervised learning* that identifies patterns in unlabeled data making it suitable for dynamic environments where new anomalies may emerge and can detect it [29], *semi-supervised learning* that combines both labeled and unlabeled data for enhancing detection capabilities in scenarios with limited labeled examples [30].

Abusitta *et al.*, [31], have suggested deep learning-based anomaly detection system for IoT. It is capable of learning and capturing strong and significant traits that are unaffected by unstable environments. The classifier then uses these features to increase the precision of sensing false IoT data. When comparing the proposed framework to the most modern IoT-based anomaly detection approaches, testing results based on real-world IoT datasets show how successful it is at enhancing the accuracy of recognizing dangerous data. Figure 11.3 shows the different types of anomalies detection.

Table 11.1 shows the comparison between all the above-mentioned methods such as rule based, threshold based, signature based, machine

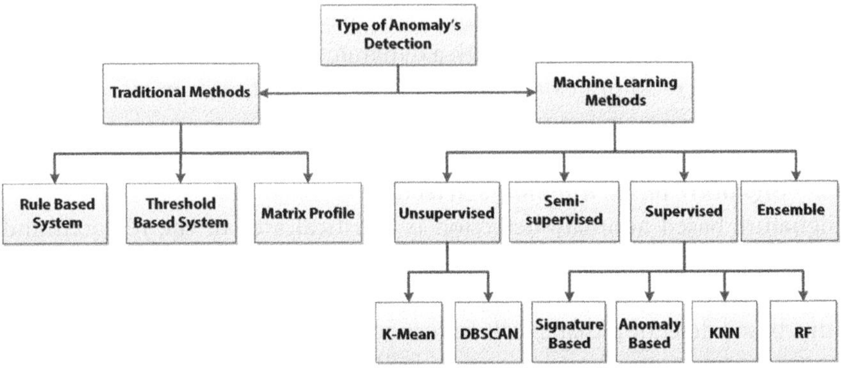


**Figure 11.3** Various anomalies algorithms.

learning based; it also presents a summary of the various methods for anomaly detections.

Each method has its strengths and weaknesses, often making hybrid approaches more effective for comprehensive anomaly detection.

## 11.4 Emerging Trends and Opportunities

Emerging trends in dynamic anomaly detection within cloud and IoT networks are revolutionizing how these systems operate, offering significant opportunities to enhance security, efficiency and resilience. The traditional static models of anomaly detection are proving inadequate for real-time and adaptive environments as cloud-IoT networks become increasingly complex and interconnected. Dynamic anomaly detection has influenced advanced technologies such as artificial intelligence (AI), machine learning (ML), and edge computing to identify and address irregularities in real-time. AI-driven models are particularly impactful, enabling systems to learn and adapt continuously to new patterns and threats. Techniques such as deep learning and federated learning are gaining attraction that allow anomaly detection systems to process vast amounts of data, uncover hidden patterns and operate effectively in distributed environments without compromising data privacy. Edge computing also plays an important role by reducing latency and enabling faster detection of anomalies directly at the data source such as IoT devices. This shift minimizes the bandwidth usage and enhances response times which is particularly valuable in latency sensitive applications like autonomous vehicles, healthcare monitoring and the industrial automation. The integration of blockchain

**Table 11.1** Comparison between different methods.

| Criteria | Rule-based | Threshold-based | Signature-based | Machine learning-based |
|---|---|---|---|---|
| ***Definition*** | It uses predefined rules to identify anomalies. | It uses fixed set thresholds for metrics; flags deviations. | It matches against known patterns or attack signatures. | It learns patterns from data to identify anomalies dynamically. |
| ***Adaptability*** | Low; requires manual updates for new scenarios. | Low; fixed thresholds often fail with changing workloads. | Low; cannot detect unknown or zero-day threats. | High; can adapt to new patterns and environments. |
| ***Accuracy*** | It depends on rule quality; prone to false positives. | It is prone to false positives and negatives in dynamic systems. | It is accurate for known threats; ineffective for novel ones. | High; reduces false positives with sufficient training data. |
| ***Scalability*** | Limited in handling large, dynamic datasets. | It scales poorly for highly variable systems. | It scales well but limited to known datasets. | It scales effectively with modern computational power. |
| ***Complexity*** | Simple to implement. | Easy to implement; limited by static nature. | Moderate; requires maintaining signature databases. | High; requires expertise in model training and deployment. |
| ***Use Cases*** | Basic policy enforcement, known fault detection. | Monitoring CPU, memory, or bandwidth spikes. | Malware detection, IDS in known environments. | Complex systems, zero-day threats, fraud detection. |

technology is another emerging trend which adds a layer of security and transparency to anomaly detection systems by ensuring data integrity and preventing tampering. Additionally, the hybrid detection models that combine signature-based and behavior-based approaches are becoming more prevalent, enabling systems to identify both known and novel threats with higher accuracy. Furthermore, these advancements enable the compliance with stringent regulatory requirements for data protection and privacy. By implementing robust anomaly detection frameworks, the organizations can demonstrate their commitment to security, and it also builds trust among users and stakeholders. The rise of 5G networks further amplifies these opportunities by providing the high-speed connectivity and low latency required for real-time anomaly detection across a vast network of devices.

## 11.5 Conclusion and Future Direction

Dynamic anomaly detection in cloud and IoT networks represents a foundation of modern digital infrastructure that address the escalating challenges of security, scalability and operational efficiency. With the interconnected ecosystems continue to evolves, the ability to detect and respond to anomalies in real time becomes increasingly critical. The conclusion of this exploration highlights the importance of dynamic approaches that influence advanced technologies such as machine learning, artificial intelligence and edge computing to monitor vast data streams, identify deviations and take proactive measures. The dynamic anomaly detection adapts to the ever-changing behavior patterns of cloud-IoT environments, enables systems to maintain reliability and security while fostering user trust. This adaptability ensures the resilience of critical applications in areas such as healthcare, smart cities, and industrial automation, where any delay or oversight in detecting anomalies could lead to severe consequences, including compromised safety, financial losses and reputational damage. The future scope of dynamic anomaly detection in cloud-IoT networks is vast and promising. Figure 11.4 shows the number of papers published in Scopus from 2020 to 2024, with keyword *Dynamic Anomaly Detection* and it clearly shows that the number of papers published is increasing year by year. Figure 11.5 shows the different types of documents published from 2020-2024. Figure 11.6 shows the number of articles published from 2020-2024 from top ten countries.

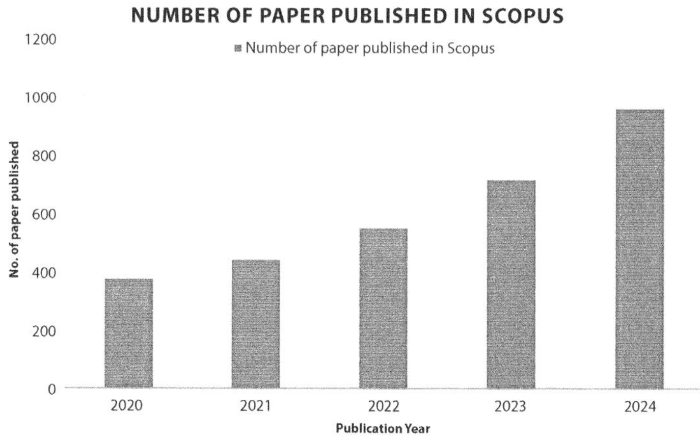


**Figure 11.4** Number of papers published in scopus from 2020 to 2024.

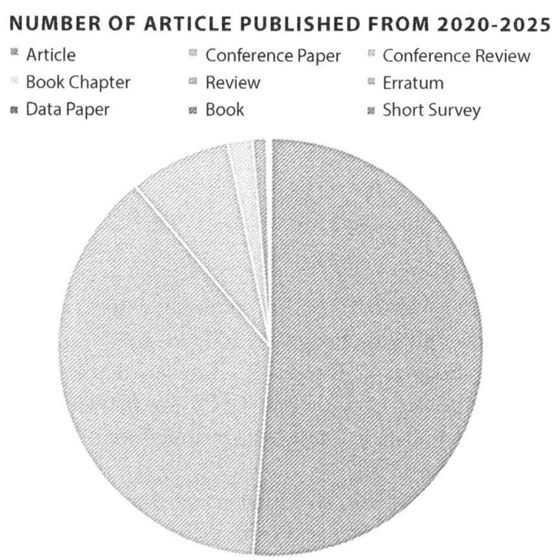


**Figure 11.5** Different types of documents published from 2020–2024.

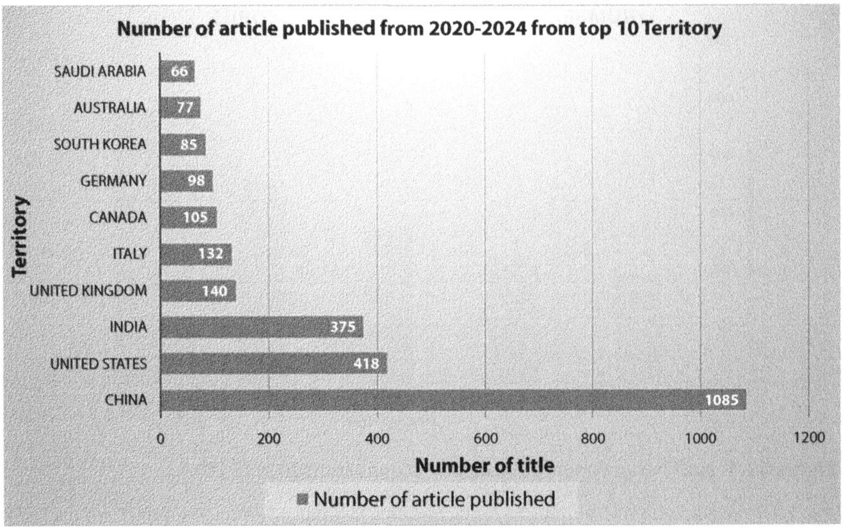


**Figure 11.6** Number of articles published from 2020-2024 from top ten countries.

**AI disclosure statement:** The author acknowledges the use of AI-based tools for minor language editing or grammatical correction. However, all intellectual contributions, analyses, and conclusions presented in this chapter are entirely the author's own.

## References


1. Chatterjee, A. and Ahmed, B.S., IoT anomaly detection methods and applications: A survey. *Internet Things*, *19*, 100568, 2022.
2. Dhadhania, A., Bhatia, J., Mehta, R., Tanwar, S., Sharma, R., Verma, A., Unleashing the power of SDN and GNN for network anomaly detection: State-of-the-art, challenges, and future directions. *Secur. Priv.*, 7, 1, e337, 2024. doi: 10.1002/spy2.337.
3. Ansari, M., Ali, S.A., Alam, M., Internet of things (IoT) fusion with cloud computing: current research and future direction. *Int. J. Adv. Technol. Eng. Explor.*, 9, 97, 1812, 2022.
4. Adel, A., Unlocking the future: fostering human–machine collaboration and driving intelligent automation through industry 5.0 in smart cities. *Smart Cities*, 6, 5, 2742–2782, 2023.
5. Al-kateeb, Z.N. and Abdullah, D.B., Unlocking the Potential: Synergizing IoT, Cloud Computing, and Big Data for a Bright Future. *Iraqi J. Comput. Sci. Math.*, 5, 3, 25, 2024.

6. Landril, E., Valente, S., Andersen, G., Schneider, C., Ransomware detection through dynamic behavior-based profiling using real-time crypto-anomaly filtering, 2024.
7. Pal, T.L., Kumari, M., Singh, T., Ahsan, M., Semantic representations in text data. *Int. J. Grid Distrib. Comput.*, 11, 9, 65–80, 2018.
8. Pandey, M.K., Pal, T.L., Gupta, P., Deep Generative Models in Alzheimer's Research, in: *Deep Generative Models for Integrative Analysis of Alzheimer's Biomarkers*, vol. 2024, pp. 341–360, 2024.
9. Fahim, M. and Sillitti, A., Anomaly detection, analysis and prediction techniques in IoT environment: A systematic literature review. *IEEE Access*, 7, 81664–81681, 2019.
10. Cook, A.A., Mısırlı, G., Fan, Z., Anomaly detection for IoT time-series data: A survey. *IEEE Internet Things J.*, 7, 7, 6481–6494, 2019.
11. O'Reilly, C., Gluhak, A., Imran, M.A., Distributed anomaly detection using minimum volume elliptical principal component analysis. *IEEE Trans. Knowl. Data Eng.*, 28, 9, 2320–2333, 2016.
12. Ahsan, M., Kumari, M., Singh, T., Pal, T.L., Sentiment Based Information Diffusion in Online Social Networks. *Int. J. Knowl. Discov. Bioinf.*, 8, 1, 60–74, 2018.
13. Mahajan, S., Chen, L.J., Tsai, T.C., Short-term PM2. 5 forecasting using exponential smoothing method: A comparative analysis. *Sensors*, 18, 10, 3223, 2018.
14. Ding, C., Sun, S., Zhao, J., MST-GAT: A multimodal spatial–temporal graph attention network for time series anomaly detection. *Inf. Fusion*, 89, 527–536, 2023.
15. Alghanmi, N., Alotaibi, R., Buhari, S.M., Machine learning approaches for anomaly detection in IoT: an overview and future research directions. *Wirel. Pers. Commun.*, 122, 3, 2309–2324, 2022.
16. Jaiswal, S. and Pandey, M.K., A comparative study of various digital image watermarking techniques: Specific to hybrid watermarking. *Recent Adv. Comput. Sci. Commun. Bentham Sci.*, 16, 8, 2023. ISSN 2666–2566. https://doi.org/10.2174/2666255816666230522155134.
17. Dunne, M., Gracioli, G., Fischmeister, S., A comparison of data streaming frameworks for anomaly detection in embedded systems, in: *Proceedings of the 1st International Workshop on Security and Privacy for the Internet-of-Things (IoTSec)*, Orlando, FL, USA, 2018.
18. Jaiswal, S. and Gupta, P., Diabetes Prediction Using Bi-directional Long Short-Term Memory. *SN Comput. Sci.*, 4, 373, 2023. https://doi.org/10.1007/s42979-023-01831-z.
19. Jaiswal, S. and Pandey, M.K., A Review on Image Segmentation, in: *Rising Threats in Expert Applications and Solutions. Advances in Intelligent Systems and Computing*, vol. 1187, V.S. Rathore, N. Dey, V. Piuri, R. Babo, Z. Polkowski, J.M.R.S. Tavares (Eds.), Springer, Singapore, 2021, https://doi.org/10.1007/978-981-15-6014-9_27.

20. Jaiswal, S. and Pandey, M.K., Digital Watermark Extraction Using RS-KNN and RS-LDA with LWT and Statistical Features. *SN Comput. Sci.*, 4, 496, 2023. https://doi.org/10.1007/s42979-023-01924-9.
21. Pandey, M.K., Kar, N.K., Gupta, P., *Federated Learning: Introduction, Evolution, Working, Advantages, and Its Application in Various Domains*, P.R. Chelliah, A.M. Rahmani, R. Colby, G. Nagasubramanian, S. Ranganath (Eds.), Elsevier, Wiley, 2024, https://doi.org/10.1002/9781394219230.ch6.
22. Hernandez Aros, L., Bustamante Molano, L.X., Gutierrez-Portela, F., Moreno Hernandez, J.J., Rodríguez Barrero, M.S., Financial fraud detection through the application of machine learning techniques: a literature review. *Humanit. Soc. Sci. Commun.*, 11, 1, 1–22, 2024.
23. Benaddi, H., Jouhari, M., Ibrahimi, K., Ben Othman, J., Amhoud, E.M., Anomaly detection in industrial IoT using distributional reinforcement learning and generative adversarial networks. *Sensors*, 22, 21, 8085, 2022.
24. Chakraborty, S., Pandey, S.K., Maity, S., Dey, L., Detection and classification of novel attacks and anomaly in IoT network using rule based deep learning model. *SN Comput. Sci.*, 5, 8, 1056, 2024.
25. Sangeetha, S.B., Selvarathi, C., Mathivanan, S.K., Cho, J., Easwaramoorthy, S.V., Secure Healthcare Access Control System (SHACS) for Anomaly Detection and Enhanced Security in Cloud-Based Healthcare Applications. *IEEE Access*, 2024.
26. Nayer, T., Figueroa, E., Vishnu, P., A., S., Kolandapalayam, S., Kiran, K., V., S., Sengan., A., Melgarejo, B,.C., Adaptive Approach to Anomaly Detection in Internet of Things Using Autoencoders and Dynamic Thresholds. *J. Mach. Comput.*, 2024. doi: 10.53759/7669/jmc202404001.
27. Goenawan, I.H., Du, Z., Wu, C., Sun, Y., Wei, J., Bader, D.A., Dynamics signature-based anomaly detection. *Softw.: Pract. Exper.*, 53, 1, 160–175, 2023.
28. Rani, P.S., Ahamed, M.V., Chaithresh, K.S.S., Srinivas, S.K., Vivek, P.V., Utilizing Machine Learning Techniques for Detecting Anomalies in IoT Networks, in: *2024 5th International Conference on Recent Trends in Computer Science and Technology (ICRTCST)*, IEEE, pp. 105–110, 2024, April.
29. Kumar, G.R., Kulkarni, A.D., Kumar, B.S., Singh, N., Revathi, V., Kumar, T.C.A., Machine Learning Approaches for Anomaly Detection in IoT Networks, in: *2024 International Conference on Advances in Computing, Communication and Applied Informatics (ACCAI)*, IEEE, pp. 1–5, 2024, May.
30. Harish, G.N. and Annapurna, H.S., Survey on machine learning based anomaly detection in cloud networks, in: *2024 International Conference on Knowledge Engineering and Communication Systems (ICKECS)*, vol. 1, pp. 1–9, IEEE, 2024, April.
31. Abusitta, A., Silva de Carvalho, G.H., Abdel Wahab, O., Halabi, T., Fung, B.C.M., Al Mamoori, S., Deep Learning-Enabled Anomaly Detection for IoT Systems. Available at SSRN: https://ssrn.com/abstract=4258930 or http://dx.doi.org/10.2139/ssrn.4258930.

12

# Immunity against Intrusion: Introducing an Agent-Based Blockchain Mechanism in Cloud IoT Environment

**Amitabha Mandal[1]* and Pramit Ghosh[2]**

[1]*Panihati Mahavidyalaya, West Bengal State University, West Bengal, India*
[2]*RCC Institute of Information Technology, Kolkata, West Bengal, India*

***Abstract***

Wireless Sensor Networks (WSNs) were originally designed for specific applications. They were not intended to support modern household devices or provide additional features. Their internet use was limited, and WSNs struggled to meet new demands as technology advanced. Due to these restrictions, the Internet of Things (IoT) was developed, which uses the internet to transmit commands and data between objects. However, the need for extensive infrastructure and high deployment costs has slowed the adoption of IoT solutions. Cloud IoT emerged as a cost-effective alternative, offering data storage, analysis, and web services to connect diverse devices. However, its reliance on public networks exposes it to intrusions and attacks *via* web service interfaces. Malicious actors can inject fabricated data or overwhelm web services, compromising system reliability. While secret key or passcode-based strategies offer a basic defense, they fail to address insider threats and become unmanageable as the network scales. Blockchain technology provides a robust alternative by utilizing dynamic transaction records for data validation instead of static keys. However, its computational demands exceed the capabilities of many IoT devices. To overcome this limitation, an agent-based approach is proposed. In this system, a high-capacity node, designated as an agent within the local network, maintains transaction records and manages dynamic keys or passcodes. These keys enable smaller IoT devices to access cloud IoT services without direct blockchain interaction securely. This agent-based Blockchain mechanism enhances security and mitigates intrusions in cloud IoT environments. It addresses the inefficiencies of traditional methods, leverages Blockchain's strengths, and ensures the

**Corresponding author*: amitabha.1982@gmail.com

Partha Ghosh, Rajdeep Chakraborty, Anupam Ghosh and Ahmed A. Elngar (eds.) Strategic Approaches to Intrusion Detection in Cloud-IoT Ecosystem, (301–330) © 2026 Scrivener Publishing LLC

participation of resource-constrained devices in a secure ecosystem. This solution promotes the broader adoption of cloud IoT technologies, instilling trust and advancing IoT's role in modern applications by providing a scalable and efficient agent-based Blockchain security framework.

***Keywords***: Wireless sensor network, internet of things, cloud IoT, blockchain, intrusion detection system (IDS), encryption, OFMC, CL-AtSe

## 12.1 Introduction

This section is organized into several interconnected subsections, including the evolution of digital systems, distributed sensor environments, intrusion, and intrusion detection [1]. As digital systems evolve from their initial development phases and begin to offer real-world benefits, they inevitably attract negative attempts to undermine their advantages. The subsection on intrusion and intrusion detection will explore these malicious activities and the methods used to safeguard systems, ensuring that the positive impact of digital technology is preserved.

### 12.1.1 Evolution of Digital System

In the mid-20th century, digital systems [2, 3] emerged to address automatic decision-making challenges. These systems rely on digital logic gates as their fundamental components, processing binary inputs to produce outputs based on specific operations. However, basic gates alone are insufficient for complex logic, leading to the development of combinational circuits. These circuits are made up of input variables, logic gates, and output variables and the output of these circuits are entirely dependent on the current inputs. Examples include adders, subtractors, decoders, encoders, multiplexers, and de-multiplexers.

As system requirements grew, sequential circuits were introduced to handle more advanced tasks. Unlike combinational circuits, sequential circuits depend on both current inputs and previous outputs, integrating memory elements to maintain state information. While combinational circuits perform predefined tasks efficiently, sequential circuits enable more dynamic operations.

The availability of integrated circuits (ICs) for common tasks saves time and cost. However, customized circuits are necessary for complex operations. These circuits combine combinational and sequential elements but require complete replacement for even minor modifications. The stored program concept addressed these challenges by allowing data and instructions to coexist in memory, enabling efficient, automated operations; the system's block diagram is shown in Figure 12.1.

Modern microprocessors have revolutionized digital systems. These devices integrate millions of transistors and key components such as the arithmetic logic unit, control unit, and registers, performing four essential steps: Fetch, Decode, Execute, and Store. Their programmability enables them to handle input, execute operations, and produce outputs efficiently.

The advancements in digital circuits and microprocessors have enhanced the capabilities of distributed sensor environments, where networks gather information and analyze them in real-time. These innovations continue to shape modern computing, enabling large-scale monitoring and processing.

### 12.1.2 Distributed Sensor Environment

Modern engineering advancements have led to innovative sensor designs, wireless systems, and information technologies, bridging the physical and digital worlds. Sensors are vital in devices, industries, and machines, preventing failures, boosting productivity, and enhancing security. To address

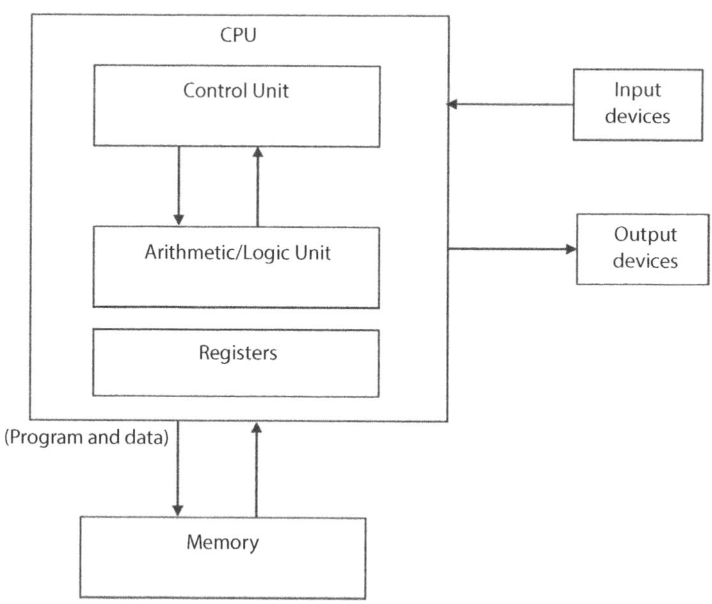


**Figure 12.1** Store program architecture of a typical system.

these needs, wireless sensor networks (WSN) [4–6] were developed. A WSN consists of interconnected sensor nodes. These nodes monitor, gather, and wirelessly send data to a base station, which uses Internet to process and share the data.

WSN architecture has three primary layers:

- **Physical Layer**: Utilizes Bluetooth, radio waves, and infrared for sensor-to-base station connectivity.
- **Data Link Layer**: Ensures reliable communication using protocols like IEEE 802.15.4.
- **Application Layer**: Formats and transmits data for applications like environmental monitoring or industrial control.

A schematic diagram of a wireless sensor network with its components is shown in Figure 12.2.

In combination, these layers provide a wireless sensor network's seamless operation and data flow, enabling effective data gathering and monitoring across various applications.

WSN monitors a variety of environmental conditions similar to temperature, pressure, and sound and distributes the information wirelessly [7–9] acquired from the base station or various nodes. WSN will be suitable for a wide range of applications in the domains of industry monitoring,

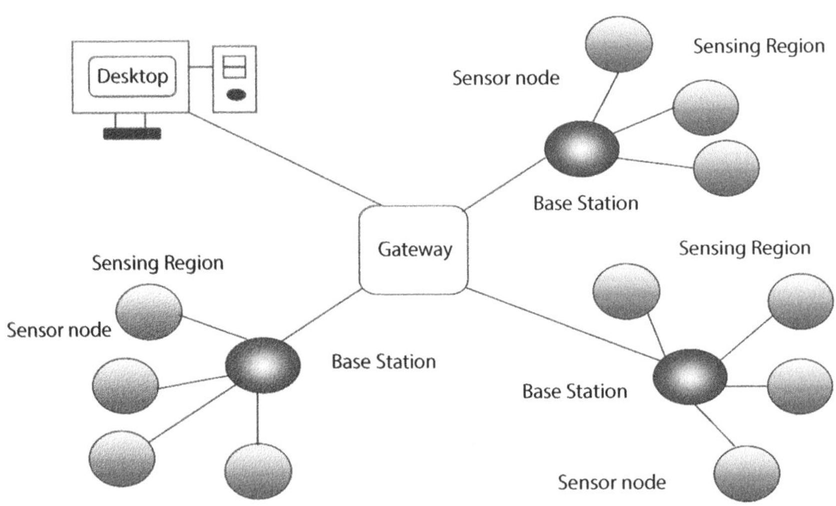


**Figure 12.2** Diagram of a wireless sensor network that includes computing nodes, gateways, and sensor nodes.

health monitoring, agriculture (crop monitoring), military, and industrial automation etc.

### 12.1.3 Intrusion and Intrusion Detection

Wireless Sensor Networks (WSNs) offer cost-effective solutions for diverse monitoring tasks but face significant security challenges due to open wireless media, decentralized communication, and deployment in vulnerable areas. These vulnerabilities make WSNs susceptible to unauthorized access, attacks, and malicious activities, necessitating early detection and mitigation strategies.

An intrusion detection system (IDS) [10, 11] identifies unauthorized behaviors or threats within the network. IDS monitors user activities and network behavior across layers, serving as a passive defense mechanism. Instead of preventing attacks, IDS alerts administrators, enabling timely responses to mitigate damage. Intrusion detection accuracy is determined by reducing false positives (false alarms) and false negatives (undetected attacks).

IDS operates in two key forms:

Signature-based IDS: Matches threats against a database of known signatures, effective for known attacks but limited against new ones.
Anomaly-based IDS: Monitors system activities and traffic patterns, detecting new threats but occasionally missing known vulnerabilities.
IDS modes include standalone operation on individual nodes and cooperative cluster-based operation, where nodes monitor neighboring activities and report issues to a cluster head. These approaches enhance WSN security and reliability.

### 12.1.4 Internet of Things (IoT)

Wireless Sensor Networks (WSNs) were initially developed to address specific problem domains and were not designed to provide value-added features for common household devices. The usage of the internet within WSNs is limited, and as requirements have evolved over time, WSNs have struggled to meet new demands.

To address these limitations, the internet of things (IoT) [12–14] emerged as the successor to WSNs. The IoT includes more than merely networking or connecting devices; rather, it involves the transfer of meaningful data between devices to achieve specific goals.

Internet of Things (IoT): A network of interconnected devices that can communicate with one another and exchange data, is known as the internet of things (IoT).

These gadgets may be people or animals, as well as common household objects and industrial tools. IoT links devices, helps data collection from different sources, communicates data, analyzes data from multiple sensors and devices, and produces flawless results quickly.

The internet of things (IoT) comprises interconnected subsystems, including data acquisition devices, local servers for data processing, cloud systems for advanced analytics, and internet connectivity for user access. Key characteristics of IoT systems include:

Connectivity: IoT connects devices like computers and mobile phones, enabling real-time information access from anywhere.
Identity of Things: Unique identifiers differentiate devices, ensuring precise communication and command execution.
Intelligence: Sensors enhance IoT device intelligence, enabling smart tasks through frequent updates and added features.
Dynamic Behavior: IoT devices adapt to their environment, such as ACs adjusting temperature or cameras optimizing for light conditions.
Scalability: IoT efficiently manages vast data volumes, enabling insightful analysis.
Self-Upgradation: IoT devices autonomously update software and integrate new devices seamlessly.
Architecture: IoT's architecture supports diverse devices, ensuring compatibility, data security, and device integrity (Figure 12.3).
Security: IoT prioritizes data privacy and mitigates risks like unauthorized data transfer, maintaining secure and reliable systems.

Protocol stack:
The Internet of Things (IoT) protocol stack [15, 16] is a collection of layered protocols that enable communication between devices. Like the traditional network stacks, the IoT protocol stack has seven layers, each performing a specific function in device communication (Figure 12.4). This design is similar to the standard protocol layers in wired and wireless technologies. Let's go through each layer in detail.

Physical/Sensor Layer: Interfaces with sensors (e.g., temperature, humidity, pressure) to gather data from the environment. Sensors are selected based on application needs and cost-effectiveness.

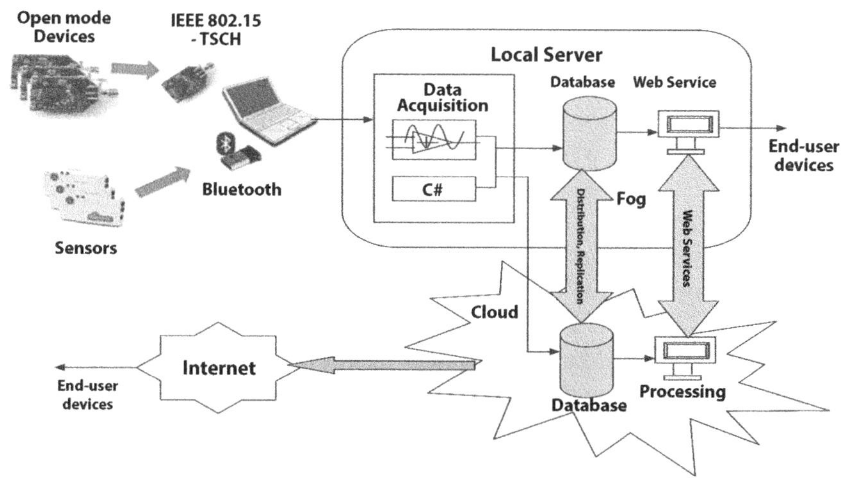


**Figure 12.3** Heterogeneous architecture of internet of things (IoT).

| |
|---|
| Application Layer |
| User Experience Layer |
| Session Layer |
| RF Layer |
| Hardware Interface Layer |
| Processing and Control Action Layer |
| Physical or Sensor Layer |

**Figure 12.4** IoT protocol stack.

Processing and Control Layer: Processes sensor data using microcontrollers, processors, and operating systems like Arduino, Linux, and iOS. Executes tasks based on inputs.

Hardware Interface Layer: Manages device communication using protocols like RS232, SPI, and CAN, ensuring synchronized and reliable data transfer.

RF Layer: Handles wireless communication by means of technologies namely GSM , Bluetooth, WiFi, and 5G, enabling data transmission over electromagnetic waves or light (LiFi).

Session/Message Layer: Uses protocols like MQTT and HTTP to transmit messages between devices and cloud servers.

User Experience Layer: Enhances usability with rich graphical interfaces and analytics tools.

Application Layer: Develops real-world solutions, including smart cities, agriculture, and waste management, leveraging IoT's interconnected ecosystem.

IoT Security Challenges
The rapid growth of IoT has introduced critical security challenges:

Lack of Encryption: Many IoT devices lack robust encryption due to limited resources, making them prone to data manipulation.
Insufficient Testing and Updates: Rapid deployment often leads to inadequate testing and delayed updates, increasing vulnerability to breaches.
IoT Malware and Ransomware: These attacks lock users out or hold data hostage, exploiting the expanding IoT ecosystem.
Botnets and Cryptocurrency Threats: IoT botnets can compromise data privacy and blockchain security.
Weak Device Security: Outdated software and weak passwords make devices easy targets.
Lack of Standardization: Absence of standard protocols hinders secure communication across devices.
Network Vulnerabilities: IoT devices are prone to network-based attacks like DoS, risking data theft.
Unsecured Data Transmission: Insufficient protection exposes data to tampering; encryption and secure protocols are essential.
Privacy Concerns: Transparent practices and strong security measures are necessary to protect personal data.
Software Vulnerabilities: Regular updates and secure coding are vital to mitigate risks.
Insider Threats: Monitoring access and enforcing security policies reduce internal risks.

Addressing IoT security challenges is crucial for its safe integration into daily life. Measures like encryption, secure authentication, regular updates, and standardized protocols are essential to safeguard systems and devices. IoT system design faces obstacles in interoperability, security, scalability, reliability, power efficiency, and privacy.

Interoperability enables diverse devices to communicate seamlessly. Common protocols and standards are necessary to avoid fragmentation and inefficiencies, fostering integration across industries like healthcare and smart cities.

Security remains a top concern as IoT devices are prone to cyberattacks. Safeguarding data, ensuring device integrity, and employing encryption, firewalls, and regular updates mitigate vulnerabilities.

Scalability is vital as IoT expands, requiring systems to handle growing data and devices. Scalable cloud architectures and efficient storage solutions address these needs.

Reliability ensures uninterrupted performance, especially in critical applications. Redundancies, regular maintenance, and failover mechanisms maintain consistent operation.

Power efficiency is critical for battery-powered devices, necessitating energy-efficient designs and power management strategies to extend lifespans and reduce costs.

Privacy is essential, as IoT devices gather a lot of personal data. Robust privacy policies, encryption, and user education protect sensitive information.

Cloud-based IoT [17–19] solutions enhance scalability, security, and cost-efficiency. By centralizing data storage and management, they simplify deployment, improve functionality, and support seamless integration. Adopting innovative protocols and efficient strategies ensures IoT systems achieve secure, scalable, and high-performing outcomes.

### 12.1.5 Cloud IoT

The rapid adoption of IoT infrastructures for applications [20, 21] like smart homes, cities, and healthcare has significantly increased the demand for robust data storage, processing, and management services. Cloud IoT has emerged as a critical enabler in this domain, offering elastic computation and advanced data handling capabilities that complement the growing complexity of IoT systems. By integrating IoT devices with cloud data centers, a unified infrastructure is established, providing a cost-effective and scalable platform for IoT applications. This integration allows IoT devices equipped with sensors to interact seamlessly with cloud technology, facilitating remote monitoring, application development, and efficient data management.

However, the reliance on public networks for communication between IoT devices and the cloud introduces vulnerabilities. Attackers can exploit these public networks to infiltrate cloud systems, injecting fabricated data to disrupt analytics and compromise system integrity. Such intrusions can lead to significant misjudgments and undermine the reliability of IoT ecosystems. To address this, robust encryption mechanisms are essential in cloud IoT.

Encryption safeguards sensitive data by transforming plaintext into unreadable ciphertext, decoded only with a decryption key. Symmetric encryption [22, 23] uses the same key for both processes, suitable for bulk data but requiring secure key exchange. Asymmetric encryption, employing public and private keys, enhances security and supports IoT-cloud communication.

Cloud IoT can experience threats from attackers exploiting public networks, confused about data authenticity and confidentiality. This integration of IoT with cloud technology not only unlocks new levels of automation but also experiences the challenges posed by unauthorized access and intrusion.

### 12.1.6 Blockchain

Cloud IoT systems face security risks, particularly through web service interfaces, where attackers may inject false data or launch overwhelming assaults, compromising system integrity. Traditional secret key or passcode strategies offer limited protection, struggle with scalability, and fail to detect insider threats. Blockchain technology [24, 25] enhances security by using dynamic transaction records for data validation, ensuring transparency and resilience. However, its high computational demands challenge smaller IoT devices. An agent-based service addresses this, designating a high-capacity node to manage transaction records and dynamically provide secure keys, enabling smaller devices to access cloud services securely without heavy computational requirements.

Before going into details, brief discussion on block chain is given below.

Blockchain is a decentralized technology enabling secure, peer-to-peer data exchange, commonly used in financial transactions and industries like supply chain management. It works similarly to a distributed ledger and records transactions on several computers, making it visible and tamper-resistant. Blockchain data is stored in immutable ledger entries within a peer-to-peer network.

Blockchain architecture includes blocks, each containing a timestamp, version, Merkle root, difficulty target, nonce, and a previous hash linking it to the prior block. These blocks are secured using cryptographic functions like SHA-3, ensuring data integrity and tamper resistance. Consensus algorithms validate new blocks and prevent malicious changes.

There are three types of Blockchain: public (open to all), private (exclusive to one organization), and federated (controlled by multiple entities).

Nodes in Blockchain can be full (storing and validating all transactions) or partial (used for lightweight tasks).

Challenges in public Blockchain include complexity, slow transaction speeds, high resource usage, and security risks like 51% attacks. The first block is the Genesis Block, and any type of modification in the chain changes the hash, ensuring data security.

## 12.2 Contribution of the Authors

It is clear that wireless sensor networks (WSNs), IoT systems, and cloud IoT systems suffer from security vulnerabilities, particularly external intrusions. To enhance security, Blockchain technology can serve as a solution for IoT or cloud IoT systems. However, Blockchain technology requires significant computational power, which becomes a burden for small IoT devices. Therefore, an agent-based service, where a higher-capacity node manages transaction records and dynamic keys, allows smaller IoT devices to securely interact with cloud IoT services. This approach improves security, scalability, and fosters wider adoption and trust in IoT technologies.

## 12.3 Proposed Agent-Based Blockchain Mechanism in Cloud IoT [ABBM Cloud IoT]

This section discusses the proposed ABBM-Cloud IoT in detail. First, we provide an outline of the proposed scheme, followed by an in-depth discussion of each phase.

### 12.3.1 Proposed Scheme

The overview of the proposed ABBM-Cloud IoT is addressed in the following sections. To enhance the security of the key management and generation processes, in a private Blockchain using multiplicative and product operations, we have developed a one-way hash chain to set up the IoT devices and the Blockchain-based Region-wise Agent.

In the proposed scheme (Figure 12.5), IoT devices connect to a region-wise agent for authentication before transmitting the data to the cloud. The system's computing and communication setup begins once IoT devices and the region-wise agent, integrated with a private Blockchain, are initialized. All nodes in the data acquisition layer must register with their respective

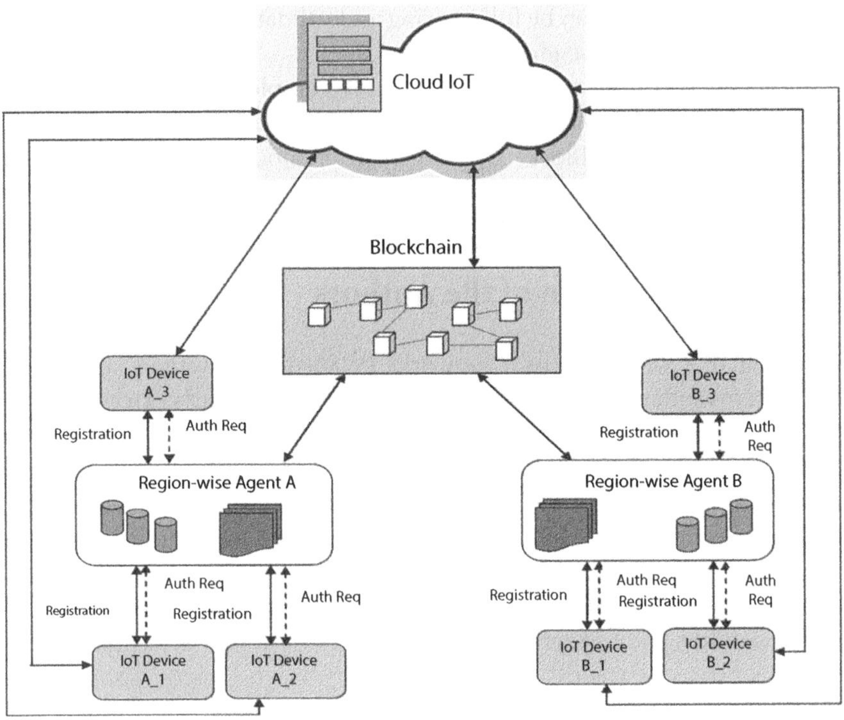


**Figure 12.5** System architecture of proposed scheme.

region-wise agent for future communication with cloud IoT. These registering IoT nodes can be any smart devices in the data acquisition layer. Upon successful registration, nodes can communicate through secure key management. Authentication requests from IoT devices are handled by the region-wise agent, which uses the private Blockchain to store key pairs and other critical information securely. This approach ensures efficient authentication and secure communication within the IoT network.

The proposed ABBM-Cloud IoT process, illustrated in Figure 12.5, begins by initializing the computing environment with a region-wise agent and a private Blockchain. IoT nodes are then registered with the region-wise agent by sharing their credentials. In the case study, one IoT devices, A_1 used as a node to the cloud IoT. When device A_1 needs to communicate with cloud IoT, the region-wise agent A processes the request. It verifies the details and checks the Blockchain for an existing key pair. If a valid key pair exists, it is reused within its lifespan; otherwise, a new key pair is generated using the identification numbers of A_1. The region-wise agent then forwards the request, including the key pair and other encrypted credentials, to cloud IoT *via* blockchain for further action. Upon receiving the request from cloud IoT, Blockchain verifies the credentials and generates a key at both ends upon successful authentication.

The ABBM-Cloud IoT scheme operates in two major phases: one of them is the Device Registration phase, and another one is the Authentication with Key Management phase, both of which are discussed in detail in subsequent sections.

### 12.3.2 Phase I: Device Registration

The leaf layer nodes must first be registered with the region-wise agent prior to their access to cloud IoT or communicate with one another. This process is part of trust management. The registration starts with every device choosing a random number and selecting its unique identity. This random number will be used as the private key (Pri), and a corresponding public key (Pub) will be generated [26] *via* $Pub_i = xy$. Once the device has both a permanent public and private keys, it will communicate the public key along with its identification number to the region-wise agent and store the private key locally. After receiving the credentials, the region-wise agent keeps them and distributes the public keys and identity numbers to all other registered devices for later use. Key generation requires significant computational effort, which can be challenging for small IoT edge devices with limited resources. In the proposed model, since the region-wise agent and the IoT edge devices are within the same local area network, the region-wise agent can handle the computational workload of generating keys for the edge devices. Private (Pri) and public (Pub) keys will be utilized for the encryption and decryption operations in the future. The process of device registration is given in Algorithm 12.1.

---

**Algorithm 12.1** IoT node (Edge Device) Registration

---

**Input:** $D_i$, Region-wise Agent

**Output:** IoT node (Edge Device) Registration successful with Region-wise Agent

1: BEGIN
2: The device ($D_i$) selects an $ID_i$ and chooses random numbers as s and t.
3: Set one of the random numbers as private key ($Pri_i = s$).
4: Calculating public key for the device ($D_i$) by using random generator 't' as $Pub_i = t^s$.

5. Store the permanent key pair with Identification number ($ID_i$, $Pri_i$, $Pub_i$) in its local database.
6: Send the pair ($ID_i$, $Pub_i$) to Region-wise Agent
7: The Region-wise Agent receives and stores ($ID_i$, $Pub_i$) in its own database.
8: It broadcasts the pair ($ID_i$, $Pub_i$) to all registered devices.
9: The Region-wise Agent also forwards ($ID_i$, $Pub_i$, $Pri_i$) to Cloud IoT *via* Blockchain.
10: END

### 12.3.3 Phase II: Authentication with Key Management

The registered IoT devices are able to exchange data and communicate, but they must agree on the keys. Initially, If device A is willing to communicate with B; it must request and get B's approval. After both edge devices have been successfully authenticated, the final session key is generated at each device. The key pair of the end devices is the primary determinant of the session key generation.

**Algorithm 12.2** Authentication of device A by Region-wise Agent

**Input:** $Pub_b$, tt, $ID_a$, $ID_b$

**Output:** Edge Device authentication with Region-wise Agent

1: BEGIN
2: Device A selects random number $Rand_a$
3: Encrypt the $Rand_a$ by $Pub_b$ using standard encryption method to compute $Rand_a$*
4: Send the pair ($ID_a$, $ID_b$, $Rand_a$*, ts1) to Region-wise Agent at time stamp ts1
5: Region-wise Agent receives the pair at ts1* from device A
6: if( [ts1*- ts1] <= tt) then
7:     Check the availability and validate the database of Region-wise Agent for ($ID_a$, $ID_b$)
8:     if available
9:         Accept the request from Device A
10:     else
11:         Reject the request as an unauthenticated device
12: else
13:     Reject the request based on out of time-bound
14: END

The region-wise agent will utilize a one-way hash function for the creation of the key pair of each requesting node. Furthermore, the generated key pair is stored in the blockchain and later used for session key generation at edge devices, subsequently the region-wise agent shares it. The process of key management by generating the final session key upon authentication is shown in Figure 12.6. The device $D_a$ has to select any random number and encrypt it using the public key of $D_b$ (The public key of edge devices is made available to all registered devices in the registration phase) and then transmit the request to the region-wise agent with the encrypted random

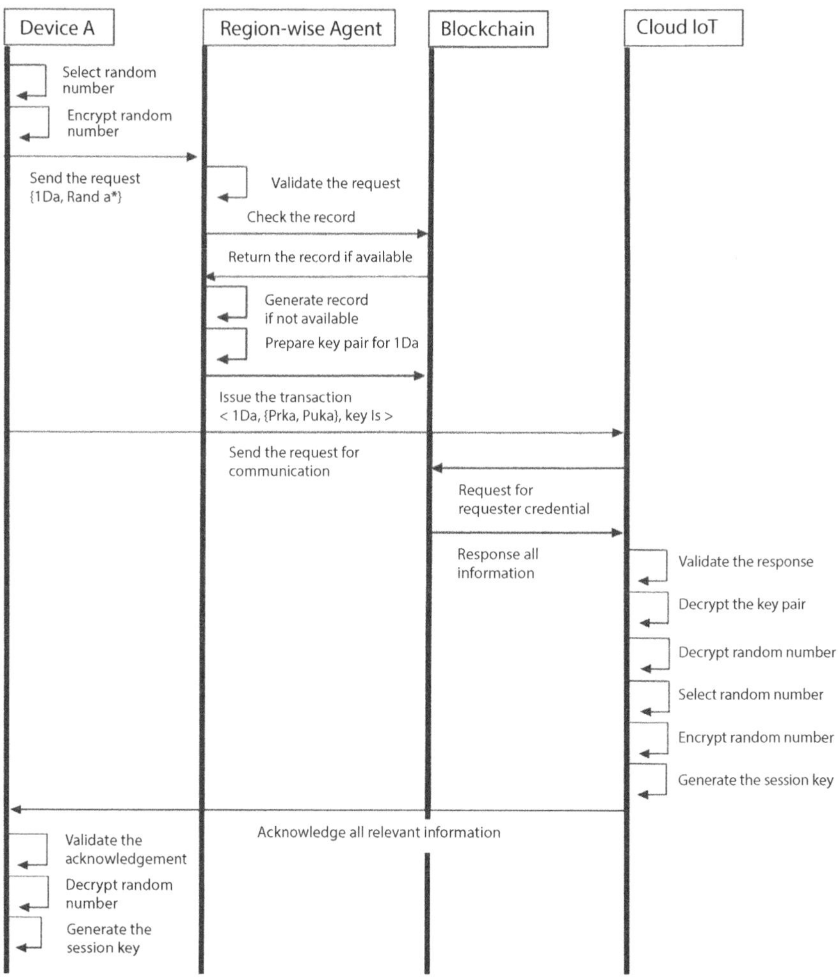


**Figure 12.6** Sequence diagram of key generation.

number identifying the requester and recipient. The region-wise agent checks the identity using its stored data and validates the request depending on the time of arrival. It is explained in Algorithm 12.2.

Upon success, if the region-wise agent finds a pair of the requester and recipient's IDs in the Blockchain, it will extract the necessary key pairs from the blockchain. The key pair in a transaction that is kept on the Blockchain has a lifespan; after that, it will no longer be functioning correctly. The region-wise agent will produce the key pairs for Da and Db based on the corresponding IDs if this is the first time the Da is requesting Db, or if the key life span has ended, a blockchain containing the produced key pairs, their corresponding ID pairs, and their life span will be recorded as {(IDa, IDb), (Prka, Puka), (Prkb, Pukb), key_ls}. According to their public key, the region-wise agent also distributes the key pairs in an encrypted format to the appropriate edge nodes. The detailed explanation appears in Algorithm 12.3.

---

**Algorithm 12.3** Key pair generated and sharing by the region-wise agent

---

**Input:** $ID_a$, $ID_b$, $Rand_a$*, $Pub_a$, $Pub_b$

**Output:** Successful sharing for private and public key pair with devices

1: BEGIN
2: Region-wise Agent has to verify the Blockchain for a record based on ($ID_a$, $ID_b$)
3: if found then
4: Fetch the record form Blockchain
5: { ($ID_a$, $ID_b$ ), ( $Prk_a$, $Puk_a$),($Prk_b$, $Puk_b$), key_ls}
6: if (key_ls) then
7: Make use of the record's key pair, go to step 13
8: else
9: go to step 10
10: else
11: Using one way hash function to generate $Prk_a$, $Puk_a$, $Prk_b$ and $Puk_b$
12: Issue { ($ID_a$,$ID_b$ ), ( $Prk_a$, $Puk_a$),($Prk_b$, $Puk_b$), key_ls} into Blockchain
13: Encrypt using standard method and send the key pair to $D_a$ at ts2 {($Prk_a$,$Puk_a$), ($Puk_b$), ts2}
14: Encrypt using standard method and send the key pair to $D_b$ with an encrypted random number at ts2 { ($Prk_b$,$Puk_b$), ($Puk_a$), $Rand_a$*, ts2}
15: The Device A receives { ($Prk_a$,$Puk_a$), ($Puk_b$) } at ts2*
16: The Device B receives { ($Prk_b$,$Puk_b$), ($Puk_a$) , $Rand_a$*} at ts2*

if( [ts2*- ts2] <= tt) then
    Key pair sharing is success
else
    Abort the process
END

The shared key pair and other credentials will be sent to the edge nodes, which will decrypt them after validating them according to arrival time. Finally, use a one-way hash function [27, 28] to construct the session key at both ends based on the key pairs and random numbers of both edge nodes as follows: Session Key = Hash (Puka, Ra, Pukb, Rb) as given in Algorithm 12.4.

**Algorithm 12.4** Session key generation at edge devices

**Input:** $Rand_a$*, ($Prk_b$,$Puk_b$), $Pub_a$,$Pri_b$, tt, $Pri_a$

**Output:** Generation of session keys on both end devices.

BEGIN
Device B selects $Rand_b$
$Rand_b$* = Encrypt $_{PBa}$($Rand_b$)
$Rand_a$ = Decrypt $_{PRb}$($Rand_a$*)
Decrypt $_{PRb}$(Encrypt $_{PBb}$($Prk_b$,$Puk_b$))
Decrypt $_{PRb}$(Encrypt $_{PBb}$($Puk_a$))
Session Key = Hash (Puka, Ra, Pukb, Rb)
Send { $Rand_b$*, Hash ($Rand_a$* , $Rand_b$), ts) to Device A at ts3
The Device A receives { $Rand_b$*, Hash ($Rand_a$* , $Rand_b$) } at ts3*
if( Difference(ts3*, ts3) <= tt) then
    if(Hash ($Rand_b$*, $Rand_a$) = Hash ($Rand_a$* , $Rand_b$) ) then
        $Rand_b$ = Decrypt $_{PRa}$($Rand_b$*)
        Decrypt $_{PRa}$(Encrypt $_{PBa}$($Prk_a$,$Puk_a$))
        Decrypt $_{PRa}$(Encrypt $_{PBa}$($Puk_b$))
        Session Key = Hash (Puka, Ra, Pukb, Rb)
    else
        Abort the process
    else
        Abort the process
END

### 12.3.4 Incorporating Blockchain in Key Management

In this section, we talk about the use of the private blockchain in the proposed key management system. Each block comprises a data field that has been encrypted, it's hash value, and the hash value of the Blockchain's preceding block. The genesis block does not contain any hashes from earlier blocks because it is the first block. The data field of the genesis block contains the meta-data, including the number of blocks and the blockchain limit. Transactions issued by the region-wise agent are the data field in the remaining blocks.

## 12.4 Results and Discussion

The performance assessment of the **Agent-Based Blockchain Mechanism in Cloud IoT (ABBM - Cloud IoT)** is analyzed based on security, overhead metrics, and blockchain efficiency. The results demonstrate the effectiveness of the proposed mechanism in addressing key management and authentication challenges in cloud IoT environments.

### 12.4.1 Security Analysis

The ABBM-Cloud IoT mechanism was tested against known attacks, including man-in-the-middle, denial-of-service attacks, and replay, using the AVISPA tool under the Dolev-Yao model. The analysis, performed *via* OFMC and CL-AtSe backends, confirmed the scheme's robustness, showing no attack traces. The time taken for security analysis varied slightly, with OFMC processing 370 nodes in 8.9 seconds while CL-AtSe analyzed 9 states in 0.23 seconds indicating computational efficiency.

Table 12.1 shows the security features and resilience analysis for ABBM - Cloud IoT; it is clear that the ABBM - Cloud IoT mechanism effectively addresses multiple security threats through robust design and advanced cryptographic techniques. Replay attacks are mitigated by incorporating random numbers and session-based timestamps, ensuring intercepted messages cannot be reused. Protection against man-in-the-middle attacks is achieved through ECC-based encryption and mutual authentication, safeguarding the integrity and origin of communications. Distributed architecture reduces the impact of denial-of-service (DoS) [29, 30] attacks by eliminating reliance on just one node, while forward secrecy ensures that past session keys remain uncompromised even if current keys are exposed. Additionally, the system prevents privileged insider attacks by

**Table 12.1** Security features and resilience analysis for ABBM - Cloud IoT.

| **Security feature** | **Description** | **Effectiveness in ABBM-Cloud IoT** | **Explanation** |
|---|---|---|---|
| **Replay Attack** | Prevents attackers from reusing intercepted data to deceive devices. | Resilient | Incorporates random numbers and timestamps in every session, making data replay attempts invalid. |
| **Man-in-the-Middle Attack** | Prevents middlemen from intercepting and changing device-to-device communication. | Resilient | Uses ECC-based encryption and mutual authentication to ensure message integrity and origin verification. |
| **Denial-of-Service (DoS) Attack** | Avoids service disruption by overloading the network or agent node with unnecessary requests. | Resilient | Employs distributed architecture with private blockchain, reducing reliance on single points of failure. |
| **Privileged Insider Attack** | Prevents misuse of privileges by authenticated insiders. | Resilient | Keys and session credentials are session-based and not reusable post-session, limiting insider misuse. |

(*Continued*)

**Table 12.1** Security features and resilience analysis for ABBM - Cloud IoT. (*Continued*)

| Security feature | Description | Effectiveness in ABBM-Cloud IoT | Explanation |
|---|---|---|---|
| **Forward Secrecy Attack** | Ensures that compromise of long-term keys does not compromise past session keys. | Resilient | Session keys are independently generated for each session, combining random numbers and time-sensitive parameters. |
| **Ephemeral Secret Leakage Attack** | Protects against exposure of short-term credentials used in session key generation. | Resilient | Combines short-term random values with long-term keys, ensuring secrets are secure even if one component is exposed. |

using session-specific keys that cannot be reused post-session. Ephemeral secret leakage is addressed by combining short-term random values with long-term keys, maintaining secure session key generation. Finally, robust mutual authentication between devices ensures trust before initiating data exchanges, making the system highly resilient to a wide range of attacks.

### 12.4.2 Overhead Metrics

The overhead of the ABBM-Cloud IoT mechanism was assessed by examining computation, communication, and storage costs. The results are summarized in Table 12.2 below, followed by an explanation of each category:

#### *12.4.2.1 Computation Cost*

Computation cost focused on operations related to authentication and key management, excluding registration. The total computation time was 6.54

**Table 12.2** Overhead metrics analysis for ABBM - Cloud IoT.

| Overhead metric | Value | Comparison improvement |
|---|---|---|
| Computation Cost | **6.542 ms** | **8% to 16% reduction** |
| Communication Cost | **2,470 bits** | **11% to 19% reduction** |
| Storage Cost | **950 bits (device)** | **9% to 18% reduction** |

milliseconds, which involved, 4 hash operations [31–33], and 6 encryptions and decryptions. When compared to similar mechanisms, this proposed solution reduced computation costs by 8% to 16%, making it more efficient for edge devices.

The following formula is used to calculate the entire computation cost for ABBM-Cloud IoT based on each primitive's execution timings, as displayed in Table 12.3.

$$4T_{prod} + 4T_h + 6T_e + 6T_d$$
$$= 4(0.474)+4(0.032)+6(0.398)+6(0.355)$$
$$=1.896+0.128+2.388+2.13$$
$$=6.542 \text{ ms}$$

The total computation time was 6.542 milliseconds, which involved, 4 hash operations [31–33], and 6 encryptions and decryptions.

If we compare the methods numbered [34–37] to the **ABBM - Cloud IoT** method, it is found that the latter is better optimized due to its **significantly lower computation cost (6.542)**. This proves its greater effectiveness in

**Table 12.3** Execution duration with MIRACL.

| Primitive | Description | Time (ms) |
|---|---|---|
| $T_h$ | One-way hash function (SHA-512) | 0.032 |
| $T_{prod}$ | Elliptic curve point product | 0.474 |
| $T_e$ | ECC-based encryption | 0.398 |
| $T_d$ | ECC-based decryption | 0.355 |

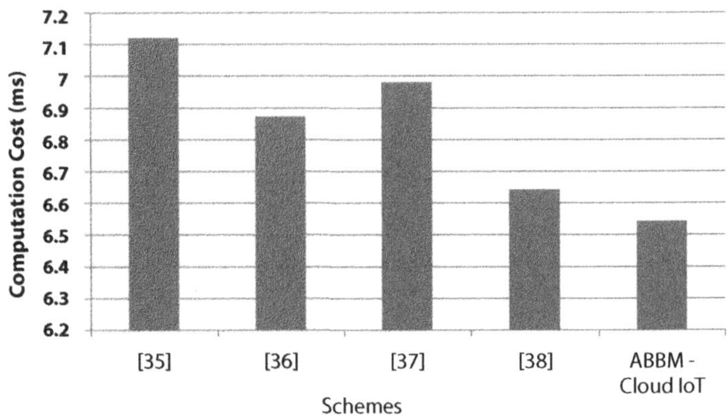


**Figure 12.7** Computation cost comparison.

terms of resource utilization. The other methods show higher computation costs (Figure 12.7) (ranging from 6.64 to 7.12), whereas **ABBM-Cloud IoT** attains the same or better performance with reduced computational overhead and better cost-efficiency. This suggests that **ABBM-Cloud IoT** is able to deliver processing times that are faster, using less system resources. This makes it the perfect real-time solution and resource-constrained environments such as IoT applications. By reducing the computational load, the **ABBM-Cloud IoT** method is also more appropriate for scalability and deployment in a variety of IoT and cloud-based applications.

#### *12.4.2.2 Communication Cost*

Communication cost was determined by the total number of bits exchanged during the key management process. The mechanism exchanged a total of 2,470 bits, achieving a reduction of 11% to 19% compared to previous methods. This was largely due to efficient message encoding and minimized transaction overhead.

As a result, a total of 2416 bits were exchanged during the communication process.

**ABBM-Cloud IoT** has the **lowest number of bits exchanged** during the key management process **(2416 bits)**, which is significantly lower than the other methods shown in the below Figure 12.8.

This shows that ABBM - Cloud IoT method, is the most cost-effective method, requiring fewer bits to be exchanged, making it more efficient for key management processes. In terms of communication overhead and energy usage, fewer bits exchanged typically implies lower resource

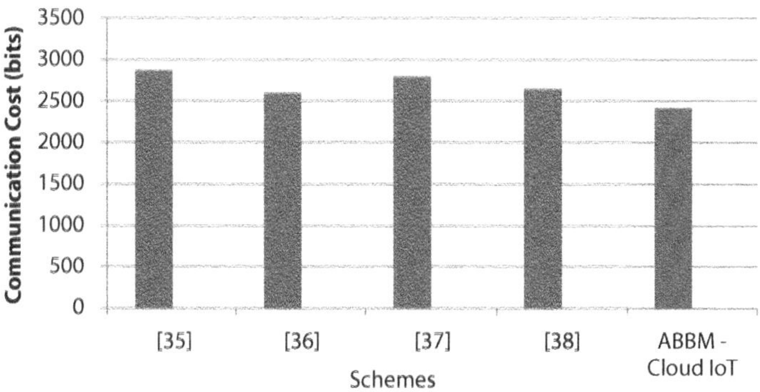


**Figure 12.8** Communication cost comparison.

**Table 12.4** Parameters of communication with size.

| Parameter | Description | Size (bits) |
|---|---|---|
| $ID_a$, $ID_b$ | Device Identifiers | 128 |
| $R_a$, $R_b$ | Random Numbers | 160 |
| Prk, Puk | Private and Public key-pair | 160 |
| PR, PB | Private and Public keys of a device | 160 |
| h(.) | Hashed data | 512 |
| Cts1, cts2, cts3 | Timestamp | 52 |

consumption, which makes ABBM - Cloud IoT a superior choice compared to other methods in Table 12.4.

### *12.4.2.3 Storage Cost*

Storage overhead was evaluated both for the devices and the agent node. Devices required 950 bits for storage, while the agent node allocated 336 bits per device. This led to a reduction in storage costs of 9% to 18% when compared to similar solutions, contributing to more efficient resource usage. These findings highlight the effectiveness of the ABBM-Cloud IoT mechanism in reducing overhead across all evaluated dimensions, ensuring faster and more resource-efficient operations, particularly on edge devices.

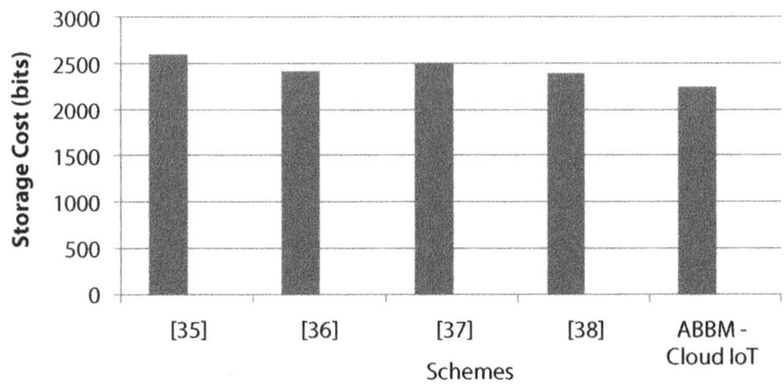


**Figure 12.9** Storage cost comparison.

Since **lower storage overhead** typically translates to more efficient use of resources, ABBM - Cloud IoT is the most storage-efficient technique in this comparison (Figure 12.9). It will require a smaller amount memory for data storage, which contributes to reduced system cost and improved scalability, particularly in resource-constrained IoT environments.

### 12.4.3 Blockchain Efficiency

The efficiency of the blockchain [38, 39] was evaluated using the Truffle framework, focusing on transaction handling and block preparation time. Table 12.5 summarizes the key findings, with further explanations provided for each category:

**Table 12.5** Proposed blockchain efficiency analysis.

| Blockchain efficiency metric | Value | Comparison improvement |
|---|---|---|
| **Transaction handling time** | 0.00062 seconds (average) | Low latency |
| **Block preparation time** | 50 transactions/block: 0.17-1.50 sec | 12% to 28% improvement |
| | 100 transactions/block: 0.23-2.10 sec | |
| | 150 transactions/block: 0.31-2.96 sec | |

#### *12.4.3.1 Transaction Handling*

Transaction handling was optimized to minimize latency, with each transaction requiring an average processing time of 0.00062 seconds. This low processing time ensures fast and efficient addition of requests to the blockchain, contributing to the overall system's high throughput.

#### *12.4.3.2 Block Preparation Time*

The block preparation time was analyzed for different transaction block sizes. For blocks containing 50 transactions, the preparation time ranged from 0.17 to 1.50 seconds; for 100 transactions per block, it ranged from 0.23 to 2.10 seconds; and for 150 transactions per block, the time varied from 0.31 to 2.96 seconds. This performance indicates a scalable system that handles larger block sizes effectively. When compared to other blockchain mechanisms, the block preparation time was 12% to 28% lower, demonstrating the efficiency gained from an optimized blockchain design and lightweight transactions.

These results highlight the blockchain's efficiency, particularly in its ability to handle transactions with minimal latency and prepare blocks quickly, even as transaction volume increases.

The **ABBM-Cloud IoT** technique stands out as the best method because it takes the shortest preparation time compared to all the other transaction volumes. As the table clearly shows, **ABBM-Cloud IoT** dependably demonstrates the lowest preparation times compared to the methods named [34–37]:

- For 250 transactions per block, **ABBM-Cloud IoT** takes 0.17 seconds which is faster than all other methods, the next best being **0.3 seconds**.
- At 500 transactions, **ABBM-Cloud IoT** requires only **0.22 seconds** again the quickest, compared to **0.36 seconds** from method [37].
- As the transaction count increases, **ABBM-Cloud IoT** continues to maintain the fastest preparation times: **0.4 seconds** for 1000 transactions, **0.59 seconds** for 1500 transactions, **0.86 seconds** for 2000 transactions, and **1.5 seconds** for 2500 transactions.

Therefore, in Figure 12.10, we see that, **ABBM-Cloud IoT** surpasses the other methods in preparation time, which also makes it the most

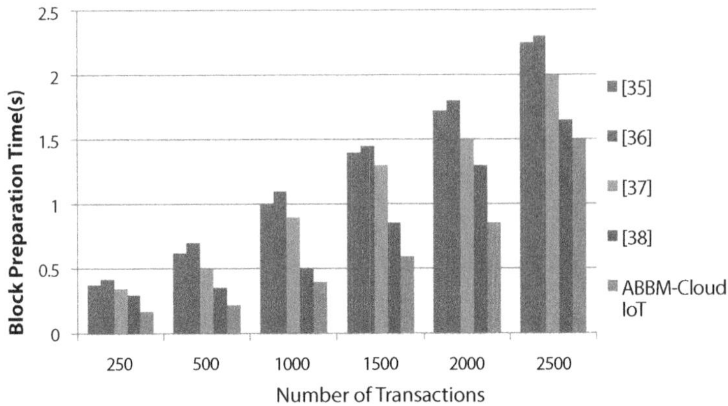


**Figure 12.10** Block preparation time (50 transactions per block).

time-efficient solution for processing IoT transactions at any block size. Thus, **ABBM-Cloud IoT** is the ideal choice when minimizing preparation time is a critical factor.

Likewise, the block preparation time for scenarios with 100 and 150 transactions per block is displayed in Figures 12.11 and 12.12, respectively. The outputs demonstrate that the proposed **ABBM-Cloud IoT** scheme does better than schemes [34–37], achieving an average reduction in block preparation time by 28.69%, 28.88%, 16.19%, 14.81%, and 16.33%, respectively. This confirms that the **ABBM-Cloud IoT** method is more effective in terms of block preparation time compared to the other methods, proving its effectiveness.

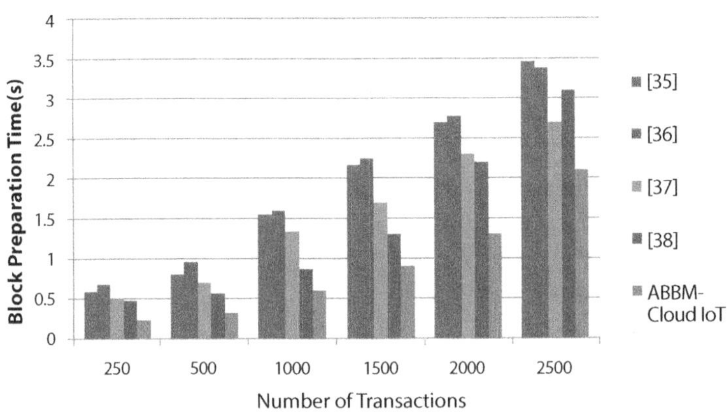


**Figure 12.11** Block (100 transactions per block) preparation time.

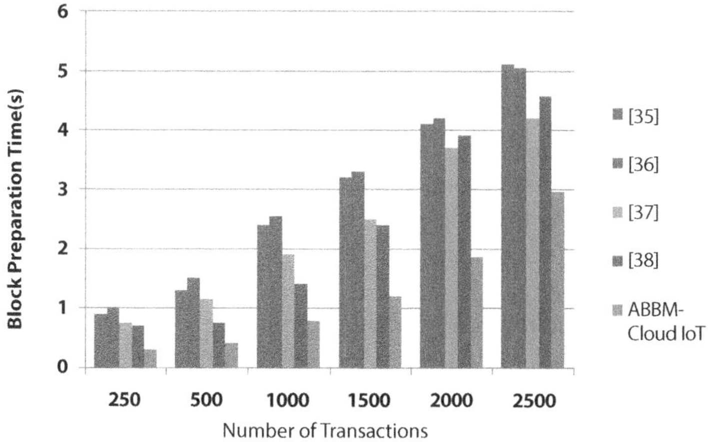


**Figure 12.12** Block (150 transactions per block) preparation time.

### 12.4.4 Summary of Results

The ABBM-Cloud IoT mechanism effectively enhances security, reduces computational burdens, and demonstrates scalable blockchain performance. Improvements across all performance metrics, including computation, communication, and storage costs, validate its suitability for cloud IoT environments. Further refinements, such as incorporating multi-agent node communication and distributed consensus, will enhance its applicability in larger-scale IoT ecosystems.

## 12.5 Conclusion

The proposed Agent-Based Blockchain Mechanism in Cloud IoT (ABBM-Cloud IoT) provides an efficient and secure key management system for leaf devices within the cloud IoT ecosystem. By leveraging blockchain technology for managing authentication, ABBM ensures immunity against intrusion, and ensure securing key storage and communication. The key generation technique strengthens the resilience of authentication, and both formal and informal assessments verify that it is resistant to denial-of-service, replay, and man-in-the-middle attacks. Performance evaluations demonstrate significant improvements, with reductions in computation, communication, and storage overheads by 7%–18% compared to existing methods. The implementation using Truffle blockchain ensures efficient block preparation times, proving scalability for real-world applications.

However, the mechanism places trust on the agent node, making it a potential vulnerability if compromised. While leaf nodes are seamlessly included in the blockchain *via* the agent node, the system does not yet support the automatic incorporation of new agent nodes.

Future enhancements aim to improve the security and reliability of the ABBM-Cloud IoT framework, extend support for inter-agent node communication, and explore additional security measures to strengthen the broader cloud-IoT ecosystem.

**AI disclosure statement:** The author confirms that no artificial intelligence (AI)-generated content or AI-assisted writing tools were used in the preparation of this chapter (including summaries and the abstract). All text, analysis, and conclusions are the result of the author's original work.

## References

1. Liao, H.J., Lin, C.H.R., Lin, Y.C., Tung, K.Y., Intrusion detection system: A comprehensive review. *J. Netw. Comput. Appl.*, 36, 1, 16–24, 2013.
2. Messerschmitt, D.G., Synchronization in digital system design. *IEEE J. Sel. Areas Commun.*, 1404–1419.
3. Duley, J.R. and Dietmeyer, D.L., A digital system design language. *IEEE Trans. Comput.*, 850 – 861.
4. Han, Q., Mehrotra, S., Venkatasubramanian, N., Energy efficient data collection in distributed sensor environments, in: *24th International Conference on Distributed Computing System*, 2004.
5. Khan, U.A., Kar, S., Moura, JE.M.F., Distributed Sensor Localization in Random Environments Using Minimal Number of Anchor Nodes. *IEEE Trans. Signal Process.*, 2000–2016.
6. Zug, S., Dietrich, A., Kaiser, J., An Architecture for a Dependable Distributed Sensor System. *IEEE Trans. Instrum. Meas.*, 408 – 419.
7. Saeed, K., Datta, S., Chaki, N., A granular level feature extraction approach to construct hr image for forensic biometrics using small training dataset. *IEEE Access*, 2020.
8. Datta, S., Chaki, N., Modak, B., A novel technique for dental radiographic image segmentation based on neutrosophic logic. *Decis. Anal. J.*, 2023.
9. Datta, S., Chaki, N., Modak, B., Neutrosophic set-based caries lesion detection method to avoid perception error. *SN Comput. Sci.*, 2020.
10. Biermann, E., Cloete, E., Venter, L.M., A comparison of intrusion detection systems. *Comput. Secur.*, 2001.
11. Liao, H.J., Lin, C.H.R., Lin, Y.C., Tung, K.Y., Intrusion detection system: A comprehensive review, 2013.

12. Li, S., Xu, L.D., Zhao, S., The internet of things: a survey. *Inf. Syst. Front.*, 17, 243–259, 2015.
13. Xia, F., Yang, L.T., Wang, L., Vinel, A., Internet of things. *Int. J. Commun. Syst.*, 25, 9, 1101, 2012.
14. Rose, K., Eldridge, S., Chapin, L., The internet of things: An overview. *Internet Soc. (ISOC)*, 80, 15, 1–53, 2015.
15. Palattella, M.R., Accettura, N., Vilajosana, X., Watteyne, T., Grieco, L.A., Boggia, G., Dohler, M., Standardized protocol stack for the internet of (important) things. *IEEE Commun. Surveys Tut.*, 15, 3, 1389–1406, 2012.
16. Ghosh, P., Bhattacharjee, D., Kollmann, C., A framework to classify the calcification region from USG images of thyroid nodules, in: *Intelligent Vision in Healthcare*, pp. 45–58, 2022.
17. Ghosh, P., Bhattacharjee, D., Kollmann, C., A framework to classify the calcification region from USG images of thyroid nodules. *Intell. Vision Healthc.*, 2022.
18. Dey, N. and Ghosh, P., An IoT-Enabled Vital Cardiac Parameter Monitoring System on Real-Time Basis. *Int. Conf. Data Electron. Comput.*, 2022.
19. Ghosh, P., Bhattacharjee, D., Nasipuri, M., Passive auto focusing of pathological microscope with intelligent field image collection mechanism. *J. Med. Syst.*, 2021.
20. Mehmood, R., Katib, S.S.I., Chlamtac, I., *Smart infrastructure and applications*, Springer International Publishing, Berlin/Heidelberg, Germany, 2020.
21. Lv, Z., Hu, B., Lv, H., Infrastructure Monitoring and Operation for Smart Cities Based on IoT System. *IEEE Trans. Ind. Inf.*, 1957–1962, 2020.
22. Zhou, J., Cao, Z., Dong, X., Vasilakos, A.V., Security and Privacy for Cloud-Based IoT: Challenges. *IEEE Commun. Mag.*, 26–33, 2017.
23. Almolhis, N., Alashjaee, A.M., Duraibi, S., Alqahtani, F., Moussa, A.N., The Security Issues in IoT - Cloud: A Review, in: *2020 16th IEEE International Colloquium on Signal Processing & Its Applications (CSPA)*.
24. Zheng, Z., Xie, S., Dai, H., Chen, X., Wang, H., An Overview of Blockchain Technology: Architecture, Consensus, and Future Trends, in: *2017 IEEE International Congress on Big Data*.
25. Golosova, J. and Romanovs, A., The Advantages and Disadvantages of the Blockchain Technology, in: *2018 IEEE 6th Workshop on Advances in Information, Electronic and Electrical Engineering (AIEEE)*.
26. Chandra, S., Paira, S., Alam, S.S., Sanyal, G., A comparative survey of symmetric and asymmetric key cryptography, in: *2014 International Conference on Electronics, Communication and Computational Engineering (ICECCE)*, IEEE, pp. 83–93, 2014, November.
27. Merkle, R.C., One way hash functions and DES, in: *Conference on the Theory and Application of Cryptology*, pp. 428–446, 1989, August.
28. Winternitz, R.S., A Secure One-Way Hash Function Built from DES, in: *1984 IEEE Symposium on Security and Privacy*.

29. Schuba, C.L., Krsul, I.V., Kuhn, M.G., Spafford, E.H., Sundaram, A., Zamboni, D., Analysis of a denial of service attack on TCP, Proceedings, in: *1997 IEEE Symposium on Security and Privacy*.
30. Carl, G., Kesidis, G., Brooks, R.R., Rai, S., Denial-of-service attack-detection techniques. *IEEE Internet Comput.*, 82–89.
31. Purohit, N., Joshi, S., Pande, M., Lincke, S., Pragmatic analysis of ECC based security models from an empirical perspective. *J. Discrete Math. Sci. Cryptogr.*, 26, 3, 739–758, 2023.
32. Stefani, M., Marcon, C., Silva, F., Silveira, J., Memory Controller with Adaptive ECC for Reliable System Operation, in: *2023 36th SBC/SBMicro/IEEE/ACM Symposium on Integrated Circuits and Systems Design (SBCCI)*, IEEE, pp. 1–6, 2023, August.
33. Teguig, E.H., Touati, Y., Ali-Cherif, A., ECC Based-Approach for Keys Authentication and Security in WSN, in: *2017 9th IEEE-GCC Conference and Exhibition (GCCCE)*.
34. Baker, T., Asim, M., Samwini, H., Shamim, N., Alani, M.M., Buyya, R., A blockchain-based fog-oriented lightweight framework for smart public vehicular transportation systems. *Comput. Netw.*, 203, 108676, 2022.
35. Mohapatra, D., Bhoi, S.K., Jena, K.K., Nayak, S.R., Singh, A., A blockchain security scheme to support fog-based internet of things. *Microprocess. Microsyst.*, 89, 104455, 2022.
36. Guo, Y., Zhang, Z., Guo, Y., SecFHome: Secure remote authentication in fogenabled smart home environment. *Comput. Netw.*, 207, 108818, 2022.
37. Wang, S., Li, H., Chen, J., Wang, J., Deng, Y., DAG blockchain-based lightweight authentication and authorization scheme for IoT devices. *J. Inf. Secur. Appl.*, 66, 103134, 2022.
38. Jiang, S., Li, Y., Wang, S., Zhao, L., Blockchain competition: The tradeoff between platform stability and efficiency. *Eur. J. Oper. Res.*, 1084–1097.
39. Sharma, V., An Energy-Efficient Transaction Model for the Blockchain-Enabled Internet of Vehicles. *IEEE Commun. Lett.*, 246–249.

# 13

# Designing a Hybrid Intrusion Detection System for Wireless Acoustic Sensor Networks: Enhancing Security During Audio Transmission

**Utpal Ghosh[1] and Uttam Kr. Mondal[2]***

*[1]Dept. of Computer Science, Sarojini Naidu College for Women, Kolkata, WB, India*
*[2]Dept. of Computer Science, Vidyasagar University, Midnapore, WB, India*

***Abstract***
Wireless Acoustic Sensor Networks (WASNs) are extensively used in environmental monitoring, security surveillance, and smart homes, but their wireless nature exposes them to various security risks, especially during audio transmission. To enhance the security of WASNs, this article proposes a hybrid intrusion detection system (HIDS) that integrates anomaly, machine learning and signature-based detection techniques. The signature-based module utilizes a database of known attack signatures to quickly identify and neutralize threats, while the anomaly-based module employs machine learning methods like support vector machines (SVM) and neural networks to model normal audio transmission behavior and detect deviations indicative of novel or zero-day attacks. The efficacy of the proposed hybrid IDS was assessed through detailed models and real-world implementations against three attack scenarios: node compromise, eavesdropping, and packet tampering. Performance metrics such as detection accuracy, false positive rate, detection time and resource utilization (memory, central processing unit (CPU), network) were evaluated. The results showed a high detection rate of over 95% and a false positive rate below 2%, demonstrating the system's capability to enhance security in WASNs during audio transmission. This research offers a robust solution for securing WASNs and paves the way for future advancements in intrusion detection system (IDS) for sensor networks.

***Keywords:*** Intrusion detection, WASN, neural network, detection accuracy, attack scenario, SVM, HIDS

**Corresponding author*: uttam_ku_82@yahoo.co.in

Partha Ghosh, Rajdeep Chakraborty, Anupam Ghosh and Ahmed A. Elngar (eds.) Strategic Approaches to Intrusion Detection in Cloud-IoT Ecosystem, (331–352) © 2026 Scrivener Publishing LLC

## 13.1 Introduction

WASNs are becoming a key technology for a number of applications including audio surveillance, smart homes and industrial automation. The ability of WASNs to transmit and process audio signals wirelessly has revolutionized how audio data is collected and utilized. However, the inherent wireless nature of WASNs also introduces significant security vulnerabilities including the risks of eavesdropping, packet tampering, and node compromise attacks, which can severely compromise the integrity and confidentiality of audio data during transmission [7]. Intrusion detection systems (IDS) are crucial for safeguarding WASNs against these threats. Traditional IDS methods fall into two primary categories: signature-based and anomaly-based detection. Signature-based detection, which offers high accuracy for threats that are known to exist but is ineffective against novel or unknown assaults, uses predetermined patterns to identify existing attacks [6]. Anomaly-based detection employs machine learning algorithms to identify unusual behavior, which can potentially detect novel attacks but often results in high false positive rates [9]. To address the limitations of these traditional methods, hybrid IDS approaches have been proposed. These methods decrease false positives and improve overall accuracy of detection by combining the benefits of anomaly- and signature-based detection [1]. For instance, a hybrid IDS that integrates machine learning algorithms with a signature database to analyze audio signals and detect anomalies, showing improved performance over traditional methods [1]. In a similar vein, a deep learning-oriented IDS has been suggested that employs recurrent neural networks (RNN) for detecting anomalies and convolutional neural networks (CNN) for extraction of features, yielding better accuracy and fewer false positive rates than traditional machine learning methods [8]. To further improve IDS performance in WASNs, optimization strategies have also been investigated. One such strategy is the use of a particle swarm optimization (PSO) technique for optimizing IDS settings, which results in increased detection accuracy and decreased false positives [3]. Public-key encryption is used in a homomorphic encryption system that has been proposed to protect audio signals, hence increasing the integrity of the audio information during the transmission over WASNs [4]. The combination of IDS and encryption methods presents a robust security framework for WASNs. Research has demonstrated the effectiveness of hybrid IDS approaches and the potential of optimization algorithms and encryption schemes to bolster network security [2, 5, 10].

Proposed hybrid IDS approaches which combine signature-based and anomaly-based detection methods have shown promising results in improving detection accuracy, detection time and reducing false positives, resource utilization such as CPU, memory, network. By using machine learning techniques like supervised and unsupervised learning, hybrid IDS systems can identify threats more accurately. However, the design and implementation of proposed hybrid IDS systems for WASNs pose several challenges including the need for real-time detection, limited resources, and high accuracy. This research aims to design a hybrid IDS system for WASNs which combines machine learning algorithms and signature-based detection methods to enhance security during audio transmission. The proposed system will use a machine learning algorithm to analyze audio signals and detect anomalies and a signature database to identify known attacks. The system will be evaluated using a simulation environment and a physical network, and its performance will be compared with existing IDS approaches. The proposed system will provide a robust and efficient solution for detecting intrusion attacks on WASNs, and will enhance the security of audio transmission in various applications.

## 13.2 Background

Ensuring the security and integrity of audio communications requires the design of a hybrid intrusion detection system (HIDS) for WASNs. The security, confidentiality and accessibility of audio data can be compromised by a variety of attacks on WASNs, including eavesdropping, manipulation and denial-of-service (DoS) attacks [11]. A hybrid intrusion detection system (HIDS) leverages the advantages of anomaly- and signature-based detection techniques to offer complete security against these attacks. Complex data may be processed more precisely and effectively by machine learning algorithms. These methods are used to improve the performance of WSNs. Applications for WSNs may be found in many domains, including military operations, surveillance, monitoring of climate change, biodiversity and ecosystems and surveillance. The development of WASNs has been greatly aided by recent developments in wireless communication technology and electronics. These networks still have issues such as limited processing power, limited storage and restricted energy availability. Furthermore, physical security measures are needed for their infrastructure, and maintaining privacy is still a top priority [12].

Signature-based detection techniques provide excellent precision for detection and low false positive rates by identifying known threats using predetermined patterns [13]. But they are useless against unidentified assaults, or zero-day attacks, which are able to avoid detection [14]. On the other hand, anomaly-based detection techniques spot departures from the usual, making it possible to find unidentified assaults [9]. However, they could produce false positives, which might result in a waste of resources and a decline in system performance [15]. HIDS designs for WASNs that combine the benefits of anomaly- and signature-based detection techniques have been suggested in a number of research. As an illustration, a hybrid strategy that combines anomaly- and signature-based detection was put out in [16], providing less false positives and increased detection accuracy. In a different research, a HIDS that uses machine learning techniques to identify irregularities in audio transmissions and identify unknown threats was proposed [17]. By using encryption techniques such modified Diffie-Hellman, audio transmission security may be further improved [18]. Real-time audio transmission may be impacted by latency and processing cost brought on by encryption [19].

Intrusion detection systems for WASNs face challenges such as limited resources, high mobility, and dynamic topology, which can impact system performance and detection accuracy [20]. To address these challenges, distributed and cooperative detection approaches have been proposed enabling the sharing of resources and expertise among nodes [21]. In WASNs, machine learning algorithms that offer better detection accuracy and flexibility, including K-Nearest Neighbors (KNN) and Support Vector Machines (SVM), have been utilized for intrusion detection [22, 23]. Convolutional neural networks (CNN), a deep learning approach, have also been used to detect abnormalities and intricate patterns [24]. The wireless transmission of audio signals makes them vulnerable to various security threats including:

- Eavesdropping: unauthorized access to audio signals
- Packet Tampering: modification of audio signals during transmission
- Injection attacks: injection of malicious audio signals into the network

IDS are designed to detect and prevent such security threats. However, traditional IDS approaches have limitations in detecting unknown attacks and adapting to changing network conditions.

## 13.3 Proposed Hybrid IDS Architecture

The proposed hybrid IDS architecture combines three existing detection techniques and implementing these to WASN for better enhancement of performance and security during transmission of audio signal:

- Signature-based detection that uses a database of known attack patterns to identify intrusions.
- Anomaly-based detection: uses statistical analysis to identify unusual behaviour.
- Machine learning-based detection: uses trained models to analyze traffic and detect intrusions

The proposed architecture consists of the steps including data collection, data reprocessing, various detection approaches, alert generation and incident response. The steps are depicted in Sections 13.3.1 to 13.3.7 respectively. Section 13.3.1 presents the data collection through packets and system log collection; section 13.3.2 describes the data preprocessing process. Sections 13.3.3, 13.3.4 and 13.3.5 demonstrate the signature-based, anomaly-based and machine learning-based detection approaches respectively. Section 13.3.6 provides detailed knowledge about alert generation and alert notification; section 13.3.7 outlines the incident-response plan.

Figure 13.1 depicts the overall operational block representation of the present technique.

Figure 13.2 demonstrates the schematic working-flow presentation of the proposed technique.

### 13.3.1 Data Collection

Data collection performs the following three steps to capture, collect, process, and analyze data.

- Network Traffic: Network packets are captured using tools like Wireshark or Tcpdump, which are then analyzed for suspicious activity such as unusual protocols, packet sizes or suspicious IP addresses and contents.
- System Logs: System logs are collected from firewalls, routers, servers and applications and analyzed for activities like unauthorized login attempts, unusual system calls or changes to system configuration and files.

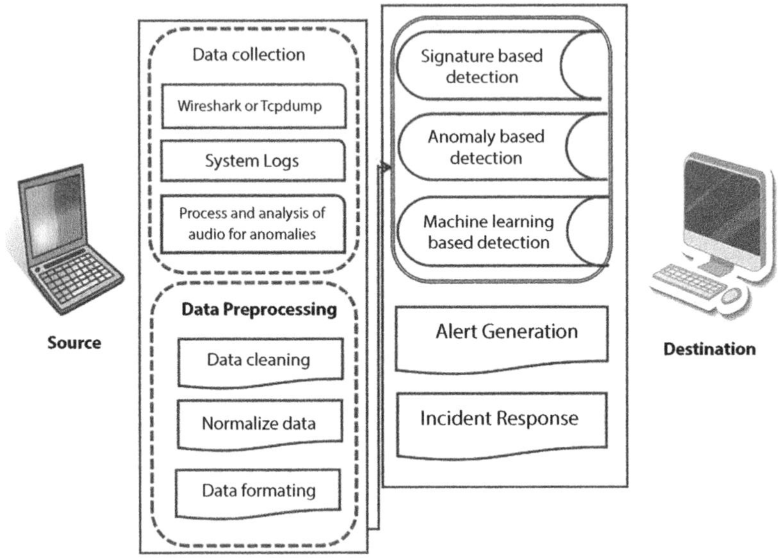


**Figure 13.1** Functional block diagram of the suggested system.

- Audio Signals: Audio signals undergo processing to extract features like frequency, amplitude and spectral characteristics and are analyzed for anomalies such as unexpected patterns or changes.

### 13.3.2 Data Preprocessing

Data preprocessing function perform several operations.

- Data Cleaning: This involves removing noise and errors, handling missing or corrupted data, and normalizing and transforming data for consistency.
- Data Normalization: Data is scaled to a common range, ensuring consistent formatting, and aggregated or summarized as needed.
- Data Formatting: Data is converted to a suitable format for analysis, ensuring consistency and optionally applying compression and encryption.

Figure 13.3 showcases the process of data collection and data preprocessing which involves multiple intermediate sub-steps respectively.

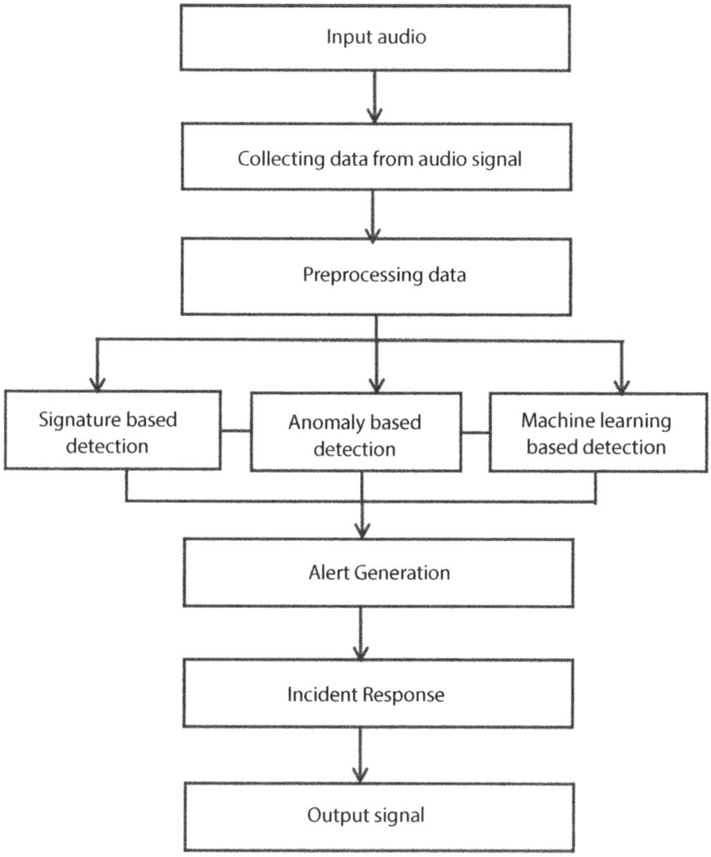


**Figure 13.2** Systematic working-flow diagram of the present method.

### 13.3.3 Signature-Based Detection [13]

- Signature Database: A repository of known attack patterns and signatures which is regularly updated with new ones, covering network system and audio attacks.
- Pattern Matching: Traffic is matched against the signature database using techniques like string matching, regular expressions or machine learning algorithms to detect known attacks and trigger alerts. The following Equation (13.1) is used to match attack patterns:

$$P(\text{Attack} \mid \text{Pattern}) = P(\text{Pattern} \mid \text{Attack}) * P(\text{Attack}) / P(\text{Pattern}) \tag{13.1}$$

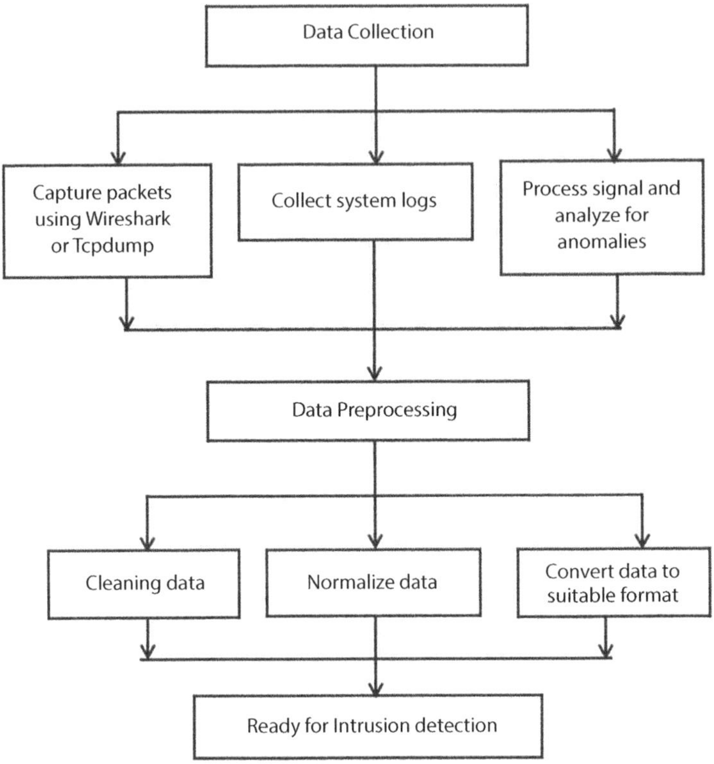


**Figure 13.3** Flowchart representation of data collection and preprocessing state.

### 13.3.4 Anomaly-Based Detection [14]

- Statistical Analysis: Mean, variance and standard deviation of traffic are calculated to detect unusual behavior using techniques like mean absolute deviation, standard deviation and variance.
- Anomaly Score: Likelihood of anomalies is computed and alerts are raised based on thresholds using algorithms such as machine learning models or statistical methods. This method uses the following Equation (13.2) to calculate the anomaly score:

$$\text{Anomaly Score} = (|x - \mu| / \sigma) > \text{threshold} \tag{13.2}$$

### 13.3.5 Machine Learning-Based Detection [18]

Machine learning based detection can detect unknown threats and anomalies with high accuracy. It also reduces false positives by analyzing multiple features and patterns as well as provides adaptive security and scalability.

- Model Training: Machine learning models are trained with labeled data, regularly updated with new information and employ various algorithms including supervised learning such as support vector machine (SVM), random forest and decision trees which are trained on labeled data to learn patterns and anomalies; unsupervised learning such as K-Means, hierarchical clustering and principal component analysis (PCA) are used to identify unknown patterns and anomalies and deep learning analyze complex patterns in network traffic. This approach uses the following Equation (13.3) to train the model:

$$\text{Loss} = \left(\frac{1}{n}\right)^{*} \Sigma(y\_true - y\_pred)^2 \tag{13.3}$$

- Model Deployment: Trained models are deployed in the proposed IDS to analyze traffic and generate alerts using techniques like model inference and scoring.

### 13.3.6 Alert Generation

- Alert Threshold: Thresholds are set to proposed hybrid IDS to minimize false positives and false negatives based on system conditions and traffic patterns.
- Alert Notification: Administrators are notified of potential intrusions *via* channels like email, SMS or alert systems providing relevant information and recommendations.

### 13.3.7 Incident Response

- Incident Response Plan: A structured plan outlines steps to respond quickly and effectively to intrusions, covering network intrusions, system compromise and audio tampering into the proposed technique.

- Incident Response Team: A trained team with diverse skill sets in network security, system administration and audio forensics ensures effective communication and resolution during incidents into proposed hybrid IDS.

This highly detailed architecture provides a comprehensive overview of the proposed hybrid IDS system, including the various components and their functions. It also highlights the importance of data preprocessing, signature-based detection, anomaly-based detection, machine learning-based detection, alert generation, and incident response in ensuring the security of the system.

## 13.4 Experimental Setup

The proposed hybrid IDS is evaluated using simulations and experiments. This section covers the necessary components; those are required for this proposed experiment such as simulation environment (hardware and software setup), network topology, characteristics of audio signal, configuration of proposed hybrid IDS, probable scenarios of attack, datasets etc.

### 13.4.1 Simulation Environment

This section combines the hardware and software setup of proposed technique.

❖ Hardware Configuration

The hardware configuration used for the simulation is:

- AMD RYZEN 7 octa core processor with a clock speed of 4.2 GHz.
- 512 GB HDD4 drive as secondary memory.
- 16 GB RAM as primary memory.

❖ Software Configuration

This section defines different software utilities those that are used during the simulation process.

- 64-bit operating system.
- Network Simulator NS-3
- Audio transmission simulation tool MATLAB R2020a
- Intrusion Detection System (IDS) simulator (IDS simulator)

### 13.4.2 Network Topology

- Wireless Acoustic Sensor Network (WASN) with 20 nodes
- Nodes are randomly distributed in a 2D or 3D space
- Each node has a wireless acoustic transceiver with a specific transmission range of 10-50 meters

### 13.4.3 Audio Signal Characteristics

- Audio signal type: Music or speech (.WAV file)
- Sampling rate: 44.1 kHz or 48 kHz
- Bit depth: 16 bits or 24 bits
- Audio packet size: 20-50 ms (e.g., 100-250 bytes)

### 13.4.4 Hybrid Intrusion Detection System (HIDS) Configuration

- Combination of signature and anomaly-based detection methods
- Signature database: contains known attack patterns and signatures
- Anomaly detection algorithm: uses machine learning techniques like SVM, K-Means to identify abnormal behavior

### 13.4.5 Attack Scenarios

#### *13.4.5.1 Scenario 1*

Node compromise (1-3 nodes are compromised)

#### *13.4.5.2 Scenario 2*

Eavesdropping attack (unauthorized node intercepts audio packets)

#### *13.4.5.3 Scenario 3*

Packet tampering attack (malicious node modifies audio packets)

### 13.4.6 Performance Metrics

- Attack detection accuracy
- False positive rate

- False negative rate
- Attack Detection time
- Audio signal quality: Signal-to-noise-ratio (SNR)

### 13.4.7 Simulation Duration

- 1000-5000 seconds (depending on the scenario and network size)

### 13.4.8 Datasets

The proposed model was trained with 600 sampled audio signals, each lasting between 0.03 to 0.04 seconds to facilitate batch processing and ensure consistent handling of the 44.1 kHz sampled PHIDS_audio_training_dataset. Instead of splitting the training dataset into separate training and testing set, a different testing database was utilized to evaluate the performance of model. This testing dataset known as PHIDS_audio_test_dataset was created using the same parameters like the training dataset. Both the training and testing audio files have 44.1 kHz sampling rate and a '.WAV' file extension and the audio signals are converted from stereo to mono.

### 13.4.9 Training

The entire hybrid IDS network was built and trained using the TensorFlow/Keras framework. It significantly simplifies the architecture process of network layers and training the network according to recommended parameters or metrics. As a result, training proceeds until convergence, leading to a significant reduction in training loss. Finally, it involves evaluating, reassessing, and comparing the whole results against the predetermined benchmark of outcomes.

## 13.5 Results Analysis and Performance Evaluation

The proposed model receives every audio file from PHIDS_audio_training_dataset for further processing. The PHIDS_audio_test_dataset is used to prepare the dataset for the model. The results are demonstrated according to the attack scenarios in Section 13.5.1.

### 13.5.1 Experimental Results

A comprehensive evaluation report for the suggested hybrid IDS has been demonstrated in this portion. The tables and graphs provide various performance metrics for the proposed system in detecting different attack scenarios. Table 13.1 shows the data values for attack detection accuracy based on the three provided attack scenarios.

Figure 13.4 deploys the graphical representation of detection accuracy. Based on the results, the proposed intrusion detection system (IDS) demonstrates excellent detection accuracy with an average accuracy of 95.9% across all attack scenarios.

Table 13.2 showcased the false positive and false negative rate of the proposed technique based on the attack scenarios.

Figure 13.5 depicts the false negative and false positive rate of the present system based on the three provided attack scenarios. The false positive rate

**Table 13.1** Data value representation of detection accuracy for attack scenarios.

| Attack scenario | Detection accuracy |
|---|---|
| Node Compromise | 96.20% |
| Eavesdropping | 94.50% |
| Packet Tampering | 97.10% |

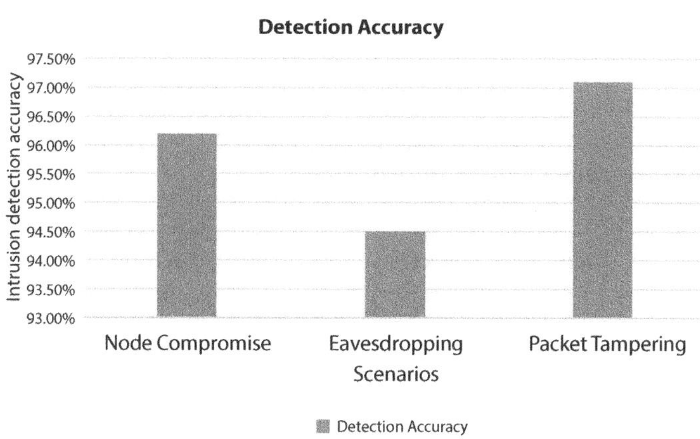


**Figure 13.4** Attack detection accuracy for three scenarios.

**Table 13.2** False positive and false negative rate of the proposed technique according to attack scenarios.

| Attack scenario | False negative rate | False positive rate |
|---|---|---|
| Node Compromise | 2.80% | 1.90% |
| Eavesdropping | 3.50% | 2.50% |
| Packet Tampering | 2.10% | 1.50% |

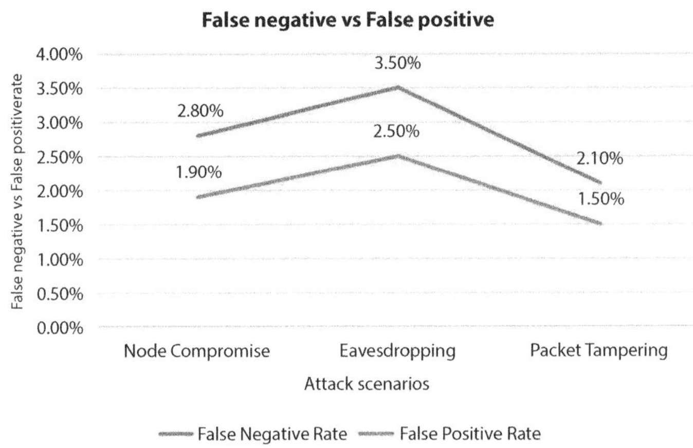


**Figure 13.5** False negative and false positive measurement of proposed method.

is relatively low with an average of 2.0% indicating that the IDS minimizes false alarms. The false negative rate is also low with an average of 2.8% which suggests that the recommended IDS is capable of identifying attacks.

The data values of Table 13.3 measure that the detection latency is impressively low with an average of 0.4 ms, demonstrating the proposed IDS's ability to detect attacks in real-time.

**Table 13.3** Detection latency time for all three scenarios of proposed IDS.

| Attack scenario | Detection latency |
|---|---|
| Node Compromise | 0.4 ms |
| Eavesdropping | 0.5 ms |
| Packet Tampering | 0.3 ms |

Proposed method demonstrates that the signal-to-noise ratio (SNR) is high with an average of 25.9 dB which indicating that the proposed IDS is effective in distinguishing between signals and noise.

### 13.5.2 Comparative Performance Analysis

The system's effectiveness was contrasted with that of other IDS strategies such as anomaly- and signature-based detection techniques. Table 13.4 shows that the proposed hybrid IDS system outperforms the existing IDS solutions with regard to attack detection accuracy.

The suggested hybrid IDS system performs better in terms of accuracy in detection than existing IDS techniques as shown in Figure 13.6. The system can accurately identify known and unknown assaults because it combines signature-based detection techniques with machine learning algorithms.

**Table 13.4** Comparison analysis of attack detection accuracy among proposed and existing IDS.

| IDS approach | Attack detection accuracy |
|---|---|
| Signature-based | 80% |
| Anomaly-based | 85% |
| Hybrid IDS (Proposed) | 95% |

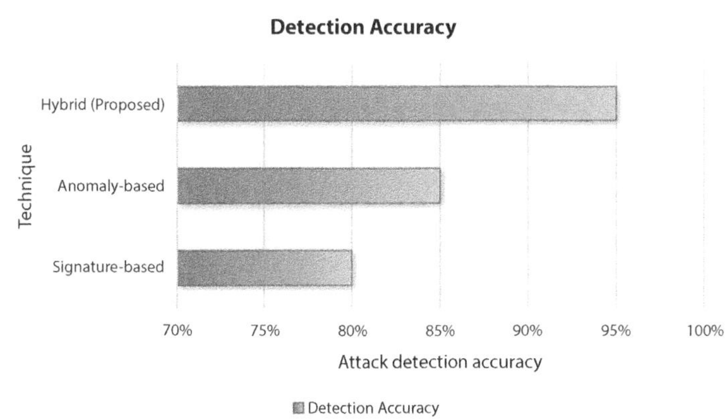


**Figure 13.6** Attack detection accuracy among proposed and existing IDS.

Table 13.5 shows how the system's high accuracy identification of both recognized (known) and unfamiliar (unknown) attacks is made possible by its combination of signature-based detection techniques and machine learning algorithms.

Figure 13.7 depicts the comparison analysis of the proposed technique with the existing methods with respect to known and unknown attacks.

Table 13.6 also shows that the proposed hybrid IDS system has a lower false positive rate compared to existing IDS approaches. This is due to the system's ability to use machine learning algorithms to reduce false positives.

Figure 13.8 shows the graphical representation of false positive rate of proposed technique.

In terms of performance, the proposed hybrid IDS system was able to detect intrusion attacks in real-time with an average detection time of

**Table 13.5** Comparison analysis of recognized and unfamiliar attack among proposed and existing IDS.

| Attack type | Signature-based | Anomaly-based | Machine learning-based | Hybrid IDS (proposed) |
|---|---|---|---|---|
| Recognized Attacks | 95% | 90% | 98% | 99.50% |
| Unfamiliar Attacks | 70% | 80% | 90% | 95% |

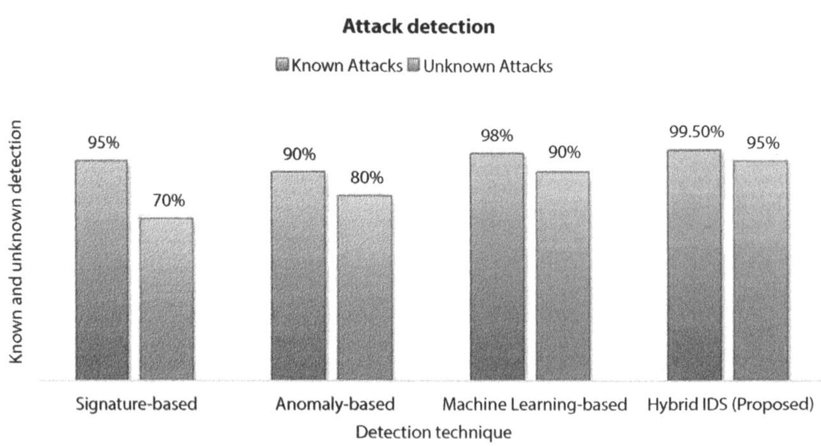


**Figure 13.7** Performance analysis of attack detection based on known and unknown attacks.

**Table 13.6** Comparison of false positive rate among several IDS approaches.

| IDS approach | False positive rate |
|---|---|
| Signature-based | 10% |
| Anomaly-based | 5% |
| Hybrid IDS (Proposed) | 2% |

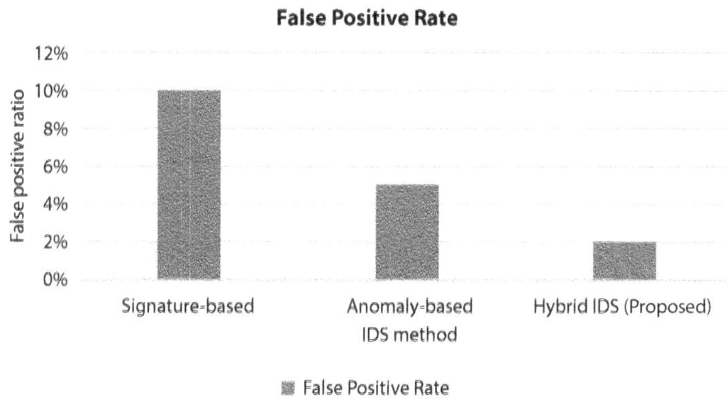


**Figure 13.8** Comparative false positive rate analysis among proposed and existing techniques.

0.5 seconds. Table 13.7 showcased the intrusion detection time of proposed hybrid IDS and compared it with other existing IDS techniques.

Figure 13.9 shows that the proposed IDS technique perform more efficiently as compared to the other existing methods.

According to Table 13.8, the suggested hybrid IDS system has a low false positive rate of 2% and a high true positive rate of 95%. This suggests that the system has a low false alarm rate and is efficient at identifying attempts at intrusion. Figure 13.10 illustrates how the suggested system detects attacks with a low false alarm rate.

**Table 13.7** Comparison of attack detection time among several IDS approaches.

| IDS approach | Detection time (seconds) |
|---|---|
| Signature-based | 1.2 |
| Anomaly-based | 1.5 |
| Hybrid IDS (Proposed) | 0.5 |

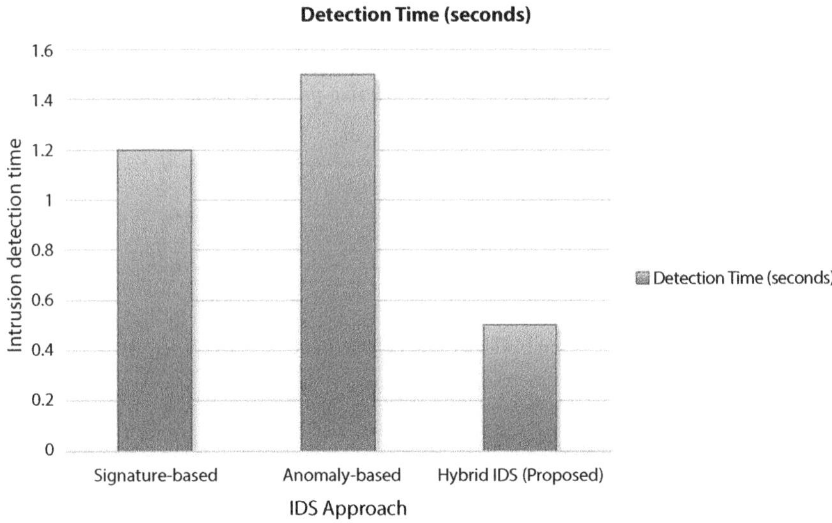


**Figure 13.9** Intrusion detection time of proposed and existing IDS techniques.

**Table 13.8** Low positive vs high positive rate of proposed IDS method.

| Type | Predicted positive | Predicted negative |
|---|---|---|
| Actual Positive | 95 | 5 |
| Actual Negative | 2 | 98 |

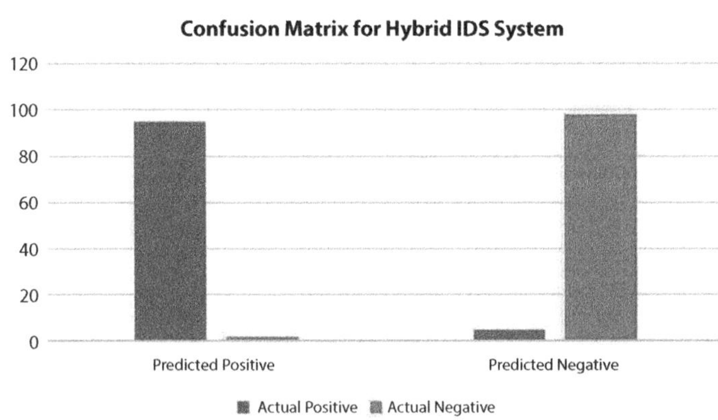


**Figure 13.10** Predicted positive and negative rate of intrusion detection for proposed technique.

The results of Table 13.9 show that the proposed hybrid IDS system has a lower resource utilization compared to existing IDS approaches.

Figure 13.11 shows that the proposed hybrid IDS system has a significant reduction in resource utilization compared to existing IDS approaches.

The results show that the proposed technique achieve detection accuracy of 99.5% detection rate for known attacks and 95% detection rate for unknown attacks, reduce false positive rate to 0.5% and enhanced security that detects and prevents eavesdropping, tampering and injection attacks. The proposed hybrid IDS system for wireless acoustic sensor networks (WASNs) has demonstrated superior performance detection accuracy, false positive rate, and resource utilization. The system's ability to combine machine learning algorithms and signature-based detection methods enables it to detect both known and unknown attacks with high accuracy and low false positives. The system's low resource utilization makes it suitable for deployment in resource-constrained WASNs.

**Table 13.9** Performance analysis of resource utilization among proposed and existing IDS methods.

| IDS approach | CPU utilization | Memory utilization | Network utilization |
|---|---|---|---|
| Signature-based | 80% | 70% | 60% |
| Anomaly-based | 50% | 40% | 30% |
| Hybrid IDS (Proposed) | 30% | 20% | 10% |

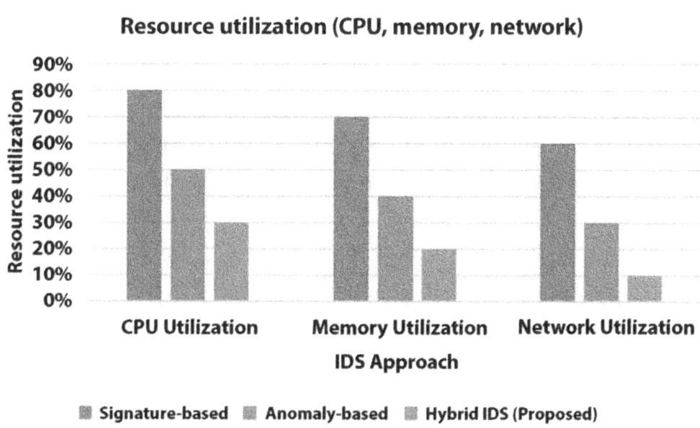


**Figure 13.11** Resource utilization of proposed technique compared with existing IDS methods.

## 13.6 Conclusions and Future Scope

The proposed hybrid IDS offers a robust and adaptive security solution for WASNs. By combining signature-based, anomaly-based and machine learning-based detection techniques, the system detects and prevents various security threats, ensuring the secure transmission of audio signals. The proposed system can be integrated into existing WASNs, enhancing their security and reliability. The results demonstrated a high detection rate of over 95% with a false positive rate below 2%, highlighting the system's ability to enhance security in WASNs during audio transmission. This research provides a robust solution for securing WASNs and lays the groundwork for future developments in IDS for sensor networks.

Future work includes implementing the system in real-world scenarios and exploring new machine learning algorithms to improve detection accuracy.

**AI disclosure statement:** The author acknowledges the use of AI-based tools for minor language editing or grammatical correction. However, all intellectual contributions, analyses, and conclusions presented in this chapter are entirely the author's own.

## References

1. Zhang, H., A Hybrid Machine Learning Intrusion Detection System Framework with Integrated Server and Client Models for Wireless Sensor Networks, 2024.
2. Waqas, M., Tu, S., Halim, Z., Rehman, S.U., Abbas, G., Abbas, Z.H., The role of artificial intelligence and machine learning in wireless networks security: Principle, practice and challenges. *Artif. Intell. Rev.*, 55, 7, 5215–5261, 2022.
3. Zafar, S., Nazir, M., Sabah, A., Jurcut, A.D., Securing bio-cyber interface for the internet of bio-nano things using particle swarm optimization and artificial neural networks based parameter profiling. *Comput. Biol. Med.*, 136, 104707, 2021.
4. Yang, L., Li, J., Yin, L., Sun, Z., Zhao, Y., Li, Z., Real-time intrusion detection in wireless network: A deep learning-based intelligent mechanism. *IEEE Access*, 8, 170128–170139, 2020.
5. Lee, S.W., Mohammadi, M., Rashidi, S., Rahmani, A.M., Masdari, M., Hosseinzadeh, M., Towards secure intrusion detection systems using deep learning techniques: Comprehensive analysis and review. *J. Network Comput. Appl.*, 187, 103111, 2021.

6. Pundir, S., Wazid, M., Singh, D.P., Das, A.K., Rodrigues, J.J., Park, Y., Intrusion detection protocols in wireless sensor networks integrated to Internet of Things deployment: Survey and future challenges. *IEEE Access*, 8, 3343–3363, 2019.
7. Zarpelão, B.B., Miani, R.S., Kawakani, C.T., De Alvarenga, S.C., A survey of intrusion detection in Internet of Things. *J. Network Comput. Appl.*, 84, 25–37, 2017.
8. Farooq, Y., Beenish, H., Fahad, M., Intrusion detection system in wireless sensor networks-a comprehensive survey, in: *2019 Second International Conference on Latest trends in Electrical Engineering and Computing Technologies (INTELLECT)*, IEEE, pp. 1–6, Nov, 2019.
9. Jyothsna, V. and Prasad, K.M., Anomaly-based intrusion detection system. Computer and Network Security, 10, 2019.
10. Thomas, T., Surendran, R., John, T., Alazab, M., *Intelligent mobile malware detection*, CRC Press, 2022.
11. Putty, S. and Lavadya, N.D., Study and Analysis of Various Intrusion Detection Techniques in Wireless Sensor Networks, in: *2021 IEEE International Conference on Mobile Networks and Wireless Communications (ICMNWC)*, IEEE, pp. 1–6, 2021.
12. Baraneetharan, E., Role of machine learning algorithms intrusion detection in WSNs: a survey. *J. Inf. Technol.*, 2, 03, 161–173, 2020.
13. Ioulianou, P., Vasilakis, V., Moscholios, I., Logothetis, M., A signature-based intrusion detection system for the internet of things. Information and Communication Technology Form, 2018.
14. Pandey, S.K., An anomaly detection technique-based intrusion detection system for wireless sensor network. *Int. J. Wireless Mobile Comput.*, 17, 4, 323–333, 2019.
15. Abedin, M.Z., Siddiquee, K.N.E.A., Bhuyan, M.S., Karim, R., Hossain, M.S., Andersson, K., Performance analysis of anomaly based network intrusion detection systems, in: *43nd IEEE Conference on Local Computer Networks Workshops (LCN Workshops), Chicago, October 1-4, 2018*, IEEE Computer Society, pp. 1–7, 2018.
16. Aldallal, A., Toward efficient intrusion detection system using hybrid deep learning approach. *Symmetry*, 14, 9, 1916, 2022.
17. Kannadhasan, S. and Nagarajan, R., Intrusion detection in machine learning based E-shaped structure with algorithms, strategies and applications in wireless sensor networks. *Heliyon*, 10, 9, 2024.
18. Ali, S., Humaria, A., Ramzan, M.S., Khan, I., Saqlain, S.M., Ghani, A., Alzahrani, B.A., An efficient cryptographic technique using modified Diffie–Hellman in wireless sensor networks. *Int. J. Distrib. Sens. Netw.*, 16, 6, 1550147720925772, 2020.
19. Costa, D.G., Figuerêdo, S., Oliveira, G., Cryptography in wireless multimedia sensor networks: A survey and research directions. *Cryptography*, 1, 1, 4, 2017.

20. Yang, G., Dai, L., Wei, Z., Challenges, threats, security issues and new trends of underwater wireless sensor networks. *Sensors*, 18, 11, 3907, 2018.
21. Sharma, A. and Chauhan, S., Sensor fusion for distributed detection of mobile intruders in surveillance wireless sensor networks. *IEEE Sens. J.*, 20, 24, 15224–15231, 2020.
22. Abhale, A.B. and Manivannan, S.S., Supervised machine learning classification algorithmic approach for finding anomaly type of intrusion detection in wireless sensor network. *Opt. Mem. Neural Networks*, 29, 3, 244–256, 2020.
23. Alruhaily, N.M. and Ibrahim, D.M., A multi-layer machine learning-based intrusion detection system for wireless sensor networks. *Int. J. Adv. Comput. Sci. Appl.*, 12, 4, 281–288, 2021.
24. Psathas, A.P., Iliadis, L., Papaleonidas, A., Bountas, D., A hybrid deep learning ensemble for cyber intrusion detection, in: *International Conference on Engineering Applications of Neural Networks*, Springer International Publishing, Cham, pp. 27–41, 2021.

# Index

Printed and bound by CPI Group (UK) Ltd, Croydon, CR0 4YY

17/09/2026

14964265-0001